Making Energy Markets

Ronan Bolton

Making Energy Markets

The Origins of Electricity Liberalisation in Europe

palgrave
macmillan

Ronan Bolton
School of Social & Political Science
University of Edinburgh
Edinburgh, UK

ISBN 978-3-030-90074-8 ISBN 978-3-030-90075-5 (eBook)
https://doi.org/10.1007/978-3-030-90075-5

Cover illustration: smartboy10

This Palgrave Macmillan imprint is published by the registered company Springer Nature Switzerland AG.
The registered company address is: Gewerbestrasse 11, 6330 Cham, Switzerland

Acknowledgements

While writing this book I have been lucky to have been involved in a number of research projects and collaborations which have provided me with a great deal of insight and inspiration. I want to thank all of those colleagues I have worked so closely with over the years, in particular those participating in the following research projects: *Transition Pathways*, *ClimateXChange*, *InGrid*, *Reframing Energy Demand* and *UKERC*.[1]

I was lucky to have the opportunity to travel to Bergen to interview Einar Hope; thank you to him for being so generous with his time. Stephen Littlechild was extremely helpful and pointed me to key sources early on. Both Einar and Stephen also read and commented extensively on an earlier draft of the work. This was greatly appreciated. Stephen Thomas and David Parker also helped me to source material. Thank you also to Andrew Claxton and Rickard Nilsson for sharing their experiences of working in power exchanges. I benefited greatly from the excellent work of Sally Horrocks and Thomas Lean who led the British Library's 'Oral History of the Electricity Supply in the UK' project. A number of others commented on draft chapters: thank you to Helen Poulter, Chris Dent, Vincent Lagendijk, Mark Winskel and a number of anonymous referees. I greatly appreciate all of these helpful contributions, whilst taking full responsibility for the published work.

The Science, Technology and Innovation Studies group at the University of Edinburgh has been a great place to work over the years. I am particularly grateful to Steve Sturdy, Cathie Lyall and James Mittra who have led this group since my arrival and helped to create a supportive environment for research.

I want to thank in particular a number of colleagues who provided me with help and advice at crucial stages of my career: Tim Foxon, Joseph Murphy, Peter Pearson, Frank Geels, Robin Williams and Jan Webb.

Line, Oskar and Louie; this book is dedicated to you.

Ronan Bolton Edinburgh, June 2021

Note

1. UK Research Councils: EP/F022832/1, EP/K005316/1, EP/M008215/1. EP/S029575/1. Norwegian Research Council: 243994/E20. Scottish Government: ClimateXChange – Integration of Power Transmission Grids.

Contents

List of Figures

CHAPTER 1

Introduction: Making Energy Markets

The introduction of competition to western European electricity supply industries during the 1980s and 1990s was a political act which fundamentally reordered the relationship between states and national electricity systems. Fuel shortages in the immediate post-WWII period and rapidly growing economies in subsequent decades had prompted governments across the region to become tightly coupled with integrated generation and transmission organisations who controlled the industry. 'Electric nationalism'[1] became a key strategic tool for building the macroeconomy and powering the consumer revolution across western Europe in the post-war era. For many during this period the idea of competition in the electricity supply industry was an anachronism. It harked back to the late Victorian era when the industry first emerged as fragmented and small-scale undertakings, with uncoordinated developments resulting in the duplication of assets and inefficiencies. Competition had been swept aside by rationalisation and more modern forms of industrial organisation, enabling, in Alfred Chandler's words, 'Economies of Scale and Scope'.[2] There seemed to be an inherent centralising logic behind the growth of large-scale and centralised systems like electricity supply, with the engineers and technocrats who controlled them seeming to be 'autonomous' from political and democratic influence.[3] Why then did the idea of competitive electricity markets gain such traction during the late 1980s and 1990s across western Europe? Why were some countries so keen to privatise and liberalise (structural reform and competition) their electricity systems during this particular period? What different market designs emerged and why? This book seeks to answer these questions and to account for the

R. Bolton, *Making Energy Markets*,
https://doi.org/10.1007/978-3-030-90075-5_1

transition to competitive electricity markets across western Europe during the final two decades of the twentieth century.

From Monopoly to Competition

The economic rationale of supressing competition in industries with high fixed costs, such as electricity supply, was that the economists' ideal of marginal cost pricing would be insufficient to cover total industry costs. It was also thought that pure competition would create uncertainties, to the extent that investing in and maintaining a sufficient level of spare generation capacity to meet demand at peak periods would not be economically viable, thus threatening security of supply. Regulation and centralised control seemed to be the obvious solutions to the economic and coordination challenges posed by these large and increasingly complex interconnected systems. The 'triumph of the systems' required the conventional laws of economics to be suspended, and in many respects politicians became enrolled into the logic of the systems themselves, by introducing monopoly rights and legally protected market shares for integrated utilities, or by nationalising entire electricity industries. From the early 1900s powerful utility managers succeeded in convincing regulators that electricity systems ought to be categorised as 'natural monopolies' granting them exclusive rights to supply power within certain geographic areas, enabling them to capture economies of scale and scope as they expanded and integrated across different functions of the electricity chain.[4] This settlement was made on the basis that the gains from the more efficient organisation of the industry would be shared with customers, thus providing a rationale for regulated pricing.

Strong state-industry alignments arose from, and were sustained by, a common interest in reducing competition and providing stability, enabling long-term investments to be made in what were highly capital-intensive and technologically complex industries. In the words of the sociologist Neil Fligstein, for powerful industry elites these structures provided a 'conception of control';[5] a mutually agreeable and commonly understood normative basis for organising the electricity system which enabled highly capital-intensive investments to be made and for complex systems to serve the interests of wider society. As such, 'national electricity regimes'—referring to the relationship between a state and dominant electricity industry actors in a national context[6]—were not simply technocratic achievements, rather they were politically and culturally shaped, becoming deeply embedded in the institutions and logics of industrial capitalism.

While classic electricity system histories, such as Hughes' *Networks of Power* and Granovetter and McGuire's *The Making of an Industry*,[7] have provided us with rich accounts of the formation and early development of these integrated electricity supply systems, the breakdown of the alignments of technologies, industry structures and political frameworks which led to the creation of competitive electricity markets from the 1980s has been much less studied from a history of technology perspective.[8] Although the relative performance and efficiency of different electricity liberalisation models has been discussed extensively in the vast energy economics literature on the subject, there has not yet been a systematic historical account of the origins and establishment of these markets in a European context.

The western European context is particularly interesting because the transition to markets was so pronounced and disruptive. Political control of electricity systems became a crucial economic lever for the post-WWII reconstruction of the region, its subsequent industrial transformation and rapid economic growth. Systems had developed a strongly national character, and in some cases national electricity companies were adopted as symbols of the technological prowess of the nation. However, following the reforms which largely took place during the 1990s, Europe is now seen as the home of liberalised electricity markets, with the examples of Britain (covered in Chaps. 2, 3 and 4) and the Nordic region (Chaps. 8 and 9) being held up as exemplars for the sweeping tide of marketisation which, by the late 1990s, seemed destined to engulf the entire world. Another interesting feature of the European context has been the *Europeanisation* of electricity markets, a process encouraged and facilitated by the European Commission (covered in Chaps. 5, 6 and 7). Despite the presence of deeply embedded national electricity regimes (France and Germany are discussed in detail in Chap. 6), the period of study saw the creation of a common approach to liberalising electricity supply industries amongst European Economic Community (EEC) Member States. This was in the context of the drive to implement the Single European Act by 1992, but an internal energy market (IEM) of some description had been muted as far back as the founding of the EEC in 1957.

The empirical chapters of the book analyse the reconfiguration of the complex web of state-mediated economic interdependencies which had underpinned national electricity regimes and the undermining of natural monopoly as a key organising principle for the electricity supply industry. Before embarking on the cases of *Making Energy Markets*, we must first account for the various causal factors which influenced the trend towards markets and competition during this particular period.

A Socio-technical Approach

For some, the move towards electricity liberalisation was primarily driven by technological changes. Innovations in combined cycle gas turbine technologies (CCGTs)[9] enabled private investors to gain a foothold and compete against the incumbent monopolies. Parallel developments in ICTs reinforced this trend towards decentralisation. This new dynamic changed the economic fundamentals of electricity generation; liberalisation was essentially an institutional response to this technology-driven change.[10] An alternative framing places economic knowledge at the centre; ideas from regulatory economics, initially arising from the US deregulation movement of the 1970s, questioned the natural monopoly doctrine. These ideas were first applied in pioneering cases (Britain and Norway) and later filtering up to the European level.[11] A third common approach to the liberalisation narrative characterises the change as inherently political; right-wing politicians dismantled and privatised public electricity monopolies in order to reduce the role of the state in the economy, as part of an ideologically driven neoliberal political project.[12]

This work frames the transformation from monopoly to competition as a *system dynamic*. So, rather than there being a single driving force—technology, politics or economics—leading to the creation of these markets, there was an interplay of causal factors which shaped the liberalisation process. In reality, it is difficult to disentangle economic, technological and political factors as drivers of long-term and structural changes to complex technical systems such as electricity supply, rather they come together in different ways to shape these varied transformations; their influence and relative importance is a matter of empirical investigation which takes into account the particular context and timing of transformation. As Rip and Kemp outline, such a 'coevolutionary' approach to the study of long term system transformations assumes that 'overall changes result from several interacting developments together, rather than from a point source of change forcing itself upon the rest of the world'. This *socio-technical systems* perspective was first proposed by the historian of electricity Thomas Hughes and later developed in the expansive large technical systems (LTS) field.[13]

Also relevant to this study is a similar *socio-technical* approach to the study of market creation which has been proposed by actor-network theorists Koray Çalişkan and Michel Callon.[14] They use the term *economisation* to characterise processes of constructing markets through socio-technical work; that is, 'the processes through which behaviours, organizations, institutions and, more generally, objects are constituted as being "economic"'.[15] Markets, in their terminology, are socio-technical *agencements*; or arrangements of heterogeneous elements; transmission grids, economic theories, market devices,[16] ideas, regulations and laws, and so on. Similar to the Hughesian LTS approach, constructing markets (or systems) is viewed as a messy process, involving the building of connections between these heterogeneous elements—both people and materials—and once these networks are stable, they enable things—such as a megawatt hour—to be valued and for prices to be ascribed. The 'pragmatics of valuation', again using Çalişkan and Callon's terminology, involves the study of how these heterogeneous elements are assembled in practice.

There is much to say about the nuances of, and differences between, these theoretical and analytical styles,[17] but there is a broad commonality which can be drawn out and deployed pragmatically for our purposes: that electricity markets should be characterised as socio-technical constructs, shaped through processes of interacting materialities, economic ideas, political interests and agendas. The basis of our story is how actors in diverse contexts created and manipulated these connections, recreating the organisational logic of electricity supply industries around markets and competition: a brief snapshot of each case may serve to illustrate how such a socio-technical approach can help us to tell this complex story.

In the British case, these three factors—technology, politics and economics—came together during its radical market reforms of the 1980s and early 1990s. This case is of course well known because of its place within the wider privatisation programme of the Thatcher governments. As outlined in Chap. 2 on 'Inventing Competition', as the process unfolded during the late 1980s, politicians and senior civil servants initiated a dialogue with a group of economists who were engaging with the Austrian school of Von Mises, Hayek and Schumpeter, blending this with public choice theory, property rights theory and the emerging field of regulatory economics,[18] to argue that a shift towards private ownership and competition, as opposed to state-control and regulated monopoly, would improve the efficiency of the industry. Think tanks, including the Institute for Economic Affairs and the Centre for Policy Studies, played an important role in fermenting these ideas and translating them into the policy sphere.

Later, in the early and mid-1990s, as the new market was up and running, technology began to play a key role in shaping the competitive dynamic. Newly privatised Regional Electricity Companies (RECs) began to invest in CCGTs—the famous 'dash for gas'—as a means of capitalising on the opportunities presented by liberalisation. As natural gas prices fell, this technology was reaching the point where it was increasingly competitive against conventional steam turbine generators whose innovation potential had largely been exhausted. CCGTs could be constructed quickly and were relatively low capital cost, enabling private investors to finance projects. The implication of this was that one of the key economic arguments for state-control and monopoly protection as a prerequisite for financing large-scale investment programmes, then seen as the only feasible route to low cost electricity, became undermined.

Technology and the materiality of power systems also played a key role in shaping the Norwegian market, but in this case it was more of an instigator of the reforms. Throughout the 1980s, excess production from its hydropower dominated system could not be absorbed domestically, creating an impulse to seek out export markets and for the growth of cross-border trade. As we shall see, however, this was not simply a matter of selling power to their neighbours (Sweden, Finland and Denmark) as trade created interdependencies requiring robust market institutions and contracts. There was a balance between autonomy and regional integration struck in this case as the *Nord Pool* market enabled each system operator to retain tight control over their national grids, whilst enabling cross-border exchanges and trading in financial instruments. This mixed-economy approach aligned well with the tradition of state-controlled electricity companies across the Nordic region; unlike the more radical British case, there was no privatisation of state-owned electricity companies. But similar to Britain, an alignment of politics and economics enabled the initial transition to markets within Norway in the early 1990s. A group of economists form the Norwegian School of Economics in Bergen was asked by the short-lived conservative-led administration (late 1989 to late 1990) to develop a proposal for reform. Drawing on industrial economics and the structure–conduct–performance (SCP) paradigm, they proposed a market design with the aim of using the price mechanism to achieve a market 'equilibrium', resulting, in their model, in a more efficient allocation of resources within the system.

The chapters which examine the role of the EEC in developing a coordinated approach to electricity liberalisation amongst its Member States perhaps best illustrate the political nature of these markets. Initially, the European Commission's strategy was based on the British approach of dismantling integrated monopolies and imposing, through legal means, a uniform model of competition throughout the region. As the process evolved, however, it became part of a wider political process and complex institutional dynamic associated with the construction of Europe's single market in the early and mid-1990s. A complicating factor was the institutional flux that the EEC was undergoing during the period in question; a particularly important change being the introduction of qualified majority voting to enact single market legislation and the increasing decision-making powers of its legislature, the European Parliament. After much to-and-fro, a compromise was reached to slowly phase-in competition, the outcome of a political debate in the context of an institutional dialogue between the European Commission, the European Parliament and key Member States. This was a long and drawn out process with many countries being reluctant, and some vehemently opposed, to dismantling their national electricity regimes.

A Changing Energy Landscape

While the study focuses on how technological, political and economic factors shaped the transition to markets in particular national contexts, it should be noted that broader international and structural factors had a strong influence across the cases during this period, not least changes to the relative prices of fuels in global commodity markets.

National electricity regimes—those close alignments of state institutions and electricity industries—seemed to have been reinforced by the 1970s oil crises. In many ways the relationships between states and energy industries became more intertwined as the subsidisation of domestic electricity generators and indigenous fuel sectors was increased as a means of promoting national energy security. In France, the 1973 oil crisis prompted its politicians to rapidly accelerate its nuclear expansion programme, while in Britain and Germany struggling coal mining industries were given a reprieve, as both governments increased investment and channelled subsidies into domestic sources of energy.

By the early 1980s, however, it became apparent that the assumption about persistently high oil prices proved to be flawed. OPEC—the

Organization of Petroleum Exporting Countries—following a period of dominance over world oil markets, was becoming concerned about diminishing market share, and the leading country within the organisation, Saudi Arabia, started to increase its production to squeeze out its competitors; most notably producers with operations in non-OPEC regions such as Alaska, the USSR, the North Sea and Brazil. As a result, the price per barrel decreased 'from nearly $30 in 1984 to about $14 in 1986 in money-of-the-day. In real terms, prices had more than halved'.[19] As global conditions looked less volatile and threatening for energy importers, such as the EEC countries,[20] doubts began to be expressed about the need for strong energy and industrial policies to provide a buffer for these national economies and societies against high energy prices.

Along with undermining basic energy policy assumptions, the falling oil price also had a more direct impact on the economics of electricity generation in western Europe. It reinforced a parallel trend in international coal markets as low oil prices meant that the use of coal for heating, transport and electricity generation greatly diminished. In Britain, for example, 80% of the country's electricity generation was from burning coal in 1981/82, whereas it has been as low as 66% five years earlier, before the second oil crisis of 1979. This, combined with a longer running trend in the growth of global coal production—up circa 50% by the late 1980s from early 1970s levels—and international trade led by export nations, meant that, despite continuing and often successful efforts to improve productivity,[21] domestic European coal mining industries faced an existential threat.[22]

This was compounded by growing environmental concern during the 1980s about acid rain which had led to a greater emphasis on environmental regulation to mitigate flue-gas emissions, thus adding pressure on already struggling domestic industries.[23] Environmental concerns were also damaging to the nuclear industry. The aftermath of the Chernobyl accident in 1986 amplified the voice and influence of anti-nuclear campaigners and the green political movement. A key battleground between pro and anti-nuclear lobbies was the economics of nuclear power; the resulting scrutiny of which was a key factor in de-legitimising the closed technocratic culture which had characterised this industry.[24] The reality was that the twin pillars of the post-war national electricity regimes in western Europe—national coal industries and nuclear power—were under increasing threat.

As coal prices fell dramatically during the 1980s, it became apparent that a rapid liberalisation of electricity markets, in a way which enabled utilities to source coal from the cheapest sources for burning in their power plants, would have collapsed the domestic coal mining industries of western Europe. The coal-dependent electricity markets of West Germany and Britain were particularly vulnerable and ripe for imports, as both could be easily accessed from the ports of Rotterdam and Antwerp, where much of the international coal was delivered. Productivity gains in these countries' coal industries were being wiped out by dramatic falls in international coal prices, almost halving in real terms during the second half of the 1980s; in the case of Britain, at least 60–70% below domestic sources.[25]

It had seemed that the interests of national utilities, industrial consumers and governments had been bound together around the need to promote national economic expansion. Across western European nations this set of interdependencies saw the creation of protected markets for the producers, while the large industrial consumers agreed to be tied-in to long-term supply arrangements with monopoly utilities. In return, governments structured tariffs in a way which cross-subsidised these large consumers, typically to the disadvantage of domestic users and smaller businesses. However, the cohesion of national electricity regimes was altered fundamentally as the interests of industrial consumers and dominant electricity producers began to diverge. A disconnect between regulated electricity tariffs and energy prices in international commodity markets emerged as a key tension. As we shall see across the cases, a key political driver for electricity liberalisation was the emergence of an industrial lobby arguing for the ability to access these cheaper energy sources and for the burdens of subsidising national energy industries to be lifted from them. The ability to source cheap energy also chimed with a concern amongst western European governments at the time about industrial competitiveness, being particularly strong in West Germany, which had amongst the highest industrial electricity prices across the industrialised nations, second only to Japan.

Another factor which undermined national electricity regimes was a questioning of the need for centralised planning to meet long-term growth in electricity demand. During the decades of accelerated economic growth following the war, presumptions of ever-growing electricity demand and its relationship with economic growth—like high oil prices—became somewhat engrained. A growing gap between supply and demand featured in many long-term energy planning studies, even up to the late 1980s, and investment appraisal methodologies in these state-controlled industries tended to look over very long timespans—often over 40 years—and use low discount rates. These assumptions enabled large-scale investment programmes which would not have been economic in a competitive market to gain approval from governments, who were themselves concerned about keeping up with economic growth and maintaining high living standards. Long-term thinking and central planning seemed to be a foundational pillar for these industries.

However, two factors contributed to a breakdown in these assumptions. The first was the general slowdown in economic growth in advanced industrialised nations following the 'golden age' from the early 1950s to the first oil shock of 1973. The second was the lower energy intensity of this economic growth—falling by 20% from 1973 to 1983[26]—as a result of the structural shift towards services economies and improvements in energy efficiency, partly induced by the high energy prices of the 1970s. Compared to 1973, by 1987 OECD countries were 'using 24% less energy per $1000 of GDP',[27] with industry being a key driver. Energy demand from industry actually fell across the EEC between 1980 and 1987.

Competition and markets were certainly a response to the perceived structural problems of national electricity regimes, but a sole focus on macro trends would obscure the 'micro politics' of market creation. These seemingly impersonal economic and technological 'forces' were not in fact external drivers of market liberalisation, rather they were interpreted and used strategically by agents of change in each national context and in different ways. Responses were conditioned by the particular configuration of each national electricity regime, as 'macro trends' reinforced pre-existing tensions within these industries, resulting in a severing of established state-industry ties which had previously been so deeply rooted in the post-war paradigm of state capitalism and the mixed economy. We will explore these varying responses and pathways of electricity market reform in the following chapters.

Outline

With its three parts, the book is structured in such a way that the reader can explore an individual case—Britain, the EEC or the Nordic region—or alternatively read it as a single study of a broader trend towards electricity market liberalisation across the western European context. It should be noted that the order of the cases is not indicative of their relative importance: we start with the British case simply because it was the first to enact deep structural reforms of its electricity supply industry along competitive lines in 1990. Although Norway followed shortly after, implementing its reform legislation in early 1991, the chapters covering the EEC case come next. The rationale for this is that the British experience was highly influential in shaping the European-level reform process, often being referenced by proponents and opponents of competition and structural reform during a highly politicised process which did not reach a conclusion until the mid-1990s. While there was a common reform agenda shared between the UK and the European Commission, Chap. 6 discusses the reasons why France and Germany were reluctant liberalisers. In the French case this was largely due to their tradition of state monopoly, uniform national pricing and the technical vulnerabilities of their nuclear-dominated power system. In the German case, a desire to extend protection to its struggling coal industry and the challenges posed by integrating the East German power system meant it sought to ease the transition to competition rather than disrupt the industry.

Although it is not intended as a structured cross-national comparison, throughout the book differences between these different national 'styles' of electricity liberalisation are discussed; for example how Britain and Germany approached the issue of regulation in very different ways, with Germany seeking to protect its incumbent utilities, while Britain dismantled them with a view to increasing diversity in the market (see end of Chap. 7). The Nordic case which follows can be read as a pioneering case of electricity liberalisation, similar to Britain. A key difference however was that a model of public ownership and tradition of state control was retained; the region's exchange-based market model enabled participating countries to retain autonomy over the operation of their national power systems. It is discussed at the end of Chap. 9 how this accommodation between cross-border trading and national sovereignty provided the basis of an EU-wide approach to electricity markets which was implemented in subsequent decades.

As will be discussed in the concluding chapter, the study of this phase of electricity liberalisation and system change—during the 1980s and 1990s—can provide a bridge between the early histories of electricity systems and contemporary approaches to the analysis of 'system transitions' in the context of energy decarbonisation. As our societies become ever more dependent on reliable electricity supply, the nature of the markets, rules and regulatory frameworks tasked with ensuring the stability of these systems needs to be understood. A study of the inception of electricity markets is not merely a historical exercise therefore, but crucial for understanding our contemporary dilemma of ever-increasing reliance on unsustainable energy systems and for exploring alternative ways of configuring the relationship between energy systems, politics and society. This book illustrates how electricity markets were politically shaped, but as we discuss in the final chapter, the role of these markets in directing a new phase of energy system change—towards low carbon—is by no means clear.

PART I

Britain

Part I contains three chapters on the creation of the British electricity market from 1987 and its evolution during the 1990s. Due to its emphasis on private ownership and competition, and its association with the wider Thatcherite 'neo-liberal' project, it has become viewed as a pioneering case, featuring prominently in the energy economics and policy literature on the subject. In England and Wales, the electricity industry incorporated 12 publicly owned Area Boards, each with a regional distribution/supply monopoly, operating alongside the Central Electricity Generating Board (CEGB)—formed in 1957—which was responsible for the transmission grid and the vast majority of generation assets. This hybrid configuration was instituted by the 1947 Electricity Act which nationalised the industry. The Scottish industry had developed its own identity, and by 1954 was operating under a different structure, with two fully integrated power boards: the South of Scotland Electricity Board (SSEB, formed in 1954) and the North of Scotland Hydro Electricity Board (NSHEB, formed in 1943). Across Chaps. 2, 3 and 4 we will see how political power within the English/Welsh electricity regime effectively shifted away from the CEGB as direct competition between the regional Area Boards and the newly privatised generation companies shaped the new industry into the 1990s, which later integrated with the Scottish system.

CHAPTER 2

Inventing Competition

This chapter examines how the contours of a new electricity supply industry structure began to emerge in Britain[1] during 1987 and 1988. By the time of the 1987 General Election, a number of key state-owned corporations and nationalised industries, including British Telecom and British Gas, had already been privatised.[2] But despite the political momentum behind the privatisation programme of the Thatcher governments, there remained a strongly held view that electricity was a 'natural' monopoly, requiring overall responsibility for ensuring the continuous operation of the system to be centralised within one body which had control over the major generators and the high-voltage transmission grid.

The mainstream view at this early stage within the British—and international—electricity industry was that it was an exception to arguments about the benefits of competition. Due to the coordination benefits of vertical integration and the technical complexity of the system, it was argued that separating out different functions and introducing competition would be inefficient, and even impractical, thus removing the main economic argument for the privatisation of the nationalised industry. Privatisation without meaningful competition was not seen as an existential threat by senior managers within the electricity supply industry (ESI); the expectation had been that if it was to be privatised the integrated structure of the ESI would need to be largely retained, similar to other privatisations of the early and mid-1980s, in particular British Gas which

R. Bolton, *Making Energy Markets*,
https://doi.org/10.1007/978-3-030-90075-5_2

had been sold as a single entity in 1986. This would enable the generators to pass-through operating and capital investment costs to customers via contracts with the regional distribution companies (the Area Boards); privatisation would not alter the fundamental structure of the industry and its organisational paradigm.

The view of the electricity system as an integrated whole and as an exception to the mainstream economic view of the benefits of competition became associated with the then Chairman of the Central Electricity Generating Board (CEGB), Sir Walter Marshall. Marshall, the quintessential 'man of the system', was formerly the Chief Scientist at the Department of Energy and Head of the UK Atomic Energy Authority (UKAEA).[3] At the outset, Marshall was not ideologically opposed to privatisation and early on did not envision that it would result in the segmentation of the CEGB into competing electricity generating companies and a separate grid company, as turned out to be the case. He sought to replicate the British Gas model and retain the integrity of the CEGB, but have it operate in the private sector free from ministerial diktat. This viewpoint was articulated by Marshall publicly in February 1988, during an evidence session of a parliamentary Energy Committee:

> [referring to the CEGB Board]... there is a remarkable amount of effort that we have to put in simply arising from the fact that the Minister, the Secretary of State for Energy, has an obligation to answer in the House of Commons for anything we do ... there is a real sense in which the Secretary of State for Energy is something akin to the Chairman of the CEGB, and I am just sitting in since he is too busy to come ... I do not think politicians are the best chairmen for any industry.[4]

Marshall saw that privatisation could be a means of delivering a sounder footing to realise the industry's substantial capital investment programme,[5] and in particular the plan to construct a fleet of new nuclear reactors which had been announced in 1979, during the first Thatcher government. At the time, loans to the nationalised industries were included in overall public sector borrowing and therefore subject to political control, via a mechanism called the External Financing Limit (EFL), which was decided through the Treasury's broader macroeconomic framework: the Medium Term Financial Strategy (MTFS). Breaking free from these fiscal constraints would have been attractive to Marshall and others concerned with realising the CEGB's grand technological ambitions.

Walter Marshall, since his appointment by Nigel Lawson in 1983, had developed an extremely close working relationship with Margaret Thatcher, becoming somewhat of a confidant on matters relating to nuclear power and electricity supply - she typically referred to him as 'Dear Walter'. Part of the rationale for appointing him as Chairman of the CEGB in 1983 was that he was seen as an outsider to what was viewed by tory politicians as a closed technocratic culture within nationalised industries, one which had become detached from commercial realities. Marshall had famously had a prickly relationship with the arch enemy of conservative reformists, the former labour energy minister Tony Benn, who fired Marshall as his Chief Scientist at the Department of Energy in the late 1970s, following a disagreement about Britain's nuclear power policy.[6] In the context of privatisation, Thatcher saw Marshall as an ally, as he had previously facilitated the stockpiling of coal and crucial chemicals at power plants in the run-up of the miners' strike of 1984/85, insisting that the CEGB stick to its guiding mission to 'keep the lights on'. This close relationship developed partly because of Thatcher's technocratic sensibilities, being a former scientist and an enthusiast for nuclear power.

We will see later however that Thatcher's commitment to competition, while wavering at times during the process of privatisation, resulted in the side-lining of Marshall, who was unceremoniously fired in the months leading up to the start of competition in 1990, as the CEGB's role in obscuring the true economic costs of nuclear power became clear. This outcome would have been unimaginable in July of 1987 as the new conservative government set about its plans to implement its manifesto commitment to privatise the electricity industry.

The CEGB and the Planning Mentality

Viewed in a wider European context, the CEGB was an exemplar of how to run an electricity industry around technocratic principles, successfully exploiting economies of scale and with a significant research base enabling it to develop and deploy cutting-edge technologies. The CEGB, formed in 1957, was one of the largest electricity corporations in Europe, with over 52,000 MW of generating capacity by the mid/late 1980s (see Fig. 2.1 below. Fig. 2.2 shows the regional distribution areas operated by the Area Boards); it served 95% of power demand across England and Wales and had over 131,000 employees. It controlled the high-voltage 'Supergrid'—the largest single power system in the western world—which connected the largest of its over 70 generating plants[7] and it also operated

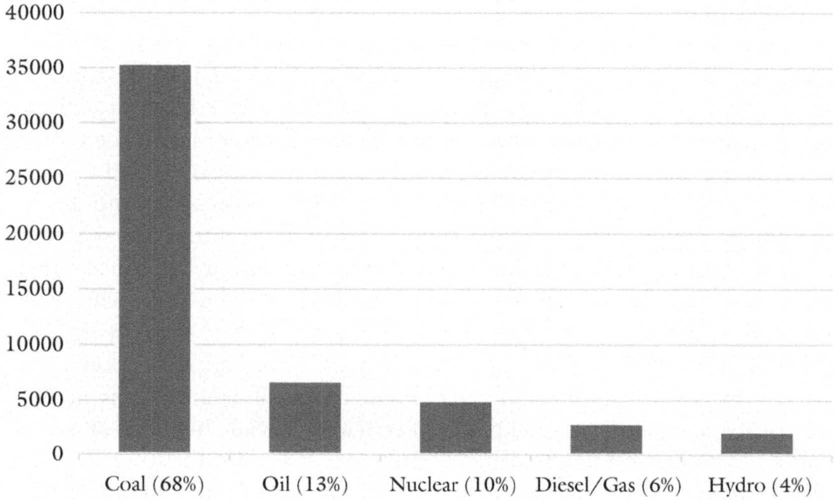

Fig. 2.1 The CEGB's installed capacity (1986/87 in MW). In capacity terms for the main sources this equated to 68% coal, 13% oil and 10% nuclear, but as oil, gas and hydro plants had low capacity factors, in output terms the figures were typically more like 80% coal and 20% nuclear. (Energy Committee (1988) *Third Report: The Structure, Regulation and Economic Consequences of Electricity Supply in the Private Sector*. HMSO. 6 July 1988 (Data from Table 1))

the interconnectors to the neighbouring Scottish and French power systems. It was significant in international terms; the second largest integrated generation and transmission company in the world, just behind *Électricité de France* (EDF), France's state-owned and fully integrated utility. In comparative European terms, the CEGB was viewed as an efficiently run utility; its financial results for 1986–87 reported 'an operating profit of £1.15 bn. This was up 22%, or £318 m, from 1985–86. Electricity sales had increased 2.9% to 219,551 GWh, with growth largely driven by a 6.5% increase in demand from the commercial sector and a reduction in its fuel costs of £278 m'.[8] It was noted at the time that CEGB 'was turning over profits which were the envy of other state utilities in Europe'.[9]

The CEGB and its culture were deeply rooted in the political economy of Britain's key nationalised industries (utilities, steel, rail and coal mining) which had become central to the country's economic model, employing 1.8 million, accounting for 16% of capital employed and for 8% of GDP.[10]

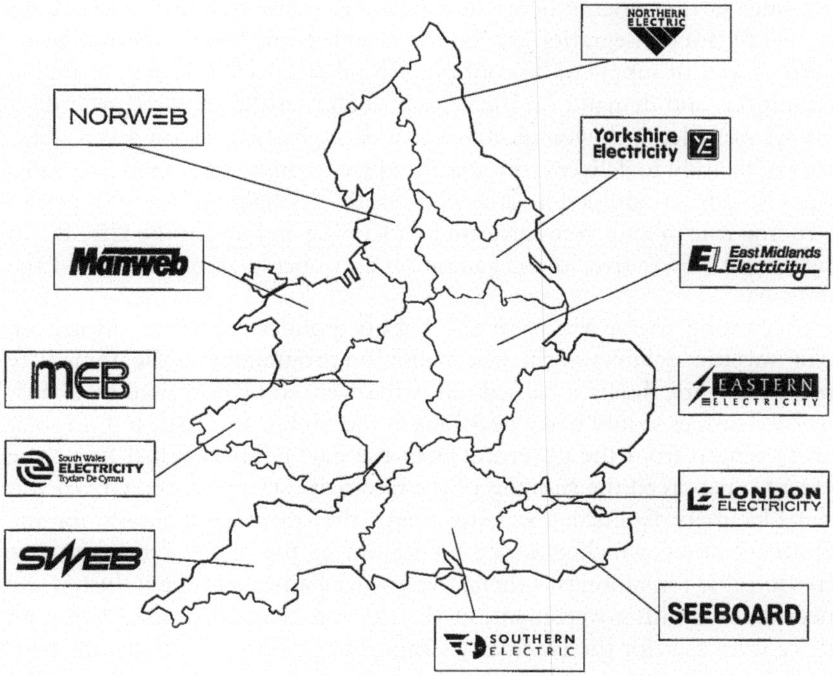

Fig. 2.2 The 12 distribution/supply regions in England/Wales. The figure above shows the branding of these as Regional Electricity Companies (RECs), formed in 1990 as the successors to the nationalised Area Boards. (National Audit Office (1992) *The Sale of the Twelve Regional Electricity Companies.* A Report by the Comptroller and Auditor General. London: HMSO, p 10. Courtesy of the National Audit Office)

Prior to the nationalisation of the ESI in 1948, the industry had suffered from chronic inefficiencies resulting from its fragmented structure, with 600 electricity supply companies and 400 stations in operation. A trend towards greater centralisation was advanced by the Weir Committee report of 1925 which recommended the creation of a national transmission system under the control of the new Central Electricity Board (CEB), which was later rebranded the British Electricity Authority (BEA) after nationalisation. The CEGB was then created under the 1957 Electricity Act which saw the separation of the Scottish industry from the BEA. Unlike power systems which achieved their coordination through collaboration—or pooling—arrangements between local or regional utilities, the CEGB's model of 'total integration', it argued, enabled 'the balance between cost and security of supply to be continuously adjusted according to changing conditions and demand on the system, such that the required security is always provided at lowest available cost'.[11] At its foundation was a statutory obligation to deliver economical and secure supplies to the 12 regional Area Boards; as outlined in later sections, this 'obligation' meant it played a central role in long-term investment planning and meant the CEGB had significant power over the organisation and operation of the rest of the industry.

According to the vision of the Labour politician Herbert Morrison, who was the architect of the nationalisation programme of the immediate post-war years, the nationalised industries were to be governed by boards whose trustees would make decisions in the 'public interest', but do so at arm's length from the government of the day. Politicians had to a large extent outsourced the running of the electricity system to the CEGB and the Electricity Council, the latter being the coordinating body for the entire industry which was set up following the 1957 Electricity Act (responsible for, amongst others, the financial aspects of the industry, pay negotiations with government, marketing and taxation issues). Although there were calls for the Electricity Council to be set up as a fully independent body, it ended up being comprised of the chairmen of the Area Boards and the CEGB, and a small full-time staff. Despite the importance of its functions, it had little or no authority over the CEGB.

One key area where direct supervision by the responsible secretary of state was retained was the approval of investment plans and financing. Tensions between the CEGB and government in relation to its financial performance had surfaced in the 1960s with the publication of two government white papers: one in 1961 on the 'Economic and Financial Obligations of the Nationalised Industries', and a second in 1967: 'Nationalised Industries: review of economic and financial objectives'. On the back of these, there was a growing scrutiny of the CEGB's investment plans, with a test discount rate applied to new projects and with capital expenditure required to be justified in relation to the financial performance of the industry. This was followed up by a later 'White Paper on the Nationalised Industries' published in 1978 which put in place stricter financial controls and targets,with the industry as a whole now required to make an annual sub-mission to the Investment and Financing Review (IFR). The IFR covered all of Britain's nationalised industries and local authorities, and through it the UK Treasury controlled their finances, imposing an overall limit known as the 'public sector borrowing requirement'.

As part of the process, the Treasury evaluated the electricity industry's investment plans against a financial metric (an average rate of return on the industry's net assets on a current cost accounting [CCA] basis) and set performance targets, often dictated by political trade-offs; for example, whether the government prioritised investment in schools and hospitals, versus defence, versus power plants, and so on. For the ESI as a whole—the CEGB and the 12 Area Boards—its financial target was a relatively generous 2.75% over 1985–86 to 1987–88.[12] A particular drag on the productivity of the CEGB had been a poorly performing fleet of advanced gas-cooled reactors (AGRs), along with a low utilisation of the board's fleet of expensive oil-fired plants which had been constructed in the 1960s and early 1970s when oil was relatively cheap.

A target rate of return of 5% had been set for the nationalised industries following the 1978 white paper on nationalised industries, but its application was less strict in the case of the electricity industry as politicians were keen to retain flexibility over the rate of the Bulk Supply Tariff (BST): the wholesale price the CEGB charged to regional Area Boards. According to economic principles, the BST should have been set according to the long-run marginal cost (LRMC) of generating power,[13] ensuring the most efficient use of resources, with new investments triggered on the basis of demand signals. However, by the early 1980s the BST had become detached from economic principles; the Monopolies and Mergers Commission (MMC) noted in 1981 that:

> the Bulk Supply Tariff is intended to reflect long-run marginal costs; but we believe that the way this principle is being applied creates the danger that the basis of the BST may become arbitrary.[14]

In reality the tariff was set in a way which enabled the industry to achieve its politically determined financial targets. Cecil Parkinson, the Secretary of State for Energy from 1987 to 1989, later highlighted the political appeal and economic limitations of this mechanism:

> As a system for concealing true costs and giving scope for price manipulation it [the BST] was superb; as a way of producing electricity efficiently, giving

accountability to the public and promoting productivity within the industry it was disastrous.[15]

While developments from the 1960s white papers onwards saw efforts to apply economic principles to the nationalised industries, the CEGB remained intact and retained its dominant position, often taking advantage of its strategic importance and mass of expertise to dictate the agenda to government. An emphasis on macroeconomic priorities over efficiency concerns prevailed, as Stephen Littlechild, an economist who later became one of the architects of the competitive electricity industry, wrote in 1978:

> In the last few years, government instructions to the nationalized industries have alternated between 'stand-stills' on prices and investment so as to combat inflation and exhortations to raise prices so as to break even or to accelerate investment so as to avoid employment. These instructions have made it clear that the micro-economic principles of the White Paper designed to promote long-run efficient resource allocation are clearly subordinate to the day-to-day requirements of macro-economic policy and demand management.[16]

Along with the wider macroeconomy, an important political consideration in long-term electricity planning was the survival of the British electrical equipment industry. At the time General Electric Company (GEC) and Northern Engineering Industries (NEI) were the key suppliers who, like many dominant equipment suppliers in Europe that had developed alongside the national utilities, thrived in a market which was effectively closed off to foreign competitors. An increase in size of power plants and a slowdown in demand growth had however diminished the size of this industry since the 1960s, and there was an ongoing process of consolidation with smaller companies like Vickers, AEI, English Electric and Metro either folding or merging. By the 1970s GEC and CA Parsons (later NEI) dominated the market for turbine manufacture, while Babcock, alongside CA Parsons, led on boiler manufacture. In order to maintain a semblance of competition, the CEGB had in place general rules of thumb to decide the allocation of contracts: according to the 'Buggins' turn' rule orders were spread reasonably evenly amongst competitors, while according to the 'X + 1 rule', the CEGB encouraged slightly more competing bidders than required. But the overarching rule was 'buy British'.

The CEGB had developed as a central node in a set of economic and infrastructural interdependencies across the entire British economy: its Bulk Supply Tariff—described by a senior CEGB executive as a 'quasi-taxation system'[17]— was used to subsidise the nation's substantial spend on nuclear R&D, its coal industry and leading engineering conglomerates. However, despite its financial heft and undoubted political clout, the CEGB was on somewhat shaky ground because of sometimes hesitant political support for its investment plans. The organisation was lobbying intensively to get government consent for the construction of a fleet of new pressurised water reactors (PWRs) to replace old gas-graphite (magnox) nuclear stations over the coming decades and generally to continue with its plans to construct ever larger coal plants. This was despite having a very healthy reserve margin of 20% and the general trend towards smaller-scale generation sets internationally. The CEGB was gearing up for an investment programme similar in scale to that of the decade from the late 1950s to late 1960s and were pressing government to invest in new manufacturing and construction capabilities, and streamline the planning process. Their envisioned programme involved 13 GW of new plant coming online by 2000, around 25% of the then installed capacity, at a cost of around £40 bn. In 1987, the CEGB submitted financial projections showing a sixfold rise in their expenditure on capital programmes by 2000. A 1988 position paper—'Meeting Demand: Options for future generating policy'—foresaw four new PWRs and two to three large coal plants with 900 MW sets which were to utilise subcritical boiler technology and be fitted with flue-gas desulphurisation systems.

There had however been unfulfilled optimism around earlier investment plans previously announced by the conservative government in 1979 for a fleet of new nuclear plants with a PWR design, costed at £15 bn in money of the day. David Howell, Thatcher's first energy secretary, had committed to ordering at a rate of one new PWR per year for 10 years, beginning in 1982, with up to 15,000 MW of new nuclear capacity coming onto the system by the end of the century. Although planning permission had been granted for the first PWR at Sizewell B, by the late 1980s the CEGB was increasingly pessimistic and scaled back its investment programme for new nuclear. A 1987 CEGB internal briefing document indicated a need for eight or nine new coal and nuclear plants in the 1990s, with four new PWRs likely. The cost of this programme in April 1987 prices was estimated at £23 bn for the PWRs and £19 bn for the coal plant. Alongside this, there was the UK Atomic Energy Authority's—the national nuclear research centre—plan to build a fast breeder fuel plant at Dounreay in Scotland, a technology which was seen to be the future of the nuclear industry.

The CEGB's view at the time, strongly expressed to government, was that there would be insufficient capacity to meet demand into the 1990s, with capacity shortfalls potentially rising to 12,500 MW by 2000. The lifetime of existing plant was a key assumption behind these projections, with 40 years assigned to existing coal plant, 30 years for the early generation of nuclear units (magnox reactors) and 25 for the newer fleet of advanced gas-cooled reactors (AGRs). The CEGB calculated that even with favourable assumptions around these figures, England and Wales would be looking at a 9 GW gap by the end of the 1990s. Based on these doom-laden messages the CEGB had embarked on a PR campaign to convince politicians to press ahead with the revised investment programme.

Sections with government and the Department of Energy were however deeply sceptical about the ability of the CEGB to deliver an efficient investment programme at this scale. A 1981 investigation by the MMC had criticised the organisation for poor decision making and lack of transparency in relation to its previous investments in large generation plants in the 1970s.[18] The MMC were particularly scathing of the CEGB's approach to investment appraisal, stating:

> While we find that the Board's demand forecasting has improved, we consider that there are serious weaknesses in its investment appraisal. In particular a large programme of investment in nuclear power stations, which would greatly increase the capital employed for a given level of output, is proposed on the basis of investment appraisals which are seriously defective and liable to mislead. We conclude that the Board's course of conduct in this regard operates against the public interest.[19]

The MMC's remit did not extend, however, to wider questions of the governance of the ESI and its relationship with government, and it was in this relationship that the industry located the root cause of the problem. Writing in 1987, Sir Philip Jones, Chairman of the Electricity Council, cited political interventions with the aim of bringing forward investment for wider macroeconomic purposes, combined with inflation control policies of the 1970s, as key factors behind the industry's seemingly poor financial performance:

> The catalogue of specific Government interventions in the E.S.I. is quite a long one. It certainly includes the earlier ordering of Ince 'B' power station in the early 1970s. The first of these - Ince - was brought forward primarily to assist the then Government's economic expansion programme. The second was advanced at Government request to help the plant construction industry. In the mid-1970s electricity ... price increases were constrained in support of the then Government's counter-inflation policy with compensation being provided to the Boards under an Act passed for the purpose in 1974. Our concern throughout has been to make sure that the industry received adequate compensation for taking decisions that were not, as we saw them, in the best economic interests of our industry and the electricity customers.[20]

Government was pressing the CEGB, and the electricity industry as a whole, to improve their financial performance, particularly in the context of the plans for future investment. Although the industry had slightly outperformed the 2.75% financial target for the first two years from 1985, its submission to the IFR in order to access external financing exceeded the Treasury's baseline expectations by over £2 bn for the financial years 1988–89 to 1990–91. The Treasury were calling for a substantial increase in this required rate of return on capital employed, with their advisors recommending a target in the region of 4% for 1988–89,[21] rising to 5% and then 6% for subsequent years.

In 1987, the clear message from government was that they were willing to sanction new investment but that higher rates of return were required to fund the programme. There was an ulterior motive to the imposition of stricter financial targets; that the improved capital structure and resulting cash flows would be acceptable to private investors. In the meantime, a higher return from the industry was desirable because of the revenue that would come back to government via the 'negative external financing limit', an effective profit tax imposed on the industry. This was the highest of any nationalised industry at the time, amounting to £1.325 bn in 1986. The Electricity Council, which represented the industry as a whole during such financial negotiations with the Treasury, was willing to strike a compromise: Sir Philip Jones had offered increases to 3.75% and 4.75% in 1988–89 and 1989–90 respectively, requiring average price increases in the region of 6–9%. This, combined with a reduction in capital expenditure, would reduce the industry's IFR bid from £2.2 bn to £233 m. A price hike would enable the CEGB's investment programme to proceed whilst meeting financial targets; it was announced later in March 1988 that price increases averaging 8.8% would be imposed and take effect on 1 April.

There was strong criticism of this outcome, which seemed to sacrifice consumer welfare to enable a questionable investment programme to proceed—constructing up to five coal stations and four PWRs during the 1990s (13,000 MW in total). Strong scepticism was expressed about the need for additional revenue to finance the programme, then at an estimated cost of £40 bn, arguing that it could be readily financed off the CEGB's existing revenues. Government 'appears', the Financial Times' *Power in Europe* publication argued, to have accepted this 'unquestioningly'.[22] The announcement by government 'appears to presume that, despite privatisation, the CEGB's power station plans will sail on regardless'.[23] The underlying criticism was that the price increases suited both parties; the CEGB got its investment programme, while government would see an improvement in the financial position of the industry, enabling it to be privatised.

This obfuscation regarding the rationale for the price increases became apparent at an Energy Committee hearing held in early 1988.[24] In his evidence Cecil Parkinson provided a rationale for the price increases as follows:

> One of the reasons for our electricity price increases has been to create what I call an income base against which the future generators, those who are going to build the new capacity we need, can make their plans.

While in supplementary evidence the Department of Energy clarified that:

> electricity prices have not been increased simply in order to fund the ESI's investment programme from current cash flows. If investment in new capacity is to be justified prices must be sufficient to earn a normal rate of return, whether the funds come from retained profits or from borrowing. Because the ESI has had unplanned surplus capacity the incremental costs of meeting extra demand have been low. This has been reflected in low electricity prices and a low rate of return (2.45 per cent) on the industry's assets. Now that the period of surplus capacity is coming to an end and new investment is required, it is appropriate that the rate of return should move towards a more normal level … The Government does not accept the argument that an increased rate of return can only be accomplished by price rises. We agree

financial targets with the Industry, and once these have been set it is up to the Industry to achieve them through cost saving, price increases or both.

From the point of view of technology choice, there were also rumblings within the industry press that the CEGB's investment planning may be fundamentally flawed. The CEGB's engineering culture had developed around the idea of optimising the thermal efficiency of its plants, requiring high capital cost investments in large turbines which expanded the steam and delivered low pressures. Although marginal to the debate at the time, a study by Walt Patterson—the prominent anti-nuclear campaigner—argued that assumptions about the economics of increasing plant size implicit in the CEGB modelling were already proving to be flawed.[25] Smaller units were beginning to make more sense economically, with scale economies starting to diminish above 660 MW. As the economic fundamentals of electricity generation were changing, the power plant refurbishment industry had begun to take off, particularly in the USA. This implied that the life of existing CEGB plant could be extended, therefore further diminishing the case for an ambitious investment programme on the back of price increases. The CEGB's investment proposals, it was argued, 'were an almost defiant defence of the "economy of scale" philosophy which the rest of the world, and even EDF, was beginning to shake off'.[26]

A Divided Industry

While the CEGB was undoubtedly the dominant actor in the electricity industry in England and Wales, as the privatisation agenda was increasingly driven by pro-competition voices the power and influence of the 12 regional Area Boards—with a statutory responsibility for the operation of the distribution networks from 132 kV downwards and for the vast majority of supply to end customers—began to shape the reform process. Tensions between these two constituent parts of the electricity supply industry had prompted various proposals and schemes to redraw the boundaries between generation, transmission, distribution and supply, well before the actual splitting of the industry and its privatisation in 1990/91.[27] One strand of thought was that the industry was too fragmented, resulting in unnecessary friction between its constituent parts. The idea of reducing this friction and streamlining decision making across the industry was behind the key recommendation of the Plowden

Committee, which in 1976 recommended to unify the industry.[28] This would have seen the creation of a single national utility, achieved by amalgamating the Area Boards and giving more powers over the distribution networks to the Electricity Council. These proposals for greater centralisation were rejected by Thatcher's first energy secretary, David Howell, prompting the then Chairman of the Electricity Council, Francis Tombs, to resign, on the basis that the organisation would not play a meaningful role in the new industry structure as he had envisioned.

A second strand of thought was that the industry should be unified at a regional level with the creation of a number of separate vertically integrated power boards, along the lines of the two Scottish Boards (South of Scotland Electricity Board [SSEB] and North of Scotland Electricity Board [NSHEB]) which had since the 1950s been separated from the British Electricity Authority and went on to develop distinct systems and engineering cultures. NSHEB had been created in 1943 following the Hydro-Electric Development (Scotland) Act and had always operated independently from the BEA, which until 1955 integrated the large generators and transmission lines across England, Wales and southern Scotland. Due to the low population density of the northern region the NSHEB's 'social clause' required it to pursue regional 'economic development and social improvement' across the Highlands and Islands; as such it was seen to have a distinctive social mission. The SSEB was created out of two distribution regions previously within the BEA system, the South Eastern and South Western Electricity Boards, and once it was formed it developed a vertically integrated system. It also operated a power pool with the NSHEB through which the mainly thermal and nuclear output in the south could be balanced with the north's highly distributed hydro-based system, with 54 hydro stations in operation by the late 1980s. Exchanges between the two boards were settled via the 'joint generating account' and there was also a joint planning committee; the large pumped hydro scheme at Cruachan, for example, was developed by the NSHEB in the 1960s for the specific purpose of improving the utilisation of a new nuclear station (Hunterston A) in the south. Despite its willingness to collaborate closely with the NSHEB, the lack of joint planning and cooperation between the SSEB and the CEGB had been criticised by successive parliamentary energy committees. The UK Department of Energy and other proponents of privatisation and competition south of the border were keen to tap into the SSEB's generating surplus and improve the level of interconnection between the two systems, with only 0.8 GW available via two lines connecting Stella in Northumberland and Harker in Cumbria to the Scottish system.

While there were advocates of the Scottish regional power board model, with the SSEB often cited as an efficiently run utility with a well-diversified power plant mix, the trend south of the border had in fact been in the opposite direction. Throughout the 1980s, under Marshall's chairmanship, the CEGB's five regional transmission centres in England and Wales which had been created in 1971 were in the process of being disbanded and their functions centralised within a new National Control Centre, with the operation of the 132-KV distribution power lines being transferred to the Area Boards who would coordinate with the national level via 'Area grid Control Centres'—the so-called two-tier project. The centralisation process resulted in a reduction in power stations from 108 in 1981 to 78 in 1987. Organisationally the CEGB was rationalised and reorganised into four functional divisions— Operations, Engineering, Generation and Transmission — and was beginning to resemble more closely its highly centralised European neighbour, EDF. There was speculation that the main rationales for the CEGB's centralisation drive was to remove the local loyalties that many staff members had to regional control centres and to ensure that opposition to the intended shift away from AGR to PWR nuclear technology was suppressed; it was well known at the time that many of the CEGB's 'middle ranking managers were not convinced about the benefits of PWR and remained committed to AGRs'.[29]

In a 1987 report the MMC was highly critical of this reorganisation, stating 'The history of the "two-tier" grid control project is a catalogue of managerial and technical mistakes which have had serious consequences at the level of both national and area control'.[30] Marshall's rationale for this reorganisation was what he viewed as the ongoing trend towards fewer and larger power plants, stating that 'At present we have five regions with a loose federal control from the centre. That was quite right and proper for the period of time when we operated over 250 power stations'.[31] His view on the trend towards greater scale and centralisation was however questioned, as the reduction in the number of power plants—at privatisation the CEGB had 71 power plants—had already happened in the 1970s 'without any need for other than an evolutionary change in the CEGB's regional structure'.[32]

Within the cabinet and amongst the circle of advisers to the PM, there were advocates taking a more disruptive approach to industry reform. However, during the first two Thatcher governments the general view was that while they were keen on promoting competition in the generation market, it was best to leave well enough alone with respect to the basic organisation of the industry, retaining the CEGB at the apex. As Parker notes in his 'Official History of Privatisation', the first Thatcher government took the view that use of discretionary powers, rather than primary legislation, was the most practical means of improving efficiency and introducing an element of competition and 'it was really only in 1981/2 that attitudes towards the state-owned utilities began to change within Government'. Keith Joseph, the Secretary of State for Industry, was pushing for more radical reform of the nationalised industries and had, in 1980, 'tabled a paper including an ambitious list of possible state sell-offs', although at this time 'there was no suggestion of privatising the electricity industry'.[33] Aside from the technical challenges, the sheer scale of the electricity industry—in the region of four times the size of those industries privatised in the earlier 1980s—meant it was unsurprising that it was towards the back of the queue for privatisation and competition reform.

The following year, 1981 (September), the moderate Howell was replaced by the more radical Nigel Lawson in the Department of Energy. Lawson had a clear vision of energy as a tradable commodity and early on in his tenure called for the removal of public control over the energy supply industries.[34] The major change under his term in office, before he moved on to the Treasury in June 1983, was to introduce competitive reforms at the upstream end of the gas and electricity industries. The 1982 Oil and Gas (Enterprise) Act[35] and the 1983 Energy Act[36] introduced 'common carriage' to the transmission networks, whereby British Gas and the CEGB were obliged to provide terms of access to competitors and publish tariffs for utilising the networks, whilst the Area Boards were required to publish tariffs for the purchase of power and its sale on to end customers. The 1983 Act was however seen as a failure in terms of introducing competition to these industries. Writing in 1986, Hammond et al. summarised that

> the legislation has failed to induce any significant new competition into the industry. Private generation of electricity has remained marginal, confined in the main to small by-product generation and to small-scale combined heat and power (CHP) schemes. There are no large-scale privately owned power-stations, and no one has started supplying electricity directly to final customers by renting use of the transmission system (as envisaged by the Act).[37]

In fact, independent generation had actually declined since the introduction of the Act, from 5.2 to 4.7% between 1982 and 1986. A key reason for this failure was that the 1983 Act didn't fundamentally alter basis of the relationship between the CEGB and the Area Boards, which had at its core the Bulk Supply Tariff (BST). The tariff included a capacity charge which was split into a peak and baseload component which varied annually, along with unit charges which represented the short-run incremental costs of generating. These unit charges were differentiated depending on season, weekday/weekend and time of day, with charges defined for specific 3/4 hour blocks. There was also a fixed charge known as the 'system service charge' which reflected the CEGB's costs of running the transmission system. These varied geographically depending on the cost of transporting power to each of the Area Board's system supply points. The CEGB had the autonomy to vary these different charges in a way which limited the scope for competitors to undercut them and sell to Area Boards below the BST level. This left the CEGB 'with effective control of price and entry conditions',[38] and thus limited the effectiveness of the 1983 competition reforms.

Under the terms of the Act independent generators were to be paid the 'avoided costs' of supply via the BST—the variable component of the BST—and therefore by adjusting the ratio of fixed and variable components making up the tariff, the CEGB could reduce the revenue stream for investors in independent plant by almost one quarter. The CEGB justified its increases in fixed charges in 1984 and 1987 on the basis that its contracts with British Coal had resulted in a lower marginal cost of fuel supply and therefore it needed to increase the fixed component to recover its costs. In 1987 the average payment to an independent power producer was 2.76 p/kWh while the CEGB's own unit generating cost was 3.37 p/kWh.

The partial reform of 1983 retained the centrality of the BST as a reference price for the market, along with the power of the CEGB over the entire industry as it retained the autonomy to vary these charges. As we discuss later in this chapter, the removal of the BST and the freedom to contract for power supplies was a key reason why the Area Boards were keen to promote the splitting up of the CEGB and for meaningful competition to be introduced to the industry. In this respect, their views aligned with those of Cecil Parkinson, the Secretary of State for Energy who succeeded Peter Walker following the 1987 General Election.

Another key source of the CEGB's power which was not reformed in 1983 was its statutory obligation to supply the Area Boards. With the aim of ensuring securing security of supply, an issue of critical national importance, it meant that the organisation could justify its investment plans, not on commercial grounds, but on the basis that they were required to meet its public service obligation. It would have the final say over investment and system planning matters, and costs could then be recovered from the Area Boards via adjustments to the BST. The 'obligation' implied that the CEGB needed to retain control over the transmission system as otherwise security of supply for the system could not be guaranteed.

The future of the obligation to supply was therefore not a mere practical question, it was about who would hold power over the future of the industry. If it was with a successor organisation to the CEGB, despite being a private company with fewer power plants, its control of the transmission grid would mean it could continue to play a central role in formulating long-term investment plans to meet its obligation. Whether privatised or not, it would continue to be the organisation with the central source of information and expertise about the security of the electricity system that ministers would turn to for advice and guidance.

In his evidence to a parliamentary Energy Committee, Walter Marshall clearly spelled out that a privatised version of the CEGB organisation, retaining the overarching goal to 'keep the lights on', would provide it with the ability to override the market in the event that security of supply was in question:

> The other factor is to consider what is the obligation to maintain the system in the longer term. If the distributors are buying, placing orders for new power stations and all that work is developing well, fine, but if you discover that it is not likely to provide the capacity that is needed ten years ahead, who is the generator of last resort? Who actually must build if it is actually necessary? That is if the market forces do not produce you an answer that you think is satisfactory.[39]

Although Lawson did not privatise and restructure the ESI along the lines of his broader vision of 'a market for energy', during his time the initial ideas for the eventual reorganisation of the industry started to be discussed and relationships between senior civil servants and economists proposing more radical ideas about the organisation of the industry were initiated. One of his first decisions upon entering the Department of

Energy was to initiate a study into the privatisation of electricity. The eventual study, conducted by the consultancy firm Coopers and Lybrand,[40] and published in May 1983, proposed two models: a regional model where 'the electricity industry in England and Wales should be gathered into a single body, and then, gradually, split up into a series of self-contained utilities along the lines of Scotland's SSEB'[41]—Nigel Lawson himself rejected this model—while a second involved splitting up the CEGB and separating out the transmission system.

Coopers and Lybrand advised against the regional option because they predicted that there would be substantial power imbalances due to north-south flows, with high-consuming regions in the south becoming reliant on those in the north. In any case, the trend at the time was towards more centralisation of control over the high-voltage transmission system. The study advocated something close to the eventual outcome: splitting the CEGB into a number of separate generators and the creation of a separate grid company. It was highlighted in the report that in order for competition to be feasible certain safeguards may need to be put in place, including long-term electricity supply contracts between the Area Boards and the new generation companies, and the retention of a degree of protected monopoly for Area Boards to ensure continued investment in the industry. As we shall see in the next chapter, these safeguards featured prominently in the reform debate as the practicalities of transitioning to a competitive model began to be discussed in minute detail.

In flagging up the inherent tension between a large nuclear power investment programme and a competitive electricity market, the report rightly identified nuclear power as a key potential obstacle to the favoured model. Coopers and Lybrand advocated against a single nuclear power company and noted that the need for a large organisation to manage the nuclear plants was the only argument in favour of an entity like the CEGB with a diversified portfolio and a large balance sheet. It is unsurprising therefore that, from an organisational survival point of view, the CEGB were advocating strongly in favour of nuclear power being included in the privatisation programme. Following the release of the Coopers and Lybrand study, Marshall wrote a letter to the secretary of state in May 1983 outlining his preference for amalgamating the Area Boards and abolishing the Electricity Council altogether.

Lawson was also in direct contact with Stephen Littlechild. Littlechild had spent the 1970s and 1980s as an academic economist at the University of Birmingham developing proposals for 'denationalisation'[42] and advising government on the economic regulation of privatised industries, most notably for telecoms.[43] In 1983, Littlechild sent Lawson a copy of his joint work with Michael Beesley—'Privatisation: Principles, Problems and Priorities'—and on the back of this a seminar was organised by Ian Byatt—also an academic economist who was a senior economic advisor at the Treasury[44]—to discuss the paper and put the ideas directly before ministers. While the focus of the economic analysis within the Treasury had for many years been on the introduction of marginal cost pricing within the nationalised industries, by the mid-1970s there had been a loss of faith in this approach to 'rational' pricing and attention shifted to the design of incentives and achieving productive—rather than allocative—efficiency. Littlechild, who by this time was explicitly writing with a view to influencing the policy of privatisation, had links with both Byatt in the Treasury and his former lecturer at the University of Birmingham, Alan Walters, who in the early 1980s was the chief economic advisor to Margaret Thatcher. At this early stage, Littlechild and Beesley were proposing something much more radical than the 1983 reforms: splitting up the CEGB and the introduction of retail competition in electricity.

After Lawson was moved to the Treasury later in 1983, the political momentum behind reform of the electricity industry was lost. Between Lawson leaving and another pro-competition minister taking office in the energy department in 1987 (Cecil Parkinson), there was somewhat of a hiatus in the debate about electricity privatisation, partly because of the dominance of the miners' strike as a central issue, but also because of Thatcher's appointment of Peter Walker as Secretary of State for Energy, who was less inclined towards radical structural changes to the industry. Like Howell, his preference was to work with industry, as evidenced by his decision to privatise British Gas as a single monopoly in 1986.

The argument that privatisation wouldn't be 'politically acceptable' was a strong one in the context of the early to mid-1980s, when it was industrial unrest and the future of the coal industry which was top of the energy department's agenda. Walter Marshall had a good relationship with Peter Walker during this period and was seen to be an ally of the government in its battle against the coal mining unions. During the 1984/85 miners' strike, the CEGB and government developed a common stockpiling strategy at coal stations, and this later developed into a policy known as 'endurance', which ensured power plants could run using stockpiled coal for a nine-month period. As part of this strategy, the CEGB had invested in a number of oil burning stations, expanding this capacity to the equivalent of almost 50 million tonnes of coal.

During this interim period, following Lawson's tenure at the Department of Energy, the privatisation and liberalisation agenda was mainly driven by a number of think tanks, most notably the Institute of Economic Affairs (IEA) and the Centre for Policy Studies (CPS). CPS, founded by Keith Joseph and Margaret Thatcher in 1974, had a small team working on the issue and which was receiving advice from Stephen Littlechild. An October 1987 CPS report by Robinson and Sykes[45] argued that competition would result in savings (operation and capital costs) of £1.2 bn/year. They proposed that ownership of the CEGB should pass to the Area Boards, which would be amalgamated into a smaller number of entities and then sold to the private sector, with the condition that the power plants would later be separated from these integrated utilities and sold off through auctions.

A more influential CPS report published in May 1987 was written by Alex Henney.[46] This work, which was being discussed within the Department of Energy, advocated the splitting of the CEGB into nine or ten separate competing private companies—with nuclear retained in the public sector—and the creation of a grid company, fully independent of the generators. In order to maintain diversity in the generation market, there would be a ban on any single company having more than a fifth of the entire market. The privatised Area Boards would not be able to own generation or to merge with each other. Henney's idea was to radically decentralise the industry; *Power in Europe* predicted that 'whatever else emerges by the end of this year, it will not be that'.[47] Senior figures within the department were not in favour of such a radical model and the department even wrote a critical paper on it. It was seen to be too disruptive and would take too long to implement; it would certainly not be possible to achieve in one parliament, the envisioned timescale for privatising the industry. Also, at the time the idea of separating the grid from the generators and operating it independently was seen to introduce unnecessary technical risks and would lead to inefficiencies from a lack of coordination across the different parts of the industry.

During this period the Electricity Council was also working on privatisation and reform questions. With the expectation that a third Thatcher-led conservative government would likely look to privatise electricity, since May 1985 the Electricity Council had been convening a working party on electricity privatisation under the chairmanship of Roger Farrance, a full-time Council member responsible for industrial relations. As part of the initial work a study tour to the USA was conducted to explore different models of private utility ownership, and on the back of this they identified four scenarios for the future of the industry:

1. *The Status Quo: Privatisation of the Boards with as little initial disturbance as possible to the present structure of corporate bodies.*
2. *Unification: Establishment of a unitary organisation, either on the lines recommended by Plowden or by the creation of a holding company.*
3. *Fragmentation: Retention of part of the Industry in the public sector, or the creation of power boards, or the encouragement of maximum competition based on a number of generation and distribution undertakings.*
4. *Piecemeal Privatisation: The disposal of assets such as power stations in a gradual and maybe random manner or the hiving off of board activities such as contracting and sale of appliances.*[48]

However, while the working group was useful in terms of background analysis and identifying possibilities, no clear consensus on the best way forward for the industry could be agreed in advance of the final report submitted to the Electricity Council in May of 1987, just before the election. The Electricity Council's clear preference was 'Unification', to have the Area Boards and the National Grid operate under a single holding company of which the existing 12 regional boards would be subsidiaries. As the Area Boards themselves were understandably pushing back against this and keen to retain their autonomy, the single holding company option could not become the official position of the Electricity Council, but it was recommended to government by the Council's central members, those not affiliated with the boards. Cecil Parkinson, the Secretary of State for Energy appointed after the election, later described this proposal as a 'classic Whitehall solution'.[49] The main rationale for it provided by the Electricity Council's chair, Philip Jones, was that concentration at the distribution side of the industry would be an effective counterweight to the powerful generators:

> Certainly the Area Boards may be able to bring in generation at the lower end of the scale, but if one is talking about bringing in new, say, 2,000 megawatt stations, one will need a larger company with a financial strength so to do. So that is one very large reason … So when we look at it against those considerations, and indeed the practicality of floating 12 boards as

> opposed to one, we are driven to favouring very strongly a single distribution holding company.[50]

In the run up to the 1987 General Election two models were seen as feasible: to create a single holding company and privatise the industry as a unified entity, similar to the gas privatisation which took place the previous year—known as the *en bloc* model—or to have separate sales for the CEGB and the Area Boards, with the likelihood being that the latter would be amalgamated into a single distribution holding company controlled by the Electricity Council—referred to as the 'two company' solution within the Department of Energy. This 'two company' approach had also been studied by Coopers and Lybrand who had identified it as a possibility if more competitive models were ruled out. In this model the distribution company would control the grid and have the obligation to supply all customers in each respective area, whilst also having the right to generate power.

In April 1987, a report for the secretary of state had been written based on these discussions with industry, including the two company model and Henney's proposals. These identified problems associated with industry fragmentation and highlighted concerns about implications for other nationalised industries, in particular the knock-on effects for state-owned companies which, in various ways, relied on their contracts with the CEGB for their profitability. This included the British Coal Company (BCC), British Nuclear Fuels Limited (BNFL), the Atomic Energy Authority (UKAEA) and British Rail.

The failure to achieve industry consensus around a preferred model meant that its various components—the Electricity Council itself, the Area Boards and the CEGB—were free to propose their own models and pursue their own interests, contributing to a highly politicised process. These constituent parts of the industry began to mobilise, exposing in particular the fractures and tensions between the CEGB and the Area Boards; the latter were unsurprisingly much keener on competition as they felt somewhat 'under the thumb' of the CEGB and its BST. The Electricity Council meanwhile was keen to ensure its own survival, but had to be cognisant of its role in representing the entire industry and to maintain a sense of impartiality. The CEGB, on the other hand, seemed to be on the front foot, initiating a strong public relations campaign and extensive lobbying of MPs. *Power in Europe* reported that 'The first, and most effective, card played was that of the industry's complexity'.[51] The CEGB was arguing 'that it would be impossible to unravel the centralisation process which it had been carrying out over the last five years or so within the timescale necessary to sell the industry in the life of one parliament'.[52]

As somewhat of a superficial nod to competition, Marshall was putting forward the notion of 'kick start for competition': to privatise the CEGB intact and enable competition through (a) allowing CEGB to contract with private generators, and (b) to transfer some smaller power stations connected at 132 kv and below to the Area Boards. He argued that the role of the CEGB should be to act as a central purchasing agency for independent generators; these non-CEGB plants would not be subject to centralised dispatch and their total combined capacity would be limited to around 4000 MW. The argument made in favour of this was that it would be impossible to subject non-CEGB plant to a central 'merit order'—with plants dispatched based on their marginal costs of operating—and that if this level of generation went above 15% the system would be unworkable, in effect a technical barrier to competition. Crucially, the CEGB would retain its statutory obligation to 'keep the lights on'. The logic behind this limited view of competition was put forward by the CEGB to the Energy Committee in early 1988:

> Privatisation can bring benefits for consumers by freeing the CEGB from Government constraints, and allowing it to reduce fuel and other costs by adoption of a stronger commercial approach. The CEGB is anxious to exploit these opportunities ... Although the nature of electricity supply constrains the extent to which competitive market theories can be applied, the CEGB recognises the potential value of competition for consumers. There is scope, under regulatory supervision, for the early development of effective competition in generation alongside retention of the benefits of an integrated power system.[53]

They went on to dampen expectations around the prospects of 'competition' in the electricity supply industry:

> The term "competition" needs to be carefully understood in so far as it relates to electricity supply. An extensive study of overseas practices recently completed by the Board has not identified anywhere in the world a model of electricity supply based upon genuine competition or where the operation of market forces obviates the need for a significant degree of consumer protection: in simple conceptual terms, electricity utilities are not like supermarkets which compete to sell goods to the consumer ... No examples were found which supported the viability of the idealised concept of competing

> generators, representing a substantial proportion of available capacity, able freely to enter and exit the market for electricity at will in response to market forces. No country in the world has attempted a complete separation of generation from transmission.[54]

There was however some level of scepticism about the CEGB's measured narrative around the prospects of competition, as expressed in the pages of the FT's *Power in Europe*:

> To show its deep love of competition, the CEGB revealed that it was considering plans for a number of private power stations, only one of which seemed to have any substance to it, and that but little. A well-timed application for Hinkley C brought the nuclear card to the table while, just days before this week's top-level meeting, Marshall's deputy Gil Blackman was letting press know what havoc a competitive system would wreak in the British coal industry.[55]

Meanwhile, the Electricity Council's now updated proposal involved selling the CEGB as a single generating unit, but to separate the National Grid and transfer its ownership, either to the unified national distribution company, via the Electricity Council itself, or an independent holding company. *Power in Europe*, once again, were critical of the industry's proposals: 'The striking similarity between the two "rival" schemes', they argued, 'is that both the CEGB and the Council come out of them more or less in one piece. The difference between them centres on control of the grid'.[56] The Electricity Council were hedging their bets somewhat: Sir Philip Jones later sought to influence Cecil Parkinson, Jones playing a role as a mediator between the department and the Area Board chairmen, with a view to creating a rival power block to challenge the CEGB.

Options

In the run up to the general election of June 1987 debates about the future structure of the electricity industry moved beyond a discussion of concepts. The key decisions that needed to be made were about, firstly, whether there would be a commitment made to privatise the industry and, secondly, the extent of competition. As part of a drafting process for the Conservative Manifesto, Nigel Lawson had been chairing a series of discussion groups—a sounding board—involving experts and stakeholders sympathetic with the Conservative Party's agenda of the time—including Stephen Littlechild[57]—with the aim of identifying the main policy priorities. One of the key topics discussed was whether to privatise the electricity or coal industry first. Although a general view at these meetings was that coal should be first—this was often referred to as 'the ultimate privatisation' in conservative policy circles—in the end they decided against this sequencing as it would have been impossible for investors to evaluate the prospects of coal investments if the main market for British coal, electricity generation, had a major structural question handing over it.

In parallel to this consultation process there were meetings taking place between the Department of Energy and the PM to discuss options and whether to include electricity privatisation in the manifesto for the June election. A meeting between Thatcher, Lawson (treasury), David Young (trade secretary after election), Malcolm Rifkind (Scottish secretary) and Cecil Parkinson (energy secretary after election) was reported as having 'included a review of possible options for the post-privatisation structure of the industry, but no definite decision on this was taken'.[58] The Conservative Manifesto therefore included a vague aspiration 'to bring forward proposals for privatising the electricity supply industry subject to proper regulation'.[59]

So, although the commitment to privatisation was made, the future structure of the industry was still all to play for. But there were two underlying factors which began to condition the political room for manoeuvre: the first was the increasingly negative view of the gas privatisation which had taken place in 1986 under Peter Walker's term as secretary of state. The second political calculation was the view that electricity privatisation needed to be completed within the term of the new parliament. June 1987 was Thatcher's third consecutive election victory; if an incomplete privatisation was passed on to a subsequent Labour government, the risks of it being watered down, or even reversed, were viewed as extremely high. The PM and the chancellor were therefore keen to appoint a stronger advocate for competition to the Department of Energy. Cecil Parkinson was their man. Parkinson had previously chaired the Conservatives' 1983 General Election campaign and was subsequently Secretary of State for Trade and Industry for a brief period. Prior to entering politics, Parkinson had built a career in the construction industry, heading up a successful sub-contracting firm in the 1960s.[60] Parkinson, at the outset, understood the basic trade-off at the heart of electricity privatisation: more competition would introduce risks, thus reducing the value of the companies to investors and the proceeds from the sale for the taxpayer. Following an early meeting with the PM and the chancellor, it was made clear to him that his remit was to favour 'competition over cash'.[61]

Three options for electricity industry reform were on Parkinson's desk when he took over at the Department of Energy: unifying the industry and an *en bloc* sale, regionally integrated utilities (the Scottish model) and the 'two company' model (separate sale of generation/transmission and distribution sides of the industry). The main advantages and disadvantages of each, as viewed by Parkinson and department officials, were as follows:

The *first option* of creating a single electricity company encompassing the CEGB and 12 Area Boards was, as Parkinson described at the time, the 'least likely option'.[62] The ESI was already fragmented, consisting of 15 separate companies, including the two in Scotland; amalgamating them would create one of the largest electricity companies in the world. Regardless of the practical challenges, previous *en bloc* sales of nationalised industries without fundamental restructuring, in particular British Telecom and British Gas, were by this point in the privatisation programme viewed as a mistake. The gas supply industry, shortly after privatisation, had encountered problems as customers accused the British Gas Corporation (BGC) of price discrimination and anti-competitive behaviour in the market for contracts to supply large consumers.[63] Already, by 1987, BGC had been referred to the MMC, which in 1988 'found that this discrimination was an abuse of monopoly power, and recommended that prices both for supply of gas to the contract market and for conditions of carriage of gas by competitors via its pipelines to be published and made non-discriminatory'.[64] Around this time, problems with British Telecom's dominant position in the market were also emerging: a July 1987 report by the Telecoms regulator criticised the company heavily for its poor quality of service to customers.

There was a view that the gas industry, led at the time by Denis Rooke as the Chairman of BGC, had got the upper hand against the government and Peter Walker during the 1986 privatisation. It should be noted however that the gas privatisation, rather than resulting from Rooke imposing his solution, reflected Walker's personal political philosophy. Peter Walker was not aligned with the radical right of the Tory Party and the monetarist doctrine of the first Thatcher government; although in favour of privatisation, he preferred a more cautious 'middle way' on policy issues, 'a balance between compassion and efficiency',[65] in line with a brand of 'One-Nation Toryism' of previous leaders such as Macmillan and Heath. Walker had been critical of the view that the nationalised industries were inefficient and during his time as energy secretary came into conflict with Lawson in the Treasury who wanted to cut the budgets of British Gas and the CEGB. Walker had argued that electricity and gas needed more capital investment if they were to become efficient. But the caricature of Walker and Rooke had taken root and Parkinson in his memoirs recounts that he was wary of damage to his reputation as a reforming minister if he was seen to fall under the influence of Marshall in a similar way.

The *en bloc* model did align to some extent with a sceptical view about the need for a radical reform which was held within senior levels of the Department of Energy and the Prime Minister's Policy Unit; that splitting the CEGB ought not to be an end in itself, rather the majority of available cost savings in the industry could be achieved by liberalising fuel purchasing and plant construction, not necessarily requiring a wide-scale structural reform of the entire electricity industry.[66] It was argued that more transparent decisions and accountability in these very specific areas would go a long way towards achieving the objectives of those proposing competition. But Parkinson had firmly set out his stall and stated clearly at the Conservative Party conference of that year that the ESI 'would not be privatised as a "block monolith"'.[67]

The *second option* of creating a number of separate utilities integrated at a regional level would have seen the Scottish electricity boards become the template for the new industry. The SSEB, run at the time by the highly respected engineer Donald Miller, was viewed as a highly efficient organisation. Replicating the Scottish model in England and Wales would however create structural imbalances, requiring arrangements for import and export between the different regions. Arrangements to enable the different power boards to trade had been actively discussed within the department; one possibility would have seen a separate grid company acting as a neutral common carrier, while an alternative proposal would have involved a more active role for the transmission grid operator in the market, acting as a 'market maker' by purchasing and selling power from the regional utilities and smoothing out the imbalances. However, the largest coal plants in England were clustered close to the mining areas around Yorkshire and Nottinghamshire, whilst demand was rising rapidly in the conservative heartlands of the south, largely due to the shift towards a financial/services-based economy. The model therefore raised difficult practical and political questions about electricity pricing and the ability to create an efficient merit order of plant dispatch in some regions. The Scottish model worked because the SSEB had a balanced portfolio of generation sources across the Central Belt and, despite some tensions, the two Scottish Boards had collaboration arrangements in place to balance the largely hydro output in the north with the nuclear and thermal generation in the southern region. It was felt that it would be difficult to replicate this model in England/Wales.

The *third option*, the two company model introduced previously, involved an amalgamation of the 12 Area Boards into a single distribution company. This had been Peter Walker's and the Electricity Council's preferred option and was the basis for much the analytical work that had been taking place within the department before Parkinson's arrival in June 1987. The logic behind the model was that the single distribution unit would be large enough to negotiate on equal terms with the CEGB, thus creating a competitive tension between the two sides of the industry. Marshall favoured the model because it left the CEGB intact; he had expressed confidence that the privatised CEGB would thrive under this structure and would have likely accepted it if the CEGB could have retained control of the grid under the arrangement. The Area Boards meanwhile were largely against it, seeing it as a dilution of their autonomy; a report by London Economics commissioned by the boards in order to inform these early debates had the title: 'Electricity Privatisation and the Area Boards: the Case for 12'.[68]

Although the position of the Area Boards strengthened as the process evolved, at this time it looked as if they were not in a strong position to influence the final outcome. *Power in Europe* reported that 'it now appears likely that four or five distribution companies will be created out of the 12 Area Boards which now distribute and market electricity. The boards appear to have lost their battle – launched rather too late in the day – to retain their present identities'.[69] However, as the process unfolded the Area Boards became increasingly central to Parkinson's vision for the new industry - that they be provided with the freedom to purchase electricity from whom they wished. He even wanted them to have an obligation to supply, thus entrusting them, rather than government, with responsibility for the overall security of the system.[70] According to Parkinson's vision, the freedoms conferred upon the Area Boards would be the central driver of competition.[71] Once the Area Board Chairmen realised that privatisation was on the cards and that the government favoured retaining them as independent companies, they communicated their general support for privatisation directly to Parkinson. As discussed later in this chapter, this was a decisive moment in the process as it created a strong alliance between the Area Boards and government, reducing the political power of the CEGB.[72]

In the meantime, these three options had been well rehearsed within the department, and when Cecil Parkinson took up office in June of 1987, he found, to his surprise, that little of the analytical groundwork had been done for restructuring the industry along truly competitive lines.[73] Shortly after this, in July, initial steps were taken to create a dedicated branch within the department's Electricity Division to drive the privatisation and competition agenda: William Rickett, a young civil servant who had previously been working as a private secretary to the prime minister,[74] was drafted in to lead the unit—known as B Division—under the overall charge of John Guinness, Deputy Secretary at the department. A second privatisation branch was created later in September 1987 focusing on consumer and nuclear issues, along with drafting the necessary legislation and updating the electricity supply code.[75]

A crucial second step taken early on after the 1987 election victory was the appointment of outside advisors. At the time the key expertise in the economic and financial aspects of privatisation was within the London merchant banks and a small number of consultancy firms. The main advisors hired by the department were Kleinwort Benson (financial aspects), Touche Ross (regulatory and accounting issues), Slaughter and May (legal advice) and Merz and McLellan (engineering and technical aspects). Rothschilds had advised the government on the gas privatisation, and partly because of this, the main advisory role went to their competitor, Kleinworts; although Rothschilds did play an important role later on in advising the Area Boards. The Electricity Council appointed Price Waterhouse while the CEGB appointed Lazard Brothers as key advisors. As we shall see, the role of advisors to the government, the CEGB and the Area Boards became crucial at a later stage when the privatisation programme had progressed to the finer details and the department began to organise civil servants, key industry personnel and advisors into a number of working groups. The civil service culture of the time enabled a close working relationship between senior officials and private sector advisors and it was viewed as a good career move for a civil servant to spend a period of time in the private sector on secondment. Rickett himself, for example, had worked at Kleinwort Benson's for a number of years in the mid-1980s.[76]

At this early stage, within the Department of Energy, there had been little consultation with industry and only one meeting at ministerial level which, as mentioned previously, took place in April 1987, before the election. The Electricity Division decided to establish consultations with industry via the Electricity Council who were asked by the department to arrange an industry-wide consultation, bringing together the views of the Area Boards and the CEGB. Meanwhile, Parkinson began to hold informal conversations with the Area Board Chairmen, who by this time had begun to organise as a collective body, with one of them—Dr. Jim Smith of Eastern Electricity—acting as chair.

Parkinson then met Walter Marshall of the CEGB later in September. At this meeting, Marshall articulated what became his main line of attack against the notion of splitting the CEGB and introducing meaningful competition, as Parkinson saw it; that a split of the generation and transmission sides of the industry would lead to cost increases and likely power failures. In these early conversations with Parkinson, Marshall went into some detail about the complex interactions between generation and transmission, which he argued were required to maintain the stability of the grid: the need for the grid operator to call on power stations to adjust their output at short notice to maintain frequency levels, for the ability to produce reactive power in order to stabilise voltage, and the importance of a centralised system operator to prevent localised faults from 'cascading' across the entire system. Marshall had described the idea of a separate grid company as 'a very exciting experiment, which had never been tried before'.[77]

While Marshall and senior CEGB representatives eventually conceded that separating the grid was technically feasible, their argument was that a central organisation needed to have the obligation to supply and hence overall control of the high-voltage grid. The 12 separate Area Boards, they argued, would be unable to fulfil such an obligation to supply, and if the CEGB was split, fulfilling this role would be more complex as the two or three generating companies would need to contract with each other, introducing added complexity and expense. The CEGB estimated that separating the grid would cost £270–700 m/year, getting more expensive the more diverse the generation market was.

Particularly important therefore, at this early stage, was the department's technical advisors' independent appraisal of the feasibility and likely transaction costs of separating generation from the grid. Based on Merz and McLellan's early work, the department's estimation of the costs of separation was much lower than the CEGB's, more in the region of £100 m/year, which would be more than offset by the efficiency savings from greater competition. While these technical challenges were of course not to be dismissed lightly, what grated with Parkinson and department officials during these early discussions was Marshall's lecturing and somewhat patronising tone, as they experienced it.[78] Parkinson recounted: 'He treated them [the early meetings] as a series of seminars at which I was the pupil and he was the teacher. Hours passed during which I was schooled in such subjects as the working of the national grid, reactive power and megavars'.[79] His main worry though was that that Marshall would go over his head and speak directly with the PM, using his leverage as a confidant on nuclear power and energy security issues to influence her.

Decisions

The Electricity Division's work on privatisation, led by Rickett, was presented to the entire cabinet at a seminar at Chequers, the prime minister's country residence, in September 1987. The seminar was a major milestone in the decision-making process as various options for industry reform were laid out on the table, and through the discussions the political impetus for a competitive industry model started to be revealed.

Two main papers were prepared in advance of the meeting: one factual/background and the second on structural considerations for the industry. The structural question was divided into two broad options: one which kept the CEGB broadly intact and had 'competition by growth'—replacing the BST with initial contracts between the Area Boards and the CEGB which would progressively taper away over time, gradually bringing about competition—and the second which created 'competition by division' of the CEGB. These were further distilled down into four feasible options which were presented to the ministers by Rickett. As Rickett himself recalled, he was very nervous and Parkinson had asked the prime minister to go easy on him and not interrupt as he made his presentation. He outlined the following four possibilities:[80]

- Option A: Keep the CEGB intact and privatise as it stood.
- Option B: As with A, but a number of power plants to be separated off and sold separately, with a view to creating a smaller competitor to the CEGB. The relevant analogy was the British Telecom privatisation where a limited version of competition was introduced by enabling a competitor (Mercury) access to local wires and to sell equipment to end-users, but with BT remaining by far the dominant player.

- Option C: As with B, but to separate the transmission grid from generation.
- Option D: As with C, but to split the CEGB into four or five competing generators of roughly equal size.

Other proposals, including the *en bloc* sale of a unified industry and the creation of integrated utilities at the regional level, were not included. In the case of the former, it was because it would not lead to competition, and the latter because it was seen as impractical and would take too long to implement. Keeping the CEGB intact, they felt, would not lead to competition. While Rickett and his team noted industry support for the 'two company' model and discussed how it could be developed to bring about competition, the expectation at the time was that a significant restructuring of the industry would take two parliamentary periods deliver. Parkinson was clear however that he wanted it done in one parliament. The dilemma was that the further down the competitive industry model route the government went, the longer the privatisation would take to deliver.

Based on initial modelling analysis, two key issues were identified by the Department of Energy officials at the meeting which would later play a crucial role in deciding the structure of the industry and the extent of competition. The first was the viability of the CEGB's planned nuclear investment programme and the likely price rises that would be required to deliver it, a key part of the strategy to fill the estimated capacity gap out to 2000. A more competitive industry would increase the risk premium demanded by private investors, and hence the raise the discount rate used for investment appraisal. As nuclear costs are skewed towards the initial capital investment, a high discount rate could make new nuclear uneconomic and would put in jeopardy the PWR investment programme. Based on their (limited) understanding of nuclear costs at the time, the department estimated that at a discount rate of 10%, coal would replace PWRs as the investment of choice. Rickett raised the possibility that the nuclear plants may need to be retained in the public sector. However, it was made clear by the prime minister that she was strongly in favour of privatising the nuclear industry,[81] in line with Walter Marshall's wishes.

The second issue identified by Rickett was the viability of the British Coal Corporation (BCC) if private generators were free to purchase coal at world prices, then much lower than the price per tonne paid by the

CEGB (see next chapter). The British coal industry received a large effective subsidy from its sales to the CEGB and its supply curve was relatively flat, meaning that a minor change in its contracted prices to supply the CEGB would make many of the pits uneconomic. It was estimated that up to 30,000 jobs could be lost across the coal industry if coal trade was liberalised, resulting in a 25 million tonne (mt) drop in output. The electricity industry was at the centre of a set of key economic interdependencies between the nuclear and coal industries, the latter employing over 70,000 people, and the former being a key strategic national industry since the development of the world's first civil nuclear power plant at Calder Hall in 1956. An intact CEGB would be beneficial to coal and nuclear, and therefore, there would be a strong political drive to limit competition in a way to protect these sectors. However, based on the department's analysis presented at the Chequers seminar, the main benefits of competition came from the severing of these ties, resulting in lower coal prices and a significant reduction in the ambition of the nuclear new build programme, leaving it up to the market to decide when and where to build new plant, and of what type.

At the seminar both the Chancellor of the Exchequer (Lawson) and Secretary of State for Trade and Industry (Lord Young) were adamant that 'genuine competition had to be introduced'[82] and that they would be willing to extend the timetable for privatising the industry over two parliaments if necessary. Both saw the separation of the grid and power stations as essential. The chancellor was in favour of option D above, involving a split of the CEGB into four or five competing generators, and thought that they would find a way to protect the nuclear programme. Meanwhile, Margaret Thatcher was less convinced, questioning whether deep structural reform was in fact necessary to bring about more efficient and competitive fuel purchasing and power plant investment decisions, somewhat in line with Marshall's 'kick start for competition' mantra. The cabinet agreed at the seminar to rule out option A and focus on C and D, and committed to passing legislation within the lifetime of the current parliament. The next step was to publish the government's decisions by March 1988, with a view to introducing legislation in the 1988/89 parliamentary session.

After the Chequers meeting, the Department of Energy's advisors began producing more in-depth analyses of options C and D. Both Touche Ross and Kleinwort Benson advised that a separation of the high-voltage transmission grid from the CEGB would be necessary if competition was to be at all feasible. If the grid was kept within the CEGB, they argued, the need to regulate and oversee its activities in the area of common carriage (monitoring, setting prices, etc.) would make it, in effect, a separate entity. Also, Kleinwort Benson gave advice not to merge the Area Boards, rather to sell them as separate entities. Meanwhile, Touche Ross was investigating two potential models of a separate grid company: (1) to operate as a sole purchaser buying the output of the generators or (2) to operate as a power pool, through which contracts between generators and distributors would be organised and settled. In this second model the grid company would dispatch the generators based on their bids and according to their marginal costs of operating, but the distributors would purchase their power from the generators at pre-arranged contracted rates. There would then be a mechanism whereby the generators who had contracts but were not included in the dispatch could pay lower cost generators to supply the distributors on their behalf. We will discuss in Chap. 4 how this initial idea for a competitive power pool—later referred to as the 'two pool' model—became so complex that it was found to be unworkable and was a key factor in delaying the move to competition.

At this early stage the department came to the view that the nuclear industry would need some form of protection, either through a subsidy or an obligation on the Area Boards to purchase a proportion of the output of the nuclear plants. Kleinwort Benson advised that a nuclear company on its own would not be sellable to the private sector, but if the nuclear plants were combined with some of the thermal stations, it may be possible to float. In the event that the CEGB was split into two, according to Option C, Kleinwort proposed a 70/30 split (Big G and Little G), with the bigger of the two generating companies having a large enough balance sheet to accommodate liabilities for nuclear fuel reprocessing, waste and decommissioning, beyond those which were known and quantified at the time of privatisation.

A subsequent departmental seminar was held at Nuneham Park with the purpose of discussing the work of the Electricity Division. This seminar was notable for two reasons: firstly, because it was attended by Stephen Littlechild, who had been recently appointed as an economic advisor to Cecil Parkinson. Littlechild had previously exchanged letters with Parkinson regarding the privatisation programme. This had followed a recommendation to Parkinson by Alan Walters, who had been the chief economic advisor to the prime minister and Littlechild's former lecturer at the University at Birmingham in the early 1960s. At the seminar Littlechild recalled that an anonymous straw poll was conducted on the four options: 13 were in favour of option C, while Littlechild himself voted for B.[83] Surprisingly, he didn't vote for option D, this was on the basis that, as it was then presented, the nuclear plants would be owned collectively by the competing generators. He was later reported to have 'conceded' that option C would constitute effective competition, meeting minimum criteria.[84] But he was frustrated that a genuinely competitive option, in his view, was not presented at the seminar. The failure to consider this option was because of the PM's strong preference for a privatised nuclear industry.

Another point of note was that at the seminar Parkinson was informed of a threat by the CEGB Board to resign *en masse* if the organisation was to be split up. The prime minister was known to be reluctant to agree to privatisation at all if Walter Marshall was not on side. This prompted the Electricity Division to quickly draft what later became the famous 1988 White Paper as a means of presenting the government's view in a unified and coherent way before the CEGB's threat might water down the political drive for competition. In advance of this, Parkinson met with Thatcher to present his views on 15 December 1987 and subsequently a draft paper was presented to ministers in January 1988 outlining option C as the preferred way forward. However, at the meeting Nigel Lawson argued in favour of option D as the large generating company in option C would be in a dominant market position. Thatcher was of the view that option C could promote effective competition because under the department's model the Area Boards could generate a proportion of their own demand themselves, thus competing against the dominant generators. As expressed at the Chequers seminar, she was concerned about the future viability of the nuclear programme under the model, but she was persuaded following a discussion with senior civil servants - her Principal Private Secretary and the Department of Energy's Permanent Secretary.[85] Following a meeting between Parkinson and the PM in February 1988, they agreed to proceed on the basis of option C.

The White Paper, *Privatising Electricity*, was then published on 25 February 1988, with a set of proposals for the later privatisation of the Scottish industry published on 2 March.[86] *Privatising Electricity* was based on option C above, involving a split of the CEGB into two competing generators, a separate transmission grid company to be owned collectively by the Area Boards, and with the Electricity Council abolished. Noting that this was a relatively short document, of 16 pages, it was commented in the FT that 'Rarely can the fate of such an important industry have been disposed of in so few words'.[87] Rickett himself played a key role in writing the document, having spent a weekend after the Nuneham seminar at the tail-end of 1987 writing the first draft. The 'six principles' which framed the document were as follows:

1. *Decisions about the supply of electricity should be driven by the needs of customers.*
2. *Competition is the best guarantee of the customers' interests.*
3. *Regulation should be designed to promote competition, oversee prices and protect the customers' interests in areas where natural monopoly will remain.*
4. *Security and safety of supply must be maintained.*
5. *Customers should be given new rights, not just safeguards.*
6. *All who work in the industry should be offered a direct stake in their future, new career opportunities and the freedom to manage their commercial affairs without interference from government.*[88]

Despite the emphasis on competition as a general principle, at this stage the idea that the new electricity industry would see competition between suppliers for each and every customer was not the central idea that it later became. The White Paper stated, 'The Government's proposals will end the effective monopoly in generation and give more influence to the distribution companies and their customers'.[89] While customers would be given rights and their needs would be 'reflected' in the decisions of the distribution companies, it was generally accepted that only the very largest industrial users would participate directly in the market. The prices charged to end-users of electricity were to be regulated via regular price controls, and the profits of the distribution companies would be dependent on their ability to reduce their costs, either relative to previous performance or in relation to other distribution companies (yardstick competition). The distributors would also own the transmission grid company as they would have a strong incentive to promote competition and reduce the costs of generation.

Crucially, rather than responsibility for electricity supply being left entirely to the market, the obligation to supply was retained, but placed with the 12 distribution companies (the former Area Boards). This would ensure that the contracts with generators were sufficient to meet demand and, according to Parkinson, would have de-risked the electricity industry from a political point of view as customers would no longer look to government to ensure security of supply.[90] We will see in Chap. 4 how the new market in fact operated without a statutory 'obligation to supply', rather it was coordinated via a series of contracts between generators and distributors and an inventive mechanism built into the market which ensured a reserve margin was in place. The later decision made not to have an obligation imposed was partly because brokers communicated to the Department of Energy that any company operating under such a restraint would be difficult to sell to city investors.

Under Parkinson's early model, set out in the White Paper, the independent distribution companies would be free to generate themselves or contract for power supply, either via their collectively owned grid company, which would in turn instruct the cheapest mix of power plants to run during each settlement period, or via direct contracts with generating companies. We will see later in Chap. 4 how the complexity of operating these two forms of contracting side-by-side caused problems at the market design stage later in 1989. Situating the distribution companies so centrally in the new industry in this way tallied with Cecil Parkinson's view that for the vast majority of customers it would be through the freedoms granted to the distribution companies to operate in the market that the benefits of competition would be achieved. Addressing the House of Commons on 7 March Parkinson stated that:

> the distribution companies will be the key to change. With a turnover of between £500 million and £1,500 million each last year, they will be among the largest private sector companies in their region. They will have a strong local identity and a real incentive to strike the best deal for their customers. Our proposals will give them the freedom to use that initiative. They will become a force for development in their local economies. They will become real independent companies looking after local interests, not just the distributors of the CEGB's electricity … Because the CEGB's monopoly will be ended, and because its obligation to supply will be removed, the distribution companies will no longer be obliged to take all their electricity from one supplier. Because the companies will own the grid, they will be able to bring new suppliers on to the system. They will be able to buy in the cheapest electricity and will have plenty of choice. The customer cannot have more than one switch, but the distribution companies can and will have more than one supplier.[91]

With the CEGB to be broken up, the view of the FT's *Power in Europe* was that 'The chairmen of the 12 Area Boards … emerge as undisputed winners'.[92] They were to remain intact and 'be sold separately', while 'The clear loser in this scheme is the CEGB. Its arguments about the importance of an integrated generation/transmission system have been wholly discounted, and its robust lobbying campaign has proved an expensive waste of time'. With the obligation to supply, a largely captive customer base and the ability to contract freely for power, the FT went so far as to predict that the 'The Boards will, in effect, become integrated utilities in all but name; local monopolies, deriving their supplies from a specified group of power stations, with the two Gs [the two generating companies] acting as their contractors for the construction and operation of power plants'.[93]

We will discuss later how the concept of retail competition moved into the centre of the debate, in a large part due to Stephen Littlechild's growing influence within the Department of Energy. At this stage, however, around the publication of *Privatising Electricity*, the notion that each and every electricity customer would be able to choose their supplier, regardless of geographical location, was not the view of even the most ardent proponents of competition. Littlechild later recollected how at this time he and Rickett discovered that their views were similar and had begun to work closely together.[94] They thought about how to insert wording into the White Paper which would keep open the possibility of more radical ideas around competition as the privatisation process evolved. The key sentence in that document that Littlechild later referred to is as follows:

> And large users will also be able to buy electricity direct from generators, by-passing the distribution companies but using their transmission and distribution systems for 'common carriage' of the electricity.[95]

That customers connected to one of the regional networks could 'bypass' the local distribution company and purchase electricity from an alternative supplier was based on experience in the telecoms sector where, shortly after privatisation, it became possible for BT's competitors to gain access to their local lines and phones and offer services directly to customers. Extending this concept to electricity and offering the choice of supplier to the 22 million electricity customers in England and Wales was not seen to be a feasible, or even desirable, proposal. We shall see later that as Littlechild and Rickett's group within the department worked to make full retail competition more central to the debate about privatisation, it raised difficult issues about the feasibility of selling electricity companies whose customers would have freedom to switch to competitors. These ideas were being developed surreptitiously at this stage however.

Immediately following the publication of the White Paper, work began within the CEGB, with Marshall's consent, on the creation of shadow boards for the two new companies, then termed 'Big G' and 'Little G'. Marshall's resistance to the proposals was perhaps assuaged by him being invited by the secretary of state to be the chairman designate of Big G. It was agreed that the roles of Chairman and Chief Executive of the new companies should not both be held by CEGB insiders. One each - a CEGB insider and an outsider - would fill the key roles, with Ed Wallis, Director of operations at the CEGB, being appointed as CEO of 'Little G'. Meanwhile, the existing Area Board Chairmen were announced as chairmen designate of the new companies, but their official appointments were not confirmed by government until late on in the process, most likely as a way of keeping them on board with the government's plans.[96] Marshall remained central to shaping the new industry at this stage and proposed ideas around the split of generators between Big and Little G, with the larger company to have 30,876 MW (62.2%) of the non-nuclear capacity and all of the nuclear plants. This was analysed by Touche Ross and seen as reasonable. Marshall was keen to ensure in these discussions that the two companies would remain intact and not be asset stripped by an overly powerful regulator. In particular, that they could retain control of the greenfield sites that the CEGB owned and had in mind for future development.

Following this early conceptual phase, when ideas about the future of the industry were being put forward, the next chapter takes the story forward from the point when the White Paper *(Privatising Electricity)* was published in late February 1988. It covers the period from this point up to late 1989, when key political decisions were made about the economic relationships between component parts of the new electricity industry whose structure had been broadly sketched out in that document.

CHAPTER 3

Trade-Offs: Competition or Cash?

With the White Paper published in early 1988, the general timetable for the privatisation was to have the new companies operating (vesting) by 1 January 1990, the flotation of the Area Boards—to be rechristened as Regional Electricity Companies —in the first half of 1990, with flotation of the first generating company in autumn 1990 and the second in spring 1991. In the run up to this, the degree to which competition would jeopardise the sale of the new generating companies and the Area Boards become the central tension at the heart of the politics of the privatisation process.

Although the instruction given to Cecil Parkinson as he took office in the summer of 1987 was to favour 'competition over cash', there was a significant grey area between the extremes of monopoly and competition which needed to be navigated by departmental officials and their advisors. The debates and decisions taken focused on three key areas: firstly, the liabilities and economic performance of the nuclear component of the industry, raising fundamental questions about whether the nuclear power plants could even be privatised; secondly, the future of the coal industry if generators were subject to competitive forces; thirdly, the implications for retail competition if the new Regional Electricity Companies (RECs)[1] were obliged to purchase power in a way which would provide a measure of protection to the nuclear and coal industries. If the RECs were saddled with these contractual obligations, whilst being subjected to the full forces

R. Bolton, *Making Energy Markets*,
https://doi.org/10.1007/978-3-030-90075-5_3

of competition, they could not have been floated in the London Stock Exchange at a reasonable share price and the return to the taxpayer would have been minimal.

This chapter explains how a contractual structure for the new electricity industry was eventually arrived at. This involved long-term contracts between the two generating companies and British Coal for fuel supply at pre-determined prices, running out to 1993, along with an obligation on the RECs to purchase nuclear output at above-market prices for a period of eight years. These contracts meant that the ability of the RECs to purchase electricity from competing generators freely in the market, so central to the initial vision for the competitive industry outlined in the White Paper, needed to be curtailed. It also meant that limits had to be placed on Littlechild's ideal of full retail competition, thus enabling the RECs to retain a significant proportion of their customers who were, controversially, not given access to the market. This mitigated the risk to the RECs that competing suppliers, not bound by such contracting obligations, would take their customers away, whilst ensuring that prospective investors in these companies had greater certainty over future revenues.

Decisions made during this period had real-world effects in terms of who were the winners and losers from the reform process. The decision to subsidise nuclear via a levy on customer bills and the domestic coal industry via long-term contracts, combined with the limitations placed on access to the market in its early years, meant that, contrary to the intentions of the White Paper, domestic customers did not benefit initially from the new market. Rather, it was shareholders in the new companies who benefited, along with a relatively small number of large electricity customers who could access competitive tariffs, and to some extent taxpayers who were no longer obliged to keep the nuclear and coal industries afloat.

The first sections of the chapter explain in detail the reasons why the coal and nuclear industries required protection from market forces. Then the chapter follows debates about how protection of coal and nuclear were to be accommodated within a competitive industry model; this was around the time of the publication of the Electricity Bill in November 1988 and continued up to September 1989. The decision not to privatise nuclear, made late in the day, meant that the necessary payments to keep this industry afloat could be made via rather traditional means; a subsidy to a publicly owned nuclear company funded through an additional levy on consumer bills (the Fossil Fuel Levy [FFL]). A challenge which needed to be addressed was how to channel payments into the coal industry if the coal generating plants were to be operated by private companies who were themselves subject to competition from new entrants into the market. A key question was therefore how long-term contracts for coal supplied to the generators could be accommodated within a competitive market structure. The overall issue was how to make the British coal industry more competitive and efficient, thus enabling subsidies to be wound down, whilst ensuring that the generators and the RECs were attractive investment propositions. Ultimately, as part of a contract package tabled later in September 1989, it was agreed to introduce financial 'contracts for differences' between the generators and the RECs. As will be explained in the next chapter, this required that all power be traded centrally via a competitive power pool through which a 'system price' was determined. This price was then used as a reference for the financial contracts which enabled additional revenues, above the typical market price, to be channelled from captive consumers, through the RECs, and into the generating companies, thus covering the costs of their coal contracts.

The next chapter will explain how this contractual arrangement and market structure, which was designed to address a number of competing and ultimately incompatible political priorities, stored up problems for the future. As the competitive market got up and running, the market became undermined due to a combination of the earlier structural decision to split the Central Electricity Generating Board (CEGB) into only two competing generators—Big G and Little G were later christened National Power and PowerGen—along with the centralised nature of the market, which meant that the private generators could exert their market power over the power price, thus de-legitimising it as a trusted reference for the entire market. The RECs felt the need to hedge the risk that the incumbent generators' market power would be exerted to their disadvantage and went their own way by integrating upstream and constructing their own power plants. This approach to managing risk became a driver behind the famous British 'dash for gas' of the 1990s, and the start of a trend towards consolidation and re-integration of the industry from the late 1990s onwards.

Coal's Problems, Contracts and Constraints on Competition

To understand the existential threat facing the British coal industry one needs to look back at the development of an interdependency between the CEGB and the British Coal Corporation (BCC) which had, by 1987, resulted in a significant effective subsidy due to a long-running trend of declining world coal prices. At the time of privatisation almost 80% of the output of the British coal industry was sold to the CEGB for electricity generation, in the region of 78 mt annually. This share had increased significantly since nationalisation, when only 14% of British coal was used for electricity generation. By 1986/87, as coal's share in heating, transport and industrial markets diminished, '77 per cent of British Coal sales were at power stations; coal provided over 70 per cent of the power stations' total fuel requirements; 45 per cent of CEGB's total costs and 55 per cent of their operating costs were accounted for by supplies of British coal'.[2]

Despite the significant industrial strife of the early and mid-1970s which contributed to the collapse of the conservative-led government in 1974, by the early 1980s the British coal industry's position seemed to have strengthened. The Labour-led minority government's 1978 'Plan for Coal' had envisioned an increase in coal production to 135 mt by 1985, and by 1980 the volume of output from deep mines was at its highest for three years. Capital investment in the industry was over £600 m, significantly higher than the £69 m invested in 1973/74. Meanwhile, Europe's largest coal plant at Drax in Yorkshire was ordered in early 1978.

The early years of the first Thatcher government saw a broad continuation of the high levels of investment in the coal industry, and with the 1980 Coal Industry Act, the energy secretary, David Howell, was seeking to use public investment as leverage to get BCC to close its unprofitable pits. The industry was also put under increasing financial scrutiny as the government demanded that it increase productivity and break even, and over time to use its own resources for capital investment, reducing the burden on the public sector borrowing requirement.

This resulted in a pushback by the powerful National Union of Mineworkers (NUM) and in somewhat of a climbdown the conservative government relaxed these financial constraints in 1981. Part of the rationale for this was that the government felt it was not prepared for a full-on confrontation with the NUM. However, with the appointment of the right-wing Nigel Lawson as Energy Secretary in September 1981 and the hard-left Arthur Scargill in 1982 as President of the NUM, the stage was set for a confrontation. The strategy of the conservative government shifted from capital investment and incentivising productivity improvements towards stockpiling of coal and chemicals used for electricity generation at power stations in expectation of a national strike. The prolonged miners' strike of 1984/85 resulted in a clear defeat for the NUM.

The fallout from this coincided with structural changes to international coal markets which, along with the deployment of labour-saving technologies, had a greater negative impact on the domestic industry than the miners' strike itself. As part of its 1979 'joint understanding' with BCC—an agreement between two nationalised industries, not a legal contract—the CEGB had agreed to limit its coal imports and purchase 95% of its supplies from British mines, and by the mid-1980s only 1 mt was being imported. The CEGB agreed to purchase annually 75 mt for the next five years from 1980 and this was followed in 1986 by a 'five-year accord' for 72 mt, which an average price of £42/t.

By this time, Marshall's strategy was, in his own words, one of 'progressively driving British Coal's prices down towards world prices',[3] and in order to reflect this in the deal with BCC, a tiered pricing structure was agreed. So, rather than a set price for the entire quantity, in the first year 50 mt (£46.88/t) was linked to production costs, 12 mt (£29.50/t) was linked to world prices and a further 10 mt (£33/t) was linked to the cost of imported coal delivered to accessible power stations. There had been ongoing rounds of discussion between the CEGB and BCC about how these quantities and pricing methodologies would change over the course of the five years; for example, the 50 mt linked to production costs would drop to 47 in the second year. The tiered approach fitted a policy of 'broad alignment' with world prices; alignment would only be applied to that British coal which could be practically replaced by imports via Rotterdam at this time.

Despite its 'Byzantine structure', there was a strong economic and political rationale for the agreements; they created stability for BCC, who could invest in improving productivity and reducing costs at the mine; the CEGB had price stability and a reliable source of fuel, while for the government it avoided the prospect of a major disruption to the coal industry and mass unemployment. A key advantage from BCC's point of view was that the contracts were negotiated for output from the entire coal industry, rather than on a pit-by-pit basis, which would have exposed the high marginal costs of the many deep mine operations.

The CEGB, partly due to pressure from government, was hedging its bets however, having signed a contract with Shell, SSM and Carbocol for just over 1 mt of coal and announcing it would also buy on the spot market for delivery into Rotterdam. The generator had begun to actively seek out alternative sources of fuel supply internationally, as a diversification strategy following the miners' strike of 1984/85; however, the scope to take advantage of cheaper international sources was limited by the lack of import terminals and means of delivery to inland power stations, particularly those in the North of England and the Midlands. The hybrid coal/oil plants located along the Thames (Kingsnorth, West Thurrock, Tilbury and Littlebrook) could be more readily accessed, but the scope was limited on a national basis. As we will discuss in the next chapter, while the logistical challenges of using imported coal at inland power stations in the North and Midlands remained, the operation of a competitive wholesale power market based on marginal costs meant that those plants using cheaper imports moved higher up the merit order of plant dispatch, having a particularly negative impact on the large inland coal plants.

In Scotland, more intense pressure had come on these types of arrangements as the South of Scotland Electricity Board (SSEB), the lager of the two Scottish utilities, had a much more acrimonious relationship with BCC than the CEGB south of the border. Two major SSEB plants, Cockenzie and Longannet, had associated with them long-term take-or-pay contracts with BCC for coal supply, but by the late 1980s SSEB was refusing to pay, demanding a closer link to world coal prices in its contracts, some of which dated back to the 1960s. Despite that Scottish coal was relatively low cost, the SSEB was being charged 12% more for its supplies than the CEGB. Part of the reason for this was that due to the much larger size of the CEGB relative to the SSEB, the CEGB would always demand a lower price than the Scottish utility. As Walter Marshall spelt out:

> the CEGB is the largest customer that British Coal have. Indeed, we are the largest user of coal in the western world. Since we are the largest user of coal, I would expect British Coal to give us the best commercial deal that is going and I would be upset if South of Scotland got a better deal than we did … if Don Miller [SSEB's Chairman] makes one agreement with British Coal, I want a better one.[4]

The SSEB invited tenders for coal imports to supply the two stations, threatening the BCC monopoly. BCC then obtained a court order demanding the payment, and in response SSEB signed an initial contract for 1 mt of imported coal and threatened to mothball the stations and replace the capacity with its back-up oil plants at Kincardine and Inverkip. In some respects the SSEB had more leverage than the CEGB because of the location of its large coal plants along the Firth of Forth, and the fact that the mining industry in Scotland was, by this point, much smaller[5] and less politically powerful than that south of the border. Also, the new advanced gas-cooled reactor (AGR) nuclear station at Torness, commissioned in 1988, meant that the SSEB had a huge capacity margin and could continue to meet demand without its coal plants. Subsequently, in July 1988, SSEB and BCC came to an agreement which involved a nine-month pricing agreement.

From the CEGB's point of view, certainty about future coal prices was more of a priority than buying from the cheapest source. Fuel price stability was central to its long-term investment planning which, as discussed previously, had become increasingly focused on the delivery of a large-scale PWR (pressurised water reactor) investment programme. The agreed prices for coal supply served as a crucial input into its investment appraisal calculations, at this time based on its 'Net Effective Cost' (NEC) method.[6] Based on appraisals conducted by the CEGB in the late 1970s and early 1980s, it had been estimated that in order for new nuclear to be selected over coal plant in its NEC modelling, the real price of coal would need to increase by '36% between 1980 and 1986/7'.[7] This was during the period when it had been envisioned that many of the new nuclear plants would be at the construction phase, so the relative costs of nuclear versus coal would have been highly sensitive to fuel price variations. The CEGB annual reports presenting these investment appraisals were later heavily criticised for obscuring key assumptions made about rising coal prices, upon which the financial viability of the nuclear programme relied.

The implications for the economic future of the coal industry following privatisation had been raised during the Chequers seminar on options for the future structure of the electricity industry (see previous chapter). While some within the department, including within Rickett's group, had explored the possibility of removing BCC's implicit subsidy immediately and relying on the inertia within the market to protect the coal industry for a few years,[8] this was never a realistic political proposition. It was clear that contracts between the generators and BCC would need to continue in some form.

The BCC were initially looking for ten-year contracts with the generators, with a similar structure to the previous deal with the CEGB (prices linked to inflation and an overall industry-wide volume, with tranches progressively reducing down to the prevailing world prices). Government was also amenable to long-term contracts, the logic being that the price stability would improve the prospects of privatising the coal industry further down the line. However, if the electricity industry was to be truly competitive, coal industry privatisation was highly unlikely given the competitive pressure that the private generators would be under. The shadow boards of the new generators were looking for three-year contracts with station-by-station deals, rather than a single industry-wide volume and pricing structure. If the generators were to sign long-term contracts, they would be vulnerable to new entrants who could undercut them with imported coal. Unsurprisingly, the reaction of the RECs was that in order to protect against competitive entry into their supply markets they would need to retain a monopoly over a significant share of their customer base if they were to be tied to long-term electricity supply contracts with the generators.

As discussed in more detail in the next chapter, as the wholesale electricity market became organised around power plants being dispatched at their marginal costs of operating, the generators needed greater flexibility in these coal contracts, especially the ability to source cheap fuel to make a profit from their plants lower in the merit order. The battle lines were drawn. As was written in *Power in Europe* at the time, 'The generators want freedom; the coal board wants stability. The government wants to open up the market, which at the same time it wants a British coal industry left in sellable form'.[9]

Jumping forward, by the end of 1989, a deal was brokered by the secretary of state—John Wakeham—where the two private generators and the BCC came to a three-year agreement, purchasing 70 mt in 1990/91 and 1991/92, reducing to 65 mt in 1992/93. These contracts amounted to a £1 bn/year payment above-market prices to the coal industry for these three years. PowerGen, the smaller of the two generators, would take 28 mt in the first two years, while National Power would purchase 42 mt. The coal was to be priced in two tranches, a broadly similar pricing structure to the last years of the BCC 'joint understanding' with the CEGB: across all three years 40 mt was to be sold at £1.85/GJ (at the pithead rather than delivered to the station) while the remaining volume (30 mt in the first two years, then reducing to 25) would be closer to world prices, at £1.50/GJ. These prices would rise in line with inflation, and an agreement was reached whereby the two generators were protected from this inflation risk to a significant degree, with the BCC absorbing the first 5–6% of the price rise,[10] measured against the Retail Price Index (RPI). This was significant given that inflation was projected to be in the region of 8% in 1989/90. The contracts ensured that generators' costs, along with the coal prices, would decline in real terms once privatisation commenced.

Although the ambition was that both sides would continue to negotiate and come up with an agreement for years 4 and 5, at this stage the view of the department was that longer coal contracts at vesting would threaten the flotation of the generators. This was done with the knowledge that it would put the BCC under financial strain and result in the closure of 10–12 pits and the loss of about 25,000 jobs over four years, but as the department's own record states, 'The Secretary of State had been able to persuade Sir Robert Haslam [the BCC Chairman] to accept the deal only by assuring him that further financial support from the Government would be forthcoming'.[11]

The British Coal Corporation were willing to sacrifice contract longevity for prices in the interests of maintaining employment levels. It also seems that they were of the view—incorrectly, as outlined in Chap. 4—that low prices on the international markets were temporary, mostly due to sterling's appreciation against the US dollar and lower energy demand due to economic recession. Although the price of coal delivered into Rotterdam had by 1988 halved over a two-year period, in the medium term, as the commodity cycle took its course, the assumption was that British mined coal would once again be competitive against imports. Due to the low prices, the supply glut would be eaten away as marginal coal mines dedicated to export, which had received significant investment following the first oil crisis, would be mothballed or closed down. BCC believed that, in time, as energy demand picked up and the dollar recovered, the privatised generators would place a premium on contracts priced in sterling. They also predicted that these deflationary factors would have an effect before National Power or PowerGen were able to construct the port and infrastructure required to transport large volumes of imports directly to inland power stations, thus avoiding the additional costs of shipping from Rotterdam. While the prevailing low prices may have been temporary, international competition was changing the dynamic of coal markets, as BCC themselves recognised in their submission to the Energy Committee on privatisation in 1988 (published on 27 July):

> everything therefore points to a rise in the present price of international steam coal. On the other hand, substantial under utilised capacity exists in the world which could be brought back into production if there was confidence in a sustained level of higher prices. The large potential of Eastern US mines, given higher prices, effectively puts a ceiling on international coal prices.[12]

As discussed further below, another key reason that the deal between the generators and the BCC ended up being three years, rather than the ten-year period initially proposed, was that following the publication of the White Paper, retail competition had risen up the agenda to become a realistic prospect at this stage. This would have made it difficult for the costs of long-term take-or-pay contracts for coal supply to be passed through to end customers. The view was that the tonnage in the contracts had to be linked to a protected market share; otherwise, it was unlikely that the industry could be floated at all. The logical consequence of locking-in the generators to long-term contracts with the BCC was that the costs of meeting the obligations in these contracts would need to be passed on to customers in some way. How this was done would have a determining effect on the extent of competition in the new market: if full retail competition was introduced, whilst the costs of meeting the obligations in the coal contracts were passed on to customers via the RECs, the value of these distribution/supply companies would diminish and their viability as private entities would be called into question. This is because the RECs would be subject to the full force of competition on one side of their operations (retail sales) but would have ridged take-or-pay contractual obligations on the other (electricity purchasing).

A key question which arose prior to the signing of the coal supply and vesting contracts was the extent to which the two generators, who were to hold the vast majority of the country's generation capacity, would be able to set the terms of the contracts entered into for bulk electricity supplies to the RECs. The RECs were wary of being trapped in an arrangement similar to the CEGB's old Bulk Supply Tariff (BST). A key concern was that National Power and PowerGen, along with other new entrant generators accessing the market via common carriage, would out-compete the RECs in the market for large customers, as they could dedicate their most efficient plant to these users and offer contracts on the basis of low marginal prices. The RECs would be stuck on long-term contracts based on less favourable terms; similar to the BST but with open competition for their largest and most lucrative customers. This risk to the RECs as viable businesses would be worsened if, as had been proposed in the White Paper, the obligation to supply all customers was transferred to them. The question for government was whether some form of regulation of the electricity supply contracts between the generators and large consumers of power would be required.

At a departmental seminar on regulation held in July 1988, the RECs had claimed that given the availability of cheap fuel sources and technological innovations, new entrant independent power producers could produce power at a level 30% below the BST. The department's financial advisors, Kleinwort Benson, were clearly of the view that National Power and PowerGen could not be sold if prices were pushed down by competitive new entrants in this way. There was therefore a dilemma facing the government: low market prices for electricity generation would enable the RECs to become competitive and for retail competition to be introduced, but this would make the generators unsellable as they would be saddled with binding obligations in the long-term coal contracts.

The view at this time was that in order to provide a measure of stability to the industry, contracts between the generators and the RECs for bulk power supply would need to be introduced for a duration of 5–15 years, at a level broadly in line with the existing BST, and cost recovery would be enabled by price controls which would be imposed across the whole customer base. At this early stage, thinking around retail competition and the need for price controls was very much in flux, reflecting the fact that there were radically different views within the department itself. The White Paper had envisioned competition to be limited to large customers, with the RECs as the main market makers, but shortly after its publication, at a meeting of a 'Joint Department/REC Regulation Working Group' held in March 1988, a proposal was made by the department that full retail competition could be introduced on day one.[13]

A particular concern of the RECs during these early negotiations was the way in which the contracts with the generators would be structured, in particular with respect to how the costs of electricity generation would be covered. Their concern was that if capacity charges—as opposed to energy charges—were high, new entrants purchasing their supplies on the free market would have a competitive advantage as they could purchase closer to the marginal cost prices of generation. The generators were of course keen to have steady capacity payments in order to cover their fixed costs, but if they were given freedom to allocate these costs between customers, they could potentially discriminate against the RECs and 'cherry-pick' their large customers. In order to assuage these fears they proposed linking the RECs' contracts with eligible customers to generation contracts, so if the user switched, the REC would not be saddled with the contract payments. They also proposed a tapering mechanism whereby contracts would fall off if generators began supplying large users in a REC's region. The RECs were, on the other hand, proposing a 'net-back' mechanism whereby the capacity charges in a certain proportion of contracts were linked to spot prices. They had agreed on the broad outline of this mechanism and were negotiating the percentage of 'net-back' contracts of the overall supply, with the RECs proposing 20% for five to eight years and the generators proposing 10% for three years.[14] In the end, these negotiations came to nothing as BCC were not willing to subject themselves to the uncertain revenues implied with such mechanisms. As outlined earlier, they preferred shorter contracts but with steady cash flows.

Alongside the issues of retail competition and generator market dominance, a key concern of the RECs in signing long-term supply contracts was how fuel price fluctuations would be treated. As discussed earlier, a proportion of the coal contracts were linked to fluctuating world prices; the pertinent question was how potential price increases would be passed through to customers via the RECs. The intention was to utilise the RPI-X formula for regulating the RECs' price increases; this was a formula initially developed by Stephen Littlechild for regulating the British Telecom monopoly in 1983. According to it, the monopoly company's prices would increase in line with the RPI inflation index and adjusted according to an efficiency factor 'x'. If a negative 'x' was applied for the regulatory period, it would be based on a presumption that the company could operate more efficiently and reduce its prices relative to the economy-wide average. The formula was seen to be successful because it provided an efficiency incentive through adjusting the x-factor, and a structure through which regulatory intervention would be somewhat predictable from an investor's point of view.

The issue with applying this to the RECs, however, was that the key cost driver for electricity prices—generation costs, which in turn were strongly influenced by coal prices—was largely out of their control. Electricity generation accounted for about three-quarters of RECs' overall costs, with fuel costs being in the region of 50% of the operating costs of the electricity industry as a whole. The balance to be struck was between getting the RECs to be efficient in terms of how they purchased power, but with some form of cost pass-through, without which investors would not be protected against unforeseen and potentially significant fuel cost increases due to changing international conditions. Depending on the length of the generation contracts, the price that the RECs would pay for power via the energy component of the contract would vary, the question was how this fluctuation would be dealt with given that the RECs were to have an obligation to supply the captive customers.

A number of ideas were proposed at the July 1988 seminar on regulation: both the generators and the RECs were in favour of full cost pass-through, achieved by adjusting the pricing formula to RPI-X+Y, with 'y' being the cost of generation. However, government was reluctant to agree to this, on the basis that if this protection was in place there would be little incentive on the RECs to purchase power in an efficient way. There were discussions about having a fixed percentage of cost pass-through (partial pass-through), but the percentage of pass-through would need to be close to 100% to manage the risk for the RECs. On the other extreme, the option of not having a 'y' factor was discussed; that is, letting prices fluctuate within a range around the general rate of inflation. But this was also seen as inflexible and risky, in the event of a severe price shock. Another idea was to index 'y' to world fuel prices. However, with an index a challenging scenario could arise if prices on the international coal market rose just as those for domestic sources were falling, due to the effects of competition on the British coal industry. This would provide the generators with an unwarranted windfall. In any event, given the complexity of the international coal market, the department felt it would be too difficult to construct a reliable index. The department had favoured at this time a third option: a 'yardstick approach', where price increases would be linked to a baseline of costs incurred across the sector of 12 RECs, placing an incentive on each company to perform in line with this average.

Stephen Littlechild proposed an alternative to these three models which, rather than calculating a single price for the full costs faced by the RECs—generation, distribution and supply costs—would involve a split of costs related to generation and those related to distribution and supply. There would be separate pricing formulae applied to each, one involving the application of basic RPI-X regulation to the wires business, a largely non-competitive activity, with a different approach being taken to the treatment of supply, where the cost base and risk profile were different. By the end of 1988, Littlechild's idea of having different pricing formulae for distribution and supply began to win favour; a decisions paper, including draft proposals on licencing and regulation, published in December of 1988, 'proposed that distribution of electricity to both tariff and contract customers should be subject to a RPI-X formula; whereas prices for the supply of electricity should be subject to the RPI-X+Y formula (with Y relating to average system generating costs, ie the yardstick approach)'.[15] The paper was also clear that regulation would only apply to the tariff component and not the contracts supply market through which large users could transact directly with generators.

Following the implications of the long-term coal supply contracts down through the system revealed the political limitations of competition as originally envisaged. The rigidity of these contracts meant that generators' room for manoeuvre was curtailed, so if the RECs were free to choose their generation sources, National Power and PowerGen would have been risky propositions for private investors. The vision set out in the White Paper, where competition resided in the freedoms provided to the RECs, was now largely defunct. This opened up a new window of opportunity for proponents of full retail competition; competition could reside with the consumer instead. The separation of regulatory treatment of the RECs' core monopoly networks, with different tariffs applied for accessing the networks and supply to the end-user, was a key conceptual shift made around this time which opened up this possibility.

Littlechild's interventions following his first engagement at the Nuneham seminar in November 1987 and contributions to the subsequent regulation seminar of July 1988 seem to have resulted a crucial change in direction. A small network of economically minded members of the Electricity Division, in particular William Rickett and Geoff Horton—an economist seconded to the Electricity Division—began to work closely with Littlechild. This economists' alliance became increasingly influential as the old network dominated by Marshall and senior CEGB officials became de-legitimised. As described in the next section, this came about as the department began to scrutinise the CEGB's claims about the economic viability of nuclear power. The CEGB, under Marshall, had been so committed to the PWR expansion programme that it was willing to accept privatisation. Marshall, as Chairman Designate of National Power, and still influential with Thatcher, could have shaped the new industry, but by the end of the process Marshall was sacked and the path was clear for competition as we now know it today to be pursued.

End of the Old Order: Dropping Nuclear

The discussion around the future of nuclear power in the early years of planning for privatisation (1983–86) was on the basis that a new investment programme would certainly take place and that it should be included in the wider electricity industry privatisation. If it wasn't, it would have called into question the rationale for the whole privatisation programme as the largest investment component across the industry to take place over the course of the next two decades would have been excluded. On the surface, Lord Marshall was confident about the prospects of the new PWR programme under privatisation, stating at an energy select committee hearing that 'the benefits of nuclear power will survive that change [privatization]'.[16] However, as outlined in the following paragraphs, the inclusion of nuclear power in the sale was increasingly questioned as the extent of its potential financial liabilities were exposed during the process of preparing the industry for privatisation. Private investors required transparency, so these costs could no longer be hidden, as *Power in Europe* summarised: 'Dragged out from the shelter of the electricity industry's vast cashflow, left exposed to stand or fall on its own merits, nuclear has fallen'.[17]

The privatisation programme coincided with a difficult period for the nuclear industry in Britain. This was, firstly, because the industry was facing significant costs associated with the closure of old magnox stations. As part of a first nuclear reactor programme announced in the 1955 document 'A Programme for Nuclear Power'—with the ambition of 12 plants by 1965—nine magnox plants were constructed from 1962 to 1971 and the first of these—at Berkeley, Bradwell and Trawsfynydd, totalling 920 MW—were due to come off line in the mid-1990s. Another group of reactors were due to come off in the early 2000s, totalling just over 1600 MW, and the youngest of the plants, Wylfa, was due to follow in the mid-2000s. There ageing magnoxs were the 'workhorses' of the nuclear fleet, providing over 22,000 GWh output out of just under 33,000 GWh in total. These plants used natural uranium as fuel (with a gas-graphite reactor), a decision based on the incorrect assumption made in the 1950s that the UK would struggle to source large enough quantities of enriched uranium.[18] As a result, the magnox reactors involved large back-end costs for fuel processing and waste management.

The British magnox fleet was initially developed, in part, to produce plutonium for military purposes. It was envisioned that spent uranium could be used as a feedstock in fast breeder reactors, thus constituting a 'plutonium credit' which would make nuclear competitive against coal by the end of the first nuclear programme in 1965. The amount of waste produced by these plants was significant; as later pointed out by Walter Marshall, 'the British Magnox programme has probably produced more nuclear waste than all the rest of the world put together'.[19] However, rather than a 'credit', this turned out to be a significant cost which hung over the industry for decades and, as outlined below, damaged the credibility of the nuclear industry as a viable private undertaking.

The first nuclear programme was based on a broader industrial strategy; the UK economy would benefit from being a nuclear pioneer by capturing global markets. As we shall see later, the opposite turned out to be the case as there was little international demand for magnox technology. In fact, being a nuclear pioneer turned out to be a disadvantage as the power plants came to the end of their lives and needed to be decommissioned - Britain was dealing with first-of-a kind costs with little scope to learn from international experience.

A second fundamental problem for the industry was the poor performance of the advanced gas-cooled reactors (AGRs) which had succeeded the magnox plants as the British reactor design of choice since the decision to embark on a second nuclear programme in 1964. The AGR plants, which used enriched uranium, were at one time the 'great hope' of British industry and started to come online from the mid-1970s. The programme encountered difficulties early on however, as there had only been one small prototype plant developed based on this indigenous technology, and due to the technical uncertainty which was faced in the early stages, three different variants of the AGR design were ordered initially, significantly adding to the costs of the programme. The average plant load factor of the AGR fleet in 1987–88 was extremely low—57.2% compared to 74.6% for the older magnoxs—and acted as a drag on the CEGB's productivity. While the newest AGRs at Heysam B and SSEB's Torness performed well, Dungeness B, Hartlepool and Heysham A were poor, with Hunterston B in Scotland and Hinkley B in England somewhere in the middle. Hartlepool 1 had a load factor of 19.1%, while Dungeness B, the first plant ordered which then took 22 years to come into operation, had been described as a 'basket case'.

Along with poor reactor performance, the economics of the AGRs was not helped by the arrangements for fuel storage and reprocessing. The initial idea was that the CEGB's—and the SSEB's—spent fuel from the AGRs would be expensively reprocessed and be used to fuel the next phase of fast breeder reactors, which it was envisioned, again incorrectly, would be the future of the nuclear industry globally.[20] On the back of this, approval had been attained by British Nuclear Fuels Limited (BNFL, under public ownership until 1996) in 1978 for a facility to reprocess spent fuel from AGRs—a Thermal Oxide Reprocessing Plant (THORP)—with its main customers being the CEGB, SSEB and a number of Japanese utilities. Although the Japanese signed a contract in 1978, the CEGB and SSEB didn't agree terms until 1986. This ten-year, cost-plus contract was on a take-or-pay basis, so the British utilities would face penalties if they didn't send fuel to BNFL in sufficient quantities, amplifying the negative effects of poor AGR performance. There was a general view that both the CEGB and SSEB had been 'wrangled' into signing the long-term contract for 1,850 tonnes, at cost in the region of £1 million/t. There was much acrimony and friction between the CEGB/SSEB and BNFL because this contract was on much less favourable terms than what had been offered to German, French and Japanese companies.

The spent AGR fuel was in wet storage at the Sellafield site while the THORP plant got up and running, then due for completion in 1993. SSEB were continually in dispute with BNFL about this issue. They were looking at the option of investing in their own dry storage facility and may have taken this route if they had the choice. Due to leaks published in *Time Out* magazine in 1989, wet storage at the Sellafield site was highly controversial at this time. These reports revealed that spent fuel from AGRs had been 'lying in storage ponds at Sellafield' and 'revealed problems with corroding spent fuel elements at the Sellafield nuclear plant'.[21] Anti-nuclear groups were arguing that permanent dry storage would be a better option than liquid storage followed by reprocessing.

While back-end fuel costs for the magnox plant were to a large extent fixed (approx. 75%), as the existing BNFL plant was the main cost driver and there was little variation based on throughput volume,[22] in relation to AGRs, the nuclear generators were being forced to accept open-ended risks that would not be viable in a privately run industry. A pertinent example was BNFL's decision to fully decommission its fuel cycle facilities to meet new environmental standards, necessitating a significant increase in provisions by the CEGB and SSEB for 1988–89 to cover the substantial increase in decommissioning costs, to over £4.5 bn.

The ability to manage this risk by passing on additional costs to captive customers would of course be greatly diminished by competition. With little incentive to manage such costs, BNFL were being protected from risks associated with the market through their long-term, cost-plus contracts and specific supports offered by government to this particular component of the industry.[23] So, along with decommissioning of magnox plants, an effective nuclear waste policy and more favourable terms with BNFL were likely to be key issues affecting the viability of a privatised nuclear industry.

A third problem facing the nuclear power industry at this time was increasing scrutiny of the economics of the third nuclear investment programme. The previous Labour-led government had chosen another British design—the steam generating heavy water reactor (SGHWR)—which had been developed at prototype scale in the 1970s and, in advance of its scaling up, decided in 1978 to build the two final AGRs at Torness and Heysam. Wary of hubris surrounding the benefits of indigenous nuclear technology, the subsequent conservative government opted for the tried and tested PWR design and it was announced in December 1979 that, at a cost of £15 bn, the country would construct 15,000 MW of new nuclear capacity over a decade from 1982 (see previous chapter).

The envisioned programme of PWR plants had encountered difficulties following a controversy over the first of these plants at Sizewell B which had run into severe cost overruns. A public inquiry was undertaken by government which revealed significant problems with the project and called into question its economic feasibility.[24] The inquiry, which lasted from 1982 to 1985, and didn't report until 1987, was supposed to smooth the way for future PWRs in Britain by settling the question of their economic benefits to the country. However, the processes called into question the societal benefits of preferential treatment for nuclear and the prevailing government narrative around 'fuel diversification'. Sir Frank Layfield, the chief inspector, was surprisingly liberal in allowing a wide range of evidence to be presented and the inquiry dragged on for two years. In response to the question of whether the plant at Sizewell B should have been built on economic grounds: 'He said "yes"; but only just'.[25] On the surface, this laid the ground for the PWR programme to go ahead; Sizewell B was given consent and the CEGB promptly submitted an application for a second PWR at Hinkley C. By the time of privatisation over £1 bn had been spent on the project at Sizewell B.

In reality, however, the Sizewell Inquiry opened up to independent appraisal the CEGB's approach to the economics of nuclear power. At the beginning of the 1980s, the CEGB had been publishing economic appraisals which showed that a new fleet of nuclear plants was economic in all scenarios, even in the event of demand not rising. Future planning was based on a 'net effective cost' (NEC) figure which analysed the long-term impacts of new plant on the entire system and was based on the CEGB's model which looked 40 years out into the future. The NEC incorporated capital costs over the plant lifetime plus the operational fuel costs, minus the fuel savings from lower load factors of plant with higher marginal costs. The argument was that new plant would displace less efficient units and push them down the merit order, so new investment was deemed economic regardless of whether demand rose. The underpinning economic logic of the approach was to appraise proposals on the basis of their marginal effect on the entire system—the 'economic resource cost'—and not on the full costs of a stand-alone project which would include construction costs, private sector financing costs and corporate overheads.

These CEGB investment appraisals were heavily criticised as they were not based on a full cost analysis 'in which all the capital charges are added to operating costs at the prices of one year'. Rather, 'it concocted a hybrid analysis, which appeared to constitute a full-cost analysis but in reality was nothing of the sort'.[26] The CEGB was calculating fuel costs at current values while adding capital charges at historic values, the latter therefore appeared lower in current terms as they were not inflation adjusted. This gave the appearance of nuclear as a more economic option against coal as the capital costs of nuclear were much higher relative to fuel costs.

Following criticisms of their basic accounting and investment appraisal methods,[27] the CEGB had ceased publishing comparisons of the relative economics of coal and nuclear plants in their 'Grey Books' in the mid-1980s, so the economics of nuclear became somewhat obscured. Due to these poor accounting practices and the emerging evidence of escalating back-end costs, 'it was impossible to gauge by how much the economic status of operating nuclear stations had worsened by the time of the run-up to privatisation'.[28] The conclusions of the Energy Committee following its 1990 investigation into the costs of nuclear were unambiguous:

> We are convinced that there has been a systematic bias in CEGB costings in favour of nuclear power, both in ignoring risk and failing to provide adequately for contingencies, and, in respect of investment, in putting forward 'best expectations' rather than more cautious estimates.[29]

Regardless of whether this was deliberate obfuscation, there were radically different and conflicting financial appraisal frameworks around the question of nuclear costs. For example, in a submission to the Energy Committee in 1990, Lord Marshall outlined the differences between a 'public sector price' and a 'private sector price' for a new PWR plant. The 'private sector price' would be significantly higher—at 6.25 p/kWh compared to 3.22 p/kWh in 1987 prices[30]—due to the fact that in the nationalised industries no provision was made for interest payments during construction, a significant additional cost for nuclear pants. Additional components of the private sector price were an increase in the rate of return 'from an 8 per cent real internal rate of return (IRR) (i.e. based on net asset values) to a 10 per cent current cost accounting (CCA) return (i.e. based on replacement cost)'[31] and depreciation calculated over a 20-year period, as opposed to 40 years in the public sector. These calculations were heavily criticised by Gordon Mackerron, an economist consulted by the Energy Committee. Based on his calculations, which reduced the difference between the public and private sector discount rates and added-in interest during construction, the public sector unit cost of a new PWR would be in the region of '5.62 p/kWh (or 4.91 p/kWh at an 8 per cent instead of 10 per cent discount rate), and extra building costs and lower availability could raise it further to 6.82 to 7:12p/kWh (or 6.11 to 6.41p/kWh at an 8 per cent rate), compared to a private sector price of 7.57 to 7.87 p/kWh'.[32]

The Energy Committee's investigation did not take place until 1990. Back in early 1988 the Department of Energy's assumptions and estimates around the time of the White Paper of early 1988 were that the nuclear plants, which accounted for just under 20% of overall electricity output, were to be privatised and taken over by National Power. This was the main rationale behind the 70:30 split between the two companies; National Power's balance sheet needed to be large enough to convince investors that it could handle the liabilities associated with the nuclear plants. While not to the fullest extent, the department was aware of the industry's problems, and after the publication of *Privatising Electricity*, it began discussing ideas about how to allocate nuclear-related risks between National Power, electricity customers and taxpayers. This included proposals such as amending the terms of the CEGB contract with BNFL, tighter regulation of prices charged to National Power for back-end costs, a trust fund for all nuclear liabilities, with the generator's contribution capped, or a government guarantee on its debt.

The initial advice to the department by their financial advisors, Kleinwort Benson, that the nuclear power industry could be feasibly privatised had been given back in September 1987, without full knowledge of the likely industry structure and extent of competition in the sector. All of the international examples of nuclear plants in the private sector which were continually referred to by proponents—such as Duke Energy in the USA, Germany's VEBA and Tractebel in Belgium—were cases where the owning utility had a monopoly arrangement with exclusive rights to supply customers within their areas, enabling costs to be fully passed through. What was not recognised until later on in the process was the inherent trade-off between a viable privately owned nuclear industry and competition in the new electricity market.

The general approach which was decided upon early on in these discussions within the department was to identify and isolate nuclear costs, then contract at 'cost-related prices' and address any additional costs over and above these via a levy on electricity bills. Given the projections of cost reductions in fossil fuels and the liabilities associated with nuclear waste and decommissioning, it was estimated that nuclear would require an additional £100 m/year. This funding mechanism later became known as the Non-Fossil Fuel Obligation (NFFO). It placed an obligation on the RECs to source a proportion of their power from nuclear plants, with the costs recovered from the levy (the FFL). This basic idea was first proposed in early 1988[33] and was originally designed as a contract between National Power and the RECs, through which the RECs recovered the premium on nuclear power through the FFL. As will be outlined later, this was subsequently redesigned to align with the operation of the new trading system (the Electricity Pool) and the reality that nuclear could not, in the end, be privatised.

In the meantime, doubts were beginning to be expressed about the viability of nuclear in the private sector. Kleinwort Benson were increasingly of the view that the nuclear plants would put the financial viability of National Power under threat. In September 1988 they circulated a letter to John Guinness, then Deputy Secretary at the Department of Energy, saying Big G (National Power) would need a government cap on liabilities if it was to be floated, warning that the company would not be viable if liabilities over and above the base case model exceeded 200 m/year, highlighting that there wasn't much room for manoeuvre. In the paper they floated 'the idea of a separate nuclear company, with the majority ownership vested in the government and the minority in Big G and with risks being borne in the proportion of shareholdings'.[34] They also explored the possibility of removing back-end risks all-together and having either 'a fixed price contract with BNFL for reprocessing (guaranteed by government) or by a cash payment to the government which, in return would take over responsibility for fuel reprocessing'.[35]

Despite the strong reservations of the financial advisors, the approach at this stage was to privatise nuclear, in line with Thatcher's wishes, whilst introducing measures to share risks. Following discussions with the PM, a more detailed exploration of the issues was written up later in 1988 (November) and, following this, it was agreed to write a provision in the Electricity Bill limiting government liabilities at £2.5 bn (later schedule 12 of the 1989 Electricity Act), an amount which, it was estimated, would cover accumulated back-end liabilities over the first five years of privatisation. It was subsequently decided to set the FFL to deliver 12.5 GW of new capacity by 2000, ensuring that the first four PWRs of the replacement programme would be delivered. However, the scope for new build PWRs paid for through a levy was seen as a risky proposition for the government. Estimates conducted by the department around the time showed that the FFL would cost on average £280 m annually (equating to 2% added onto consumer bills) out to 2005, that was if eight new PWRs were built and a discount rate of 8% was assumed. A more negative scenario was outlined which assumed a higher discount rate (12%), more aligned with private sector rates of return, and compared this against investment in gas turbines, the most competitive alternative investment. This would involve a subsidy of £1350 m/year, translating into a levy rate of 10% on bills.

A broad scheme for risk sharing was devised within the Department of Energy. This would involve a cap on liabilities associated with the back-end fuel costs of the older magnox stations and would be linked to the provisions which were made in the CEGB accounts on 31 April 1990, the eve of 'Vesting Day' when the new companies would become operational and competition would commence. Ninety per cent of cost increases above this benchmark would be covered by the Treasury and 10% by BNFL. A similar approach was outlined for the decommissioning costs of the magnox plants. For the newer magnox units and fuel already contracted for use in AGR plants, there would be an 80:10:10% split between the Treasury, BNFL and National Power. The logic behind this unbalanced split, with the government taking the lion's share, was that cost increases were most likely to arise from stricter environmental, health and safety regulations. For uncontracted AGR fuel and fuel from the PWRs, it would be up to National Power to make adequate provisions for these costs. The Electricity Bill was also to provide for direct subsidy of the nuclear industry in the form of grants and guaranteed loans, but only in the areas of waste disposal and decommissioning.

A lot therefore hinged on, firstly, the level of provisions in the CEGB accounts on 1 April 1990, becoming a key indicator of the financial viability of National Power, and secondly, how the scheme would translate into actual costs and the levy on customer bills. Throughout these discussions, the Treasury was generally unhappy with the commitments being entered into by government. Nigel Lawson's view was that future customers should pick up these costs as they arose, rather than facing them upfront before privatisation. Meanwhile, National Power's view on the above approach to risk sharing was that they remained far too exposed to the risk of significant changes to these initial cost estimates. The department's advisors generally agreed with National Power in this view; that they would be exposed to risks well beyond their control and investors would face open-ended liabilities, putting the privatisation programme under threat. However, government was reluctant to side completely with National Power on the matter as there was an expectation that BNFL would be privatised further down the line.

If nuclear was to be privatised and risks shared, a lot depended on the accuracy of the initial cost estimates in these areas if government was to fulfil its backstop role. However, the levels of CEGB's existing provisions were called into question and later found to be highly suspect. The CEGB accounts for 1987–88 were published in July of 1988, showing an increase (£740 m) in provisions for back-end costs (storage, reprocessing and disposal of waste). The CEGB still had an optimistic outlook for AGRs; based on assumptions of long operating lifetimes and improved performance, the fleet would earn enough revenues in the market to cover ongoing costs. As the process unfolded, however, the figures for nuclear liabilities and required provisions began to escalate. The FT, for example, in 1989, produced an estimate that the total liability for AGR and magnox plant might be in the region of £20 bn.[36]

The privatisation of nuclear began to unravel once negotiations between BNFL and National Power/SSEB got underway. The prices charged by BNFL were crucial as they would dictate the baseline provisions for nuclear liabilities upon which the risk-sharing mechanisms outlined above would kick in if costs were exceeded (as of 1 April 1990). In March 1989 BNFL tabled an offer to the generators for the fixed prices of Magnox reprocessing to take effect from 1 April 1989, covering historic fuel (£1.47 bn), committed fuel (£2.5 bn—later reduced to 2 bn) and for decommissioning of BNFL plant (£550 m). Their rational for increasing unit charges was that risks could not be passed through if contracts were not on a cost-plus basis.

National Power reacted badly to the prices quoted by BNFL. The company would have to commit to a 25-year contract for AGR fuel with BNFL and would not have the option of building their own dry store for spent fuel. Marshall called for responsibility for spent fuel to be simply transferred to BNFL; further discussions between National Power and BNFL then reached a stalemate. National Power's board concluded that it would be better for magnox not to be privatised at all.

A crucial turning point came when the CEGB's annual accounts were published in March 1989. In these updated accounts the provisions for magnox stations rose significantly, from £2.8 bn to £6.9 bn, accounting for a significant share of the CEGB's annual turnover of £8.9 bn. The majority of this (£3.1 bn) was to cover increases in fuel cycle costs mostly associated with BNFL's own decommissioning costs to meet higher standards, while £0.9 bn was for magnox plant decommissioning. The total decommissioning cost for the eight magnox plants for which provisions now needed to be made had increased from £2.496 bn to £4.79 bn (discounted to £1.835bn, some of which would be paid for from income from operating the plants). The main drivers for the increase in projected decommissioning costs were findings of a recent study into the actual costs of decommissioning a magnox plant at Berkeley, an additional allowance for contingencies (30%), and a recommendation made by the UKAEA that an additional allocation be made for business overheads.[37]

For the Department of Energy this had 'alarming implications',[38] especially given that National Power's decommissioning provisions would be subject to taxation. The particular concern was that 'the size of provision in relation to profit' would mean 'that the effective tax rate on declared profits would be anomalously high': there was a scenario that the need to 'gross up ... could in time unbalance National Power's capital structure'.[39] In a leaked letter sent by John Baker (National Power CEO-designate) to John Guinness at the department, Baker outlined the danger of nuclear liabilities spend (if taxed) consuming the business: 'unless suitable steps are taken regarding taxation of nuclear provisions, the total profit before tax could be consumed by tax payable with the result that there was nothing left over to distribute to shareholders, or retained in the company'.[40]

The department became concerned about the financial stability of National Power and the ability of its balance sheet to withstand cost increases much above the provisions contained in the baseline. Nigel Lawson, the Chancellor of the Exchequer, received these results and held a meeting with Parkinson at which he recommended that the Magnox stations be pulled from the privatisations, later recalling that 'officials in both departments were astonished, presumably thinking that I would never oppose privatisation of anything'.[41]

Marshall and Baker were then asked to provide to the department 'projected historic cost balance sheets' which were produced on 10 May 1989 by KPMG and communicated to John Guinness. The figures reportedly 'gave the Department a shock'.[42] Based on the quoted BNFL contracts for

fixed prices, required provisions in the accounts for back-end nuclear costs would need to be £10 bn at 31 March 1990, far in excess of the £3.2 billion in the CEGB accounts at 31 March 1988.

Parkinson, the chancellor and the Secretary of State for Scotland (Malcolm Rifkind) met on 29 June 1989 and set up a joint group of senior officials to look at options which then met with the PM on 4 July. A paper subsequently produced by the joint group came to the conclusion that it was unlikely to be able to privatise the magnox plants unless significant cash injections by government were made. The chancellor (Nigel Lawson) came out against cash injection as he felt it would be impossible to defend to the public; a number of senior ministers also agreed. The magnox plants were pulled from the privatisation on 24 July 1989, incidentally the same day that Cecil Parkinson moved to the Department of Transport and three days before the Electricity Bill received royal assent on 27 July. The rationale given was that removing magnox from the sale would enable National Power to focus on future nuclear construction and for the true cost of electricity supply to be reflected in bills.[43]

Until November 1989 it was still expected that the AGRs would be assigned to National Power and SSEB, and that National Power would construct Sizewell B. As part of the reformulated proposals for the nuclear sector, the government would increase the provisions under schedule 12 of the 1989 Electricity Act from £1000 m to £2500 m. The main concern for government was how this cost escalation would translate into prices and ultimately the levy on bills. The indicative prices for nuclear output provided by the CEGB/National Power to the department would be crucial for the prospects of nuclear in the private sector. Over the course of late 1988–89, the CEGB/National Power provided four sets of indicative prices for AGRs and PWRs:[44]

1. October 1988: The CEGB provided average price ranges for all reactor types ranging from 6.6 p/kWh in 1990–91 to 4.2 p/kWh in 2000–01. The department noted that they 'included no special allowances for the risks associated with nuclear power generation', and pressed for figures 'which would reflect a private company's assessment of those risks'.
2. April 1989: These indicative prices included more detail for magnoxs and AGRs for 1989/90 and took into account BNFL's quotes for fixed price contracts. On the basis of a 10% (CCA) real rate of return, the figures were magnoxs—5.8 p/kWh and AGRs—7.5 p/

kWh, with an average of 6.6 p/kWh, 'but substantially more if the nuclear provisions were not tax deductible when established'.

3. October 1989: 1989–90 prices for AGRs and PWRs with a 10% return and the 'repayment of PWR construction costs over 20 instead of 40 years'. The price for AGR output ranged from 8.37 (1989–90) to 7.66 (1993–94), while the 'levelised cost' for PWRs was 6.20 p (based on revenue required to recover lifetime costs over a 20-year period).
4. November 1989: The secretary of state requested a revised set of figures with a broader set of assumptions incorporated. As part of this National Power produced a 'best case scenario' set of 1989–90 prices: for AGRs: 5.20–5.96 p/kWh for 1989–90 to 1993–94, and for PWRs: 5.7–7.6 p/kWh for 1996–97 to 2000–01. The 'levalised cost' of a PWR was lower in this estimate (5.5 p) due to a change in the assumptions which provided for a longer amortisation period.

Prior to these National Power figures, CEGB estimates had put the unit cost of an AGR at 2.9 p/kWh, to be competitive with coal—priced at 2.50–2.62 p/kWh—once their load factors were increased, while the unit cost of the new PWR had been estimated to be 2.24 p based on the 'economic resource cost' (not including private sector financing costs, construction costs or corporate overheads) during a public inquiry in 1988. As discussed earlier, the CEGB had calculated these prices on the assumption that most of the risk would reside with the government or the RECs, and it did not include interest payments accrued during construction of the PWRs. The 20-year (as opposed to 40) amortisation, the 10% CCA return, along with the higher fuel reprocessing charges, which only became apparent in May 1989, were the key drivers. The figures came in for particular criticism by the department and the Energy Committee:

> Mr Guinness, the Deputy Secretary at the Department of Energy in charge of electricity privatisation, told us that "We knew that costs were going to be higher in the private sector than the public sector. We did not know that they were going to be so high that they could not be privatised, and we did not agree with the figures which National Power put forward finally in October [1989]" ... We acknowledge that the Department could reasonably have expected more assistance from the CEGB/National Power. One of the problems was the CEGB's own apparent ignorance in some areas.[45]

The October 1989 calculations seemed to have been somewhat of a turning point within the department, with officials becoming increasingly sceptical as their own estimates had PWR unit output priced at 5–5.5 p/ Kwh. While the CEGB figures were revised somewhat, the fundamentals were not changed; the final set of indicative prices were provided by National Power on 2 November and the decision to pull the whole nuclear privatisation programme was made one week later on the 9th.

Although National Power was still a shell company within the CEGB, its incentives to downplay nuclear costs were no longer in place, given that government was discussing the possibility of sharing risks and it was concerned with its own viability in a competitive market. In relation to PWR prices, there seemed to have been a game of cat and mouse between National power and the department. The department had requested a draft contract for PWR delivery in February 1989, but this 'was never received'; the rationale that National Power provided was that they required more certainty from the department on the 'risk environment' that they would face in the private sector. Operating under such uncertainty, the department were trying to 'smoke out' National Power, but the strategy led to paralysis for many months.[46]

The prices quoted meant that the levy—the FFL—would need to be around 20% 'about double what had previously been assumed publicly; and an increase of around 8% in electricity prices'.[47] Parkinson had earlier, in June 1989, made a commitment to maintain existing price levels until vesting of the companies. The explanation for the price increases provided by National Power that this was due to the higher risk premium demanded by private investors. However, these projections of significantly higher costs purely on the basis of a private sector risk premium and a shorter plant lifetime (20 years, as oppose to 40 years used in the CEGB modelling) were controversial. They were later criticised heavily by the parliament's Energy Committee's report on the costs of nuclear. The report concluded:

> We reject the view of the CEGB/National Power and the Department that the cost of electricity from a reactor could be almost doubled by privatisation, and we are profoundly concerned that the CEGB should have put forward a low figure to a public inquiry in support of the case for a major public investment and one almost twice as high shortly afterwards for power from the same reactor in the private sector.[48]

In any case, the news dealt a devastating blow to the idea of a privatised nuclear industry. Once the figures became known, Walter Marshall was reportedly 'horrified, apoplectic and very upset'.[49] He refused to communicate the figures to the minister and instructed Baker to do this on his behalf. John Wakeham, who succeeded Cecil Parkinson the secretary of state, subsequently met Marshall on 8 November to inform him of his view that a government-owned nuclear company to run existing plants was what would be required and that he would not commit to new PWRs. Instead, he would pursue a policy of fuel diversity which could be achieved with existing nuclear at a 20% share, achieved if the lifetime of magnoxs were extended.

Wakeham, upon taking up office, had been convinced that nuclear as a whole could not be privatised and had been working through Alan Walters, the PM's economic advisor, to try to convince her of this. He succeeded, and his recommendation was endorsed by the cabinet. Wakeham announced on 9 November that the AGRs and Sizewell B would not be included in the privatisation, stating: 'unprecedented guarantees were being sought … I am not willing to underwrite the private sector in this way'.[50] There were calls for the privatisation programme to be revisited more fundamentally as the initial rational for creating National Power had now disappeared, but it was felt that this would introduce further uncertainty and require an extension of the privatisation deadline. Getting privatisation over the line before the next election was seen as a political imperative.

Marshall, of course, fundamentally disagreed with the separation of nuclear from National Power and shortly after was sacked by Wakeham,[51] with John Baker being asked to take over as Chairman of National Power. Baker was known to be one the only senior CEGB executive sympathetic to the competition agenda. A public sector nuclear company, Nuclear Electric, was subsequently formed and plans for the new PWR programme were shelved as ministers would not commit to setting the levy in a way which could fund it, while decisions about the future of the nuclear industry would have to wait for a review which was to take place in 1994.

It wasn't privatisation which killed off the ambitious plans for the nuclear industry, rather the prospect of competition. In order to finance new PWRs, 'bankable contracts' between the RECs and National Power for nuclear output underwritten by government, involving a commitment to effectively socialise the back-end risks, would have been required. In order for National Power to operate the underperforming AGRs, government would have needed to write-down the value of these under-performing assets and accept lower proceeds at sale, as was done in the Scottish case, enabling the private company to earn a high rate of return. For all of this to be viable, an extremely strict obligation to procure nuclear output would have had to be imposed on the RECs, with them being financially liable for a failure to meet these obligations. Similar to the coal contracts, this would have tied the hands of the RECs. In the end this would not have been compatible with the model of competition envisioned. It was clear however that the Treasury wanted to avoid such exposure but to use the NFFO/FFL mechanism to ensure that the assets would hold value and be sellable further down the line.[52]

The FFL, which was eventually introduced for only an eight-year period (1990–98), enabled the RECs to avoid having such a contractual obligation, as all customers, aside from those qualifying for an exemption, would have to pay regardless of their supplier. This, in theory, would enable competition to unfold. The fact that the levy was to be set by the secretary of state and revised annually by the regulator meant that it could not form a stable basis for investment in new PWRs.

In a speech given at the Nuclear Energy Society in late 1989,[53] Marshall identified the problem as one of 'sharp conceptual difficulties' involved with introducing competition. A viable national nuclear power programme, Marshall argued, 'is best pursued by a large generator which has an obligation to supply in a defined geographical area'. This model of vertical integration over a 'defined geographical area', combined with an obligation to supply, provides a counterweight to a monopoly position. Nuclear power in the public sector, he argued, 'is an interference with the market mechanism'. He identified correctly the fundamental conflict between competition and his conceptual model of the industry:

> The distributors cannot now know what is the shape of their businesses and what is the profitability of their businesses in eight years' time. How can they willingly give lifetime contracts to buy nuclear power? Obviously this is difficult, and if the government obliges them to contract for new nuclear power then their shareholders will be worried about the imbalance between long-term commitments and short-term uncertainties.

Retaining nuclear in the public sector however meant that National Power could be sold. But as the decision came so late in the day, the 70:30 split between National Power and PowerGen was not to be revisited. As discussed in the next chapter, this created a path dependency as the resulting lack of diversity in the generation market stored up problems for the future.

The Road to Competition

Stephen Littlechild personified the opposition to Walter Marshall's concept of an integrated electricity industry and it was during the period when nuclear costs were being exposed that his influence over the emerging contours of the new electricity market grew. He, by this point, had been appointed to be the first electricity regulator once the new legislation came into force—officially titled the Director General of Electricity Supply (DGES)—and thus his views were increasingly important. He would have significant scope to interpret the terms of the companies' operating licences under the 1989 Electricity Act, so potential investors were taking note of his views and the industry was of course keen to have a 'happy' regulator in office once competition got underway. The role of the department changed once the Electricity Bill received royal assent in July 1989; rather than leading the reforms, key officials, John Guinness in particular, became the mediators between the regulator and the industry players as they negotiated the future of the industry. Government were also constrained somewhat because of the traditional status of the nationalised companies as arm's length bodies governed by independent boards.

Detailed discussions about the nature of regulation in the post-privatised electricity supply industry (ESI) had gotten underway following the publication of the White Paper in early 1988 and, as referred to earlier, a seminar on regulation was held in July 1988. With nuclear out of the way, so to speak, the contours of a new industry were emerging as the trade-offs between coal industry protection and competition were negotiated between the generators and the RECs from late 1988 to September 1989, when a final contracts package was agreed. At the centre of this was discussion about the type and duration of bulk electricity supply contracts between the generator and the RECs and the extent of retail competition. As outlined earlier, in December 1988 the generators and the RECs had come to broad agreement on the need for long-term contracts with a proportion of these having a 'net-back' clause to cover the risk that the generators could undercut the RECs in the retail market for supplying large electricity consumers. The length of these contracts—5–15 years—was decided on the basis of an expectation that the fuel supply contracts between BCC and the generators would extend over such a timeframe. However, as we discussed earlier, British Coal were indicating that they would be willing to accept shorter-term contracts at a better price, of a three-year duration (signed in November 89). On the back of this, the department, increasingly influenced by Littlechild, was keen to push the case for retail competition. As discussed in the following sections, the generators and the RECs became concerned about the destabilising and uncertain effects of a rapid switch to retail competition and increasingly sought to manage the transition by putting forward joint proposals to the secretary of state, making the argument that the introduction of full competition on day one would negatively affect the proceeds from the sales, as the RECs would be exposed to more risk. By September 1989 an agreement had been reached to phase-in competition over an eight-year timeframe.

In the months prior to this final agreement, the department began to reorganise itself to tackle the various questions emerging from the earlier discussions about bulk supply contracts and retail competition. Following the publishing of a draft regulatory framework and licences in January 1989, two key working groups were initiated to flesh out the details of the contracts: the 'Contracts Working Group' was set up in February 1989 and chaired by Brian Pomeroy of Touche Ross, the department's regulatory advisors. He had been seconded to the Department for Trade and Industry in the early 1980s where he was an under-secretary advising the government on its BT privatisation programme, focusing on consumer protection and regulation. Pomeroy's role was to be an arbitrator between the RECs and the generators, and to make recommendations to the secretary of state.

Alongside this, a 'Pooling and Settlements Working Group' was set up, with Slaughter and May chairing, the department's legal advisors. Sitting above these working groups was a 'High Level Monitoring Group' (HLMG) which was formed in July 1989 and chaired by William Macintyre, Permanent Secretary of the Department of Energy. This looked at the 'top level management of the whole project' and essentially took over the main role of the previous two steering committees. Also important was the 'Project Management Group' (PMG), in charge of a number of technical working groups—35 separate work areas were identified. The PMG was chaired by Rickett of the Electricity Division, who was by then promoted to a higher grade. A weekly report on progress against the timetable was circulated up to the PMG who then passed on particular items up to the HLMG as needed. Based on this reporting, Macintyre updated the secretary of state each week. Advising on the project management aspects of the electricity privatisation was Nicholas Coleman, who had been seconded in from British Petroleum.

David Parker, the historian of British privatisation, notes that at this time the view within government had evolved towards support for retail competition following a meeting of ministers in July 1989.[54] A 'contracts package' had been proposed which included full retail competition and shorter duration contracts between the generators and the RECs, of six months to five years, with options to terminate 10% of the contracts every six months, enabling a rapid switch to competition If the industry parties agreed. This was influenced by the work of Littlechild and Rickett who were now working closely with the economist Geoff Horton on modelling the effects of competition across the industry. What was at stake was the degree to which the RECs' customer base would be opened up to competition and the scope for the generators to become active in the supply market. It is not clear whether this radical proposal was a negotiating position, or whether, once it began to be scrutinised and the impacts on the flotation value of the companies and the ability to privatise British Coal became apparent, the government backed away.

By September 1989 there was somewhat of a collective industry view on these issues. The two generators and the 12 RECs, who were represented as a single grouping by Jim Smith of the Area Boards' Chairmen's Steering Committee, wrote to the secretary of state with a proposal. Essentially, the accommodation was that the RECs would have a franchise—a protected market share, on a regulated tariff—while the generators would get long-term contracts for their output linked to coal contracts in order to cover this demand. On 6 September they sent a letter to Wakeham proposing limitations on the competitive operation of the market. As part of this the RECs would retain a monopoly for the supply of customers with a load of 1 MW and below, equating to 70% of the market, and they would enter into long-term contracts for bulk supply with the generators to cover demand from this protected franchise. These contracts would be for 10–15 years with the overall amount of contracts tapering off after 5 years as the industry became more competitive. For the remaining 30% of end-users, they would be able to choose supplier, but the generators would be limited to serving on average 15% of demand in any one REC area via direct contracts, while the RECs' ownership of generation would also be limited to 15% of demand in their area. As Littlechild later recollected: 'The Government was now torn. It was concerned to ensure proceeds, investment and coal privatization. And it felt unable to dictate terms to the industry parties because it needed their acceptance of the contracts that would underpin privatization'.[55]

This figure of 15% of the market being open to generation other than the National Power/PowerGen duopoly was by 'a strange and amusing coincidence' exactly the same as the limit on own generation which was to be imposed on the RECs. With 70% of demand covered by contracts, there were clear signs of a 'quid pro quo between generators and distributors':[56] the generators' ability to pick off the RECs' most lucrative customers would be limited, while the RECs would have limited scope to contract with new entrant generators. Clearly, as the wheels of the reform process got into gear and the minds of former CEGB executives and Area Board Chairmen turned to competition, it became clear that it was in their interests to come to an accommodation. This accommodation meant that the generators and the RECs would essentially split the direct contracts market between them, so that between these contracts and the protected franchise, the role of short-term contracting in the generation market would be very limited initially. The main argument the RECs made for the protected franchise was that without it they would be unable to enter into long-term contracts with generators to cover the costs of the coal contracts and would be forced to buy at spot prices due to demand uncertainty. With the resulting collapse in power prices, the generators would not be floatable on the stock exchange.

The PM had seen press coverage of the industry's proposals to constrain competition in this way and became concerned. However, John Wakeham, who had taken over from Cecil Parkinson at the Department of Energy in July 1989, was more amenable to such an accommodation. He was a pragmatist by nature, being referred to as a 'fixer',[57] and had the tight timetable for delivering privatisation in mind. This was already four months behind schedule, so Wakeham was conscious of the need to make compromises with industry and to accept some limitations on competition. Following a meeting with the PM on 13 September, at which it was agreed to press for a greater emphasis on competition, Wakeham came back to the RECs and generators with a counter-offer, involving a choice of two options:

- Option 1: For premises with annual demand of 1 MW and below, a five-year restriction on competition. After this period government would review the situation and have the option to open up competition over a three-year timeframe. During the initial period, direct contracts between generators and eligible customers would be limited to an average of 15% of demand in a REC area. Long-term generation contracts between National Power/PowerGen and the RECs for 10–15 years would cover 50% of the market (not 70% as per the industry proposal), with the remainder covered by shorter-term contracts (including a mix of spot, six monthly, three- and five-year-duration contracts). Contracts stretching out to 15 years would only be available for plant which had been retrofitted with flue-gas desulphurisation equipment. One-fifth of the generation contracts would run for a maximum of five years, and a quarter for four to eight years.

- Option 2: Same as the above but only a three-year restriction on competition to supply premises below 1 MW, then a phased reduction of the limit to 0.1 MW over the next two years, and competition extended to all customers after a further three years.

Wakeham rejected the idea of a permanent limitation on competition for sites below 1 MW, as the RECs had wanted, and threatened to revert to the department's earlier July proposals for full retail competition if agreement could not be found. Littlechild, who by this point had become a key veto player, was consulted and was unwilling to accept either of Wakeham's options, writing a letter to the secretary of state on 25 September 1989 indicating he was unhappy with the two variants. He was more inclined towards option 2, as it locked in a process leading to more competition, rather than option 1, which had no such commitment, and proposed that there should only be a two-year limit on the 1 MW threshold, following which the threshold should be reduced to 0.025 MW rather than 0.1 MW. This would encompass most industry and commercial users. He was also concerned about the 15% restriction on direct contracts in any one area as he couldn't see a justification for this.

Many of the Area Board Chairmen had been in Canada attending an international energy industry conference, but were hastily summoned back to London by Wakeham for a showdown meeting on 25 September. Based on these discussions, the industry came up with a modified proposal, including a four-year limitation on competition for 1 MW and below (approx. 5000 customers, accounting for circa. 30% of generation output[58]), another four-year limit on those at 0.1 MW and below (approx. 50,000 customers), with no limitations thereafter. The 15% limitation on direct contracts between eligible customers and the generators would be in place, but would be raised to 25% after four years and subsequently completely removed. Littlechild would have some amount of autonomy in relation to the lifting of this threshold, with the 15% level being 'subject to over-ruling by the regulator and … the secretary of state for energy will retain the discretion to give second-tier (direct contract) supply licences to premises with a load under 1 MW'.[59] All of this meant that 'from vesting nearly one third of the electricity market in England and Wales would be opened up to competition from suppliers other than the distribution companies. After four years, about half of the market would be opened up. After a further four years, it would be completely opened up'.[60]

Despite further criticism from Littlechild, the secretary of state recommended the revised proposals in a letter to the PM on 26 September 1989. Littlechild was still unhappy about the franchise remaining in place for many customers and had wanted the 1 MW to 0.1 MW drop to be introduced after two years, rather than four, and to allow premises to aggregate their loads if it meant they could exceed the threshold. In a later reflection, Littlechild recognised that, in retrospect, the phased introduction of competition over eight years which bound the industry to full liberalisation proved to be crucial:

> The choice made in September 1989 turned out to be critical. Suppose the industry's initial proposal had been accepted, or the Department's first option (review of the retail monopoly after five years) had been chosen. The political pressures posed by the coal industry in the mid-1990s would undoubtedly have led to deferral or abandonment of the prospect of full competition and of the ending of the coal subsidies … In the end, some phasing of competition was not necessarily a bad idea, even from the perspective of those who argued for the 'competitive model'. It enabled electricity privatization to take place on time, with manageable risks to the companies, and later coal privatization. It allowed time for all parties to learn from experience, and for later regulatory provisions (e.g. metering, profiling and data transfer) to make retail competition effective for residential users.[61]

As the contracts with the BCC were being finalised, there were further discussions between the RECs and the generators. By this point BCC had clarified their position and opted for shorter fuel supply contracts at higher prices: three years, as opposed to four to eight years which had been on the table. These contracts were linked to the 12 GW of coal generation capacity required to meet the RECs' monopoly franchise. The generation contracts were then revised somewhat, with 70% of the generators' output being covered by three-year contracts with the RECs, in place to cover the fuel supply contracts between the generators and the BCC. Any further fuel supply contracts would need to be linked to the extent of competition, more competition reducing the scope for such arrangements. Alongside these three-year contracts between the generators and the RECs—lasting until March 1993—were shorter one- and two-year contracts (10% of overall generation) and the contracts for nuclear power output, covered separately by the levy on customer bills (20% of overall generation). The shorter contracts (one to two years) needed to be more flexible because they were linked to the non-franchise market, so each party had the option to terminate with three-month notice, and if this was the case, competition to supply the larger customers who were linked to these contracts would be opened up.

The contracts were in the form of contracts for differences (CfDs), through which the generators would receive a predictable cash flow to cover their fixed fuel costs via the option fees paid by the RECs. The main coal contracts, which largely fixed generation costs, were backed up by one-way CfDs between the generators and the RECs, with the RECs paying an option fee and receiving a rebate from generators if the spot price exceeded the strike price. This enabled prices for the franchise customers to be effectively frozen and provided a guarantee that the generators could cover their fixed fuel costs. The remainder were shorter-term and more flexible two-way contracts through which the generators and the RECs made exchanges depending on the fluctuations in the spot price around the contract strike prices. Nuclear Electric also offered CfDs to the RECs, aside from the physical output covered under the NFFO. In terms of electricity output (TWh), in 1990/91 the RECs purchased 124 from National Power, 75 from PowerGen and 38 from Nuclear Electric.[62] In total, 97% of load was covered by CfDs. As the coal contracts wound down, after March of 1993, some of the original two-way CfDs covering the coal contracts were subsequently renewed out to 1998, but they played less of a role, with the volume covering coal decreasing to just under 72 TWh by 1996/97.[63]

Based on modelling work conducted by the Electricity Division, by early 1990 it was clear that the contracts package would result in price increases for franchise customers—adding £925 m in the first year, equating to a 9% increase. Franchise customers' prices were to be controlled for the next three years (linked to the RPI), with 'y' effectively being set at zero, but with separate x-factors applied to each REC. For the eligible customers, those able to switch between competing suppliers, their charges would be based on the spot market price and would therefore not reflect the costs of fulfilling the contractual obligations. There was uncertainty about how to set this price cap for franchise customers because of the difficulty of predicting REC purchase costs with a high level of certainty; a clause was written into the REC licence which allowed them to request to pass through additional costs if they were reasonable. Littlechild agreed but only if the first price control review (PCR) was brought forward one year to the end 1994, enabling cost savings to be passed through to customers sooner.

The department announced the price increases in February 1990, with the government, clearly aware of this politically sensitive issue, making the point that the increase was not much above the general rate of inflation and that, with the price controls in place, they would be effectively capped for the next number of years. This proved to be controversial: a price freeze for domestic customers meant the falling fuel costs were not passed-on in the form of lower electricity prices. The National Consumer Council later pointed out that falling coal prices—a 30% drop in real terms between 1984/85 and 1991—should have led to lower bills in real terms, regardless of privatisation. Whilst the price cap ensured that prices for domestic customers did not increase in line with inflation in the early years of privatisation, and enabled politicians to claim the process benefited normal consumers, in reality this had come on the back of significant price increases in the second half of the 1980s which ensured that the industry was earning a healthy rate of return: between 1984/85 and 1991 electricity prices had increased by just over 40% while the rate of inflation was up 35.4%.[64] There was of course an inherent trade-off here between the damaging political effects of further price increases and the value of the companies on flotation.

Additional to this, a separate one-year price freeze costing £70 m was introduced for very large industrial customers who had been supplied on favourable terms directly by the CEGB. In the region of 300 firms were in the Qualified Industrial Consumers Scheme (QUICS);[65] these mostly electricity-intensive industrial consumers would be significantly affected by the reforms and as a result a transitional scheme, the Large Industrial Consumers Scheme (LICS), was put in place for one year, enabling production sites for which electricity was a large proportion of costs (20–70%, e.g. steel, cement and some chemicals) to manage the transition away from regulated tariffs.

EC Approval and Company Sales

As a result of the protracted discussions around nuclear privatisation and the contractual structure of the new industry, the initial deadline for industry 'Vesting Day' (the operation of the competitive market) had been put back from 31 December 1989 to 31 March 1990. At midnight on 31 March 1990 National Power, PowerGen and the 12 RECs came into being and trading commenced, with the industry now being bound together by the licencing terms in the 1989 Electricity Act and the provisions in the various contracts outlined above. This deadline was of course self-imposed by government as it was felt that a general election could take place at any point from the latter half of 1991 onwards. Coinciding the sale of a nationalised industry of this magnitude with a general election campaign and a possible change of government would have introduced significant risks.

Meeting this deadline was a close run thing as State-aid approval from the European Economic Community (EEC) was just about achieved in time. Two questions had emerged in the context of the EC Treaties: whether the fossil fuel levy constituted legal State-aid and whether imports from France (and Scotland) should be priced at market rates. Discussions with the EEC had only started in April 1989 with a presentation to officials (mainly DGIV Competition) and an exchange of informal 'non-papers', following which the UK government formally notified the European Commission in January 1990 of its intention to grant state-aid approval to nuclear under Article 93(3). This included an initial 10.6% levy on bills (amounting to circa. £1.2 bn/year) and a provision of £2.5 bn for grants to Nuclear Electric, the publicly owned nuclear company. The FFL was set in a way which ensured that Nuclear Electric would be 'cash positive' by the time it was due to be privatised in 1996; at the time of vesting the company had a negative net value in CCA terms of £1.6 bn, with assets of £6.6 bn and liabilities of £8.2 bn.[66] The levy would then vary depending on the productivity of the nuclear plants.

The Scottish nuclear industry was to be treated differently, in part because of the relative size of the nuclear component of electricity supply there was much greater than in England/Wales. Imposing an obligation on the Scottish electricity customer to subsidise these plants would have been economically and politically difficult. The Scottish nuclear company (Scottish Nuclear), jointly owned by the SSEB and NSHEB, was to be underpinned by an agreement made by the two integrated utilities that they would purchase the output of the two AGR plants—the older Magnox plant (Hunterston A) was to be decommissioned—for 15 years at a rate which would be linked to market prices, as opposed to the high costs of operating the units. This would be subsidised by the UK taxpayer via a write-down of the nuclear company's liabilities, up to £1.4 bn. This subsidy to the Scottish nuclear industry provided the two companies north of the border with an advantage as they could sell below cost nuclear output to the RECs via the new English/Welsh power market; in the words of the Energy Committee, '...constitute[ing] a severe and undesirable distortion of the electricity market in Scotland and between Scotland and England and Wales'.[67]

The UK government needed approval for its proposals by end of March, but only provided full information to the European Commission on 9 February, with the Commission's standard period of two months to assess such submission only starting then. There was a particular need to convince Leon Brittan, the then Competition Commissioner, who was concerned about the nuclear supports and wanted to see the FFL phased out over time. Overall, the European Commission's main concern was to create an open energy market across the European Community and to avoid preferential treatment of any particular domestic fuel source. Brittan had in mind a maximum level of subsidy for domestic sources in the electricity sector of each Member State of 20% by 1994, which, according to Wakeham, was set at this particular level because it corresponded to the amount of lignite coal being burned in West Germany.[68]

However, under the initial UK proposals, this level would be at 22%. There was a particular issue with treating Scotland separately from the rest of Britain; if this was the case subsidised nuclear would constitute over 50% of the Scottish electricity sector. Brittan's view was that if a British approach was taken it would help to make the case for longer (15 years) nuclear contracts in Scotland as the share of nuclear in the overall mix would be significantly reduced. The UK government then provided figures to the Commission showing protected nuclear generation on the entire British system at 17% in 1990/91 and falling to 15.7% in 1997/98, and committed to 'take action' if the figure ever rose above 20% before 1994 and then 17% by 1998. Brittan proposed a time limit of eight years on the nuclear contracts (England/Wales) and wanted an assurance that it would be limited to existing plant, that is, not used to fund new nuclear plant. On this basis Brittan agreed to approve the 'Pooling and Settlevent Agreement' (discussed in the next chapter) for 15 years.

António Cardoso E Cunha, the commissioner with responsibility for energy matters and a strong advocate for energy liberalisation, was more sceptical about the FFL than Brittan, and at a meeting on 26 March 1990 suggested amendments, including a review of the amount of State-aid approved and phase-out of the FFL in one year. He also wanted to see a restructuring plan for the nuclear industry. Jacques Delors, the Commission President, decided to defer the decision by one week, 'drawing attention to the contrast between the Brittan Cabinet's support in this case and its nit-picking attitude to French competition cases'.[69] There was also quite a bit of pushback from a number of commissioners regarding the fact that the UK seemed to be getting off lightly compared to the West Germany's coal industry, which at the time was under close scrutiny for its receipt of subsidies (see Chap. 6). An initial vote didn't see the proposals approved, with only six commissioners in favour. But after intensive lobbying, the Commission eventually approved the UK package on 28 March 1990, just in time. The Commission claimed to have secured significant monitoring agreements, a digression process for the FFL and an eight-year time limit. The Commission made it clear that they would have preferred direct budgetary support for nuclear rather than the levy which was viewed as a distortion of the market.

One particular area of controversy was how imports from France would be treated. The CEGB had been trading with *Électricité de France* (EDF) via a 160 MW cross-Channel interconnector since the 1960s, and from 1986 this capacity was substantially increased with the coming on line of a new 2000 MW High-Voltage Direct Current (HVDC) link. As the French power system was increasingly dominated by low marginal cost nuclear, the majority of flows were into England and these were priced according to a 'split savings rule'; the avoided costs were shared between the two utilities. The question was how these imports would be treated if British nuclear plants were subsidised via the FFL. After much two and fro, the decision was made to exempt EDF's imports from the levy, on the grounds that the French nuclear industry would not benefit from it. This resulted in significant transfer from British consumers to the French producer once the new arrangements came into effect as EDF could now increase its revenues substantially by gaining the new market price plus a premium which they could add into their contract, as the RECs could purchase this non-fossil power at a discount on British nuclear generation.

As the original timetable had scheduled 'Vesting Day' to be on 1 January 1990, the subsequent sales of the generators and RECs needed to be pushed back also, with the RECs being sold in December of 1990 and the generators in March 1991.[70] The two Scottish companies were then sold later in June 1991. This was not an overnight transfer of the electricity to the private sector or, as some have claimed, an outright abandoning of the industry by the UK government:[71] 80% of the shares were offered within the UK and 20% to overseas investors. At least 34.4% were made available to the general public and incentives were provided to customers of each REC via share bonuses.

The National Grid Company[72] was to be a holding company owned by both the government and the RECs who were allocated ownership shares of between 5% and 12% based on the value of their businesses. The logic behind transferring ownership to the RECs was that they, rather than the generators, would have the incentive to ensure that the transmission system was run in a way which facilitated competition. Partly influenced by the views of city investors, who were concerned about systemic risk, no single organisation was given a statutory obligation to supply; the majority of demand was to be covered by the contracts between the generators and the RECs, while market mechanisms associated with the operation of the new 'Electricity Pool' (see Chap. 4) were to ensure that the lights stayed on.

Government retained a 'golden share' option on the RECs in order to avoid a situation where the generous asset valuations of the companies in place to enable privatisation would be extracted from these companies before a more stringent RPI-X price control was set in late 1994. The National Grid Company was then sold off in two tranches, in 1991 and 1995, and its highly valuable storage assets—Dinorwig and Ffestiniog—were separated out and sold to a US company called First Hydro.

At sale, the combined share value of the RECs was almost £5.1 bn, based on a sale at a fixed price of 240 p per share. This was calculated to provide a projected yield of 8.4%, yield being 'the proportion of the gross dividend to the share price'.[73] The shareholders did well very quickly out of the sale as the profit forecasts for the RECs made by the department in the original sale Prospectus[74] was exceeded by 22% during the first year of trading on average. Partly based on the evidence that the REC share price rose shortly after the flotation, the government decided to retain a 40% ownership share in the generators, which was later sold off in 1995. The generators, now with 61 power stations (40 with National Power and 21 with PowerGen, a combined generation capacity of 48,000 MW and employing 24,000 people),[75] were subsequently sold for 175 p per share resulting in proceeds of just over £2.1 bn from the sale.

The next chapter will discuss how competition was implemented in practice, focusing on the detailed practical design of a market for wholesale power and the role of the electricity regulator. It charts the evolution of the Electricity Pool during its early years of operation in the early and mid-1990s and how the dynamics of the new competitive market created further problems for the coal industry.

CHAPTER 4

Competition: A Work in Progress

As retail competition was somewhat restricted in the early years of the market, the key site of political contestation in the new electricity industry was in relation to the dominance of the two large generators in the wholesale power market. Much of the early debate centred around the design of the trading and settlement arrangements, known as the 'Electricity Pool', and the extent to which National Power and PowerGen were able to exert market power over the pool price (Figs. 4.1 and 4.2 show the division of power plants between the two companies). As outlined in the following sections, the design of the pool itself arose from a compromise between the Regional Electricity Companies (RECs) and the generators, and was constrained by the need to have long-term generation contracts in place to support the coal industry which needed to operate alongside a short-term spot market.

The new grid operator, the National Grid Company (NGC), as set out in the legislation, had responsibility for achieving an efficient economic dispatch of plant according to their marginal costs of operating. A key dilemma faced in achieving this outcome was how the various contracts between the generators and the RECs would interact with the spot market, and how a merit order based on short-run economic signals could be achieved. One of the risks faced was that, with the wrong market design, the least efficient plants would be dispatched simply because they had obligations to burn contracted British coal, whereas the newer and more efficient stations using imported coal would be lower down the merit order and left idle.

R. Bolton, *Making Energy Markets*,
https://doi.org/10.1007/978-3-030-90075-5_4

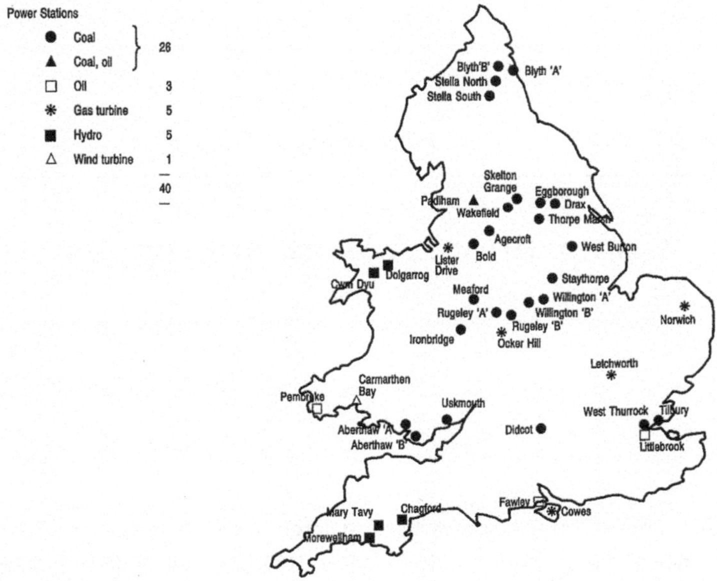

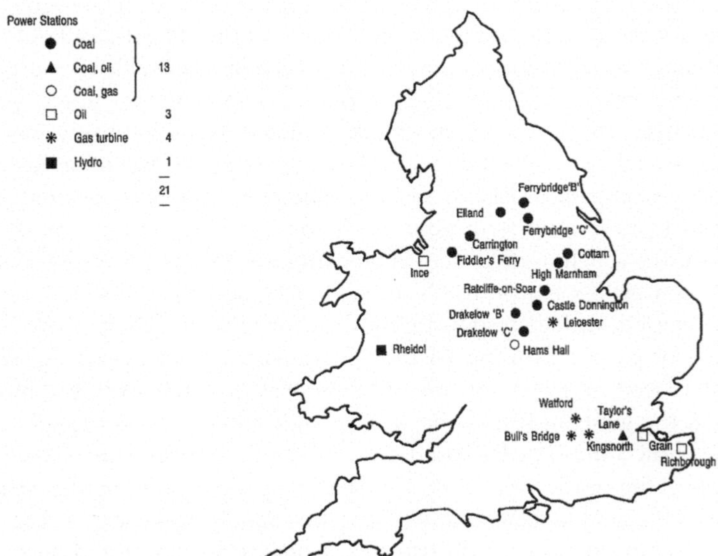

Figs. 4.1 and 4.2 Split of generation assets between National Power (above) and PowerGen (below). (NAO (1992a) *The Sale of National Power and PowerGen*. Report by the Comptroller and Auditor General. HMSO, London). An approximate 70/30% split of the former CEGB's generation capacity minus the nuclear stations. (Courtesy of the National Audit Office)

The following sections will show how key design features of the new Electricity Pool, in particular its highly concentrated structure, resulted in a politicisation of the market, prompting the regulator—the Office of Electricity Regulation (Offer)—to intervene to a much greater extent than was ever envisaged. While Littlechild himself had not been closely engaged in designing the Electricity Pool, focusing instead on establishing retail competition, he later became central to the operation and evolution of the new wholesale power market, conducting investigations into market behaviour and, eventually, forcing the two legacy generators to divest a significant proportion of their assets in order to bring about more competition in the market.

Also discussed are a number of key interventions made by the regulator during the mid-1990s which altered the distributional outcomes of the new market. In its early years (c.1990–95) significant reductions in the costs of generating and supplying electricity—mainly due to lower fuel costs, but improved labour productivity also contributed—were not passed on to the majority of customers, enabling the companies to retain a significant proportion of revenues as profits.[1] However, a more stringent price control for the RECs from 1995 onwards, the introduction of retail competition from 1999, the increasing diversity in the market and the improved productivity of Nuclear Electric—with the consequent decline in the Fossil Fuel Levy (FFL)—saw prices for domestic customers fall to 30% below 1990 levels by 2001, in real terms. This rebalancing of the market perhaps came too late as accusations of unfair profits and 'fat cat salaries' took hold. For many, this de-legitimised the electricity privatisation programme.

The Limited Market

The concept of a power pool was not a new one by the late 1980s. Such arrangements had been operating in parts of the US and continental Europe for many decades, involving 'formal and informal agreements among independent utilities to coordinate some or all of their investment and operating activities'.[2] Trading did occur between utilities in these power pools, but typically as bilateral exchanges and according to a simple 'split-savings' rule, where the price was simply calculated as an equal split between their bids and offers. The UK Department of Energy and their advisors had little precedent in terms of a competitive pool to guide the operation of an entire power system, continuously updating this for each half-hourly trading period, whilst providing long-term investment signals. The Central Electricity Generating Board's (CEGB) method of economic dispatch was to rank stations based on plant operating (thermal) efficiency, with some account taken of transportation costs from pithead/import terminal to plant. The key cost driver of electricity at the margin—variable fuel costs—was not taken into account as the system was based on 'uniform pit head pricing'. This meant that for each plant on the system a flat rate was added to account for fuel costs, so plants located near an import terminal which could access cheaper coal saw no advantage from their lower fuel costs. Plants located along the Thames, like Kingsnorth, West Thurrock and Tilbury, which had been burning very cheap coal from the North East of England at £26/t at mine, had relatively low load factors due to their low position in the CEGB's merit order system. Tilbury, for example, which was using the cheapest coal available, had a load factor of less than 30%, while Kingsnorth and West Thurrock had load factors in 1987/88 of 54.5% and 31.9%, respectively. The load factor for the giant Ratcliffe-on-Soar station further north in the Midlands was 86%, but it was paying in the region of double for its coal supplies than the Thames stations. The CEGB's dispatch system favoured the larger and newer stations like Ratcliffe-on-Soar as it emphasised 'notional thermal efficiency' rather than fuel costs, despite that the latter accounting for about 70% of the total costs of a thermal station.

With a view to designing a new market arrangement which could base the dispatch of plant on their marginal costs of operation, whilst incorporating the contracts already entered into by the generators and the RECs, the department set about designing a new type of power pool trading arrangement. Based on work by their advisors, Price Waterhouse, they initially tabled an ambitious and very complicated proposal called the 'two-pool' model—termed colloquially as 'two boxes and a bridge' by those involved in its design.[3]

The underlying concept was to think about the market in terms of both the efficient dispatch of power plants according to an economic merit order (the G-Pool) *and* the optimal allocation of contracts for the supply of generation to the RECs (the D-Pool). These two sub-markets would work alongside each other and take as a starting point pre-arranged contracts for a quantity of power at a set price between the generators and the RECs: in the D-Pool the RECs would trade their contracts between one another, such that the demand located in each region would be met in the cheapest way possible. RECs with low demand and a surplus of contracts could sell to RECs with high demand and a deficit of contracts. In the G-Pool, the generators could also trade in such a way that the contractual obligations—linked to specific units—to supply the RECs could be met by the cheapest mix of power plants.

The debits and credits incurred from trading in the two pools would be settled by National Grid who would calculate a notional dispatch of power plant based on demand from the RECs. Simultaneously, National Grid would arrange a merit order dispatch according to generator offer prices into the G-Pool and calculate a system energy price for generators (SEP(G)) based on the marginal cost of generation. The difference between the notional dispatch in the D-Pool and actual physical dispatch coordinated by National Grid would be made up through exchanges of debits and credits between generators in G-Pool which were to be valued according to the SEP(G). With a given level of payment from the D-Pool, the G-Pool would provide the generators the opportunity to minimise their costs, as through the exchange of debits and credits those generators who were included in the notional dispatch could effectively pay another generator to meet their contractual obligation. An interesting feature of the model was that the overall market price for electricity was based on the demand for contracted power, rather than price or cost bids made by the generators.

NGC had begun working on the software for this system by early 1989, but concern about the proposed bottom-up market design quickly emerged. Kleinwort Benson, the government's financial advisors, had particular concerns about the practicalities of operating such a system; running the two pools would likely involve thousands of transactions for each trading period and the problems of complexity would be exacerbated as more new entrants came into the market. *Power in Europe* commented that the system is 'unlikely to pick up any awards for elegant simplicity',[4] noting that the complexity may be justified if there was 'say, a dozen generators of roughly equal size' but with a duopoly 'it is largely nonsensical'.[5] There were rumours of a six-month delay to the overall privatisation resulting from these issues.

Ultimately, the RECs lost faith in the two-pool model and withdrew support. Before the decision to opt for financial contracts for differences (CfDs), the contracts between generators and the RECs in this earlier two-pool model were physical, involving both an energy charge and a fixed capacity charge which was to be paid regardless of whether the generator was actually dispatched. The RECs became concerned that the generators would be able to bypass the D-Pool and sell directly to customers who would not be obliged to pay the capacity charge. This, they worried, would create a viscous cycle where electricity supplied via the D-Pool would get increasingly expensive.

In the meantime, the RECs had hired consultants Hod Thornber and Larry Ruff from Putnam Hayes & Bartlett, a US firm, to advise them on market designs. Their initial idea, put forward just after the White Paper was published, was to mimic the highly unbundled US gas system, where separate markets operated for network capacity and energy, but the RECs were concerned that this model would lead to fragmentation and move the system away from their preferred outcome of regional companies integrated across generation, distribution and supply.[6]

Between May and August 1989 the RECs and their consultants worked on an alternative market arrangement which brought together the two pools (generation and distribution) into one—the 'Unified Settlements System'—largely based on the existing CEGB dispatch algorithm (GOAL—Generation Ordering and Loading). This much simpler market design was to be a mandatory pool; that is, that all physical power from plants above the 50 MW threshold was required to be sold into the pool if plant operators wanted to be dispatched. This assuaged some of the fears of the RECs that the generators could bypass the market and sell directly to large customers. The idea was that CfDs could be used to hedge against market fluctuations, with the pool price over time evolving into a recognised and trusted benchmark price, enabling the greater use of financial instruments, as in a conventional commodity exchange. The new model which emerged from discussions in the 'Pomeroy Committee'—chaired by Brian Pomeroy of the Touche Ross consultancy—was influenced in particular by Sally Hunt, a US economist working for the NERA consultancy, and Steven Roberts of Coopers & Lybrand. This later became known as the 'unified' or 'U' Pool.

Alongside the centralised design and mandatory nature of the Electricity Pool, the main difference with the two-pool model was in relation to pricing. The pool would act as a 'Fixed Price Energy Clearing House',[7] meaning that the clearing price for each trading period would be based on the bids of the generators, with the marginal plant setting the system price which was paid to all generators in the market (uniform pricing). As with the CEGB model, the demand side would not bid into the market, rather information about demand was to be communicated to the National Grid by suppliers in advance. By the beginning of September 1989 this single power pool concept was accepted by the Department of Energy.

A key advantage was that it replicated as much as was possible the CEGB's existing merit order dispatch procedure, the only significant difference being that the inputs were price bids rather than generator cost curves.[8] In many respects this market was 'engineered',[9] in the sense that it was designed in order to fit with the operational procedures embedded in the CEGB computer programme (GOAL) and to mimic a conventional market, with both a supply *and* a demand side. For Pomeroy and his Committee of 30 or so members, basing the new market on the previous CEGB computer programme had the appeal of continuity, as he later reflected:

> It had to look roughly the same to them [the generators] … the question is in what order do they call them in. It used to be costs, now it was bids. But it had to look more or less the same … we didn't want them to have to change their routine. Whereas previously they saw a number which was a cost, now they just saw a number which was a price.[10]

Despite its conservative design, the economic logic of this uniform pricing approach was elegant. In a perfectly competitive market, plants with low variable costs (baseload) would earn returns—the difference between revenue from the market and production costs—just sufficient to cover their high fixed costs, with low capital cost peaking plant receiving no rents. If the market was under-supplied and it became clear that mid or low-merit (peaking) plants were earning temporary—or quasi—rents, this would prompt new entry into the baseload level of the market where returns would be highest, thus pushing the uncompetitive mid and low merit plant out of the market. In theory this competitive dynamic would result in an economic dispatch and push prices towards the long-run marginal cost, without the need for centrally calculated tariffs or a government pricing policy. We shall see later however that this market design with uniform pricing and competition for the baseload segment of the market impacted negatively on the economics of coal plant as new entrant gas plant, built for reasons other than pure economic rationality, entered the market and pushed coal down the merit order. This then created pressure on government to intervene to 'fix' the market, in part to protect the coal industry, in a way which was fundamentally against the initial intentions of its designers.

In order to ensure that fixed costs could be recovered and an adequate reserve margin maintained, the RECs had initially proposed a separate capacity market to operate alongside this energy market, providing a more secure revenue stream to generators, particularly those which may only be used for short peak demand periods. Through this they and the generators would exchange capacity entitlements, or 'Tickets', which would be settled daily. The generators instead wanted capacity and energy under one market framework—a 'truly unified Pool'—involving an administered capacity payment. This simpler approach involved a payment based on a calculated loss of load probability (LOLP)—the probability that demand would not be met with available generation—which would be updated according to market conditions each trading period,[11] and a predefined value of lost load (VOLL) to customers—the price that consumers would be willing to pay to avoid a loss of supply, initially set at £2000/MWh, and to increase in line with inflation. This VOLL calculation conducted by Rickett and Horton of the Electricity Division was not done in a way which actually reflected the customers' preferences, rather it was reverse engineered to build the CEGB's existing reliability standard into the market; that is, 'to ensure blackouts on no more than nine winter peaks in a 100 years and brown-outs 30 winters in 100'.[12] Once the market came into operation, the ability to adjust VOLL would then provide the regulator with scope to ensure an adequate reserve margin was in place.

Following a meeting in October 1989 the RECs reluctantly agreed to the generators' proposal. The department was essentially concerned about the practicality of the separate capacity market based on the exchange of 'Tickets' and the effect that designing it might have on the timetable for flotation. The Electricity Pool was born. Essentially, what emerged was a spot market based on generator bids with the earlier D-Pool concept and the system of debits/credits dropped. Also dropped was the decentralised approach to contracts; under the 'two-pool' model these were to be station-by-station, or even unit-by-unit, but under the 'u-pool' there would be a single system price for each trading period.

Under the 'Pooling and Settlement Agreement', a private contract between licenced generators and suppliers,[13] National Grid was responsible for the scheduling of power plant and organising side payments to generators for various ancillary and system services. The market procedure would start with power plant operators submitting offer prices for power delivery for each half hour of the next day (before 10 am) from each unit. An 'unconstrained schedule' was then drawn up by the National Grid a day in advance based on the information submitted by plants—their offer price for generation and a price for maintaining plant availability on standby mode. Using the CEGB's GOAL computer optimisation model, National Grid would then act as the centralised dispatcher and develop a 'constrained schedule' for the trading period which minimised overall costs and calculated the system clearing price (announced at 5 pm for the following day's 48 trading periods). In doing so, they would take into account likely physical constraints on the transmission system.

The publicly owned nuclear operator, Nuclear Electric, would also sell into the pool, but their revenues were to be pre-determined by the secretary of state at a certain level (discussed in Chap. 3), so a premium was added to the market price for these plants. Under the Non-Fossil Fuel Obligation (NFFO), licenced suppliers would collectively purchase the required level of nuclear output via the Non-Fossil Purchasing Agency (NFPA) and a fixed charge would be levied on customers on the basis of the final sales price, apart from consumers who were designated as 'exempt', that is, those that self-generated up to 51% of their own needs. Organisationally, the NFPA would act as the suppliers' agent and contract with non-fossil generators. This collective contracting approach was to avoid a situation where one supplier was exposed to greater risks than others.

The following were the key design features of the Electricity Pool:

- The pool input price (PIP) was the price that generators would sell into the pool and the pool output price (POP) was the price buyers would pay. The difference between PIP and POP—the 'uplift'—was used to cover system costs, such as maintaining response and reserves, forecasting errors, transmission constraints, and ancillary services.
- The pool price calculated from the generator bids[14] and National Grid's demand forecast for each half hour was to be supplemented by a capacity payment to ensure that a safe capacity margin was maintained. The capacity payment was based on National Grid's half-hourly estimate of LOLP and the VOLL. It was paid to all stations who submitted bids and in doing so they committed themselves to generate if called upon.
- The formula for the pool input price represented the 'probability weighted average' of the price of meeting demand and not meeting it; that is, PIP = [SMP (1-LOLP)] + (LOLP × VOLL). The System Marginal Price (SMP) represented the clearing price, 1-LOLP the

probability of meeting demand from available generation and LOLP × VOLL the capacity payment.[15]

A critical view of the pool design was offered early on by *Power in Europe* who wryly commented that 'the Bulk Supply Tariff has been reborn'.[16] They criticised the overall market design, arguing that 'National Power and PowerGen capacity will simply be divided into contract "tranches", with a nominated price for each tranche, and these will be called up in merit order. The marginal system price, rather than a target to be aimed at and beaten by competing generators, simply becomes the twice-hourly Bulk Supply Tariff; it is an accounting tool, not a spur to competition'.[17] The argument was that the scope for competition in the new market would be severely constrained as nuclear had a protected share and was thus at the top of the merit order, while the large modern coal stations held by the duopoly, such as at Drax and Ratcliffe, would be difficult to compete with, especially if they could reduce their fuel costs as the contracts with British Coal fell away. New entrants would be squeezed into a narrow band between the mid and high parts of the merit order stack, thus making new investments extremely risky.

Gas Investment: Competition Despite the Market

This prediction proved to be overly pessimistic from a competition point of view. Very early on, just after the Electricity Pool was introduced, it immediately became apparent that there would be significant new investment in gas-fired generation capacity. This was driven, firstly, by the increasing abundance of relatively cheap gas supplied from the North Sea, enabled by the development of a common carriage regime for the British Gas monopoly network and the developments in combined cycle gas turbine technology. As we discuss further below, what brought about the investments were structural features of the new electricity market which provided incentives to the RECs to invest in new capacity as a means of mitigating the market power of the dominant generators. The market price itself wasn't the key driver for investment in these new power plants; supported by the regulator, the RECs were willing to pay a premium to avoid exposure to the pool price and the market power of the legacy incumbents.

In the CEGB's system there were a number of gas-fired plants using open-cycle turbine technology in operation, but they played a limited role, mainly operated in standby mode and used in winter as peaking plant. Prior to privatisation, the CEGB's expectations were for a further 3–4 GW gas-fired plant in the 1990s, but there was still uncertainty about the likely turbine technology; CCGB engineers had expectations that the 'coal-fired gas turbine' would be the future, using 'integrated gasification combined cycle' (IGCC) technology. A competing technology being considered at the time was 'circulating fluidised bed combustion' (CFBC). Along with the smaller plant on the CEGB system, the North of Scotland Electricity Board (NSHEB) had been operating a large oil/gas hybrid plant at Peterhead, which was planned in order to meet load growth and increase the amount of baseload capacity in the mainly hydropower-dominated northern system. This was notable because it was the first plant in Britain which involved a gas supply contract between an electricity generator and a North Sea operator other than British Gas—the consortium involved British Petroleum (BP) and Total. The plant was configured to utilise low-quality 'sour gas' (high sulphur content) from BP's Miller field, which would not have been suitable for use in the onshore gas transmission network. As the Peterhead plant was located close to the St. Fergus gas terminal it was feasible to construct a separate pipeline to the plant, bypassing British Gas. The deal between NSHEB and BP had been approved by the Secretary of State for Energy, Cecil Parkinson, prior to privatisation, in 1988.

Back in 1987 Rickett and his team were curious as to why the CEGB had not invested in combined cycle gas turbine (CCGT) technology and his team conducted some background analysis to investigate. They estimated the cost of supply from a gas turbine as 2.3–2.4 p/kWh (c. 30–40% below the BST [Bulk Supply Tariff]) and came to the view that this could fill the country's likely capacity shortage in the future. They also predicted that the RECs would invest in gas generation in order to reduce reliance on the incumbent generators. Incidentally, the officials found that this investment would likely take place with no need to raise the BST and consumer prices. We learned earlier that for reasons related to investor confidence in the privatisation programme the government had imposed price increases just prior to the flotations.[18]

By Autumn 1989 the Department of Energy were aware of discussions around 20 new CCGT projects which would add up to 7 GW; by the end of 1991, 6 GW of this had been committed in final investment decisions. While it may have been predictable that private investors, who would require a higher rate of return over a shorter investment time horizon, would look to invest in plant with lower capital cost and higher running costs, it was not until a viable business model which aligned with the new market was in place that the investment in CCGTs happened. The early business model for CCGTs developed by National Power and PowerGen was based on providing peaking plant, as their existing stations already dominated the mid-merit range of the market. Plants such as Kingholm (900 MW, online in 1992) and Rye House (780 MW, 1993) fitted into this category. However, as the take-or-pay coal contracts backed up by the RECs' franchise expired, a new business model for CCGT projects emerged and flourished during the early to mid-1990s. This involved long-term contracts between the RECs and new entrant independent power producers (IPPs), the resulting CCGT plants increasingly supplied baseload power and threatened National Power and PowerGen's dominance of the mid-merit segment of the market, beginning to push coal down the merit order.

The first contract signed between a REC (NORWEB) and an IPP (Lakeland Power) was at Roosecote (220 MW), at the site of an older CEGB coal fired unit. Lakeland purchased the gas from British Gas' Morecambe Bay field on a 15-year contract. Another large new development was the Enron-led project at Teeside which involved a partnership with four of the RECs and the chemicals giant ICI, who agreed to purchase a significant proportion of the generation output on a long-term contract. This project consisted of eight CCGT turbines, totalling 1875 MW, and a purpose-built pipeline to deliver gas from the North Sea fields.[19] Due to the scale of this plant, it became somewhat of a lighthouse project for the success of electricity competition; it was supported strongly by the Department of Energy who worked to facilitate the construction of a new transmission line through the Vale of York in order to integrate the power from Teeside.

Another important early project was the Thames Power CCGT at Barking (1000 MW). Thames was initially to be supplied gas from Norway but ended up taking British Gas supplies. Corby (406 MW) and Peterborough (405 MW) were also under construction by March 1991. The secretary of state was, at this time, considering 36 consents for new CCGT plants. By the end of 1996, as a result of this first wave of investment in gas, around 7000 MW had been brought online, with 12 different RECs involved in the various projects. Further plants were developed by National Power and PowerGen; each developed a plant at Killingholme, PowerGen also developed plants at Connah's Quay and Rye House, while

National Power had plants at Little Bradford and Deeside. Due to their scale National Power and PowerGen could finance these projects without the need for the same level of contract cover for gas supply and power purchase; they also had the benefit of being able to locate new plants at the sites of old coal stations and quickly gain planning permission.

A key driver for National Power and PowerGen's early investments in CCGTs was their cost of capital. Due to competition and uncertainty about the new regulatory regime, the two companies were viewed by investors in a similar way as a conventional company, with a risk index (beta) of 1, as opposed to a traditional electricity company operating under a rate of return regulatory regime, with a risk beta in the region of 0.7, reflecting less exposure to risk. This translated into a cost of capital for the two generators of 12%, as opposed to circa. 9% for an average electricity utility, placing a higher hurdle rate for new investments.[20] The issue was crucial due to the higher capital costs and construction times for large coal plants relative to smaller-scale CCGTs.

One key advantage that the REC-led schemes had however was their lower cost of capital as National Power and PowerGen had higher corporate overheads. Apart from a few exceptions, the RECs' involvement in these CCGT projects were as contracting partners with IPPs such as Lakeland and Enron, generally for 15 years, rather than as outright owners. Remember, initially, the ability of the RECs to own generation was limited, roughly equal to 15% of maximum demand in their area. They could part-own a power plant to fulfil the MW limit and then contract to buy all of its output via CfDs if they wished.[21] As a liquid market for financial contracts to hedge against the pool price took a number of years to develop,[22] these early CfDs with the IPPs enabled them to bypass the pool and hedge their risk; although the plants still had to bid into the pool, their prices were effectively set by the contracts with RECs. The developments were enabled by 'back-to-back' contracts, linking gas supplied form the North Sea fields down to the RECs' customers who were below the threshold for competition and were therefore tied to their local suppliers. This stable background enabled the RECs to contract for the output of the plants.

These investments in generation projects provided a means for the RECs to hedge against the risk that the incumbent generators who dominated the market could manipulate the pool price, an issue which became more salient as the majority of the vesting contracts expired in 1993. If approved by the regulator, the RECs' stakes in these generation projects supplying their own areas could be included in their regulated asset bases, which reduced the financial risk and the cost of capital for the projects, as the costs could simply be passed on to the captive customers. The guaranteed off-take agreements for 15 years enabled projects to be financed up to 90% of their costs and for the loans to be non-recourse, thus 'off balance sheet'. Off-balance sheet financing was the only means by which the RECs could finance these projects as when they were privatised the government had injected the companies with relatively high levels of debt, with debt/equity ratios at 31–43%.[23] This was to inhibit them from using their supply monopolies to finance projects off their balance sheets and tie up the market for new entrants, despite the arguments made by RECs that low debt levels would make them more attractive to investors and enable them to take more risks. High debt levels were also attractive for government as this provided a long-term cash flow for the UK Treasury.

The RECs did however have to demonstrate to the regulator that these investments met the 'economic purchasing condition' written into their licences. As Green outlines, this placed the onus on 'the RECs to demonstrate that they were buying at "the best effective price reasonably obtainable having regard to the sources available", but the RECs were able to cite the unattractive prices with which the major generators had opened their negotiations for future sales, and justify prices that, with hindsight, look expensive'.[24] Littlechild was generally receptive to such requests because of the significant uncertainty around future pool prices and the fact that the projects resulted in more diversity in the generation market.

The contracts suited the IPPs, as in their absence they faced significant risks associated with their gas supply contracts. As competition in gas supply was embryonic, the IPPs entering the market with CCGTs signed gas supply contracts called 'British Gas Long Term Interruptible (LTI) gas contracts'. At this time, they were 'the only significant contracts available with low enough prices to be attractive to power stations'.[25] So they needed in turn 'to find off-take contract arrangements which would offset the risks in the take-or-pay conditions in the LTI contracts'.[26] The LTI contracts followed a decision by the UK Monopolies and Mergers Commission (MMC) in 1987 that British Gas was discriminating against some if its industrial customers. The gas regulator—the Office of Gas Supply (Ofgas)—subsequently forced the gas monopoly to publish contract terms for common carriage across its network such that competing suppliers could access the market on fair terms. This had the effect of pushing down British Gas' tariffs; the first LTI contract (LTI1) offered

Fig. 4.3 Overall gas generation capacity (MW) in England/Wales. (Data extracted from Annex 1 of Offer (1998a) *Review of Energy Sources for Power Stations*. Office of Electricity Regulation, Birmingham)

17.5–19.2 p/therm for 15 years and shortly after they offered this at 16 p via LTI2.[27] The LTI contracts set a new benchmark for gas contracts and played a key role in compounding the effects of competition as the two markets—electricity and gas supply—interacted. All of the early CCGT developers signed LTI contracts apart from the schemes at Corby and Teeside (Figs. 4.3, 4.4 and 4.5).

Coal's Problems in the Market

The fact that many of the new gas developments were based on take-or-pay contracts for supplies via the British Gas network meant that operators had a strong incentive to keep them running and they thus competed in the baseload segment of the market, then dominated by coal.[28] This, combined with the fact that nuclear had a protected share, meant that coal became squeezed out of the market, culminating in a crisis for the coal industry as the vesting contracts expired. This, along with the increasing emphasis on sulphur emissions[29] and the need for investments in flue-gas desulphurisation (FGD) retrofits, meant the prospects for the domestic coal industry were certainly not bright.

Concerns about the future of the coal industry had resurfaced in October 1992 due to low demand and rising stocks. The closure of 31 of 50 deep mines then in operation was announced, threatening 30,000 jobs. This was not far off estimates of only 12–14 pits surviving in a competitive

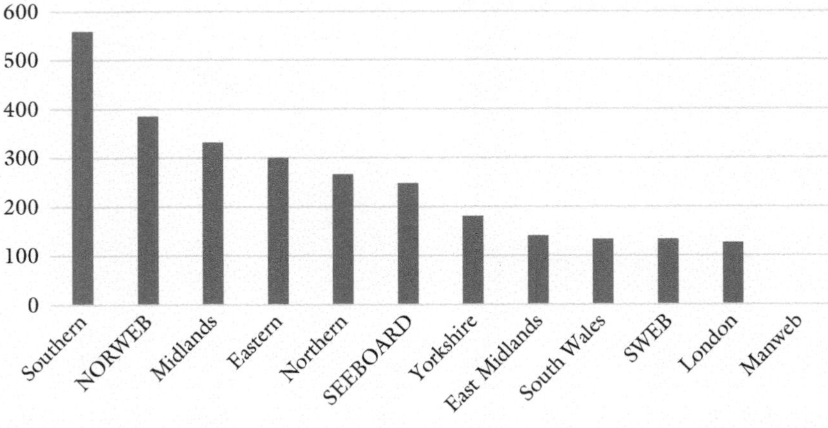

Fig. 4.4 Amount of capacity (MW) owned by the RECs by 1993 (REC total: 2799.3 MW). (Data extracted from Dieter Helm, D. (2003). *Energy, the State, and the Market: British Energy Policy since 1979.* Oxford University Press, Oxford (see footnote 13, Chapter 8). Original source cited is: Offer 1993*b*. *Review of Economic Purchasing: Further Statement.* Office of Electricity Regulation, Birmingham, p. 27)

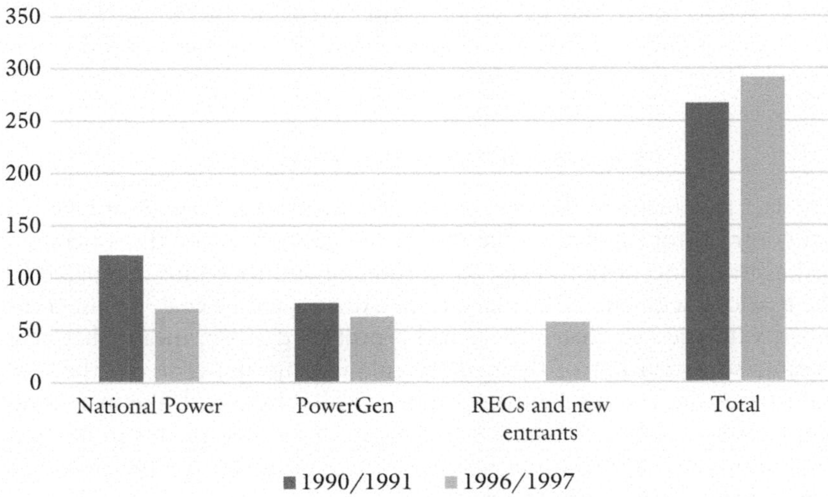

Fig. 4.5 Generation output (TWh) and changes in market shares (1990–97). (Offer (1998b) *Review of Electricity Trading Arrangements: Background Paper 1, Electricity Trading Arrangements in England and Wales.* Office of Electricity Regulation, Birmingham. Data extracted from Table 9)

environment which had been provided by Rothschilds to the Department of Energy prior to privatisation. As the April 1993 expiry date of the initial vesting contracts approached, National Power and PowerGen were put under intense political pressure by the Secretary of State for Trade and Industry, Michael Heseltine, to commit to purchasing similar amounts of British sourced coal. Heseltine intervened and announced that only ten pits were to close; the renewed contract with generators he pushed through was to enable this, but scope for a more substantial package to secure the 57,000 employed in the industry—in March 1991, down from 169,000 in 1985—was limited due to the opening up of the RECs' franchise. The renewed contract with the generators involved 40 mt in 1993/94 and 30 mt for the next four years at prices well above the world level, but the volumes were much lower than in the initial vesting contracts: at 65 mt for 1992/93.[30]

Increasingly conscious of competition from new CCGT developments, the generators were strongly pushing back against a bulk pricing contract with British Coal, demanding instead a pit-by-pit pricing approach. As a sense of crisis for the industry developed, there were calls for a ban on further investment in gas generation to protect the coal industry. Eventually, National Power and PowerGen agreed to the new five-year arrangement, but as the retail market was increasingly opened up to competition (50% by 1994), the scope for significant protection to prop up the coal industry was diminishing.[31] The 'dash for gas' continued however into the mid-1990s, and the generators in 1997 signalled clearly that they would be unwilling to enter into a new round of coal contracts. In 1998 the Labour government then put in place a moratorium on new gas plant, but the damage was done to the coal industry; by 2000, almost 40% of electricity demand was supplied by gas, and between 1993 and 1998 the already much diminished mining labour force had fallen further to 10,000.[32]

As it turned out, the main threat to the viability of British Coal in the early years of the market was not so much direct competition from imported coal, rather competition in its main market from gas-fired electricity generation which began to threaten coal's position in the baseload segment. As an Energy Committee report pointed out in 1992, 'each GW of CCGT plant potentially displaces three million tonnes of coal-burn, so 10 GW of CCGTs could by 1996 displace 30 million tonnes of coal, equivalent to 40% of British Coal's present deep mine output'.[33] British Coal argued that they were denied the 'opportunity' to compete against this new gas plant because the contracts signed by the RECs and IPPs, with 15-year off-take agreements and gas supply contracts, had effectively tied up the market. At the other end of the market, they were being squeezed by nuclear power which had a protected market share via the NFFO. Nuclear Electric's success in raising its overall level of productivity during the first half of the 1990s did not help coal; this improved by 54% between 1989 and 1993.[34]

The coal industry continually made the argument that the electricity market, with its protected market share for nuclear and contractual cover for gas, was structured in a way which discriminated against them. In a memorandum to a 1992 Energy Committee investigation on the effects of privatisation and competition, British Coal predicted that coal generation would likely be squeezed out of merit order: 'This point', they argued, will be 'reached at about 10-12 GW of new CCGT build at which point all baseload demand is taken up by CCGTs and nuclear plant'.[35] In relation to competition from nuclear, British Coal estimated that the levy paid to Nuclear Electric to keep it afloat was equivalent to 'a subsidy of £67.50 per tonne of coal equivalent'.[36] According to British Coal, the result of this market squeeze would be that 'something approaching half of the total market for electricity generation in England and Wales could soon be tied up for the rest of the century in long-term, high-cost contracts at the expense largely of existing coal-fired plant, of coal producers, and of the United Kingdom electricity consumer'.[37]

The questionable economics of the new CCGT plants came in for the most stringent criticism. The argument made by the coal industry, along with National Power and PowerGen, was that based on average pool prices (2.19 p across April–September 1991), investment in these plants did not meet the regulator's 'economic purchasing' condition; according to British Coal's estimates, 'electricity generated at a new gas-fired plant burning gas supplied under the new British Gas contract incurs costs some 30–70 per cent higher than that generated at existing coal plant'.[38]

Critics of the 'dash for gas' pointed to the risk that the new CCGTs would become stranded assets as, with their long-term take-or-pay gas contracts, they had locked in high prices and would therefore be threatened by competitive new entry at the baseload level of the market. This, the argument went, would create security of supply problems in the future as 'must-run' baseload plant bidding into the market at low prices would depress the pool price and damage the economic case for flexible peaking plant. This, in turn, would then create the need for regulatory intervention in order to fix this problem, thus undermining the operation of the 'free market'.

PowerGen submitted the following figures (see Table 4.1) to the 1992 Energy Committee investigation which subsequently became referenced widely in this argument, both by the generators and by British Coal. According to these figures, new CCGT was a higher priced source; this was on the basis that coal prices would fall as the initial vesting contracts expired in 1993 and imports increased. In PowerGen's words, the CCGTs 'represent[ed] the payment of a premium for the introduction of competition'.[39] In their submission National Power argued: 'There must be concern that because the franchise system allows the cost of economically poor supply purchasing decisions by RECs to be passed through to the franchise market customer, this could lead to a stimulus to build excessive uneconomic new capacity'.[40] In defence of his decision to allow these plants to be built by the RECs on the back of the franchise customers, Littlechild pointed out that the review of the RECs' economic purchasing decisions was not due to take place until their first price control review in 1994, but until then the threat that the regulator could refuse to pass on charges related to excessive expenditure would hang over them and discipline them.

While one can be sympathetic to these arguments, it has to be said that a good degree of blame should be attributed to the leadership of the British coal industry whose basic assumptions about the temporary nature of low world coal prices and the ability of the British Coal Corporation to

Table 4.1 PowerGen's calculation of unit costs for CCGT and coal plants in 1991. Data extracted from Energy Committee (1992) *Second Report: Consequences of Electricity Privatisation*. HMSO, London. p. xxv

	Electricity cost without FGD (p/kWh)	*Electricity cost with FGD (p/kWh)*
New CCGT with gas at 23 p/therm	2.89	–
New CCGT with gas at 20 p/therm	2.64	–
Large coal plant using British coal	2.20	2.73
Large coal plant using imported coal	1.66	2.19

compete proved to be fundamentally flawed. Since their earlier evidence provided to the 1988 Energy Committee on privatisation (see Chap. 3), imports into western Europe from Colombia and Indonesia had started to come onstream, adding to imports from traditional suppliers in Australia and South Africa, further depressing prices. The two large generators were gearing up for increasing coal imports by investing in port capacity, a move which would increase the available volumes and offset the costs of importing via Rotterdam. National Power's ambition was to import up to half of their coal by the mid-1990s, at circa. £30/t (the cheapest British coal was £45 at the mine head).

What British Coal hadn't factored in in their earlier analysis was the world coal market had reached a new equilibrium. The increasing diversity of suppliers and the ability to exploit an abundance of coal lying near the surface and accessible via open cast mines meant, in the words of John Baker, National Power's Chairman, that 'there is a lot of capacity which could come on incrementally at very modest changes in the price and that also, of course, will serve to stabilise prices'.[41] By the early 1990s imported coal was increasingly viewed as a reliable source for long-term supplies, with Baker pointing out that 'there has never been an occasion when consumers of world-traded coal have wondered from where their next tonne was coming. That has not always been the case in the UK' (Fig. 4.6).[42]

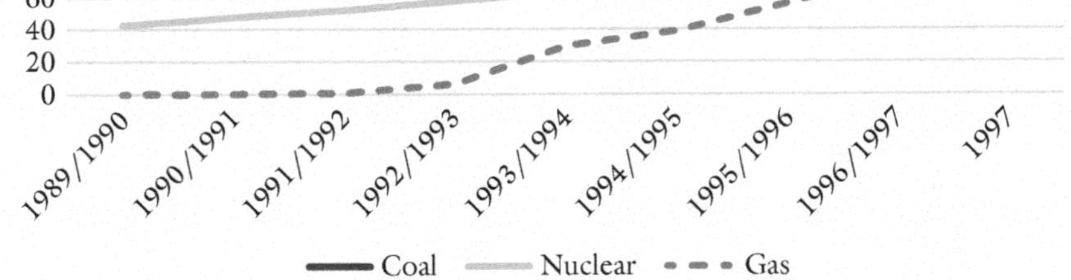

Fig. 4.6 Generation output from coal, nuclear and gas power plants in England and Wales (TWh). (Data from: Offer (1998a) *Review of Energy Sources for Power Stations*. Office of Electricity Regulation, Birmingham. Table 1)

The Realities of the Market

When the Electricity Pool was first introduced, there was in fact a concern about low prices, at times below the avoidable cost of the generators and some 25% below the department's expectations.[43] This deflation was driven by a number of factors: low international oil prices (as low as $10/barrel) meant that cheaper output from oil plants began to set the pool price more frequently. Another factor was the nature of the contracts between British Coal and the two generators. The revenues of the two incumbent generators were determined by the vesting contracts rather than the pool price, and the take-or-pay provisions in the coal contracts, along with the expectation of more stringent environmental regulation in the future and concerns about the costs of coal storage, meant they had a strong incentive to burn through the amount of coal specified in the contracts quickly. The low oil price meant that in order for these coal plants to be run they had to bid in at low prices, sometimes at below their short-run marginal costs.

Initially National Power and PowerGen in fact maximised revenues during many trading periods by keeping the pool price low, as bidding in with their costliest low merit plant may have created a risk that they would be required to produce more output than was covered by their CfDs.[44] The Electricity Pool price was actually close to zero on a number of occasions. The contracts, rather than the pool, became the key economic driver of the system, such that so long as 'the generator actually produced the volume of electricity covered by the CfD, the net effect of the CfD and its sales through the Pool would mean that its revenues would not be affected by the Pool price'.[45] The low prices of course made privatisation look good early on and were particularly beneficial for the large consumers as their prices were closely linked to the spot price. On average, this cohort saw a reduction of one-fifth in their electricity costs in real terms. Another consequence of the low pool prices was that the FFL had to be increased to 11% from 10.6%, while the long-term effects of the deflation on future investment was also raising concerns (Fig. 4.7).

However, prices began to rise as the end of the coal contracts came into view and after this point there was a clear short-term incentive on the duopoly to develop bidding strategies which raised the pool price (during one trading period on 9 September 1991 the pool purchase price rose to £160/MWh!).[46] Capacity payments also rose significantly, by a factor of three on the previous year, while uplift payments increased by 70%.[47]

Given that the market had been segmented into eligible and franchise customers, the effects of pool price increases were asymmetric, accentuating the politicisation of the market. As part of the contractual agreements agreed prior to vesting and privatisation (see previous chapter), prices for franchise customers were controlled in order to ensure that the generators could earn an attractive return on capital whilst recouping the cost of the fuel contracts, so domestic customers did not feel the effects of these increases. It should be noted however that the average price in the contracts between the generators and the RECs was significantly higher than pool prices, resulting in a significant transfer to company shareholders, at '3.4 p per kWh (in 1990 prices)', compared with 'an average Pool price of 1.7 p per kWh in April-September 1990 and 2.2 p per kWh in the same period in 1991'.[48]

The impacts of price rises on larger consumers was not uniform. The price rises were of particular concern to large users whose contracts were closely linked to the pool price (above the 1 MW threshold and not qualifying for special schemes), creating a strong lobby behind closer scrutiny of the generators by the regulator. Littlechild was under pressure to act, and following an initial investigation into pool bidding started in 1991—the first of three such investigations in the first three years of the market[49]—he came to the view in December 1991 that 'there is no doubt that the two major generators have recently been able to increase Pool Prices significantly'.[50] It was found that pool price increases were not in line with changes in the costs of electricity generation; the regulator's view was that there has been 'an element of artificiality about Pool prices which is unsettling for customers and generators alike, and which gives misleading signals to both groups'.[51]

The generators retorted by arguing that price increases were required to bring the market into long-run equilibrium, a difficult argument to make in an oversupplied market. Their logic was that contract prices—both those underpinning the new CCGTs and those covering coal generation—had been well above the pool price and that if the generators were reliant on these depressed market prices they could not cover their costs and would go bust. PowerGen estimated that if they relied on revenues from the pool they would have made a loss of £300 m in their first year. In an efficient market, the argument went, pool prices should converge with long-term contract prices as set by the CCGTs; otherwise, the market would be out of whack and the generators would not have enough

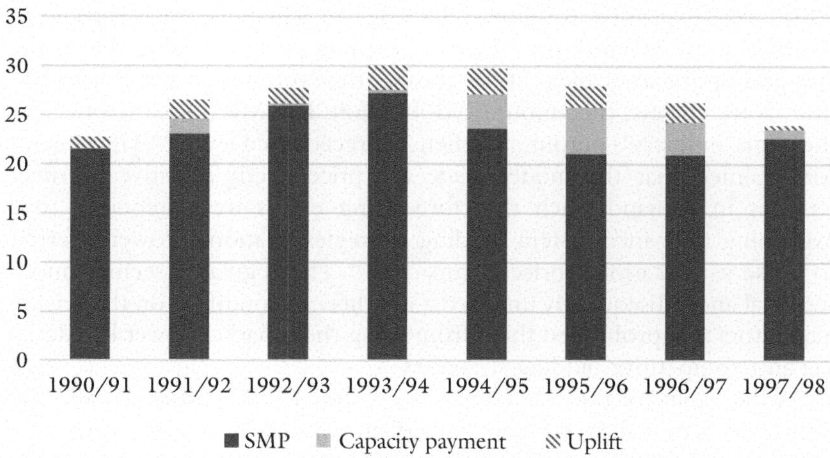

Fig. 4.7 Real annual average pool prices (£1997 £/MWh). (Data from: Offer (1998b) *Review of Electricity Trading Arrangements: Background Paper 1, Electricity Trading Arrangements in England and Wales.* Office of Electricity Regulation, Birmingham. Table 3, p. 20)

contract cover to ensure the sustainability of their businesses. Ed Wallis, Chairman of PowerGen, summarised the logic of this argument:

> The point is about how Pool price affects future contracts; of course it affects it because if somebody has a contract coming to an end he has a choice, he either negotiates and signs another contract or he buys out of the Pool and our deep concern is that we cannot achieve a proper return for our companies unless, in actual fact, the price in the Pool moves towards the entry cost of new entrants. My answer to the last bit of the question is, I believe the Pool price has to move towards that level and current contract prices which are above it need to move towards it as well and, therefore, there needs to be a convergence. What I am concerned about is that nobody will recontract ... The current profitability in the industry is the contracts that we were given when we were floated and that is where the profitability is.[52]

This regulator's first report on pool prices also identified problems with the GOAL dispatch algorithm, in particular the way in which the system 'scheduled plant, and the interaction between the schedule and the price algorithm'. Extreme price spikes, such as the one experienced in September

1991, were explained as follows: 'GOAL had scheduled a gas turbine to produce a few MWh during the early evening peak, choosing this as the cheapest option available to it, far cheaper than turning on a coal-fired station. Nevertheless, the amount bid for those few MWh set the price for the entire industry's output, at a then-unprecedented level'.[53] The generators claimed that the model made the price overly sensitive to small changes in demand, such that forecasting errors were frequent, thus explaining their inconsistent bidding strategies. National Power referred to these as 'occasional price excursions'.[54] The regulator seemed more sceptical and subsequently imposed a new licence condition on the private generators that prohibited them from using their market power by adopting anti-competitive bidding strategies.

As the expiry of the coal contracts in April 1993 approached and the output of National Power and PowerGen was less tied up in long-term CfDs which had been agreed with the RECs just before privatisation,[55] the Electricity Pool was unshackled and became more of an economic driver of the electricity system. With gas plant based on back-to-back contracts with take-or-pay provisions for fuel supply, along with increasing environmental regulation and associated FGD costs, coal became pushed increasingly towards the margins of the market. This meant that it played a more influential role in setting the pool price, thus raising concerns about market power as the legacy incumbents operated the vast majority of this plant, especially in the mid-merit segment of the market. They honed their bidding strategies around exploiting volatility and price spikes. Following a review, the regulator 'noted the growing discrepancy between rising Pool prices and falling fuel costs since vesting, and specifically the sharp increase in Pool prices in April 1993, as the previous year's contracts were replaced on 1 April'.[56]

So, although the market overall was becoming more competitive, the uniform pricing principle of the pool meant that the bidding strategies of National Power and PowerGen strongly influenced the price for the entire market—they set the price 90% of the time. Rather than seeing this as a long-term strategic opportunity to keep prices low, with a view to gaining market share back from gas plant and staving off the entry of new competitors, the incumbents seem to have adopted a strategy of bidding up the pool price to maximise returns.[57] However, this short-term strategy meant that gas plants could benefit from the resulting prices set by coal, contributing further to its diminishing market share and resulting in incentives for further investment in new baseload capacity to take advantage of the high prices. This, it has been argued, contributed to a market distortion, resulting in premature investment in gas plant—the cost of running the new gas plant was greater than the avoidable cost of running a coal plant in its place—which was not to the benefit of the average electricity customer.[58] The risk that the RECs' desire to reduce dependence on the two large generators would result in bad outcomes for customers was spotted early on by the Energy Committee, who, in their 1992 report, noted:

> There is no doubt that the RECs' interest in CCGTs results not just from potentially lower costs but from the wish to reduce their dependence on the two main generators... Clearly some CCGT projects are economically justified as replacements for existing plant and others are not. The danger is that RECs contracting with IPPs for relatively high-priced output will seek to pass on the higher costs to captive, franchise customers under the price controls in operation from 1993. The risk is heightened by the conflict of interest when RECs are shareholders in the IPPs with which they are contracting.[59]

Added to this were accusations that the legacy incumbents were able to raise their earnings by strategically holding back generation in order to exploit constraints on the transmission grid and thus gain from the associated side payments. A prominent example was National Power's plant at Fawley on the south coast which, although a high marginal cost oil plant with a low load factor, was sometimes called on by National Grid to maintain voltage levels on the surrounding transmission lines.[60] Under the pool rules, any plant like this which was not included in the unconstrained schedule, but later called on to generate, was simply paid its offer price plus an 'unscheduled availability payment' (USAV). In such cases where the generator was 'constrained-on' due to a known transmission constraint, the generator could easily game the system by submitting high bids for plant that they knew would unlikely be dispatched by the GOAL algorithm. It was found that on average National Power was submitting bids close to the costs of operating the Fawley plant which, although not generating for many hours, had fixed costs associated with the need to maintain its availability to the grid. However, PowerGen were found to have 'submitted extremely high bids from two small stations scheduled for closure. Because of the closures, NGC had to reinforce its transmission system in each area, creating temporary transmission constraints that the stations exploited',[61] earning in the region of £88 m.[62] In subsequent years National Grid took over more responsibility for these 'system support services', reducing the need for uplift payments to generators.

The dynamic during this early period was one of strategic game playing, with the generators testing the rules of the market and the willingness of the regulator to intervene. The generators of course had the in-depth system knowledge inherited from the CEGB expertise that was largely transferred over. From the outset it was clear that they could exploit these payments; once it became apparent Littlechild issued a stern warning to the companies[63] and changed the procedure by which such system services were procured by the National Grid. He also required the generators to provide a clear justification if they were to close a peaking plant.

PowerGen were also found to be holding back generation from the market with a view to raising the LOLP and their capacity payments. Shortly before the market closed they re-declared the plant to be available, a strategy known as rebidding. The generator defended this as in line with the pool rules as they stood, but it was telling that the tactic was quickly stopped on the direction of Ed Wallis once its effect on the capacity payment from the pool became apparent. On the back of this the regulator altered the method for calculating LOLP which had been determined by demand on a small number of occasions, resulting in a spikey price profile. This was changed to average it out over a longer timeframe to take into account plant availability over an eight-day period and smoothening the curve. As an aside, setting the LOLP for each half hour, 24 h in advance, turned out to be a highly complex and bureaucratic exercise. The process required input from a sub-committee of pool members and the result was often an unreliable signal for future investment; unsurprisingly, long-term contracts continued to be the mechanism through which fixed costs were covered and new plants were financed.

Concerned by these pool price developments and accusations of side-payment manipulation, the regulator began to put pressure on National Power and PowerGen to divest some of their assets as a means of making the market more competitive. The regulator had also come under some political pressure to address this issue, with the Energy Committee requesting in 1992 that he 'take steps as soon as possible to reduce the dominance of the two generators' and consider referring them to the MMC.[64] Particular focus had come on the mid-merit section of the market, a key determinant of the pool price which was dominated by the old CEGB plants. In order to avoid further scrutiny and a potential reference to the

MMC, the large generating companies agreed to a cap on pool prices for two years from 1994 to 1996[65] and to sell off some of their generation assets to competitors.

The regulator had limited direct legal authority to alter the pool rules, which were underpinned by a private contract between the members and governed by the five-member Pool Executive Committee under a Pool Chief Executive (then Margaret Thompson). As part of a 'Revised Initial Settlement Agreement', agreed in 1991, around the time of the first investigation into the pool, Littlechild gained authority to propose changes to pool rules, but not to impose them. The threat of a referral to the MMC remained the main regulatory instrument to impose competition.

With this in the background, National Power initially committed to sell 4000 MW and PowerGen 2000 MW, both to Eastern Electric. There were still concerns about market power and the pool price into the late 1990s however. This was partly because of the nature of the deal with Eastern which meant that the REC was merely leasing the plant, with National Power and PowerGen earning a payment for every MWh sold. Eastern were bidding in high in order to cover these payments, which did little to address the inflated pool price.

The pressure from the regulator on the companies to divest, along with the expiry of the government's 'golden shares' in the RECs in 1995, enabling them to be taken over, prompted a trend towards more diversity in the generation side of the market and concentration at the distribution/retail end as generators integrated downstream. The expectation of the REC Chairmen throughout the privatisation process had been that they would remain independent and over time begin to merge, leading to the creation of the regionally integrated power boards which had been an earlier model for the entire industry[66] (see Chap. 2). However, by the end of 1998 all of the RECs had been sold. Diversification into other services (e.g. water and IT), rather than regional mergers, became their dominant business strategy.

Between the expiry of the government's blocking shares and the end of the 1990s, the RECs were taken over:[67] two 'were bought by their local water and sewerage companies (also regulated utilities), one by the vertically integrated Scottish Power [Manweb, in 1995],[68] one by the conglomerate Hanson plc to become Eastern Group, and two by US utilities'.[69] Midlands 'was bought by another US utility group soon afterwards. Three more US utilities made successful bids in late 1996, and EDF, the French state-owned company, successfully bought London Electricity from its US owner, Entergy, in November 1998'.[70] British Energy (the privatised nuclear operator, successor to Nuclear Electric) bought the SWALEC retail business from Welsh Water in 2000 and later sold it on to Scottish Hydro, who in 1998 had merged with Southern Electric to form Scottish and Southern. Alongside the impending sale of their collectively held asset, National Grid, in late 1995, the large domestic customer bases (below 100 kW) that these companies held would, from 1998 onwards, be transformed into valuable retail supply businesses, making the RECs highly attractive investments.

There was also a perception that there was significant value to be extracted from the assets under the new RPI-X regulatory regime. Although unsuccessful, the first attempt to buy one of the RECs as part of this initial wave of takeovers brought to the surface the political dynamic of electricity regulation. Sparking significant controversy in 1995 was a bid of £11/share made by Trafalgar House, a construction company, to the Northern Electric shareholders, well above the share price at flotation of £2.40. This indicated that the first price control review for this company, which had been announced by Littlechild in 1994, was overly generous. On the face of it, it seemed to be a stringent target for the companies: an initial 14% price cut (Po) and an average x-factor of 2% to be applied to the RECs. But the Trafalgar bid signalled that there was significant returns to be extracted from the asset base under the new terms. There was a clamouring for the regulator to intervene, a decision which went against Littlechild's Austrian philosophy of minimal regulation and constraints on free market forces.[71] Ultimately, the Northern Electric management fought off the bid by borrowing against the assets to deliver a payout to shareholders of £5/share. As pressure mounted, Littlechild reopened the price control in March 1995 to deliver an increase in x from 2% to 3%.

National Power and PowerGen had also made bids for RECs in 1995 (Southern Electric and Midlands respectively), but these were not approved by the secretary of state on the basis that they would lead to vertical integration and reverse competition in the market, although the MMC had previously come to the view that they could go ahead subject to safeguards. This resulted in a trade-off made between the regulator and the generation companies; in return for divestment of generation assets, National Power and PowerGen could integrate downwards into distribution and retail as the market opened up. In 1996 Eastern Group, the likely buyer of this released capacity, had already purchased 6000 MW and was nearing its limit for own generation due to its equity stakes in the Barking and Peterborough CCGT plants. The regulator relaxed this constraint 'and eventually agreed that a REC could own additional stations, provided that it did not sell the power from those stations to small customers in its own area, those at most risk of exploitation'.[72] Subsequently, in order to gain approval from government to integrate with a REC (East Midlands), PowerGen sold a further 4000 MW in 1998. National Power also sold the largest plant in its fleet, Drax, 'in exchange for DTI approval of its acquisition of the retailing business of Midlands Electricity',[73] creating Npower.[74]

* * *

Following this initial period of takeovers of the RECs in the mid and late 1990s, the dynamics of the industry changed following the Utilities Act of 2000 which mandated a split of the retail and distribution areas of these businesses. There then followed a short period of industry flux when companies began to specialise in either networks businesses or generation/ supply.[75] Then a more settled industry configuration began to take shape from the early 2000s onwards, largely based on the traditional vertically integrated utility structure. The integration of the Eastern Group upstream into generation to became a large vertically integrated company had set a trend for the market, and by 2002 'there were just seven large suppliers in the domestic market: Innogy (the UK arm demerged from National Power), PowerGen, TXU (Eastern had taken on its US parent's name), London Electricity, Scottish Power, Scottish & Southern Energy and Centrica (the former British Gas). The one remaining independent REC, Seeboard, was to be bought later in the year by London'.[76] The 'Big Six' vertically integrated companies were formed later in 2002 when TXU was taken over by the German company E.ON, who had already purchased PowerGen's business, as a result of the business falling into trouble due to low pool prices. With RWE and E.ON taking over the former National Power and PowerGen businesses, the entry of EDF into the British market following its purchase of London Electricity and SWEB's retail business, and with the presence of the Scottish utilities, the British electricity industry took on somewhat of a European flavour, in terms of both its ownership and its vertically integrated structure.

The Electricity Pool failed to be the beating heart of a truly competitive market essentially because little power was purchased directly from it, this was due to the various long-term fuel contracts in place for coal, nuclear and later gas. Many of the contracts were designed around political goals, aiming to protect the coal and nuclear industries, and to mitigate market power, rather than agreed around a reliable and trusted reference price as would be the case in a functioning commodities market. It therefore failed to become a liquid market and trustworthy benchmark for new entrant generators and for long-term contracts (both financial and for physical delivery). Largely because of this, the pool was replaced by an alternative trading platform, the 'New Electricity Trading Arrangements' (NETA) in 2001, which was based around decentralised contracts and self-dispatch, moving away from uniform pricing and capacity payments (although a 'capacity mechanism' was again introduced following the 2013 Energy Act). NETA was later expanded to Scotland, in 2005, creating the 'British Electricity Trading and Transmission Arrangements' (BETTA) that operates today.[77]

The early years of the England and Wales market illustrated the effectiveness of long-term contracting as the core economic logic of an electricity system; the role of depoliticised energy markets and spot pricing in directing long-term power system change remains an economic theory.

PART II

Core Europe

Part II contains a further three chapters which examine electricity liberalisation in a wider European context over a similar timescale as the British case. Focusing primarily on the continental Member States of the European Economic Community (EEC), it pays particular attention to role that the European Commission played in opening up national electricity markets as it struggled to include power sector reform in its wider single market agenda. Despite the presence of deeply embedded national electricity regimes, the period of study saw the creation of a common, but rather loosely defined, approach to liberalising EEC Member States' electricity supply industries. As France and Germany were central to this political process, Chap. 6 is devoted to an in-depth study of these two national electricity regimes, explaining particular technical and political characteristics which led to such divergences. The lack of a central European regulatory authority, with jurisdiction to impose a single market model, meant that the diverse ways of organising national systems were carried through in the market creation process. As a result, no single European solution emerged. Markets evolved in a rather fragmented manner within regional contexts, as immediate neighbours built upon pre-existing trading arrangements and infrastructures.

CHAPTER 5

Europe: The Economic Logics of Trade

From the late 1980s, discussions were taking place amongst the European Economic Community (EEC) Member States about the possibility of liberalising electricity trade between their national systems and including the electricity supply industry in the wider project of a European single market, to be achieved by 1992. A key economic driver for liberalisation of cross-border trade in Europe at this time was the electricity imbalances which existed in many national systems, in particular in France which had a significant surplus due to its excess nuclear capacity. A second key set of drivers were developments in international energy markets, primarily the low oil price and the increasing competitiveness of international coal trade which, similar to the British case, put pressure on subsidy arrangements for national coal industries. Industrial consumers in particular viewed markets and liberalised cross-border trade as a means of accessing cheaper imports of power and breaking free from their obligations to purchase from local and national monopoly suppliers. Given the extensive interconnection of European grids, the economic drivers outlined above, and the political momentum behind the European single market, it is perhaps surprising that it took ten years from the agreement of the Single European Act for the first tentative steps towards electricity market liberalisation to be made with the adoption of the first electricity directive in 1996.

During this period, the European Commission had seen the single market programme as a guiding mission and attacked it with reformist zeal, being strongly influenced by parallel developments in the British economy.

R. Bolton, *Making Energy Markets*,
https://doi.org/10.1007/978-3-030-90075-5_5

Its efforts to align the electricity industry with the principles of the single market—'an area without internal frontiers in which the free movement of goods, persons, services and capital is ensured'[1]—started out by threatening the Member States with legal action if they did not apply existing EC law to their electricity sectors, but as the 1992 deadline to deliver electricity liberalisation passed, the Commission realised that they needed to play more of a political game and work through the decision-making procedures of the increasingly complex institutional architecture of the EEC.

Back in 1985, the European Commission published an influential study examining barriers to cross-border trade amongst the Member States, known as the 'White Book'.[2] Drafted by Arthur Cockfield, the UK commissioner responsible for the internal market under the first Delors presidency, the study was motivated by the fact that, despite the commitments to the 'four freedoms' implied in the 1957 Treaty of Rome, there remained significant barriers to cross-border trade and market integration.[3] Based on this, the Single European Act was adopted in December of 1985 and signed in February 1986, coming into legal force in July 1987. Its headline, and common objective, was the ambition to remove the identified barriers to trade by the target date of end of 1992. Key mechanisms agreed to achieve this were 'a streamlining of Council decision-making procedures on internal market matters and the enforcement of the role of the European Parliament in the review of legislation'.[4] Initially, the adoption of the Single European Act[5] in December of 1985 did not appear to have significant implications for the electricity sector as, along with other energy sectors, it was initially excluded. This was surprising given that it was 'Europe's biggest and in many ways most important industry. To exempt it from the "single market" of 1992 would be an admission of failure which the Commission could hardly countenance'.[6] In 1986 the Commission then set about its work to reform the electricity industry with the aim of including electricity, and energy more broadly, in the single market, and in 1988 a Commission working paper was published setting out the agenda for the 'Internal Energy Market' (IEM).

This chapter will examine these early proposals for electricity liberalisation in the EEC context in the late 1980s and early 1990s. A key part of the early Commission proposal was to allow 'common carriage' across transmission networks, potentially enabling consumers in one country to enter into direct contracts with producers in another. In order to enable this, the organisations which controlled access to the transmission grids, the integrated utilities, would effectively need to cede control, either to national regulators or to a central European regulatory body operating under the jurisdiction of the European Court of Justice (ECJ). If taken to its extreme, in terms of the extent of competition, it would also entail the effective dismantling of local supply monopolies. Unlike in the British context, local suppliers, often municipally owned, were an influential group of actors in many of the continental national electricity regimes and their framing of electricity supply as a public service, requiring monopoly rights over defined geographical areas, came into direct conflict with the view of electricity as tradable commodity and direct competition for end-users. As discussed in Chap. 7, this framing of electricity as a public service gained traction during the political process as it was articulated in increasingly powerful committees of the European Parliament, putting a question mark over the whole competition agenda.

We begin in this chapter with an introduction to the already extensive level of interconnection and trading between European electricity utilities which had been built up during the latter half of the twentieth century. We then discuss how the Commission's agenda for electricity competition disrupted this established market arrangement and how the Commission's proposal to introduce common carriage faced fierce resistance, eventually being watered down.

Trade Via Cooperation

It is important to recognise that prior to the liberalisation debate, there was a pre-existing market enabling cross-border electricity exchanges between European countries. This involved power flows between systems organised through power pools,[7] the largest of these was UCPTE, the 'Union for the Co-ordination of Production and Transmission of Electricity'. UCPTE had been founded in Paris in 1951, evolving out of the 'Electricity Committee of the Organisation for European Economic Co-operation' (OEEC), which had been established in 1948 in the context of the European post-war reconstruction effort. UCPTE initially had eight members: Austria, Belgium, Federal Republic of Germany, France, Italy, Luxembourg, the Netherlands and Switzerland.[8]

During the inter-war period electricity planning in Europe had featured strongly in the work of international organisations such as the League of Nations and the International Labour Office. As Lagendijk and Van Der Vleuten—historians of European technology—outline, however, 'their envisioned model of top-down construction of a European power grid, backed by political will and international financing, became a road not taken'.[9] Alternative alliances were forged between national governments and regional power companies, with the future of European electricity integration 'now seen as a patchwork of gradually emerging and collaborating national networks, rather than a supranational system to be built from scratch'.[10] The bottom-up and collaborative nature of UCPTE was a response to the failure of a number of highly ambitious 'grand visions' for the development of a trans-continental electricity infrastructure across Europe.[11]

At the time of UCPTE's formation, coal and hydropower were the dominant sources of electricity production in these countries and there were clear benefits to be achieved from coordinating the two sources. Cross-border collaboration enabled coal to be conserved, which at this time constituted 70% of all energy consumed in the six countries of the European Coal and Steel Community (ECSC), but was a scarce resource as production capacity of the mining industry was still recovering after the war. Precious coal resources could be conserved through linking thermal plants with hydroelectric power schemes, particularly in France, Italy and Switzerland, using surplus production at times of high rainfall and enabling resource use to be optimised. The ability to access thermal generation, in turn, made systems which were vulnerable to seasonal weather fluctuations more resilient. This market between utilities was based on telephone communications and developed throughout the 1950s, as summarised by UCPTE:

> In 1953 occasional electricity supplies were liberalised, i.e. supplies which were used to avoid water being lost or to help out a country whose operation was disrupted by failures in the grid. In 1956, seasonal supplies were liberalised, i.e. supplies with an obligation of less than six months, and 1959 saw the abolition of foreign exchange allocation in this area and consequently the extension of liberalisation to all electricity supplies.[12]

Over time, as national systems became more balanced and resilient, trading over longer timescales in the seasonal market 'lost significance in favour of short and medium-term mutual assistance'.[13]

Although the net volumes of trade were quite low—by 1974 amounting to 5% of total electricity supply of the original eight countries (38,700 GWh)—the systems did become very interdependent and physically interconnected, or meshed. The trading system became organised around four high-voltage transmission 'rings'—or areas of dense interconnection—including Austria-Federal Republic of Germany, France-Italy-Switzerland, Italy-Austria-Yugoslavia and France-Belgium-Netherlands-Federal Republic of Germany-Switzerland. Key sections of the UCPTE system where there was a significant trade differential included France-Italy, Spain-Portugal and Germany-Luxembourg. Switzerland was particularly well connected with its electricity neighbours as it played a crucial role as a transit system between France, Italy and Germany. Financial flows were calculated using a dispatch simulation model and utilities typically 'split the gains from trade over very short-term transactions', hence the term 'partial cost pools'.[14] These arrangements relied on information sharing regarding marginal costs, with such exchanges largely based on trust.[15]

Similar collaborations were formed at the edges of the UCPTE system and over time they became increasingly integrated with it. The system was evolving towards a pan-European collaboration, with the original UCPTE members at the core.[16] In 1963 the Franco-Iberian Union for Coordination and Transport of Electricity (UFIPTE) was formed, which operated synchronously with UCPTE, with Portugal and Spain becoming full members later in 1987. A similar organisation known as SUDEL was formed between the Austrian, Italian and the hydropower rich Yugoslav system in 1964, with Yugoslavia also becoming full UCPTE member in 1987. As we will see in Chap. 9, the Nordic countries had their own organisation, called Nordel, in operation since 1963.

A prime example of what historians of European technology have termed 'hidden integration', the expansion of these organisations was enabled by their depoliticised nature; UCPTE, for example, 'was intentionally set up as a non-governmental, coordinating body of power company and power authority representatives who participated on the basis of personal membership and voluntary adherence to UCPTE recommendations'.[17] Each system operator retained its own control centre and had autonomy over key system planning decisions. UCPTE 'merely provided coordination and facilitation'.[18] Given the risk of 'cascading' failures in highly interconnected power systems, the decentralised and loosely coupled nature of UCPTE was seen as a more resilient model than the large centralised systems in parts of the US, which in 1965 had experienced an extensive blackout in its north-eastern region.

Despite the widening geographic scope of these transnational coordinating bodies, overall, the 'nationalist paradigm'[19] remained largely dominant in Europe as, apart from Luxembourg, no country relied on trade, using it only to meet peak demand via the facility to trade in 'occasional power'. There was however a growing interdependency between the French and Italian systems; in 1987 France exported 28,806 GWh, with Italy importing just over 23,000. Generally, this was an exception as each country had invested in sufficient capacity to meet its needs, resulting in significant scope for cost reductions if a more substantive cross-border trading arrangement could be developed (Figs. 5.1, 5.2 and 5.3).

The key initial driver for improving on the UCPTE system in the late 1980s/early 1990s was a putative alliance of EDF, the French monopoly producer, and large German industrial users who faced high electricity tariffs, largely due to obligations placed on them to subsidise the domestic coal industry. They were, unsurprisingly, keen to take advantage of cheaper supplies, an issue which is covered in more detail in Chap. 6. There seemed to be an obvious rationale for direct contracts between these two parties, but this was a form of direct trade between producers and end-users which at this time could not be accommodated within the utility-controlled UCPTE system.

The European Commission meanwhile was making a strong argument for liberalising this cross-border trade, based on the relative competitiveness of the bloc in energy-intensive industrial sectors. European industries, as a whole, faced energy costs up to 40% higher than in competitor regions

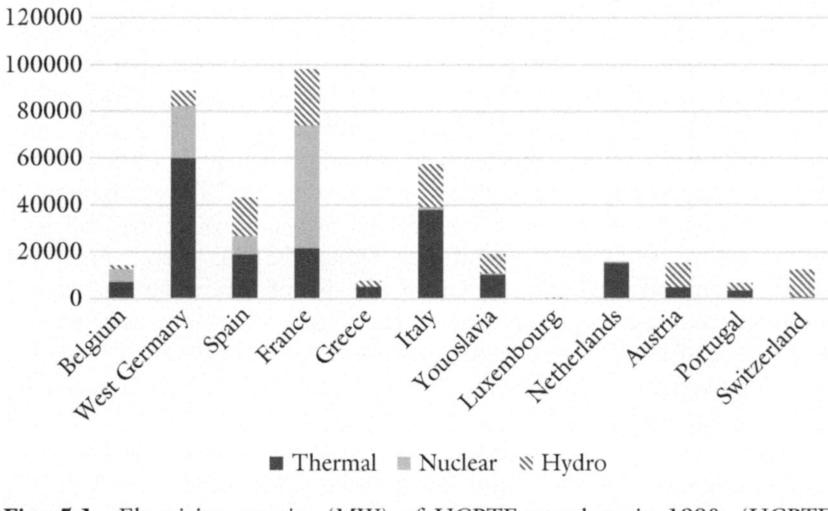

Fig. 5.1 Electricity capacity (MW) of UCPTE members in 1990. (UCPTE Annual Report, 1990)

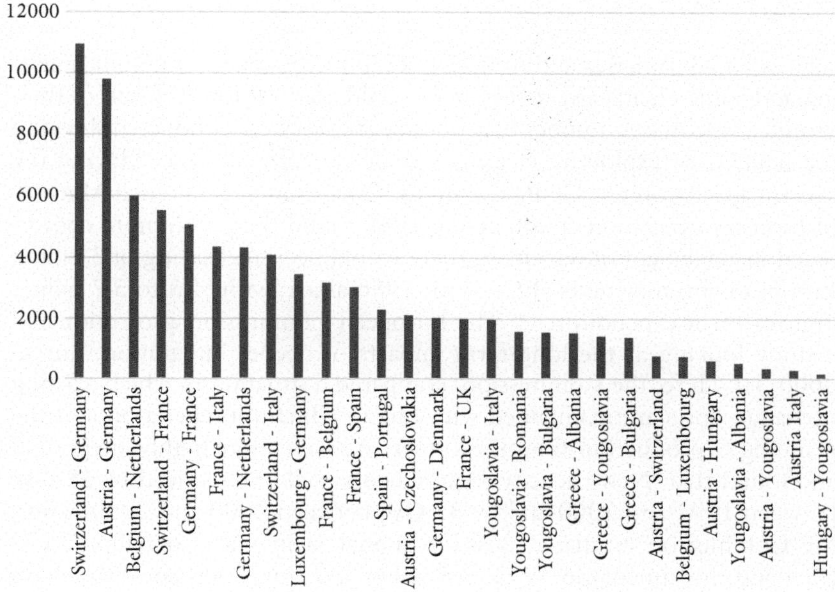

Fig. 5.2 UCPTE interconnectors and their capacity (MW). (UCPTE Annual Report, 1990)

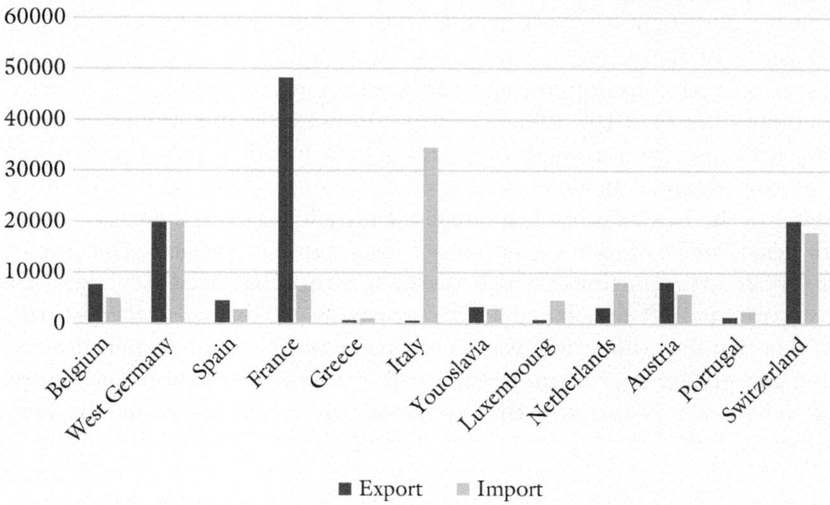

Fig. 5.3 Balance of trade for UCPTE members in 1990 (MWh). (UCPTE Annual Report, 1990)

such as North America and Australia; for industries like aluminium, smelting and some chemicals, energy costs could account for over half of their production costs. A number of economic studies were conducted showing the benefits of exploiting electricity trade differentials and reducing the excess capacity on the UCPTE systems.[20] For example, a French Ministry of Industry evaluation conducted in 1988 found that, with more coordinated management of resources, there would be a 'fuel saving of 3 billion European currency units (ECU)' for 1986 alone, with '4.3 to 5.7 billion in investment expenditure'.[21] The European Commission also conducted a study looking at the long-term impacts of deeper integration, out to 2000–10. Here, the Commission 'compared a situation in which existing exchange flows are maintained with one in which the operation and the planning of production-transmission systems were more highly integrated' and found that 'New capacity requirements could be reduced by 28 GW between 1992 and 2000 and by 37 GW between 2000 and 2010. Thus, the Commission estimated possible annual savings at 1.6 billion ECU (fuel and investment) in 1992, 3.5 billion ECU in 2000 and 3.2 billion ECU in 2010'.[22]

On the surface, and according to numerous economic studies, electricity trade was rational and mutually beneficial for the Member States. Due to the distinctive national electricity regimes which emerged in the post-war decades, there was considerable scope for enhancing the security and efficiency of these systems by exploiting complementarities and cutting down on fuel consumption and the need for excess capacity. Electricity accounted for over 16% of final energy consumption and about one-third of primary energy was used in its production, but there was a perception that the potential benefits of deeper integration between the Member States of the EEC was not being realised as trade between them accounted for 'less than 5% of total Community consumption in the case of electricity (a very great proportion of which was in the form of balanced exchanges)',[23] compared to 15% for oil and 12.5% for gas. As we discuss in the last part of this chapter, while there was a clear economic logic of deeper integration and greater coordination, there was little consensus about the nature of the market institutions though which these benefits would be best achieved.

Energy and the European Commission

Despite that electricity markets and the liberalisation of cross-border trade seemed to be marginal to the wider single market project, as it was originally conceived, energy had earlier been much closer to the core of the European integration project. The Treaty of Rome, signed in 1957, which created the EEC, was but one of three foundational treaties forming the European Communities; this stood alongside the European Coal and Steel Community (ECSC), which had been founded in 1951 in Paris, and the European Atomic Energy Community (EAEC) under the 1957 Euratom Treaty. Shortly after the Treaty of Rome came into effect in 1958, an Inter-Executive Working Group on energy was initiated in 1959,[24] which in 1965 was dissolved following the Merger Treaty and replaced by the Directorate-General for Energy (DG XVII) in 1967. The first 'Guidelines for a Community Energy Policy' were developed by the DG Energy in 1968,[25] and in this document the problem of a lack of energy coordination and cooperation was framed in terms of impacts on economic competitiveness, with energy being a major cost input for European industry at the time. The following excerpt from this document highlights this preoccupation of the Commission with the issue of energy costs and economic competitiveness, which remained high on the agenda up to the late 1980s, when electricity integration and market liberalisation reforms finally gained some traction:

> Disparities between the costs of use of energy, resulting primarily from divergences between the energy policies of the individual Member States, are increasingly distorting competition in industries with high energy consumption, and penalize certain regions of the Community when important decisions are to be taken. The attempts made to remedy this state of things by measures at national level are leading to a gradual disintegration of the Community's energy economy; uneconomic systems of aid, consumption taxes varying from country to country, and increasingly nationalist supply and marketing policies are the result. This dangerous trend can only be changed by a Community energy policy which fully integrates the energy sector into the common market.[26]

The 1968 document highlighted various barriers to trade in energy products, focusing mainly on oil, and 'assigned considerable weight to the market mechanism as a co-ordinating instrument'.[27] In the same year, an obligation was placed on the Member States 'to maintain a minimum level of stocks of oil and/or petroleum products'.[28]

The background to this document was a 1964 'Protocol of Agreement between the Member States on Energy Problems' which came out of 'a growing awareness of the global character of energy issues',[29] along with a recognition of the fragmented nature of how energy was treated across the three treaties prior to their merger. Importantly for the discussions about electricity (and gas) markets which took place later in the 1980s and 1990s, the 1968 document cited Article 37 of the Treaty of Rome as a means of opening up national energy markets to competition, Article 37 being a 'provision concerning state monopolies of a commercial character'.[30] We will discuss later how those arguing for the introduction of competition and the opening up of national electricity markets drew upon the provisions under Article 90 of the same treaty, providing an exemption to Article 37 in situations where competition would diminish the performance of a service of 'general economic interest'. At this early stage however, there was little specific discussion of electricity, with most emphasis on basic fuels (oil and gas) and nuclear. In relation to electricity, the argument was continually put forward that it was an exceptional case because of its technical complexity and networked character. The impetus provided by the 1968 document was quickly taken over by the oil crises of the 1970s, and over the next 20 odd years there was little substantive progress in achieving energy cooperation at the European level via the routes of harmonising national energy policies and taxes, and liberalising cross-border trade in electricity and other energy products.

The severe oil price volatility of the 1970s shifted the policy agenda away from open markets and towards energy security and protection from international market forces, following from which there were widely varying national responses. As a result, the EEC energy policy focus in the 1970s was constrained in its scope and ambition, focusing mainly on 'various emergency measures taken during and after the energy crises of the 1970s'.[31] Particular efforts were made in this period to reduce oil demand and promote diversification of fuels. The EEC had largely abandoned plans for energy liberalisation by 1973: 'Instead, the Commission tried to adopt a co-ordinating role between the various national energy policies, securing a number of loosely-worded objectives, such as the diversification of energy supply'.[32]

While the idea behind the Commission's efforts during the 1960s and 1970s was to create a form of centralised European energy policy, 1981 marked somewhat a shift, with the publication of 'Development of an Energy Strategy for the Community'.[33] This 'abandoned any attempt at a transfer of competence, a centralized decision-making process or the creation of EC rules on a common energy policy' and steered the focus towards 'those areas where the Community possessed specific or exclusive powers'.[34] This was followed in 1983 by a Council declaration which proposed to clarify the balance of authority between the European institutions and the Member States, which was later solidified in the 1992 Maastricht Treaty, thus setting out the notion of subsidiarity 'as a principle of general application'.[35] As we discuss in more detail later, this notion of aligning national and European energy policy priorities formed the basis of the political compromise which enabled electricity market liberalisation to be eventually introduced.

While the focus of European cooperation tended to be on energy security and crisis management, along with measures to promote energy savings and technological innovation, there was an entrenched view that a primarily national approach was justified—even required—to maintain the stability of electricity systems and their economic operation as natural monopolies. However, the association of electricity liberalisation with the broader single market agenda, along with national-level deregulation in some countries and 'the existence of a large surplus of electricity going cheap',[36] provided impetus for a radical change to the policy narrative.

In September 1986 the Council of Ministers adopted a resolution[37] on energy policy objectives for the next decade, then part of a wider programme of work within DG Energy called 'Energy 2000'. One contemporary commentator was of the view that the 1986 Council resolution was 'a significant departure in policy style from the Community's previous approach to the energy sector; an approach which had focused primarily on the formulation of common policy objectives and goals which were to be integrated into national energy policies', and 'heralded a new "market-orientated approach", with an emphasis on increasing competition as the principal mechanism for securing the Community's future energy security'.[38]

At the subsequent Energy Council meeting in June 1987, the commissioner responsible for energy, Nicolas Mosar, 'announced a wide-ranging investigation of the barriers which currently exist in the Community with the aim of establishing a timetable for the creation of an internal energy market'.[39] This announcement was made well before the structural implications of electricity liberalisation in Britain became apparent to European utilities and national governments, so it was not viewed as a threat and there was quite broad support for the agenda, with Council ministers agreeing with 'the Commission's wish first to draw up, with the help of the parties concerned, an inventory of the existing obstacles and then in due course to submit to the Council appropriate proposals for the progressive elimination of such obstacles before the end of 1992'.[40]

The Commission subsequently produced a working document titled 'The Internal Energy Market' in May 1988.[41] In the preamble to the document, the Commission inaccurately outlined the process of energy market liberalisation as technocratic and apolitical, a matter of identifying and removing 'barriers' to the desired objective. This effort to depoliticise the creation of a European energy market was perhaps behind the commission's decision not to follow the 'Green Paper' format for policy reform, involving publishing and responding to stakeholder responses, an approach that had just recently been taken in the telecoms sector.[42] The Commission was surely aware of the unique political challenges of electricity reform and the benefits of avoiding a public airing of known differences on the issue so early in the process.

The IEM document noted that in the 20 years following the 1968 'Guidelines for a Community Energy Policy', there had been 'little progress towards a genuine common market in energy'. The framing of the benefits of energy markets in the 1988 document was unsurprisingly centred around trade between the Member States, whilst being cautious about exposing the community to the vagaries of international energy markets, given the existing reliance on imports (70% for oil and 35% for gas and coal). The Commission stated:

> This natural inclination [towards free trade] must not backfire on the Community and turn it into a sort of free-trade dumping ground for unscrupulous competitors who continue to protect their markets to some extent. In the energy sphere, the Community should therefore adopt a common external and commercial policy to enable it, where necessary, to obtain reciprocal concessions from its partners ... This notion of reciprocity is essential.[43]

Substantive proposals included were a target of 20% improvement in the efficiency of energy demand by 1995, to limit oil imports by suppressing the fuel as a proportion of overall energy consumption—to 40%—and a reduction in imports from third countries to one-third of overall energy consumption by 1995. The proposals for market integration were less concrete, with aspirational statements included, such as 'greater integration, free from barriers to trade, of the internal energy market with a view to improving security of supply, reducing costs and improving economic competitiveness'.

Three broad areas for reform were identified. The first was the application of relevant treaty articles in relation to state monopolies and exclusive rights, a key structural feature of the energy sector as a whole. National energy monopolies were particularly important in the areas of oil imports and distribution within each country, and in the electricity and gas supply sectors there were often exclusive rights granted to import and export. The main areas of community law identified as applicable were (1) free movement of energy products and issues around standards (2) national monopolies and exclusive rights and (3) competition and state-aid. Secondly, in relation to the physical energy networks and their role in enabling the market, the IEM document raised the prospect of the opening up of the UCPTE system and other high-voltage lines as a 'common carriers', highlighting that arguments in favour of this had been put forward 'by large electricity consumers and large auto-producers', while in contrast, producers highlighted concerns about the technical feasibility of this. The Commission noted however that 'The definition of the obligations and application of the concept of a "common carrier" is not simple'.[44]

Along with exclusive rights and access to networks, a third key area for reform identified in the document was harmonisation of tariffs and energy-related taxation. Significant variations in end use prices documented across the Member States were attributed to taxation imposed at the national level, as opposed to differences in the cost base of electricity production. The Commission also highlighted a lack of uniformity in accounting practices for evaluating utility company asset valuations and depreciation.

Alongside these very specific areas of intervention, there was a recognition of path dependencies arising from the structural legacies of national electricity regimes; they noted that alongside nation-state-specific technical norms and industry structures, 'some of the obstacles arise from **quasi-psychological concerns** generated by markets which have traditionally been extremely partitioned: an extreme example of this is the behaviour of many national electricity companies which strive to be self-sufficient on a national basis' (emphasis in original).

Despite its efforts to depoliticise the IEM, the Commission laid out starkly the political trade-off at the heart of the new market; competition would improve the industrial competitiveness of the bloc, but the problems that this would present to monopoly utilities were made clear:

> Large electricity consumers are particularly sensitive to industrial competition and the effect of differences in electricity prices throughout the Community. Such consumers have made known their view that they should be able to obtain electricity supplies from any production source, not only their (monopoly) distributing utility, if a more economic source can be found. This implies that such supplies should be transported via the distribution and transmission networks on the basis of a supplier/consumer contract. The public supply utilities argue against such arrangements, pointing to the technical problems which may arise in ensuring continuing security and reliability of the distribution and transmission networks. It can also be argued that the "creaming-off" of the most economic production sources by consumers having the most purchasing power would result in the inequable treatment of less powerful consumers (including domestic), whose electricity prices would be more influenced by the production costs of the less economic production sources.[45]

There was a meeting of energy ministers held on 8 November 1988 to discuss the Commission's IEM document, chaired by Anastassios Peponis, the Greek minister of energy, and Nicolas Mosar. In the meeting conclusions,[46] general supporting remarks were made about the IEM proposal:

> The internal energy market should contribute to establishing the large market of 1992 and to strengthening the achievements of the Community energy policy. It should also help to strengthen the competitiveness of the European economy and the development of the Community.[47]

While typically glossed over in such documents, the contested nature of the proposals for electricity in particular was aired in the industry press at the time. Interestingly, *Power in Europe* noted that it was only France who was 'pushing hard for free trade in electricity, and other states are for the most part wary of accepting such a principle'.[48] The changing economics of international energy which seemed to be favourable to the introduction of competition, and the apparent opportunities of exploiting France's electricity surpluses, did not mask the deep divisions which existed across the industry surrounding the desirability of competition and common carriage. There seemed to be a view held, particularly amongst producer interests, that European competition was simply not possible: according to a representative of VDER (West German producers), 'Supply monopolies are indispensable because of electricity's unchangeable physio-technical characteristics'. There was some degree of pessimism about the prospects of such a European market: 'not even small steps toward competition ... are possible without first changing attitudes'.[49] According to one Member of the European Parliament (MEP), 'The bottom line of energy and the Internal Market is this: Are electricity suppliers in the EEC willing to de-monopolise their industries? I don't think so judging from the arguments we've just heard'.[50] The FT also quoted the Chairman of the 'EEC Committee of UNIPEDE' (the International Union of Producers and Distributors of Electrical Energy), Dr. Alassandro Ortis, who stated, 'The notion of [separate] electricity transfers from one point to another along the European grid is a purely theoretical concept ... It is therefore impossible to determine "a priori" a generally applicable tariff for the transmission of electricity across a power system'.[51] Ortis' preferred model of competition was to keep the national customer bases intact, but to have more competition within each market.

It should be re-emphasised here that at the time the concept of an electricity market was a conceptual leap which challenged the prevailing paradigm of electricity industry organisation and its technocratic culture. Such proposals were bound to provoke negative reactions at the outset. As we discuss later, industry perceptions and national responses to the market agenda evolved significantly as both the understanding of what a market for electricity would look like, and its implications for different industry actors, became clearer.

Early Liberalisation Proposals

Following the 1988 IEM paper, the Commission's first practical steps towards the creation of a cross-border market for electricity were taken in early 1989 with the announcement of proposals for three directives: one on transparency of electricity pricing, one on investment coordination and a third, the most significant, on transit across electricity and gas networks. In the same year a new commissioner responsible for energy, Antonio Jose Baptista Cardoso E Cunha, was appointed. Cardoso e Cunha, formerly a social democrat member of the Portuguese Parliament and minister, was very much pro-competition.[52] This viewpoint was in line with mainstream

Portuguese policy at the time; the country was concerned about its dependence on Spain for energy imports and saw a greater centralisation of policy at the EEC level as a means of reducing this, along with a means of securing structural funds and building up its energy infrastructure. Cardoso e Cunha developed a strong pro-competition alliance with the then Competition Commissioner, the UK's Leon Brittan. Upon the announcement of the draft proposals in July 1989,[53] Cardoso e Cunha stated that 'energy authorities must now jump on the wagon of liberalisation along with everyone else'.[54]

The price transparency proposals for electricity and gas would require the Member States to provide information biannually to Eurostat (the statistical service of the EEC) about large industrial customers, in order to enable the Commission to develop a comprehensive 'publication table' on industrial energy transactions and prices. This would involve the development of a classification of end-users based on size and levels of annual consumption, part of a long-running effort to improve the flow and availability of information on the extent of non-regulated tariff sales. At the time, only data on electricity consumption below 24 GWh/year were provided to the statistical body, so large installations, such as factories, were typically not included. The European Commission therefore had little information on the contracts which existed between industries and their local utilities. The Commission were proposing that 'publication thresholds above a certain consumption level would dramatically rise within the next two years to 657 GWh/yr, or 30 times the current ceiling' and to require 'national energy authorities, private or public, to publish three categories of information linked to their largest industrial consumers of energy: the price and commercial terms according to each client's size, the full range of prices in use, and the classification of users into specific categories based on annual levels of gas and electricity consumption'.[55]

Of course, transparency about existing contracts and prices would be a foundation for a competitive market, but there was some reticence about providing this information. In many European countries electricity supply formed a core part of industrial policy, so transparency around this issue may have opened up such arrangements to scrutiny regarding compliance with the articles of the EEC Treaty covering State-aid. Germany, which supported its uncompetitive coal industry through a surcharge on electricity use, was also concerned that it would undermine the future of such subsidies. Utilities were also concerned about the issue because of fears that competitors might use the information to target their most lucrative customers.

The investment coordination proposals—a draft regulation on the notification of investment projects—was an update of an earlier 1972 proposal which would have required each Member State to inform the Commission of project details and planning progress regarding key infrastructure projects in the electricity, oil and gas sectors. This proposal was eventually dropped by the Council of Ministers, partly because the purposes were vague—the role and remit of the Commission did not extend to coordinating, blocking or amending infrastructure projects across the continent—and there was also opposition from many countries. In subsequent years, backed by France in particular, the European Commission did succeed in forging such a role through the Trans-European Networks (TEN) Directive which followed the Maastricht Treaty of 1992.

The key component of the 1989 Commission proposals, and this first tentative step towards developing an IEM, was the issue of trade across borders and the necessary access to the transmission networks. The key point of contention was the operation of the high-voltage transmission grids as common carriers. As discussed previously, while major energy utilities, particularly France's EDF, had been strongly in favour of the expansion of cross-border trade, as the implications of common carriage became apparent they turned strongly against the idea. If electricity was to be designated as a tradable commodity, a key prerequisite was that transmission networks be separated out and operate under a common carriage regime, becoming neutral platforms, as oppose to strategic assets which could be managed in a way to control the entire electricity system. So, if taken to its logical conclusion, true competition would result in the demotion of the powerful integrated utilities to mere service providers to competing generators and their customers. Competition would also undermine the basic philosophy underpinning electricity systems, that a stable predictable customer base is the foundation of long-term planning of the system.

The term 'common carriage' was quite vague at this time, and much of the early debate around market liberalisation revolved around how it would be interpreted and operationalised in legal texts. Common carriage, which was mentioned as a necessary pillar of the IEM in the 1988 document, was generally interpreted as providing open access to the networks to third parties, for example, independent generators, large industrial consumers and distribution companies. If implemented, there would be a legal definition of common transit rights which would provide guaranteed and non-discriminatory access to these third parties to buy and sell power as they wished. Taken to its extreme, there would be significant implications for the existing monopoly suppliers; they would no longer have exclusive rights to supply certain customers, there would be a significant level of oversight and regulation of their operations with regard to the control of the transmission system, and they may be forced to divest a proportion of their generation assets to facilitate competition or even to fully 'unbundle' their generation and network operation activities. At this early stage, in mid-1989, the implications of competition and open access to the networks were not well understood. The British reform process was still in process and there remained significant uncertainties about the outcome, but it would have been apparent to observers that the dominant supplier, the Central Electricity Generating Board (CEGB), was unlikely to survive intact.

Unsurprisingly, there were clear statements from European utilities coming out against common carriage. For example, at the World Electricity Conference held in November 1989, major European utilities such as ENEL, RWE and EDF highlighted the need for cooperation 'rather than the damaging competition which would result from the common carriage proposals'.[56] Allesandro Ortis, Vice-Chairman of ENEL, the Italian national electricity monopoly producer, stated that common carriage would 'counter and thus diminish and nullify voluntary and responsible cooperation between utilities'. A reason put forward by ENEL against competition was that it would 'undermine the country's need to build up its own installed generating capacity and increase its dangerous dependence on electricity imports'. For ENEL, competition based on common carriage principles posed a particular threat as their lucrative customer base in northern Italy would be vulnerable to 'cherry picking' by French and Swiss competitors, leaving ENEL saddled with supplying low demand regions in the south. Italy at the time was also formulating a national energy strategy which set out an ambitious investment plan, increasing capacity by 23,000 MW, the level of their electricity deficit. This, they argued, relied on a stable and predictable demand. Ortis stated that common carriage would 'downgrade the trend towards construction, in each country or region (especially in areas with the highest electricity deficits) of power stations which generate not only kWhs but also opportunities for manufacturing, employment and local know-how'.[57]

The problem was not confined to Italy. German utilities, which had the highest industrial electricity prices in Europe, partly because of the country's levy on electricity consumption which went to support its domestic hard coal industry (see Chap. 6), were concerned that EDF would cherry-pick its large industrial customers. Meanwhile, Remy Carle, deputy general manager of EDF, labelled notions such as common carriage as 'risky experiments' and that deeper 'interconnection', not competition, would achieve 'overall optimisation'. Dirk Kallmeyer, director at RWE, stressed the German utility's energy security concerns, stating, 'The concept of common carriage seems dangerous to me, in terms of safety of supply, stability of the grid and long term costs'.[58] At a later event, Walter Fremuth, general manager of Austria's Verbundgesellschaft, which at the time had a monopoly over imports and exports, went further, describing common carriage as 'murderous competition'.[59]

Aside from these industry perspectives, there was also significant push back against the concept of common carriage at the meeting of energy ministers held in October of 1989. The UK was the only country strongly supportive at this time. Other Member States had different reasons for opposing this direction for the industry: Denmark, for example, were particularly wary because they felt that common carriage might interfere with pre-existing trading arrangements with their Nordic neighbours; these relied on bilateral agreements and good-will, rather than market determined pricing. Germany were not supportive due to the existential threat that competition posed to their coal industry. While the Netherlands were against it as they wanted to restrict transit rights for large consumers, not distributors, the opposite of the Commission's draft proposals.

Ultimately, however, the European Commission's early draft proposal to open up the networks and facilitate competition for large customers was watered down significantly. Although there was general support for more cross-border exchanges, the Member States 'want[ed] assurance that any agreement will apply only to cross-border systems in isolation. In other words, Brussels will intervene only to guarantee transit between states, while keeping its hands off the way national energy networks are operated'.[60] At a Council of Ministers meeting in July 1990, two key clauses were deleted from the Commission's draft: one which stated that the Council would consider the introduction of common carriage rights before 1993, and a second which 'implicitly recognised that the Commission could use certain powers entrusted to it by Article 90(3) EEC to exact its own Directive on open access rules'. This was seen as a 'far-reaching power' which had 'already been put to considerable use to attack monopoly privileges in the telecommunications and in the postal sectors'.[61]

The Commission did succeed in introducing a framework for 'transit' across electricity networks in cases where the buyer and seller—integrated utilities rather than individual generators or consumers—were separated by a third country. Transit only addressed a specific issue where electricity needed to be 'wheeled'[62] across a transmission grid and each country would be obliged to accept these power exchanges, but they would most likely be in the form of traditional utility-utility transactions via the existing UCPTE system. In essence, competition is between markets, rather than within them.

The problem that the transit directive was designed to solve is best explained with reference to the most prominent and controversial case of the time: electricity trade between France's EDF and the Portuguese equivalent, Electricidade de Portugal (EDP). Both national utilities had signed a deal for the supply of firm power for ten years, starting in 1994. This involved guaranteed delivery, with penalties imposed on the seller if supply was interrupted. However, the need to transit via the Spanish grid proved a stumbling block. Portugal wanted to access the cheap electricity resulting from France's nuclear surplus, allowing 'Portugal to import low-cost power during the dry summer months, avoiding costly thermal generation when production falls at hydroelectric plants'.[63] However, the Spanish grid operator was reluctant to facilitate the trade via its network and was imposing significant charges for access and transport, viewed by the Portuguese as an unearned economic rent.[64] The three countries came to an agreement in early 1990, but Portugal was still not fully satisfied as the Spanish utility was imposing a 12% transit tariff to be paid jointly by EDF and EDP. This was significantly higher than the general rate at the time around Europe, in and around 5%. The Spanish position was understandable from a self-interest point of view, as they dominated trade in and out of Portugal and were reluctant to relinquish this strategic position.

Essentially, what the European Commission was proposing was a formalisation of such exchanges which would turn the provision of transmission services into an obligation on the Spanish grid operator, subject to Commission oversight, rather than 'dependent on goodwill' and based on industry self-regulation, as had previously been the case. The Commission wanted to clarify 'the terms of such inter-utility trade'[65] and to create arbitration committees which included consumer representatives. So the Commission proposals on transit were essentially 'a procedural framework within which the Commission can oversee the conclusion of certain transit arrangements and agreements'.[66] This would in effect give the commission more information about conduct within the existing trading system and to ensure that it operates in a timely and 'fair' manner.

At this early stage of the liberalisation process, the European Commission could only use its powers in relation to ensuring transit rights, rather than intervention to open systems up to competition and for direct sales to end consumers. However, despite the dropping of common carriage, the new proposals around cross-border trade did cause some concern, particularly in relation to the definition and scope of transit. Before the measure was finally approved by the Council of Ministers meeting in October 1990,[67] the Economic and Social Committee in the European Parliament and the European Commission entered into a debate about the meaning of transit. The parliamentary committee had amended the original definition of transit as 'movement across two national boundaries',[68] not within a market or between distribution systems. This formulation was rejected by the Commission, partly because the national definition was too vague and in some cases didn't correspond to the markets that were to be governed. According to this soft interpretation, the Commission didn't win any substantial new powers to enforce the IEM according to its vision, rather an agreed process and procedure around transit was put in place.

The final 1990 directive[69] laid out the very specific circumstances in which the legal definition of 'transit of electricity between grids' applied:

- *transmission is carried out by the entity or entities responsible in each member state for a high-voltage electricity grid, with the exception of distribution grids, in a member state's territory which contributes to the efficient operation of European high-voltage interconnections;*
- *the grid of origin or final destination is situated in the Community;*
- *the transport involves the crossing of one intra Community frontier at least.*

Paragraph 2 of Article 3 (below) stated that transit should be carried out in a non-discriminatory fashion, but, crucially, that internal national security of supply concerns would take priority, leaving significant autonomy with the national utilities to judge whether this was the case and to, if they deemed appropriate, prioritise internal system management over facilitating seamless cross-border transit flows:

> The conditions of transit shall, pursuant to the rules of the Treaty, be non-discriminatory and fair for all the parties concerned, shall not include unfair clauses or unjustified restrictions and shall not endanger security of supply and quality of service, in particular taking full account of the utilization of reserve production capacity and the most efficient operation of existing systems.

One of the concerns the Commission had was to ensure that these types of technical arguments, which were difficult to disprove given that utilities could always claim greater knowledge of the operation of their grids than the European institutions, could not be used as a reason to block transit. Given the political risks of supply failure, national politicians would most likely defer to their utilities on such matters. The European Commission's proposal therefore included various obligations and arbitration mechanisms; for example, they included obligations to deal with requests for transit contracts, and if they were of a certain duration—over a year—this would require negotiations to begin within a month of the request. The Commission would have to be informed of the initiation and outcome of such discussions and would commence proceedings against uncooperative parties if negotiations were not concluded within a year. As specified in the directive, each transmission operator listed in an annex would be required to:

- *notify the commission and the national authorities concerned of any request for transit in connection with contracts for the sale of electricity of a minimum of one year's duration;*
- *open negotiations on the conditions of the electricity transit requested;*
- *inform the commission and the national authorities concerned of the conclusion of a transit contract;*
- *inform the commission and the national authorities concerned of the reasons for the failure of the negotiations to result in the conclusion of a contract within 12 months following communication of the request.*[70]

The proposal also included arbitration committees which would include network operators, consumer representatives, government, experts, and so on, to settle disputes. Paragraph 4 of Article 2 sets out the role of the conciliation body:

> The entities concerned may request that the conditions of transit be subject to conciliation by a body set up and chaired by the Commission and on which the entities responsible for transmission grids in the Community are represented.

However, the draft directives had provided for a stronger role for the Commission: 'Where a request to transport gas or electricity is refused without due reason, the Commission may, on its own initiative, or on the request of the company seeking transit rights, put in motion the relevant procedures under Community law'.[71] The European Commission's role was diminished, however, from having the autonomy to apply community law to the electricity sector, to being an arbitrator of disputes, with strong reliance on industry consultation and expert groups. This then laid the groundwork for a later institutional process whereby the Commission learned to navigate political constraints on the application of the EEC Treaty to cross-border electricity trade.

* * *

Although the transit directive was a very limited change to existing trade practice, being broadly in line with the established UCPTE market, the pushback against the European Commission's proposals for a 'Europeanisation' of electricity trade was significant and it instigated the formation of a strong anti-competition lobby led by continental utilities, in alliance with some national governments. As outlined in Chap. 7, this frustrated and delayed industry reforms during much of the 1990s.

The issue of transit, while occupying attention during 1989 and 1990, did not turn out to be a transformative change and it was not until March 1992 that the 'Committee of experts on the Transit of Electricity between Grids'[72] was actually formed. By this point the debate had moved on substantially as the idea of common carriage, by then rebranded as 'third party access' (TPA), had been resurrected by the Commission. Ultimately, there was a move towards a phase of negotiation between key Member States and the European institutions which saw the dilution of what appeared to be fundamental differences between the parties. In order to understand the dynamics of this political process which is covered in Chap. 7, we must first examine the situation regarding the two largest electricity nations: France and Germany.

CHAPTER 6

National Electricity Regimes: France and Germany

This chapter examines the French and German electricity regimes, the European Community's two largest electricity markets and most politically powerful Member States. Its purpose is to develop a sense of the why these two nations were reluctant to adopt the 'British Model' of a competitive electricity market and to explain the origins of a key political axis which was highly influential in shaping the outcome of the EEC-level reforms which were finally adopted in late 1996. Based on this understanding of the particularities of the French and German electricity regimes, the next chapter will then outline how the European Commission sought to chart a course through these embedded political interests, and how the issues were resolved, resulting in a cautious approach to the introduction competition and structural reform across the bloc. In both the French and German cases, we can see how efforts to protect the national electricity regimes, along with the nuclear and coal supply chains which relied on them, led to an ambiguous and sometimes sceptical relationship with the liberal model of electricity markets.

The two country cases begin with differing reactions to the changing international energy markets of the late 1950s. In the case of France, it sought to de-emphasise coal and exploit relatively inexpensive oil supplies, later embarking on an impressive national programme of nuclear power development. The momentum behind this nuclear expansion programme was so great that by the early 1980s there was significant excess production capacity in France. On the surface, it appeared that France's need to

R. Bolton, *Making Energy Markets*,
https://doi.org/10.1007/978-3-030-90075-5_6

find new markets for its nuclear power output and the apparent benefits to industrial customers in West Germany of cross-border trade, could be the driver of a new liberalised European power market. However, the nature of the French power system meant that the national utility, *Électricité de France* (EDF), could not enter into contracts for 'firm' power exports, as opposed to the occasional exchanges which had long been a feature of the old UCPTE (Union for the Co-ordination of Production and Transmission of Electricity) system. The increasing electrification of its domestic heating load and the reliance of its system on hydroelectric power to maintain stability meant that if a dry winter coincided with nuclear power outages caused by technical faults, which were quite common at the time, its system was highly vulnerable. This placed a technical limitation on the scope for increasing electricity trade.

In the German case the limitation was due to national industrial policy. The easing of controls on coal imports into the European Coal and Steel Community (ECSC) in the late 1950s and the changing international energy situation shook the industrial heartlands of West Germany to their core. These developments culminated in the 1958 'coal crisis' which saw substantial surplus stock develop as 'post-war coal shortages ended quickly in Europe and were replaced by mounting piles of unwanted coal at pitheads'.[1] The West German hard coal industry, which was centered around the Ruhr region, became increasingly coupled with electricity production and reliant on subsidies from electricity consumers. A form of electricity market liberalisation which threatened these sector interdependencies was to be vigorously defended against.

France: The Powerhouse of Europe?

The period of the late 1950s to the late 1970s saw a radical shift in French energy policy. Somewhere in the region of two-thirds of the country's coal mining workforce lost their jobs as the share of coal-based electricity production was halved, and by the end of this period, the country had embarked on the most ambitious nuclear power expansion programme seen to date. A key impetus behind this energy transition was the 'Jeanneney Plan' of 1960. Jean-Marcel Jeanneney, the Minister of Industry at the time, was an academic economist whose views on energy policy were strongly informed by the work of 'marginalist' economists such as Maurice Allais and Marcel Boiteux, both of whom he appointed to his Economic and Social Council.[2] As it became apparent by the late 1950s that relative fuel prices were moving in a direction which made domestic French coal seem like an increasingly expensive option—'the price of heavy fuel oil relative to French coal fell from a factor of 2.3 in 1958 to 1.2 by 1973, a reduction of 50 per cent'—a decision was taken for a phased reduction of French coal output, reducing from 58 mt to 27 mt between 1958 and 1973.[3] Domestic coal was relatively expensive to mine compared to the Ruhr and Britain, and the 1952 ECSC agreement, along with the subsequent 1958 Treaty of Rome, seemed to provide a more robust European framework, such that France could replace domestic output with coal imports from its European neighbours, along with the Soviet bloc.

The shift away from coal led to a need to reconsider France's future electricity supplies. Similar to the UK, France had developed its first reactors—initially at Marcoule in 1956—for the production of plutonium for military purposes and subsequently began its civil nuclear programme on the basis that, due to the US ban on exports of enriched fuel, it would be restricted to the use of natural uranium. Influence over government nuclear power decisions largely resided in the early years with the *Commissariat de l'Energie Atomique* (CEA), a technocratic R&D body. In 1957 a gas-graphite reactor was constructed—at Chinon—and, strongly influenced by the CEA, a further seven similarly designed reactors were ordered, the last one (St. Laurent 2) coming online in 1971. However, the indigenous reactor design could not compete for markets internationally and was based on flawed assumptions about fuel availability and the prospects for fast breeder reactors becoming economic in the future. Unlike the UK, however, the French, at an early stage, switched decisively to the pressurised water reactor (PWR) design which came out of the US. The other major player in the French nuclear decision-making apparatus was Framatome, the major plant supplier, who in 1957 had purchased a licence to supply PWR technology to the French market from Westinghouse, along with a licence to build General Electric's more basic boiling water reactor (BWR) in France.

The switch from gas-graphite to the 'light water' family of reactor designs (PWRs and BWRs) came in the mid-1960s and was based on what looked like favourable economics, following a highly competitive bid by a US utility to build a BWR at Oyster Creek. Although the CEA was still arguing in favour of the strategic advantages of gas-graphite and fast breeder reactors, a key turning point came in 1968 when the influential commission—*Consultative pour la Production d'Electricite d'Origine*

Nucleaire (PEON)—advised the French government to go for light water, and gas-graphite was effectively dropped as an option after this.

Although the CEA did have some experience with PWR technology through its role in France's nuclear submarine programme, there were initially tensions between it and EDF regarding the switch. By the end of the century, however, the French constructed 58 such plants with a total capacity of 66,000 MW, covering in the region of four-fifths of the country's electricity needs.[4] The early PWRs were essentially the Westinghouse design—the first PWR was a small 325 MW plant at Chooze on which construction was started in 1962—but later plants, those constructed from 1979 onwards, were 'frenchified'.[5] Following the decisive switch to PWRs, the key actors, including the CEA, EDF, Framatome, Alsthom (turbine and generator manufacturer) and Cogema (fuel cycle), developed systemic interdependencies,[6] creating a strong coherence and momentum behind the national programme (Fig. 6.1).

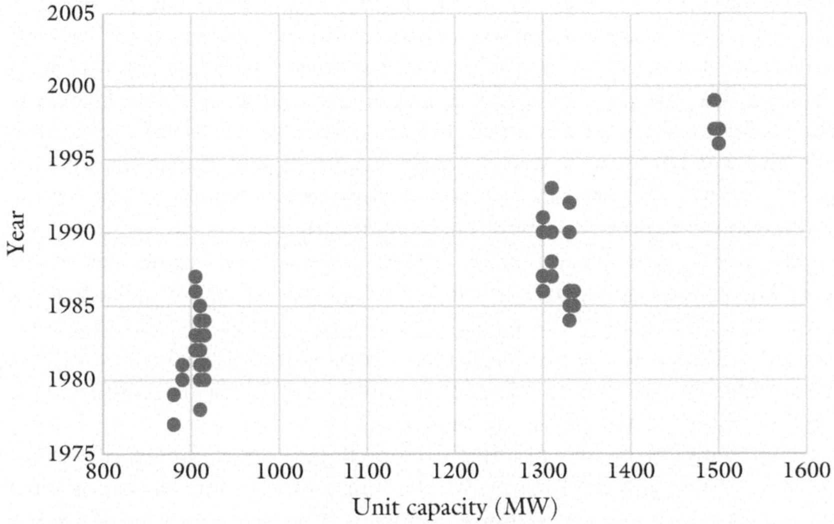

Fig. 6.1 French PWRs, showing additions of 880+, 1300+ and 1495+ MW capacity units. (Data from IAEA's PRIS database. The horizontal axis shows the reference unit capacity. The earliest PWR plant at Chooze-A (305 MW—1967) is not included, nor is the most recent plant at Flamalville-3 (under construction). A similar figure is presented in Grubler, A. (2010) The costs of the French nuclear scale-up: A case of negative learning by doing. *Energy Policy*, 38(9), Figure 1

Momentum behind the programme accelerated during the 1970s, partly in response to the threat to energy security arising from the 1973–74 oil crisis. Due to the coal phase-out, the French had been increasingly reliant on oil imports, accounting for 15% of final energy consumption in 1949, 31% in 1960 and 67% in 1973.[7] The issue was compounded, as at the same time France had a strategic concern about the potential nationalisation of its oil assets by Algeria. As a result, 'in the sixth French plan (1971–75) there was a target to order 8000 MW of LWR capacity' and subsequently after 'the PEON Commission met again in 1972 it recommended that 13 000 MW of LWR capacity should be ordered in the five years, 1973–77'.[8]

Encouraged by government, the domestic nuclear industry consolidated greatly during the period, based on the idea that it would make them more cost effective and competitive internationally. This was enabled by the 'plan contract', signed by EDF and the ministries of finance and industry in 1971, which set long-term objectives and targets for the electricity utility, providing the industry with a stable footing and long-term orientation. For the first tranche of orders between 1970 and 1974, Framatome, then part of the Empain-Schneider Group, won all of the orders, with Alsthom dominating the market for turbines. Later, the CEA purchased a 30% stake in Framatome from Westinghouse, BWRs were abandoned and Framatome were effectively given a monopoly in PWR reactor supply. Meanwhile, Cogema, an offshoot of CEA, handled the fuel cycle.

EDF was the leading body in this nuclear transition, being described as a 'state within a state'.[9] PWRs were ordered at a rate of 5/6 per year from 1975 into the mid-1980s; this trajectory had been set out in the 1974 Messmer Plan—Messmer being the French Prime Minister from 1972 to 1974—which emphasised a strong role for nuclear power and a concern about an over reliance on imported oil. During this phase of the nuclear construction programme, Framatome terminated its licence agreement with Westinghouse in 1981 and progressively the reactor designs became more 'French' throughout the decade. By the mid-1980s France had over 33,000 MW of nuclear capacity (39 units) compared to 5825 (22 units) in the UK and 16,068 (16 units) in West Germany.[10] Such was the speed and magnitude of the French nuclear transition that by the late 1980s, EDF's nuclear plant fleet consisted of '34x900 MW plants, 14x1,300 MW, 4 graphine-gas, 1x300 MW and 2 fastbreeders'.[11] Eight new plants were expected to be completed from 1990 to 1993 (Fig. 6.2).

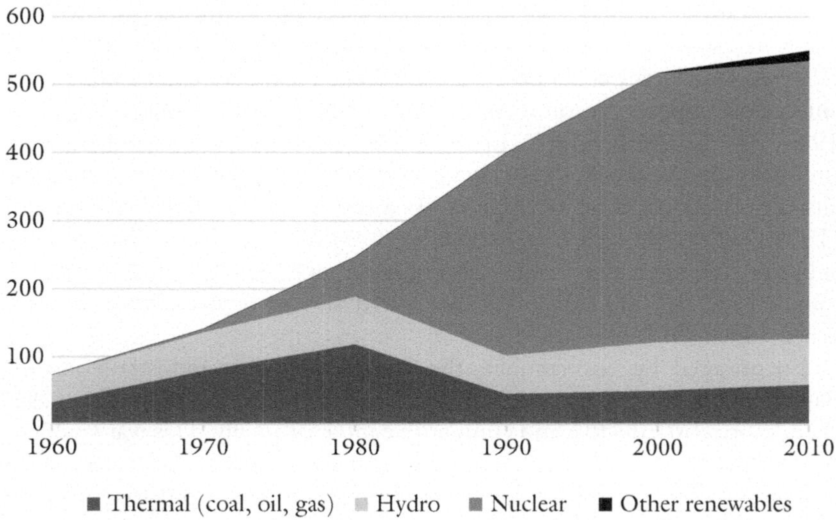

Fig. 6.2 French electricity production (TWh). (Own chart with data from Percebois (2013). *The French Paradox: Competition, Nuclear Rent.* In Sioshansi, F. (Ed.) Evolution of Global Electricity Markets. Academic Press, Cambridge, MA)

The coming into power of François Mitterrand in 1981 heralded an era of 'adjustment and consolidation', with the rate of new plant orders slowing down.[12] Although Mitterrand had been rather cool on nuclear prior to winning the presidential election, criticising 'the autocratic nature of the procedures, the apparent over-investment in plant and the concentration of resources on nuclear development to the exclusion of other options',[13] when in office he made one of his famous U-turns; in part legitimised by a framing of nuclear power as an export opportunity for the struggling French economy, with the slogan of making France the 'Powerhouse of Europe' being put forward. In 1982 an 'Energy Advisory Working Group' was tasked with advising government on new nuclear capacity, and in their interim report of October of that year, they recommended a significant reduction in the rate of ordering, with no new units required to meet demand until 1991. In the interests of retaining industrial capacity, they did however recommend to have one new plant ordered per year. Unsurprisingly, there was a significant pushback from industry conglomerates, and the final report of July 1983 'brought forward the date at which reactors would be required on demand grounds to 1987 although maintaining the recommended programme at one unit per year'.[14] Eventually, 'the government compromised and reduced orders for 1983 from the previously agreed level of three to two units, with two units to be ordered in 1984 and one or two in 1985'.[15]

The general economic slowdown and recession of the mid-1980s were however depressing demand projections. Nuclear plants were increasingly required to operate in 'load-following' mode to allow their output to fluctuate with demand—by the mid-1980s PWRs were operating in load-following mode for over 80% of the year—thus reducing their load factors and EDF's productivity levels, as costs needed to be spread over fewer units. Framatome had to introduce new control rods to the plants to make their output flexible in this way, which became a requirement for all new orders after 1983. There were also efforts to stimulate demand growth through the electrification of heating to absorb the excess nuclear production and exports were increasingly seen as a means of maintaining the momentum of the French nuclear programme. By 1985 around 10% of electricity production in France was exported (36 TWh),[16] and in 1989 this had risen to 12% (42 TWh).[17]

There was a strong political impetus behind exporting power and French politicians were pushing the agenda of electricity trade liberalisation within the European Economic Community (EEC) throughout the 1980s. In advance of taking over presidency of the Council of Ministers in the second part of 1989, Roger Fauroux, the French Industry Minister, boldly stated that that he was in favour of 'the progressive elimination of all obstacles to European energy exchanges ... the coming of the single market is not a chance to be missed, because of its impact on our electricity exports'.[18] France's industrial policy was also a key driver behind the idea of France as the 'Powerhouse of Europe'. Favourable deals between EDF and large industrial customers were part of the Socialist Government's ambition to lure heavy industry to invest in France, which also had the side benefit of absorbing some of EDF's surplus. This was however attracting increasing scrutiny from the European Commission, with France being sanctioned for illegal state-aid in relation to a deal between EDF and Pechiney, the French-owned aluminium producer, for a proportion of the output of the new Gravelines plant near Dunkirk. Leon Brittan had argued that 'the electricity price is suspiciously low ... that in view of EdF's enormous debts, it was financially too weak to enter into such a contract with Pechiney without cast-iron guarantees to cover future losses from the French government'.[19]

Aside from low demand and political support for cross-border trade, a key driver behind the growth of electricity exports from France in the 1980s was the structural characteristics and power imbalances of France's neighbours. Switzerland, with which France had extensive interconnections (see Fig. 6.3), was also a major net electricity exporter (9 TWh in 1988). Its highly flexible hydropower-based system, which could respond well to peak demand fluctuations, complemented France's largely baseload nuclear output. The Swiss system also played an important transit role for power flowing from France into Italy. Italy, which during this period had an electricity deficit, had a large 3000 MW link with France (the *Albertville-Rondissone link*). Also, as we have discussed earlier, the introduction of competition in England/Wales created a new customer for EDF, the Regional Electricity Companies (RECs), with whom EDF had signed a three-year contract to supply 1500 MW, with the remaining capacity of the 2000 MW cross-channel interconnector being used for supply on an occasional basis. France also had extensive interconnection with the West German market; its industrial consumers would have been a prized asset for EDF if European trade could be opened up to competition. Prior to the signing of the contract with the British RECs, it was

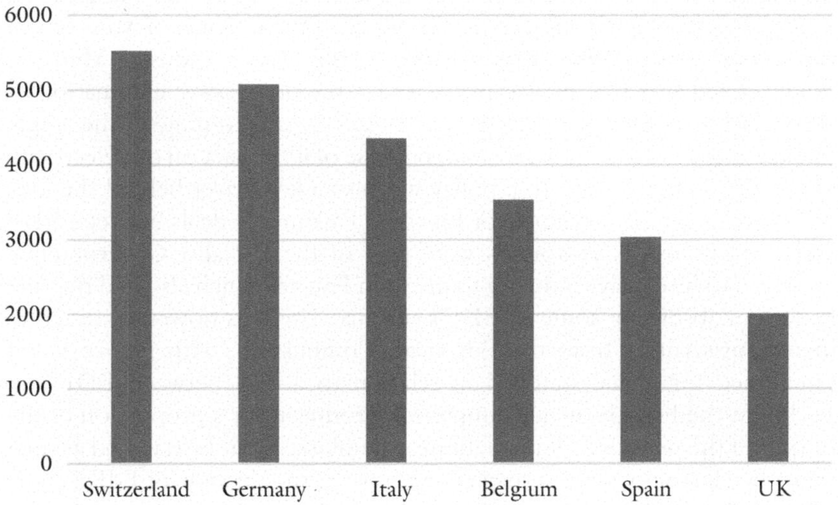

Fig. 6.3 Capacity of interconnectors with France in 1987 (MW). (UCPTE Annual Report, 1987)

reported that utilities in Germany had begun to view the French monopoly as a 'Massive predator, waiting to pounce'.[20]

However, the nature of the contract with the RECs in England and Wales would have assuaged those fears and it revealed the true intensions of EDF with regard to electricity liberalisation. Although there had been extensive discussions between large UK industrial customers and EDF for direct contracts, EDF did not enter the market in England/Wales via the direct contracting route, 'cherry picking' the large customers. This was because, firstly, it did not want to undermine its own basic model and the monopoly based industry structure it relied on for its own existence. Secondly, due to its poor financial position, EDF prioritised stable revenues via long-term contracts for bulk power, rather than commercial contracts with individual customers, which would have more likely been shorter term and entailed a greater degree of risk. EDF, as it turned out, wanted trade between utilities based on long-term contracts, essentially building on the old UCPTE model, not competition for customers.

Following the deal with the RECs, the UK become EDF's largest export market, purchasing 16.7 TWh of a total of 54 TWh (worth FFr 12.6 bn).[21] In 1991 around 14% of all electricity produced by EDF was exported. EDF's long-term view was to increase its exports to around 70 TWh/year by 2000. A key driver of this growth was expected to be eastern Europe; at the time EDF was in various commercial partnerships with German companies, including *Bayernwerk* and *PreussenElektra*, to build a nuclear plant in Hungary and for grid reinforcements to enable west-east trade across the continent.

The expectation was that after 2000 the growth in exports would then plateau. It was predicted that by the year 2000 exports could reach a ceiling of 80 TWh but then fall back to 65 soon after, after which EDF would concentrate its export strategy more on nuclear plant construction. EDF was bullish at the time and considered placing orders for up to seven new PWRs by 2000, citing a growing economy in the 1990s, success in winning new industrial clients and export opportunities as rationale. Jean Zask, EDF's 'general controller of exports' was estimating that by 1996 exports could be up to 100 TWh by 2000, 25% of France's total production.

However, within French domestic energy politics in the early 1990s, there was strong disagreement about the future rate of nuclear new build for the purposes of meeting demand from export trade. The influential advisory body, the *Commissariat a l'Energie Atomique*, delivered a report to government on nuclear power capacity, advising against building new plant solely for export. France, they argued, would not need new nuclear plant before 1995/96, estimating the current surplus at 7/8 plants (10 GW), and if EDF built the new plants its installed nuclear capacity would be up to 61,000 MW from the current 52,600 MW.[22] Jean Bergougnoux, EDF's managing director, later reformulated EDF's position, that there would no longer be a surplus after 1996 given the growing demand. The strategy was to export surpluses arising from historic investments in the system up to the mid-1990s, but after 1996 exports would be on a case-by-case commercial basis; that is, signing contracts with foreign customers tied to specific plants and additional capacity for this purpose would be strictly based on demand signals.

Also, EDF came under pressure at home to focus on investment in the transmission grid and the diversification of its generation base, rather than on continued nuclear expansion. In 1991 an update of the French long-term energy plan of 1983, 'Energie 2010', argued 'for increasing diversity in sources of electricity generation at a time of complex and uncertain supply and fluctuating demand'.[23] Along with placing the emphasis on meeting peak demand, the plan extolled the benefits of CCGTs (combined cycle gas turbine technologies), co-generation and increased hydropower. This was because, as outlined below, there was increasing concern about the vulnerabilities of the French system due to seasonal weather conditions and technical problems at its nuclear plants.

System Vulnerabilities

Behind the narrative of continuous nuclear expansion and export opportunities, there were a number of features of the French electricity system—both technical and economic—which placed constraints on EDF's move into neighbouring markets. This system, and hence EDF's revenue base, was extremely prone to volatility. While the nuclear programme provided significant amounts of overall capacity, the system relied heavily on conventional thermal and hydroelectric plant—both French and Swiss—for balancing, particularly to meet winter peak demand. The issue was becoming more acute as heating load was increasingly electrified; by the late 1980s in the region two-thirds of all new domestic premises were relying on electricity for their space heating, a demand on the system which often coincided with winter peaks. The output of the system had become highly sensitive to rainfall and temperature fluctuations, with each degree Celsius fall in temperature resulting in an increase in demand of 1000 MW at winter peak periods.

During a prolonged cold and dry weather pattern, when hydro output was limited and flows across the interconnectors to neighbouring utilities constrained, the French system could suffer a shortfall of up to 20,000 MW. The non-nuclear capacity that EDF could access to balance its system was becoming increasingly stretched (by late 1980s EDF's hydro capacity was 23,000 MW, while its conventional thermal capacity was 16,000 MW, comprising 29 hard coal stations, 3 lignite, 12 gas and 13 oil). The vulnerability of the French system at winter had been exposed on 12 January 1987 when high electricity demand associated with heating loads and the failure of a thermal unit at Cordemais saw a large number of customers in western France being cut off to avoid a cascading failure across the system.[24]

The issues were being compounded as EDF began experiencing problems with its nuclear plants. The steam generators in the PWRs were known to be a weak link and by the late 1980s the early units required replacement; Dampierre 1 (900 MW), for example, was offline for up to six months. These early steam generators generally had a lifetime of 15 years, so the expectation was that each plant would need one replacement during its lifetime, estimated to be two per year in EDF's stock from 1993. The issue fed into concerns about systemic vulnerabilities as the steam generators in the newer fleet of fourteen 1300 MW plants were becoming less reliable. During 1989, for example, the average load factor of the 14 dropped by 10%–down to 62%. In March/April of that year, four of these plants were offline and there was a question mark over whether these units would also require a full replacement during their lifetimes. The industry had been developing methods such as roto-peening and shot-peening to improve the performance and longevity of these generators;[25] the newer 1300 MW plants were inspected and allowed to continue operation, but the cost of cleaning and further inspections across the fleet was in the region of FFr 1.5 bn. The issue may have been manageable on a plant-by-plant basis, but due to the similarity of the fleet arising from the centrally coordinated nature of the construction programme, the prospect of further technical problems had to be considered a systemic risk.

As there was significant uncertainty about the future availability of nuclear capacity under different operational scenarios, there were question marks over the reliability of EDF's surplus and whether the system could cope with a significant proportion of output being committed in contracts for export. If these were 'firm', they would oblige EDF to supply foreign customers regardless of the operational situation in its domestic market. Within France there was a concern held by some at the time about the energy security implications of relying on foreign trade. If EDF was unable to deliver the power, who, if anyone, would be responsible for ensuring the customer was supplied? How would this safety-net be paid for? If system conditions deteriorated, would EDF prioritise its domestic customer base? EDF wanted long-term contracts to absorb its nuclear surplus, but was reluctant for them to be for guaranteed 'firm power'.

In order to manage the situation the company began offering interruptible contracts tied to 2000 MW of capacity to its large industrial consumers within France; these tariffs involved very high prices during the 20 or so coldest days of the year, but EDF still faced significant risks if it got the days wrong. EDF therefore had no interest in volatile spot markets or direct contracts with customers; its ideal export contract 'would be with another utility and might be for a firm 100 MW, over ten years, with the power flow being reversed on the 20 winter peak days when EdF begins to run short of power'.[26] These types of two-way contracts to deal with complex system issues and French peak demand required a strong element of cooperation—not competition—with other European utilities.

In large part due to these technical problems and seasonal factors, EDF recorded financial losses for six of the ten years prior to 1989. A contributory factor to its loss of FFr 1.8 bn in 1988 was strike action by EDF employees in the Communist CGT union during October and November of that year. This required EDF to import large amounts of power from West Germany at short notice. Drought in 1989 cost the utility between FFr 1–2 bn, due to reduced hydro output of 20 TWh, along with the steam generator issues and lack of availability of some nuclear plant which relied on river water for cooling. The deficit had to be made up by costly coal and oil substitutes and imports of 6 TWh.

The accumulated debt of EDF was also a factor: in 1982 this was over FFr 150 bn and was valued at 213bn by 1985. Currency risk was a key concern because a third of the accumulated debt was owed to foreign creditors. The company's finances had been squeezed by a falling Franc in the early/mid-1980s as 'from 1981 to end of 1983, the Franc declined by nearly 50% against the dollar',[27] recovering somewhat thereafter. Exports, in particular to countries like West Germany with stable currencies, therefore became more important to the business as they provided a source of external revenue. Another key impetus behind earning export revenues was the government's anti-inflationary drive of the 1980s, meaning EDF was restricted from raising its domestic tariffs in line with its rising costs.

By the late 1980s the company was undergoing a major debt restructuring, cutting its debt by FFr 6.4 bn between 1989 and 1990—its accumulated debt in 1990 had risen to FFr 226.1 bn, on a turnover of FFr 156 bn—and the aim was to substantially reduce the interest rate on its new debt issuings to 6–7% by the turn of the century. Speculative investments with the aim of gaining market share outside France would not have been in line with this long-term debt management strategy. But 1991 showed how crucial this export market had become: in this year EDF's overall financial position improved significantly because its electricity sales rose by 8.9% overall, with exports rising to 58.5 TWh, a staggering 22.6% year-on-year increase.

Despite its need for export revenues, EDF was increasingly sceptical of the long-term strategic implications of operating competitively and opportunistically in foreign markets. This introduced risks—both technical and financial—and undermined its own business model as a publicly owned and fully integrated monopoly. Any move towards a compulsory European electricity exchange, like the Electricity Pool in England/Wales, and/or extended European Commission powers and oversight over issues such as transit and common carriage, were to be resisted or at least delayed and watered down. The prospect of lucrative foreign markets and export potential was part of a discourse which helped to maintain domestic political support for EDF's nuclear programme during a period of demand uncertainty. While EDF were certainly in favour of an expansion of trade based on a cooperative model, akin to the existing UCPTE system, true competition in the British style threatened its core ambitions of debt sustainability and maintaining the security of electricity supply within France.

Germany: Managed Coal Decline and Regime Tensions

The hard coal mining industry in West Germany employed over half a million workers by the mid-1950s, constituting 8% of the entire workforce, and was almost entirely located in the West. From the end of the war, coal—both hard coal and lignite—had become the dominant component of energy demand, providing over 70% of primary energy consumption. However, over the following decades, this fell dramatically in relative terms, to less than 20% by the 1990s, largely due to the increasing use of oil in the economy, which had reached over 50% of primary energy consumption in 1970. Hard coal production also fell in absolute terms, form 98.7 mt in 1950 to 74 mt in 1990,[28] and this was despite the fact that oil's share had fallen back to 40% of primary energy consumption by 1990, largely due to a loss of market share in the electricity sector and competition from natural gas for the heating market.[29] Nuclear power, which had increased to almost one-third of electricity generation by 1990, also emerged as a key competitor for coal during this period (Fig. 6.4).

Coal's decline began in the late 1950s, particularly in the Ruhr region where the numbers employed in the coal mining industry almost halved over the ensuing decade—from 600,000 in 1958 to 320,000 a decade later.[30] In the late 1950s, this decline was affected by a partial liberalisation of coal trade under the ECSC agreement when, in 1958, the ECSC High Authority 'had loosened its control. It permitted Ruhr coal suppliers to sign long-term contracts, for more than one year, within the ECSC' and

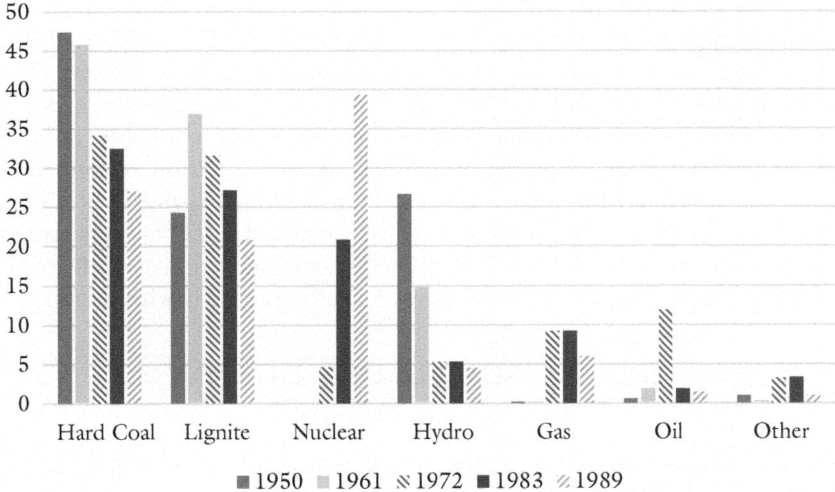

Fig. 6.4 Changes in shares (%) of power generation per source in West Germany. (Based on Table 7.6, p287, Müller, J. & Stahl, K. (1996) *Regulation of the Market for Electricity in the Federal Republic of Germany.* In Gilbert, J. and Kahn, E. (Eds.) International Comparisons of Electricity Regulation. Cambridge University Press. Data originally sourced from VDEW)

to 'adapt prices to match offers from other ECSC and third countries'.[31] This also allowed a proportion of cheaper American coal into the West German market for the first time. Along with supply-side challenges in the late 1950s, there was a general fall-off in demand from the steel industry, partly arising from a breaking of the link between particular cokeries and iron and steel works, which had long been part of an industrial policy of tying these energy-intensive industries to more expensive Ruhr coal. Compounding the crisis for the West German coal industry was a more general falling demand for hard coal; over 1957–58 there was a reduction of 2.5 m tons form the energy sector, a drop of 11.5 m tons in domestic use of coal for heating due to the mild winter of that year, and increasing competition from oil, which had been growing in market share since the 1920s. Prior to this, demand for oil for heating purposes had been artificially suppressed due to various government policies to protect domestic sources.

Unlike France, West Germany (and the UK) took assertive action to protect coal employment in the late 1950s, with the industry entering a new phase, increasingly under pressure and reliant on government subsidies. The German response to the situation in 1958 was 'a miniscule reduction in production of 0.6 million tons' and extra stockpiling. The Federal Government invoked Article 95 (1) of the ECSC Treaty and imposed 'a coal import duty of 20 DM per ton of coal imported over and above a basic quota of 5 million tons'. It also introduced 'special measures to support the financing of pit-head coal stocks', and to this end, money ($7 m) 'was made available to coal companies from 31 October 1958 to stockpile, on a monthly basis, coal produced over and above thirty-five days net production'.[32]

By late 1959 coal stocks at the pithead had increased to over 17 million tonnes, from 423,000 tonnes two years earlier. Another key response by the government to the prospect of 100,000 miner job losses and up to 12 m tons of production decline was to make 'heavy and medium grades of heating oil subject to turnover tax from which they had hitherto been exempt', although the level imposed was not hugely significant, at only 4%. Later, in 1959, a tax of 25 DM per ton was levied on 'heavy grades of heating oil and 10 DM per ton for light grades'.[33] Revenues from this tax were used to fund retraining and wage support for miners. The costs of the various labour measures, up to 800 m DM, were shared with the ECSC High Authority.

A 'coal-oil cartel' was initiated in early 1959, involving an agreement 'between the three largest mining companies and five major oil companies ... to undertake no measures before the end of December 1959 to expand the sales of heavy heating oils at the expense of solid fuels ... [and] not to sell heavy heating oil at a price below the prevailing world level before the end of December 1960'. Coal importers also cancelled existing contracts which were already agreed; cutting '8.7 million tons of American coal already contracted' and licences for the importation of 14.5 mt were cancelled. This cost 300 m DM, with government providing compensation in the form of subsidised state loans to the value of 250 m DM. This response to promote national coal was not a case of direct state intervention, rather 'state-private industry co-operation',[34] in line with 'The German Tradition of Organized Capitalism'.[35]

The rapid economic growth of the early 1960s helped the coal industry to get off its knees, with production in the region of 140 mt per annum and a significant reduction in pithead stocks. The industry had also improved its productivity, becoming amongst the most efficient in western Europe. However, coal's share in overall energy supply declined continually, dropping below 50% for the first time in 1963. The primary driver for this was the falling oil price and its growing share of the heating market. In 1963 measures were introduced to rationalise the coal industry, resulting in the closure of 51 mines, out of a total of 141, by 1967.[36] However, despite this, pithead stocks again increased in the short term, surpassing 15 mt in 1965, largely due to a fall-off in demand from the struggling steel sector. The remainder of the 1960s were characterised by efforts to support what appeared to be an industry in terminal decline; from 1956 to 1970 coal's share in West German primary energy consumption had declined to 30%.

This process culminated in the 1968 Coal Adoption Law which was introduced by the Grand Coalition Government. Measures included, for example, import tariffs and quotas, further heating oil taxes and subsidies for the use of domestic coal in the coking and steel industries. There were also efforts to consolidate the industry, particularly important being the creation of *RuhrKohle AG* in 1968, becoming the largest energy company in the Federal Republic. Later, by the 1980s, it was mining 80% of all domestic German hard coal and was the largest coal producer in western Europe. Following its creation the company quickly signed supply contracts with the major electricity utilities. These state-backed contracts had provisions in place to compensate utilities for the difference between domestic and international coal prices. As a result, the coal industry became increasingly reliant on this growing sector—electricity output 'increased tenfold from 44 TWh (1950) up to 440 TWh by 1990'[37]—as it lost out in other markets.

This policy of linking the coal and electricity sectors as a means of protecting the mining industry had earlier become explicit—in June 1965—when the government passed the 'Act to Further Coal Consumption in Power Stations', at a cost of 1.2 bn DM in tax breaks. This was followed up with the 'Second Power Act' a year later, with the aim of ensuring that German hard coal provided 'approximately 50 per cent of domestically produced electricity by 1970'.[38] However, when the country's First Energy Programme was published in 1973, its share was only 36%. The situation changed dramatically shortly after as oil prices rose unexpectedly, by over 100%, following the oil crisis of 1973/74. For the revised Energy Programme published later in 1974, energy security was prioritised and the role of oil in the economy was de-emphasised, projected now to 'fall from 55 per cent in 1973 to 44 per cent in 1985'. A publicly funded 'national coal reserve of 10 million tons' was created and the Third Power Act of December of that year saw an ambition to ramp up coal use in the electricity sector, introducing a target to burn '33 million tons of Community coal in German electricity production'. However, while putting in place an overall target, the act failed to oblige utilities to burn specific amounts of hard coal, and between 1974 and 75, hard coal's share in electricity production actually fell from 31% to 24.8%, while lignite was at 31.2%. Following the second oil crisis of 1979, renewed efforts were made to increase hard coal's share in electricity production, with utilities signing 'a new agreement guaranteeing the domestic market in electricity generation until the end of the century'.[39]

The Century Contract, or *Jahrhundertvertrag*, had been initially agreed in 1977 as a means of governing the relationship between the coal industry and electricity producers. The key contracts put in place to maintain the continuity of the coal industry involved one agreement 'between the Association of the German Coal-mining Industry (GVSt) and the Association of German Electricity Supply Companies (VDEW, *Vereinigung Deutscher Elektrizitätswerke*)' and a second 'between the German coal industry and the Association of Industrial Producers of Electricity (VIK, *Vereinigung Industrielle Kraftwirtschaft*)'. Both 'were signed under pressure from the federal government, which threatened legislation if a voluntary agreement was not reached'.[40] A levy on electricity bills, the *Kohlepfenning* (coal penny), was also introduced to fund the contract, which in 1978 financed half of total subsidies of 4.1 bn DM to the industry. As Parnell notes, the coal penny 'had initially been proposed by the coal employers and accepted by the interested parties partially as a means of circumventing EC regulations. It was to fall on private users in such a way that generation costs should be reflected in user charges that would not harm German industry's competitive position'.[41] Arrangements were put in place to ensure that competing electricity suppliers, particularly public municipal suppliers, could not gain a competitive advantage as a result of not being party to the coal-electricity agreements. In the late 1970s, this saw changes made to the Cartel Act which actually reduced competition in the electricity market.

The economic slowdown of the early 1980s and lower demand for coking coal from steel producers saw renewed pressure on the German coal industry. By the middle of the decade '5 billion DM of public aid was being made available to the industry',[42] with almost half of this funded via the coal penny, supporting the use of the fuel for 27% of electricity production in 1985. During this period West Germany's electricity sector had become largely reliant (90%) on domestic sources, primarily coal and nuclear. Worryingly though for the coal industry, oil prices were in rapid decline in the mid-1980s, and this affected the price of internationally traded coal; by the middle of the decade, this was 'available at a price which was cheaper by about 100 DM per ton', and rising to 170 DM by 1989. By 1986, 'financial support for coal was now running at over twice the level of 1984'.[43]

This was a significant exposure for the nexus of coal and electricity production, and it put pressure on the subsidy system which essentially compensated utilities for the difference between domestic and international fuel prices. By this point over half of the coal industry's output was being bought by the electricity utilities and around 40% of Ruhrkohle's turnover was linked to the subsidy payments. The coal penny accounted for 3.5% of an average electricity bill in 1983–85, but by 1990 it had risen to 8.25%. Meanwhile, from the mid-1980s, average West German industrial electricity prices had become amongst the highest in the world across the industrialised nations; significantly higher than those of competitor industrial nations such as Canada and Australia, and 'a good 30% above the European average'[44] (see Fig. 6.5). Industrial end-users, unsurprisingly, began to make their voices heard, particularly as pressure grew to maintain the Century Contract targets in the face of falling international coal prices and the apparent abundance of cheap surplus electricity from France. VIK, the electricity consumer group, were unsurprisingly highly critical of the coal

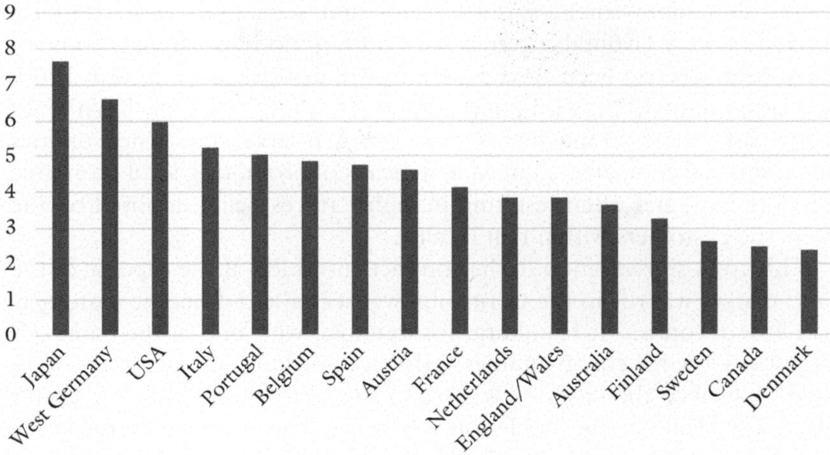

Fig. 6.5 Industrial electricity prices in p/kWh for the year 1986 (Sterling, including local taxes but not VAT). (Data from an Electricity Council chart presented in their memorandum to Energy Committee (1988) *Third Report: The Structure, Regulation and Economic Consequences of Electricity Supply in the Private Sector*. HMSO. 6 July 1988)

penny and argued that, as the levy was largely in place to protect industrial regions, it should be paid for through general taxation.

Although direct contracts between utilities and individual industrial customers were possible in the German market, there were rules in place which constrained the ability of utilities to offer lower prices to these customers. For example, where an industrial customer was being offered a contract, they were obliged to offer similar terms to the local distributor so as not to disadvantage other customers. This is not to say that utilities did not have some flexibility in their dealings with industrial customers, and the aggregate figures showing extremely high prices charged to German industry do not tell the full story. There were, in reality, exceptions to these rules for some large consumers with a high energy intensity of their production processes. Utilities had more freedom to offer more favourable terms to these 'Special Contract Customers', with an average price cut of 5% in 1990.

There were also what were colloquially known as 'Special Special Contract Customers', a very select number of high-intensity users—aluminium smelters, steel plants and such like—with contracts offered on very favourable terms, with little or no transparency. Some of these contracts had been agreed a number of decades previously, in 1960, and lasted until 1995, with prices 'reputedly as low as 2.8 Pf/KWh'.[45] In many cases these arrangements were between large city-owned utilities and industrial companies, agreed as a means of promoting local economic development, and often resulting in higher prices being imposed on the domestic customers within that locality.

This cross-subsidisation of the contract customers at the expense of the tariff market was rife in the German power sector and domestic customers had little recourse. In Hamburg, for example, with one of the country's largest city-owned energy utilities (HEW), these long-term contracts were used to finance the city's 33% share in the nearby Stade nuclear power plant. The plant became highly controversial as flaws were discovered in the containment, but, controversially, HEW decided to keep it running at least until its 'Special-Special' contract with the local aluminium works expired, resulting in the fermenting of anti-nuclear and energy industry sentiment in the locality. Things were beginning to change by 1991 however, following the introduction of new pricing rules by the Federal Cartel Office, which required utilities to justify tariff increases on the basis of changes to their cost base, as oppose to providing cheap electricity to local industries.

As the gap between international and domestic coal prices widened, it was clear that the Century Contract (*Jahrhundertvertrag*) finances were in trouble, with a deficit by the late 1980s of DM 6.3 bn. This prompted the first round of 'Coal Talks' in 1987 involving the government, the mining companies, the electricity utilities and other stakeholders, about revising the contract. Here it was 'agreed that production should be cut to 65 mt by 1995, involving the loss of 45,000 jobs'—a significant reduction in capacity of 13–15 mt. The large electricity utilities subsequently agreed in 1990 to a payment of DM 650 m into the finances of the contract on the basis that they could reduce their purchases of domestic coal, to just under 40 mt/year over the next five years.[46] The West German government then presented a Bill, 'the third Coal to Electricity Law', which included an amendment to reduce the levy on customers' bills such that it would fall from 8.5% to 7.3% by 1993, a figure which was put forward by the European Commission as a condition of approving the deal.

The government also established the *Mikat Commission* in August 1989 to advise them about designing a post-1995 subsidy regime after the Century Contract expired. This sought to balance the desire to support the indigenous coal industry with the increasingly prominent role for the European Commission in energy and industrial policy matters. When it reported later in 1990, it recommended moving coal subsidies off electricity bills and onto the public purse, whilst pursuing greater efficiency at mines. The majority of the *Mikat Commission* agreed on cuts to coal consumption in the electricity generation sector, from a level of 40.9 mt/year to 35 mt/year. There were disagreements amongst the members, however; a minority had wanted this to be cut to 25 mt/year.

The contract system had the effect of protecting a large share of the market for electricity production for domestic producers of hard coal and was unsurprisingly seen as a barrier to achieving the cross-border trading ambitions set out in the European Commission's internal energy market (IEM) proposals. Around the time of the renegotiations of the Century Contract in 1987, significant pressure was exerted from the EEC level to internationalise the German energy market, although the Commission was at this time willing to permit the continuing subsidisation of domestic hard coal. The European Commission however only agreed to sanction the contract and the coal penny payments on the basis of a plan for how these would be wound down, along with a strategy for the long-term structural reform of the coal industry, being produced. Under the ECSC framework coal subsidies were only permitted until 1993, when the treaty expired, after which the Commission would only agree to subsidies for those mines which operated within a reference unit production cost and 'cutback subsidies' for those deemed to be uneconomic. Many of the West German hard coal mines would fall below the threshold to be deemed economic as their unit production costs were DM 260/t on average, in the region of DM 40/t above the European Commission's reference price.

This decision was later appealed by the Coal Employer's Association, who in late 1989 took a case to the European Court of Justice, which, after some consideration, was eventually supported by the Federal Government. This decision by the government to join the appeal came after the European Commission had initially withheld coal penny payments for 1989, as no credible rationalisation plan for the mining industry which would see the phasing out of subsidies was delivered. The German government claimed that the measures in place to support the coal industry had previously been approved by the European Commission in 1983/84, so their action had no legal basis. A compromise was eventually reached the following year and the Commission agreed to a two-year extension. As part of this deal the German government 'recognized the inevitability of structural change in the energy sectors' and the

Commission's decision to accept the deal was 'conditional upon an acknowledgement on the part of the German government of the legality of the Commission's licensing powers and on German agreement to comply with reduced quotas'.[47]

This delayed the real decision on the post-1995 future of the coal industry until the end of March 1991; the issue was extremely politically sensitive at this time as Federal elections were scheduled for December 1990. Also, and as we discuss further below, there had been moves to liberalise the wider German economy, so the pressure from the commission 'served as an alibi for the Bonn government and was not unwelcome. Equally, Bonn exploited its domestic differences in its dealings with the Commission'.[48] The incumbent Chancellor, Helmut Kohl, had invested a good deal of his own political capital in the Century Contract and its guarantee to the coal industry of 40.9 mt annual subsidised coal to 1995. Kohl was already under pressure because he had had to roll back on a commitment made to West German miners in August 1989, just before the fall of the Berlin Wall, that their jobs would not be jeopardised.

Following the 1990 election Kohl's Christian Democrats were in coalition with the liberal Free Democratic Party (FDP) and there were early signs that the economy minister from that party, Jürgen Moellemann, was sceptical of the viability of Kohl's commitment to the miners. The FDP, as a political party, were generally critical of the circa 11 bn DM spent annually on coal support. Moellemann had argued that, given the agreement to cut back brown coal production in the East as part of the Reunification Agreement—the East was mainly a brown coal producer—it would be unfair for miners in the West to receive this level of protection against market forces. There was a demonstration of 140,000 miners on 27 September against Moellemann's 'catastrophe policies'.

Moellemann had, prior to this, set out a plan to significantly cut subsidies to the steel industry and this had unsurprisingly come under attack from the coal industry and the Social Democratic SDP. The SDP were traditional supporters of the coal miners and had majorities in North Rhine Westfalen and Saarland, both strong coal mining regions. While the FDP had an alliance with the Christian Democrats at Federal level, they were in coalition with SDP at local level in the State of Rheinland Pfalz, so they were also conscious of protecting that political flank. The Christian Democrats were also conscious of the risk of removing support for coal; if this was done the SDP would likely remove their tacit support for nuclear power, which then had widespread support amongst the centre right of the political spectrum. There were also regional-level tensions; Baden-Württemberg and Bavaria, both powerful conservative-leaning states with little direct attachment to the coal industry—Bavaria being primarily nuclear—were in favour of rationalisation of the coal industry and the abolition of the levy on bills. These political tensions were coming to the surface as questions about European Commission approval of the German arrangements arose again in 1991 as the 1989 agreement expired. The Commission, conscious of the 1992 deadline for the single market, initially indicated that it would not continue its approval of the Century Contract beyond 1993.

A key aim of the new German government was to prolong the phase-out of the subsidies to 2005, with Moellemann indicating some flexibility in terms of output levels of the industry over this timeframe. His Economics Ministry suggested cutting production back to 45 mt/year for the entire output by 2005 (30 mt for electricity and 15 for steel), significantly lower than the mining industry's plan.[49] A compromise figure of 50 mt by 2000, and staying at this level to 2005, was finally agreed after talks in November 1991. This would allocate 35 mt/year to electricity. It was also agreed that from '1992 to 1994, 40.9 mt of German coal will be supplied for electricity generation as usual. But in 1995, 1.9 mt of coal will be supplied from the coal industry's massive stocks, and 39 mt from running production'.[50]

Leon Brittan, the Competition Commissioner, later insisted that 'no more than 37.5 mt should be taken from running production, and the remaining 3.4 mt from stocks'. The 37.5 figure would mean that electricity generation from domestic sources would be down to 20% of the total, a figure which the European Commission was seeking to apply as a rule across the EEC (see Chap. 3). During the talks VDEW, the association representing the large utilities, and VIK, representing large industrial customers, had insisted that 'the subsidy system should involve no special burden on electricity prices', meaning no extension of the coal penny levy beyond 1993. However, it transpired that Moellemann and Brittan had 'agreed before the talks began that if German coal for electricity was cut to 25 mt by 1997, and production cuts began before the Jahrhundert contract expired, then the Commission would license the Jahrhundert Contract until 1995'.[51]

Leon Brittan later 'recommended to the Commission that it should license the Contract to run until its expiry date at the end of 1995, assuming that certain conditions are fulfilled'[52] and in December 1991 the commission 'licensed the contract to run its course to expiry at end-1995'.[53]

A Multi-Level Electricity Regime

Protection for the coal industry was enabled by a set of economic relationships and interdependencies between different levels of the German electricity supply industry. The industry there had historically been more diverse and multi-layered than that of France and Britain, with nine large integrated generation and transmission companies across Germany (Verbund Utilities), along with large regional and local distributors who supplied local monopoly areas. The large integrated generation-transmission companies included *PreussenElektra* (Düsseldorf based) and *Bayernwerk* (Munich based), part of the VEBA and VIAG industrial groups respectively, which together owned about one quarter of the electricity generation capacity in the west. VEBA and VIAG were founded in the 1920s, initially as holding companies owned by the Federal Government. *Rheinisch-Westfälisches Elektrizitätswerk* (RWE) was the largest single utility, with just under one-third of generation capacity. Operating out of Essen in the Ruhr industrial region, it was expanded across the surrounding region in the early 1900s, with its ownership being a mix of private investors and municipalities. Part of RWE's success was its pioneering role in developing long-distance high-voltage transmission links in the 1930s, enabling it to connect its coal-dominated capacity in the Rhine-Ruhr region with hydroelectric resources in the Austrian Alps, 600 km away.[54] These three companies—RWE, *PreussenElektra* and *Bayernwerk*—were by some distance the largest, accounting for over half of electricity generation.

Below these three was VEW (*Vereinigte Elektrizitätswerke Westfalen*), a smaller company which had been created by municipalities in the North Western region as a reaction to the growing dominance of RWE; EWAG, another subsidiary of VIAG, whilst two utilities dominated the Baden-Württemberg region (*Badenwerk* based around Karlsruhe and *Energie-Versorgung Schwaben* [EVS] from Stuttgart). Utilities owned by the city-states in Hamburg (HEW) and Berlin (BEWAG) also had shares in local generation plants and were large by national standards. The largest of these 'Verbund Utilities' operated a common dispatch centre near Cologne as part of their industry body DVG (*Deutsche Verbundgesellschaft*) which coordinated with the UCPTE system. The nine owned about 80%

of the generation assets and had a significant share of the market for supplying large industrial consumers. Typically, these companies had regional identities, and the states (*Länder*) and municipalities often had large shareholdings.

By the early 1990s ownership of the electricity supply industry as a whole was predominantly public (80%), accounting for over 90% of demand, but on the generation side the main corporate structure was mixed ownership of various forms, accounting for 70% of this market. Private ownership was mainly confined to rural areas, while distribution was 40% pure public ownership and just over 50% mixed. The distribution function and the remainder of the supply market was then split between approximately 40 medium-sized companies, covering regions or large cities, and a large number (c. 1000) of very small municipally owned utilities (*stadtwerke*). The regional companies also generated power (25% of total output) and covered about one-quarter of demand (Fig. 6.6).

This diversity meant that the attitude towards liberalisation was not shaped by its effects on a single dominant national company, such as the Central Electricity Generating Board (CEGB) in Britain or France's EDF,

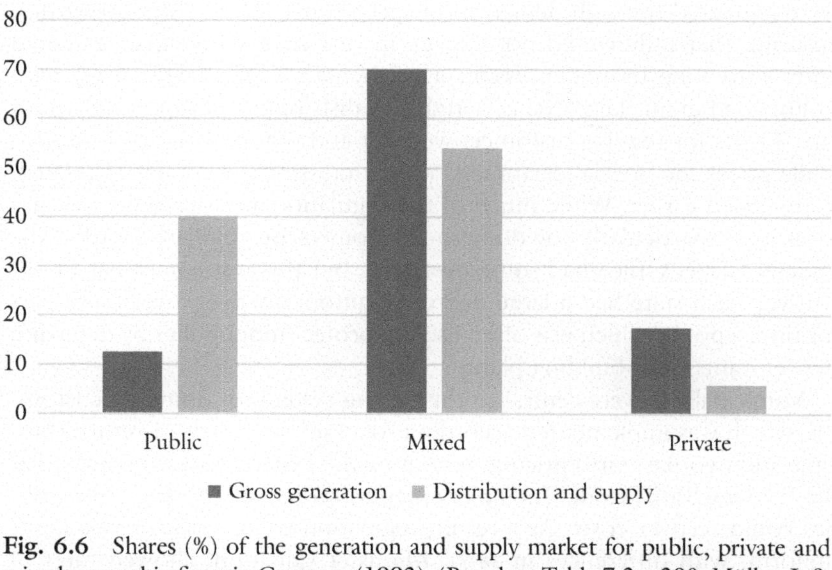

Fig. 6.6 Shares (%) of the generation and supply market for public, private and mixed ownership firms in Germany (1992). (Based on Table 7.2, p280, Müller, J. & Stahl, K. (1996) *Regulation of the Market for Electricity in the Federal Republic of Germany.* In Gilbert, J. and Kahn, E. (Eds.) International Comparisons of Electricity Regulation. Cambridge University Press. Data original sourced from VDEW)

rather by its impact on a complex set of relationships and interdependencies which governed the electricity supply industry. With little competition, the industry was structured around private voluntary agreements, or Association Agreements, between the large and small utilities. The history of these lay in the early years of the electricity industry in Germany which, like other countries pioneering the use of these new systems in the late nineteenth and early twentieth centuries, was characterised by a patchwork of localised and largely uncoordinated developments.

Following a period of competition and price wars, rivalry between the successful utilities was settled by legislation. Initially, in 1908, territories were assigned to designated utilities, and the larger players started to sign agreements not to encroach on each other's territories; for example, in 1927 RWE and *PreussenElektra* signed such an agreement. Subsequently, the industry was consolidated further following a 1935 Federal Act (*Energiewirtschaftsgesetz*—EnWG) which set out the structure of the industry, largely exempting it from cartel law. The rationale behind the 1935 act was to encourage cooperation and to protect the industry from competition, which was then seen as inefficient and destructive.

Utilities were granted exclusive rights to supply certain areas which were regulated through demarcation agreements (*Demarkationsvertrag*), ensuring that utilities did not engage in turf wars. Municipalities could enter into long-term concession agreements (*Konzessionsvertrag*) with utilities and grant them exclusive rights to distribute and supply a town or city. Tariffs for regular customers were set and regulated by each *länder*, while prices for 'special customers' (large industries) were less regulated, as discussed earlier. While much of the regulation and oversight was at a local level, particularly for domestic customers on regulated tariffs, the Federal Cartel Office had some oversight, but this was somewhat unobtrusive. Each state had a large degree of autonomy over investment permitting, a power which was often used to protect monopolies by deterring new entrants from building plant.

Municipalities were central to the pricing system for domestic customers, which was implemented according to a high level rate-of-return principle and two-part tariff pricing, set out by the Federal Government under the 'Federal Tariff Code' (or *Bundestarifordnung*—BTO), such that utilities could recover costs. As a result, regulation by the *länder* 'was never uniform, with differences in *inter alia* asset valuation, allowed rates of return, and which costs were included in the rate base'.[55] There was however some scope for the Federal Cartel Office to intervene if it was clear that large consumers of power were being subsidised and sold contracts at rates lower than the wholesale price of power.

Overall, the industry was largely self-governed and the municipalities used this leeway to cross-subsidise their other key functions (housing, transport, waste, etc.), with many municipalities evolving into powerful 'multi-utilities supplying electricity, gas, water, sewage, and waste management'. The municipalities who chose not to operate utilities 'in-house' could enter into concession contracts with private operators. These contracts were 'usually for 25 to 50 years, providing access to the rights-of-way and, in return, service to the community and sometimes sizeable concession payments'. The contracts came under increasing scrutiny at the Federal level, however, due to a lack of transparency and competition in the awarding process, and in 1990 an 'amendment to the antitrust law introduced a limit of 20 years on the term of these concessions',[56] requiring that existing contracts, many of which were for 50 years, terminate by the end of 1994.

As a result of EEC encroachment into German energy and competition policy, there was a general rush to sign contracts in the early 1990s as private operators were unsure whether this option would be cut off in the near future. Utilities were offering high concession fees and sometimes gifts, for example, to build swimming pools in the locality, if concessions were agreed. This trend towards municipal sales of local networks had begun a number of decades earlier as budgets were tightened in the late 1970s and early 1980s, with municipalities amassing large debts.

The Federal Government in 1987 had initiated a Deregulation Commission to look across the German economy and to identify regulatory barriers to competition. Their report, 'Opening of Markets and Competition',[57] discussed the electricity sector and tackled some of the arguments being made by the industry against competition, in particular that the demarcation agreements were needed in order to plan the systems effectively and ensure security of supply. The report was critical of high German electricity prices: it identified a conflict of interest between states who had a role in regulating prices, whilst owning shares in the energy companies, and was critical of municipalities for using high electricity prices to cross-subsidise other networks and services in their areas. It was also highly critical of the 'cost-plus' approach to regulation and accused utilities of extracting excessive profits, with all risks passed on to customers on regulated tariffs. They identified 'A firmly embedded cartel of power' around these complex contractual structures, involving municipalities, with their concession levies, private utilities, the mining industry, trade unions, industrial customers, Federal states and state institutions. This interlocking set of interests was characterised by the Deregulation Commission as follows:

> Despite the utterly inadequate reasons given for the regulation from a systematic point of view, despite the disadvantages to the economy as a whole which the regulation of the electricity industry causes, and despite the repeated attempts at reform, a change in German electricity policy is not in sight. It is prevented by a firmly established power cartel held together by widely branching interests. It includes: the municipalities as recipients of concession fees and as owners of supply companies, most of the electricity producing and distributing companies and their shareholders – many of whom are the municipalities–, firms supplying the electricity industry, particularly power station construction firms and coal mining companies, their employees and the trade unions, the customers who are on special rates and their advocates in local politics, the state institutions with their bureaucracies, who are entrusted with the technical inspection of the supply companies, the loss- making sectors of the cross-association companies which, like local public transport, are subsidised with the profits from the electricity industry, the Federal Länder, which block reforms mainly on regional and social policy grounds, and last [but] not least the many politicians who see their interests in offices and supervisory bodies as linked to the established electricity industry.[58]

The Deregulation Commission then proposed a number of far-reaching reforms, including, *inter-alia*, deregulation and the promotion of competition as a general goal, to forbid demarcation agreements and any rights to exclusivity in concession agreements, to create independent transmission operators, that any public contracts would need to be tendered and awarded following a competitive process, to reform retail price regulation and to shift the focus of regulation away from price caps towards addressing market externalities and countering market power.

Unlike France, therefore, many of the pressures for electricity market reform were internal within Germany, and in some instances the Federal Cartel Office was lobbying the European Commission to use its legal powers with respect to opening up the German electricity industry.[59] However, the drive for liberalisation of the energy sector was certainly not uniform across the German polity, and there were clear divisions even within the Ministry of Economics, as Padgett notes:

> The competition issue exposed differences of political perspective with the Economics Ministry … The Grundsatzahteilung (Basic Policy Division) was oriented towards the liberalization of competition in the energy sectors. The Abteilung Energiepolifik (Energy Policy Division), with its close sectoral ties, maintained that the special circumstances of the sector justified its exemptions from the full force of competition law.[60]

Discussions about a draft German energy law followed the 1991 Deregulation Commission report, potentially seeing the end of demarcation contracts and exclusive concession contracts. It was questionable however whether this would be passed before the next Federal election in the Autumn of 1994. There was significant opposition, and ultimately 'the Ministry's amendment to Federal competition law produced little in the way of liberalizing change'. A key reason being the 'inter-ministerial conflict between the Economics, Finance and Labour Ministries over state commitments to the coal industry'. Also, the issue of local gas supply created conflict with the environment ministry, which tended to be more in favour of technology-specific support, then for district energy schemes and combined heat and power (CHP). Many of the local CHP district energy schemes were locked into take-or-pay contracts for their gas supply, so without their local monopolies they could be bankrupted. These conflicts at local government level 'along with the dispersal of sectoral policy competences between the Federal government and the Länder, meant that the state lacked the necessary internal integration to confront the complex of interrelated issues facing the sector'.[61]

The debate about reform in the early 1990s made clear the divergence of interests which had developed between the different levels of the industry, which under the Association Agreements had historically been relatively harmonious. Many of the municipalities opposed the liberalisation proposals, unsurprising as they had been earning in the region of DM 5 bn/year from concession fees. On the other hand, the large vertically integrated utilities were in favour of dismantling the local monopolies and expanding their markets. They were increasingly international in focus and saw liberalisation as a way of dismantling the power of local monopoly energy distributors who were the gatekeepers to the lucrative customer base, particularly the energy-intensive industrial customers. As we discuss in the next chapter, they later began to look more favourably on third-party access to grids, as a watered-down version may favour the municipal suppliers whose business model was based on restricting competition.

The large utilities also had plans to expand into East Germany and were claiming that the expense of modernising the East German system would be very high. They used this as leverage argue for a withdrawal from Century Contract system and for an end to the 'coal penny' levy after the expiry of the existing arrangements in 1995. In advance of reunification, the 'Big Three' utilities—RWE, *Preussenelektra* and *Bayernwerk*—were planning to take a 75% stake in VEAG (*Vereinigte Energiewerke AG*), the major east German utility, which then had control of the high-voltage transmission network and a number of lignite coal power plants. Under the 'German Electricity Contract' and wider 'Unification Treaty', signed in August 1990, ownership of East German utilities would pass into a 'State Trust', a *Treuhand*, and be sold on to the West German utilities as VEAG. It was projected that VEAG would need to spend DM 40 bn on new stations and transmission grid upgrades by 2005; the western utilities were arguing that they would need access to cheap hard coal closer to world prices to achieve this expansion in the East. A dismantling of the vertically integrated structures of the western utilities and the maintenance of the obligation to effectively subsidise the coal industry, they argued, would compromise their ability to finance the upgrading of the East German system, posing a dilemma for the German government in the context of the wider push for market deregulation. There was also a strong impetus behind the expansion of nuclear power to meet the growing demand and help to phase out the most polluting brown coal plants in the East, a politically contentious issue.

The West German utilities were also to have a 51% share of the 15 regional utilities (Combines), with over 120 East German municipalities, or Communes, having the other 49%. These municipalities however objected to having a minority share, citing discontent which went back to the Nazi period when their electricity assets were appropriated and used to create the larger Combines. Following reunification, eastern municipalities were wanting to set up their own independent companies, but this conflicted with the 'German Electricity Contract'. The municipalities appealed to the Federal Constitutional Court, claiming their constitutional rights were violated. Eventually there was an agreement reached, involving the creation of a number of municipal energy companies which would be partnerships with the western utilities; however, the regional distribution companies were required to purchase 70% of their power from the large generators for 20 years. As the process of integration evolved, the western utilities looked to form closer partnerships with the eastern municipalities;

for example, Leipzig, the most powerful municipal actor in the East, decided to create its own municipal utility in partnership with RWE.

Conclusion

Despite their different political histories and technical specificities, the two electricity systems at the core of western Europe were becoming increasingly interdependent. Since the early 1980s, RWE and EDF had been cooperating in the development of nuclear power projects, in particular at the Phenix fast-breeder-reactor plant, located in the south of France, and the Cattenom PWR near the German border, while the French nuclear fuel company Cogema had a large contract with VEBA and a number of other German nuclear operators.

As German reunification approached, it was envisioned that this collaboration would be extended as German utilities, in particular RWE, were concerned that their commitment to modernise the Eastern system would lead to a lack of investment in new capacity and a supply gap in the West. There was therefore a growing mutual interdependency as EDF was willing to enter into long-term contracts for the supply of baseload nuclear and to be supplied with German power at winter peaks. In November 1989 the two governments had agreed a protocol on energy policy which set out 'a formula for agreement on the regression of German coal support phased beyond the Commission's deadline of 1993' and called for increased trade between utilities on the basis of the EEC's transit framework, seen to be 'a renunciation of the much more far-reaching principle of common carriage'.[62]

France and West Germany were of course not the only players and there were other opponents to a radical shift to electricity market competition along British lines. Spain, for example, like West Germany, was keen to protect its domestic coal industry which, like Britain and West Germany, had become heavily reliant on supplying electricity generators. It was also concerned about losing its largest export market, Portugal, to EDF. Greece was also a strong opponent of the competitive market as it wanted to protect its lignite coal industry, while Denmark was also sceptical, prioritising support for its gas monopoly and nascent domestic renewable energy sectors.

But the Franco-German relationship was key. We will see in the next chapter that as the debate about the IEM unfolded over the course of the early 1990s, what started out as a rather confrontational relationship—as

German utilities interpreted EDF's rhetoric around expanding their exports as a threat—later merged into a growing interdependency. Once Germany's problems with its coal industry were resolved, at least partially, it shifted more in favour of competition, but implemented it in a way which reinforced the strength of the dominant utilities. This was partly in order to enable them to invest in the former East, but also to equip them to compete in other European markets as liberalisation unfolded.

A common Franco-German view on cross-border trade and electricity liberalisation did eventually emerge. This came to the fore towards the end of the process and was a key factor in the agreement amongst Member States on a phased introduction of competition across the Community from the late 1990s onwards. This rather slow and cautious approach enabled France and Germany to maintain a good deal of continuity within their national electricity regimes.

CHAPTER 7

The Political Market

In Chap. 5 we discussed what appeared to be the very favourable conditions for the introduction of competition reforms to the core European market: an extensive cross-border infrastructure, structural imbalances and a reforming European Commission. However, the directive on transit appeared to be weak and not a fundamental reform to the existing UCPTE (Union for the Co-ordination of Production and Transmission of Electricity) model, with cross-border exchanges staying within the control of the integrated monopolies. By the end of 1990, the Commission had recognised that the ambition to have a single market in electricity by 1992 was unachievable and the deadline for full competition was pushed back to 2000. In the meantime, they sought to capitalise on the modest success of the transit reform and to introduce some form of open access to the networks in order to enable competition between the incumbent utilities and other generators.

The Commission still had a fight on its hands, and by the early 1990s, the coalition of actors lobbying pro- and con-electricity liberalisation centred in Brussels had grown significantly. The large electricity and gas utilities created the trade bodies Eurelectric and Eurogaz respectively; as we shall see, Eurelectric lobbied strongly against common carriage for high-voltage transmission networks and began to push for a radically different vision for a European electricity market: the 'Industrial Model'. During these early discussions and debates, they claimed that access to their transmission networks for independent third parties would undermine the

R. Bolton, *Making Energy Markets*,
https://doi.org/10.1007/978-3-030-90075-5_7

technical stability of their systems and put a question mark over the investment required to meet demand growth in the long term. The European Commission were acutely aware of the political power of these arguments. Their earlier proposal to introduce common carriage had become highly politicised and somewhat of a 'straw man'[1] in the electricity liberalisation debate, so in 1991 they had rebranded their proposal as 'third party access' (TPA).[2] DG Energy were now being more circumspect and were careful to disassociate TPA from a purely open access regime, explaining that:

> the term "open access" is used to denote that all possible users (generators, independent power producers, distributors, small and large consumers) have access to transmission services, versus the term "third party access" that is used to denote access to these services available only to certain types of customers (for example, only large consumers and distributors).[3]

This more ambiguous framing then opened the door to negotiation between the various European Economic Community (EEC) Member States and industry stakeholders about the nature and extent of competition. António Cardoso e Cunha, the Commissioner for Energy, was speaking to the two sides of the industry at this time. He spoke of the need to address 'the main technical, economic and administrative elements to be taken account of in the formulation of a Community policy on whether, and how, third parties should have access to electricity networks', but when speaking at an energy industry conference, he was more reformist, stating that citizens of Europe 'cannot accept the limitation to gas and electricity transit through networks which have technical capacity of transport available but are linked to exclusivity contracts; this is why we are insisting on some form of freedom of access'.[4]

Competing Market Visions

With a view to reframing the debate around competition, in late 1990 the European Commission set up two new 'ad-hoc' committees in order to gauge stakeholder receptiveness to TPA before an official set of draft proposals was published.[5] There were separate committees created for electricity and gas, with each being comprised of two groupings: one with the 12 Member States (*Comité Consultatif Etats Membres Electricité* and *Comité Consultatif Etats Membres Gaz*—CCEME and CCEMG)[6] and a second comprising industry stakeholders, a mix of large utilities and consumer representatives (Professional Consultative Committee on Electricity and Gas—PCCE and PCCG).[7] Chaired by the Commission, each committee met monthly throughout 1990 and early 1991, with four separate reports and a summary report published by the Commission in May 1991.[8] The composition of the groups, particularly on the industry side, meant that the reformist views of the Commission were balanced by a more conservative and sceptical industry perspective.

In a contemporary account, McGowan summarised the dynamics within these groups as follows: 'the balance of opinion was against change, though the presence of the governments of Britain and some other states (principally Ireland and Portugal) on the government inquiry, and their utilities and some industrial consumers on the technical committee, meant the Committees were unable to present a unanimous criticism of further liberalisation'. He noted that while the TPA concept wasn't rejected outright, as some had expected, both 'lobbying by opponents of the policy and the uncertain balance of opinion within the Commission meant that the proposals for further liberalization were steadily watered down over the course of 1991'.[9]

In relation to electricity and TPA, all of the national representatives were in favour of more integration between the national systems, but the majority view of the Member States' committee (CCME) was that cooperation between producers was an alternative and more desirable way of making the industry more efficient. Concern was expressed that the 'cooperative spirit', which was fundamental to UCPTE and other industry bodies, would be lost to competition. The view amongst many of the representatives was that TPA may actually reduce efficiency by interfering with existing arrangements for dispatch and adding nothing that wasn't already possible under the new transit directive. Also, that TPA would make demand for electricity more difficult to predict, hence making planning and long-term investments in assets much less efficient. The last paragraph of the CCME report stated that 'the sceptics of the possible advantages and modalities of implementing TPA significantly outnumbered those who were favourable'.

In relation to the PCCE Committee (industry stakeholders), the European Commission noted that 'the consultations have shown that clear differences of opinion exist regarding the advantages and disadvantages of the present system and those of a TPA regime'.[10] A key point of concern for the integrated utilities was the prospect of a legal obligation placed upon them to make capacity on their networks available to the market, thus requiring them to cede control of their systems, under certain circumstances, to the European Commission or some intergovernmental regulatory authority at the European level. This was 'regarded as unacceptable or illegal by most of the electricity industry representatives on the Committee'.[11]

Some potentially transformative proposals did emerge from the discussions however, particularly in relation to the coordination of trade and the prospect of greater centralisation of system operation at the European level. A key point of debate was whether a centralised merit order of some sort was included in the TPA regime; the PCCE Committee identified two possible solutions:[12] the first was termed a 'Clearing House Mechanism', which would have involved each transmission operator calculating a dispatch based on the marginal costs of generation, with financial compensation flowing to generators who could adjust their contracted output in line with this system merit order. Another proposal was to replicate the English/Welsh Electricity Pool (see Chap. 4), with each generator bidding into the market and a single system price being calculated, with financial contracts working alongside this to enable buyers and sellers hedge risks. Many representatives argued that the British approach was still too uncertain and had not been tested adequately. The general view was that neither of these options would be feasible at the European level, 'although trading between national and regional systems organised in this way would be feasible'.[13]

An alternative to these proposals was put forward by Eurelectric[14] who argued that TPA would 'impede' the mission of 'providing a service of general economic interest' and that the existing model based on cooperation between utilities could be improved 'while retaining its advantages in terms of economic and security-related efficiency'.[15] They proposed an alternative 'Industrial Model' of electricity supply system operation, essentially retaining an 'integrated production-transmission system', whilst enhancing cooperation. They criticised the TPA model where only certain 'customers' would have access to the market, that is, distributors and large industrial consumers. This would create two markets, which they described as a 'half-slave, half-free' sector.[16] In the integrated system, with 'exclusive service areas', Eurelectric argued, 'producers have little reason to apply cross subsidies as their market share is not dependent thereon'. This, they argued, required less regulatory supervision to protect certain customers as they are all essentially treated the same. With TPA, however, 'each producer will be encouraged to revert to cross subsidies, to the detriment of captive customers, in order to win or retain his share of the competitive market, and thus at least ensure global coverage of his costs'.[17]

Eurelectric argued that regulation of a TPA regime would need to be jointly at the national and European levels: 'National authorities could draw up and implement legal codes based on agreed principles laid down in Community legislation. Regulation at Community level would be necessary for cross-frontier TPA trade, as well as oversight to ensure harmonisation of national regimes. Community action would also be needed to remove any competitive distortions which were not likely to be driven out by TPA competition'.[18] So, counterintuitively, regulation would need to increase, contrary to the free market ideology.

In a broader sense, the 'Industrial Model' was framed as the one of the future. The Eurelectric document deemed direct competition for customers in the electricity supply sector an old fashioned concept, referencing the victory of centralised alternating (AC) over local direct current (DC) systems in the early years of the industry. During the inter-war years the 'Industrial Model' arose due to the inadequacies of competition, becoming 'a common industrial operating method thus appearing as the historical result of selection, introduced progressively due to competition, of forms of organization and regulation enabling the electricity supply sector to carry out its mission more efficiently'.[19] Competition, Eurelectric argued, would have a role to play, but should be limited to the purchasing of fuels in order to apply downward pressure on costs, while 'competitive' wholesale spot markets should be confined to utility-utility trade. They bluntly stated: 'Opening of the market to competition at production level – yes, but opening the electricity supply grids to third parties in general – no',[20] and cited the examples of the US and Spain where competition had been introduced, whilst keeping the advantages of the 'Industrial Model'.[21]

Whilst Eurelectric was the prominent industry voice, its single unified message masked a diversity of views and interests within the industry, which was not totally united against competition. In their submission Eurelectric tellingly referred to themselves as the 'continental members', indicating that they were not seeking to incorporate the views of the newly privatised British companies. There were also differences between public and privately owned utilities, whilst local utilities were split between those who saw the advantages of more choice in the generation market and those who were keen to protect monopolies and cross-subsidies.

Acting as a strong counterpoint to Eurelectric were consumer and employers' organisations such as the International Federation of Industrial Energy Consumers, the Union of Industrial and Employers' Confederations of Europe and the European Chemical Industries Council (IFIEC,

UNICE and CEFIC, respectively). The IFIEC, in their submission to the committees, framed the issue as one of providing the 'Power of Choice' in the electricity market, arguing that 'there are no insuperable technical obstacles to TPA'.[22] They argued that as a result of the transit reform, and other industry developments, utilities could increasingly benefit from 'choice' and the ability to access cheaper energy sources. These benefits of competition, they argued, needed to be passed on and extended to all consumers. They countered some of Eurelectric's arguments about the downsides of competition: 'Customers would be willing, indeed would seek to sign, long term contracts, and this would aid investment planning and hence, security of supply',[23] while open access would enhance energy security by providing more diversity to the system. Unsurprisingly, they made forceful arguments about the needs of industry, with energy costs being a crucial factor in determining competitiveness and the location of production globally.

The Commission's Two Routes to Reform

It was clear from the outcome of the consultation process that the European Commission would need to thread a fine line as it sought to achieve a form of TPA. The strategy it adopted was a hybrid one: on the one hand, it sought to exploit the political route via institutional mechanisms introduced as part of the Single European Act (SEA), in particular Article 100A which made provision for qualified majority voting (QMV) in certain areas, while at the same time pursuing the legal route; that is, a much stricter application to the electricity sector of the existing EEC Treaty articles covering state monopolies. As outlined below, the Commission had to play a smart game—a carrot and stick approach—with DGIV (Competition) threatening member states with legal action once DGXVII (Energy) faced blockages to its pursuit of the political route to reform.

Despite the growing recognition of the need for a political compromise, it was generally recognised by legal scholars of the time that the European Commission possessed the requisite powers under the EEC Treaty to force Member States to open up their electricity markets to a significant extent. For example, it was argued by one legal commentator that the earlier transit reform 'does little more than place those Commission powers which, theoretically, it has enjoyed for over thirty years in a more concrete procedural context'.[24] The 1957 Treaty of Rome did not exclude electricity, or energy more generally, but in practice many national utilities had been granted monopolies and exclusive rights to import and export power by national governments, and this practice had gone largely unchecked, with electricity being regarded as having some form of 'special status'. This was not a legal fact however, and based on a number of cases referred to the European Court of Justice (ECJ), electricity, like oil and gas products, had been legally classified as a good,[25] thus falling within the legal orbit of the original treaty articles. Particularly important was Article 37 which, following an initial transition period which ceased in 1970, required state monopolies of a commercial character to be adjusted to ensure no discrimination against the products of other Member States. However, there was some ambiguity with respect to 'the definition of the type of enterprise covered by Article 37'[26] and the role of the Commission in its enforcement. As a result, it took a period of time for the case law to be built up around its application.

Also relevant were 'rules of competition', in particular Articles 85 and 86[27] prohibiting 'mergers or abuse of market power to be used to distort competition'.[28] Article 90 covered the application of competition rules specifically to publicly owned companies and those which had been granted some form of exemption by a Member State, such as monopoly rights to utilities supplying essential services like gas, water and electricity. Under Article 90(1), such undertakings were prohibited from abusing their dominant position and using their special rights to restrict trade or competition (particularly Articles 37, 85 and 86). Article 90(2) set out circumstances in which there may be exemptions to this:

> Undertakings entrusted with the operation of services of general economic interest or having the character of a revenue-producing monopoly shall be subject to the rules contained in this Treaty, in particular to the rules on competition, in so far as the application of such rules does not obstruct the performance, in law or in fact, of the particular tasks assigned to them. The development of trade must not be affected to such an extent as would be contrary to the interests of the Community'.[29]

As a counterpoint to Article 90(2), Article 90(3) provided the European Commission with direct powers 'to enforce competition in the public sector either by way of decisions or special directives addressed to member states, which do not require prior Council approval'.[30]

Throughout the process of electricity market reform, opponents of electricity liberalisation drew on the provisions in Article 90(2) to argue that TPA and competition for customers would result in the cherry-picking of lucrative consumers and would compromise the ability of monopolies to achieve their state-mandated public service obligations (PSOs), thus providing a legal basis to limit the application of the EEC Treaty and the European Commission's powers to enforce Article 90(3).

However, in 1991 a decision delivered by the ECJ in relation to a dispute about competition in the telecommunications sector provided impetus to the European Commission's use of legal powers to bring about electricity liberalisation. Following the adoption of a telecoms directive in 1988,[31] France, with the support of Belgium, Italy, Greece and Germany, had challenged the Commission's powers to abolish exclusive rights to supply terminal equipment which had been conferred on its state telecoms monopoly. The ECJ published its decision on 19 March 1991[32] and essentially sided with the European Commission in this case, interpreting the Commission's powers under Article 90(3) very widely. It pointed out in its judgement that not all exclusive rights can be compatible with the EEC Treaty and that the Commission had to exert its supervisory obligations, having the ability, under Article 86, to place limitations upon exclusive rights which had been conferred by a Member State. The essence of the judgement was that exclusive rights for importing and for the commercial marketing of telecoms equipment and services were anti-competitive. In legal terms, the telecommunications network no longer needed to be treated as a single entity; certain services, such as the provision of terminal equipment, could be designated as competitive and telecoms monopolies could be prosecuted under Article 86 if they abused their position by preventing new entrants into these markets. This had clear implications for the import and export of electricity via transmission grids; the system as a whole could no longer be characterised as a 'natural monopoly'.

The European Commission was buoyed by the judgement and did not hesitate to capitalise on the new window of opportunity. Two days following the decision, on the 21 March 1991, Leon Brittan, the Competition Commissioner, sent a letter to each member state, apart from Germany and Luxembourg, 'informing them that they would now be required to abolish all statutory exclusive rights to import or export electricity'.[33] The ten countries were accused of restrictive practices in control of import/export across their territories; under Article 169 the Commission required them to, within two months, comply with the treaty 'by annulling their import/export restrictions or otherwise face further legal action by the Commission'. There were immediate implications for countries like

France, Ireland, Italy and Greece which had traditional state-owned utilities which operated vertically integrated monopolies, along with less integrated systems, like the Netherlands, which had an element of competition between generators within the market but retained monopoly rights for import and export. Although this move by the European Commission was largely symbolic, because of the absence of a legal regime for TPA at the time, it did serve the purpose of flexing the Commission's muscles and drew a clear analogy between telecoms and electricity liberalisation.

The telecoms ruling was not viewed as a silver bullet however; in reality not all electricity cases involved obvious state monopolies that could be tackled via Article 90, rather many were individual instances of anti-competitive behaviour that would have to be addressed one-by-one via Articles 85 and 86. There would be practical difficulties in doing this. There was a particular concern about the level of organisational capacity within the European Commission which would constrain their ability to pursue a legalistic and highly complex route to market reform. By the late 1980s, DG Energy had around 450 staff, but more than half of these were working in Luxembourg on Euratom nuclear safeguards.[34] Enforcing change via the legal route and fighting multiple and complex cases in the ECJ would be onerous.

Aside from the practical and administrative challenges, there were concerns that this would result in an uneven reform process where the state-dominated national industries were reformed quicker than the more complex cases where electricity industries were more fragmented and had a mixed ownership model (e.g. Germany, Netherlands and Denmark). And, even if competition could be imposed in theory, the market would need to be monitored and regulated. The Commission would have had to evolve into some form of supranational regulatory agency or competition authority for the entire electricity generation and supply sector. This clearly would not have been acceptable to the Member States who closely guarded their national autonomy and, for reasons discussed already, were threatened by the prospect of competition as it would likely result in a dismantling of their national champions and/or a process of 'cherry-picking' where the most lucrative customers would be taken by foreign suppliers. This fed into the subsidiarity agenda—limiting the scope of European-level control—which was increasingly salient at the time as the Maastricht Treaty was being negotiated, with talk of a specific energy chapter being included. As Cameron summarises: 'For the energy sector subsidiarity is a principle that has had particular significance. It has both contributed to and constrained the Commission in its attempts to promote a single market in energy'.[35] An overarching political solution via a community-wide directive seemed appealing given the nature of this complex and tortuous legal route to reform.

The Single European Act, agreed in 1985, provided the institutional platform for such a political agreement. Under this, measures to achieve a single market by the 1992 deadline would not require unanimity in the Council of Ministers, rather a qualified majority voting rule would be applied. Another important provision within the SEA was an amendment to Article 149 of the EEC Treaty which expanded the role of the European Parliament. Under the new 'co-operation procedure', the Commission's legislative proposals would now be sent to the parliament who would, following a first reading, would send notification to the Council of its opinion. With the Commission's proposal and the parliament's opinion, the Council of Ministers would then seek to take a common position, which would then be sent back to the parliament for a second reading. Then, within a three-month period, the parliament could either 'accept the common position, refrain from acting, reject it or propose amendments to the common position'. If amendments were made and the Commission decided to accept them, the Council could then ratify using QMV. However, if the parliament rejected the common position, the Council could 'only adopt the instrument unanimously'.[36] As we shall see, as the first electricity liberalisation directive was being negotiated in this new institutional context, the European Parliament, and in particular the powerful committee known as CERT—Parliament Committee on Energy, Research and Technology—became highly influential in shaping the outcome.

By 1991 the European Commission was at a crossroads; the question it faced was whether to pursue the legal or political route to reform. The strategy adopted, unsurprisingly, was to seek member state consent for a managed transition to competition in the electricity sector, but to keep the threat of legal enforcement in the background as a means of keeping the process on track. This was pragmatic given the highly complex nature and scope of the reform, and the capacity limitations already mentioned within DG Energy. But it also reflected internal differences within the European Commission. DG Energy, perhaps because it was closer to the energy sector, was more acutely aware of the fundamental differences between key stakeholders in terms of the desirability and implications of TPA and competition. Often in contrast to DG Competition, they generally adopted a 'soft approach', characterised elsewhere as 'Bargained incrementalism, with legal threats held in reserve'.[37]

The threat of using competition law to force Member States to open up their electricity markets was continually brought up however, particularly by Leon Brittan. DG Energy, at times, became frustrated that DG Competition was jumping the gun, so to speak, by threatening the industry with imposed and radical reform along the lines of the telecoms industry. The effect, from DG Energy's point of view, was to alienate those stakeholders who would have been inclined to support a limited and phased reform. The French case was highlighted in this context; 'once the main champions of the free market', but, 'because of the threats to the integrity of EdF, [have] become its main opponents'. There was a view that the reform process at the time was characterised by 'wild outbursts from DG4'.[38] All of these factors influenced a decision to opt for a politically negotiated framework directive, leaving a large degree of autonomy for each Member State to interpret liberalisation in a way which aligned with the particular circumstances of their national electricity regimes.

TPA Proposals

It was in this institutional context that the European Commission came to publish its draft proposals for TPA later in 1991. In these proposals the commission seemed to be taking a hard line, raising the prospect of forcing Member States to abolish exclusive rights by deploying Article 90, whilst also emphasising the need to develop common rules around TPA. It was commented that the proposals had 'echoes of the UK electricity restructuring', but the Commission did place emphasis on the subsidiarity principle in order to mitigate accusations of a top-down imposition of radical reforms on the industry, seeking to 'leave Member States with a high degree of flexibility to implement their own free market system'.[39] Based on security criteria, operators of transmission networks could refuse an access request if it interfered with a statutory obligation or another prior contractual commitment. Choice in the market would be restricted to large users[40] and the proposals also included an allowance for meeting 20% of electricity demand from domestic sources. *Power in Europe* commented that the 'idea of subsidiarity haunts a number of the draft Articles'.[41]

At the time the UK was the only real advocate for electricity liberalisation, but within the European Commission there was a strong meeting of minds between Leon Brittan and Cardoso e Cunha. Cardoso e Cunha, who had appointed Nicholas Argyris to lead a dedicated internal energy market (IEM) taskforce within DG 17 to progress the reforms, described British liberalisation as 'an encouraging model'.[42] He presented his plans before a more sceptical commission in July 1991, in advance of presenting it to the Council of Ministers. At the meeting of the commissioners, Cardoso e Cunha received a lukewarm response, and it was decided to push back the date for presenting the proposals until the Autumn of 1991. The commissioners were wary as the deployment of Article 90(3) implied in the proposals would in effect bypass the other European institutions during a sensitive political period in the run-up to Maastricht. This negotiation within the Commission, and the pushback against the Brittan/ Cardoso e Cunha axis, saw the origins of what became known as the 'three-stage approach' to achieving the IEM: the directive on transit had been the first stage; the upcoming second stage involved unbundling (separation of generation and transmission) and TPA, to be agreed by the end of 1992, whilst the third stage involved the extension of competition across the customer base, but this was deliberately left vague and open in terms of timescales.

However, despite these concessions, Cardoso e Cunha was 'still unable to win approval for his dossier and, instead, was instructed to present his ideas verbally to the Energy Council for some initial feedback from the Member States'.[43] At this meeting with the energy ministers (29 October 1991), he outlined the new phased approach, emphasising that the reform will involve a 'step-by-step approach' and a recognition of the subsidiary principle, outlining that 'the Community must not impose rigid mechanisms, but rather should define a framework enabling Member States to opt for the system best suited to their natural resources, the state of their industry and their energy policies'. He made it clear that Article 100A would be the main mechanism through which this reform is achieved, on the basis that 'this provides for a political dialogue with the Council and the European Parliament under the cooperation procedure, and also enables the consultations with other interested parties to be pursued'. He noted however that 'the Commission reserves the right to make use of all the powers conferred on it by the Treaty as and when appropriate'.[44]

At this stage it was foreseen that both large industrial users and distribution companies would be eligible to purchase freely in the market, but the extent of this would be limited by load thresholds yet to be agreed (or for the case of distribution companies in terms of a percentage of their overall supply). The lack of clarity around these key parameters meant that competition for customers would not be achieved by the end of 1992, rather this was pushed back to 1 January 1996. By the end of 1992—the original deadline for full competition—along with implementing directives on transit and price transparency (the first stage), each Member State would be required to end exclusive rights for the construction of energy infrastructure and power plants, to require vertically integrated utilities to be 'unbundled', involving a separate accounts and management structures for generation, transmission and distribution functions, and, ambitiously, that TPA be introduced. TPA was defined as an obligation 'to offer access to their network to certain eligible entities at reasonable rates, within the limits of available transmission and distribution capacity'. A final third stage, to be reached by 1 January 1996, was left deliberately vague; with it being 'defined in detail in the light of the experience acquired during the second … This will involve, in particular, adapting the criteria of eligibility for TPA'.[45]

The UK and Portugal were in general agreement, with France, Italy and Belgium firmly against. After this meeting the proposals were put on hold with a view to initiating a phase of bilateral negotiations with the Member States. Following these early encounters, it was questioned in the industry press 'whether other directorates, namely DG4, the competition office, will keep the free market sword at the throat of Europe's power utilities, or whether that sword is being placed slowly but surely back into the scabbard'. The more controversial aspect of the earlier proposal circulated within the Commission in July 1991, to utilise Article 90(3), 'appear[ed] now to have been consigned to the Community dustbin'.[46]

The European Commission returned with a final proposal for an electricity liberalisation directive in early 1992. A change from the first draft was that more emphasis was placed on subsidiary, with each Member State retaining autonomy for pricing in relation to non-TPA (mostly domestic) customers, for distribution (particularly related to granting exclusive rights), licencing and permitting, and whether to set up a regulatory agency or rely on its national competition legislation. The essence of the proposal was a staggered and phased approach, using the route of Article 100A, requiring approval from the European Parliament and to be endorsed by the Council of Ministers. TPA thresholds in the proposals at this point were for industrial consumers of 100 GWh/year or more and distributors who supplied 3% or more of a Member State's demand. So, based on these thresholds, competition would be limited to only 4 or 500 large consumers and 100 or so distributors. As we discuss further below, the eligibility criteria for TPA became a key sticking point in the negotiations.

A document outlining the three-stage approach was put before an informal meeting of the energy ministers in April 1992. There was still not significant support from Member States, with the UK and Portugal still in favour, and Italy, France and now Spain against any form of TPA; Denmark and Germany were somewhere in the middle. The German position was interesting at this point. As discussed in the previous chapter, there has been a drive for liberalisation and competition reforms within Germany, and politicians like Jürgen Moellemann (economy minister) and Wolfgang Schäuble (Chairman of CDU/CSU at Federal level) were now signalling a willingness to consider the Commission's reforms. There were even reports that *Rheinisch-Westfälisches Elektrizitätswerk* (RWE) had already started unbundling their accounts; they had certainly started to use the European-level liberalisation process as leverage, issuing statements calling for reforms to the German coal subsidy regime. The German government were however concerned about reciprocity, in the event that non-German utilities, which retained a protected market share, would have a competitive advantage.

At the subsequent formal Energy Council on 21 May 1992, however, most of the Member States declared their opposition to TPA. The Danish had previously signalled support for TPA, but were less inclined to support at this stage. The Danes were particularly exposed to foreign sales into their market as exiting Danish law prohibited the making of profit from electricity sales and required utilities to reinvest the proceeds. Such obligations would not apply to non-Danish companies, providing them with a competitive advantage. Also, Denmark had recently invested huge sums of money in building up its gas grid and had granted an import/export monopoly to its state-owned gas importer and pipeline operator—*Dangas*—as a means of recouping this investment. They were also lobbying strongly for a definition of public service obligations which included environmental protection. Previously, both the Dutch and Germans voted against the gas transit directive and the Dutch, French and Germans were calling on the Commission to withdraw and redraft their proposals. The Dutch were particularly concerned about the implications for the gas sector and impacts on its substantial export market, seeking separate processes for electricity and gas liberalisation. Following this, there was little progress on electricity market liberalisation at the June 1992 Energy

Council meeting. The UK, a key proponent of TPA, was due to take over the council presidency from Portugal in the second half of 1992, and this was expected to add momentum to the political process behind the IEM. In an effort to break the impasse, the UK had created a 'high level working group of senior officials', under the chairmanship of Robert Priddle, a senior UK civil servant.[47] However, in November 1992, the Council requested the Commission to 'consider modifications'—to 'revise and resubmit'.

The Negotiation Phase

Between the end of 1992 and when the first electricity directive was finally adopted at the end of 1996, there were three different commissioners with responsibility for energy matters,[48] and it is fair to say that none were as pro-competition as Cardoso e Cunha. Abel Matutes, who followed Cardoso e Cunha, was less ideologically committed to competition and was somewhat sceptical of the British approach, tending also to have a less abrasive relationship with industry. His willingness to expend political capital in enforcing a structural reform on the electricity industry was limited as his appointment was viewed as temporary, in order to fill a gap before the new European Commission commenced. He was also responsible for transport. In line with this softer approach, Matutes signalled he would be willing to water down the Commission's TPA proposal; 'negotiated TPA' would 'maintain the principle of a more competitive system but leave it to individual users to request such access; utilities would be able to refuse access on the grounds of limitations in transmission capacity and public service obligations'.[49] National authorities would arbitrate in any disputes and, similar to the transit directive, EC institutions would only intervene as a last resort.

The European Parliament became an even more important actor following the signing of the Maastricht Treaty in early 1992 which gave it 'co-decision powers'.[50] A key change arising from this was that the parliament now had the power to reject a Council position, resulting in the failure of a proposal. It required the Council to enter into direct dialogue with the parliament, in contrast to the previous procedure set out in the SEA 'under which only those Parliamentary amendments supported by the Commission could be adopted by a majority in the Council'.[51] This created the need for a closer dialogue between the three institutional pillars of the EC and meant the process of agreeing an electricity liberalisation directive began to be characterised more by institutional politics than purely technical or economic arguments. Upon leaving office at the end of 1992 to take up a role within Portuguese politics, Cardoso e Cunha pointed to this changing dynamic: 'I dare say that the main technical oppositions have been removed … We are now coming into pure political discussions'.[52]

The views of the powerful committee CERT now became of upmost importance, creating a new actor in the decision-making apparatus, one which was sceptical of competition and its impacts on the public service role of the electricity sector in many jurisdictions. CERT had been highly critical of TPA and the Commission's 'three-stage' proposal, being particularly concerned about the impacts on small consumers. Claude Desama (Belgian, Labour), CERT's Chairman and rapporteur for the proposal, was critical of what he viewed as an 'unquestioning belief in the virtues of competition as an automatic guarantee of economic prosperity', whilst recognising that 'there is nothing sacrosanct about a system based on monopolies operating in fragmented markets'.[53] CERT held an IEM hearing on 1–2 October 1992 at which at least 'three-quarters of the speakers were against TPA'.[54] Desama summed up by saying there is emerging support for two of the three aspects of the IEM proposals, accounting unbundling and exclusive rights, but not on TPA. He highlighted as major concerns the issues of long-term planning and the likely conflict between public service objectives and market access. Following this, some feared that the parliament's proposals may be rejected outright by the Commission, and Brittan was making noises about deploying the full force of competition law on the industry.

The opinion of the European Parliament was not due until June of 1993, and in advance of this, in February, CERT convened a working group to firm up its views and formulate amendments. Subsequently, Desama published the views of the committee in draft form, covering TPA and the general strategy for liberalising the sector. CERT proposed 'a substantial redefinition of the programme', seeking to 'reorientate policy by emphasizing harmonization over liberalization'.[55] Harmonisation was seen as a necessary precursor to competition and would require a considerable extension of the timeframe for introducing TPA, 'with a transition period to allow for harmonization ending in 1998'.[56] Liberalisation, as in dismantling monopolies, unbundling, competition and open network access, would have to wait.

In relation to competition, CERT proposed a 'two-track solution', based on 'transitional periods and subsidiarity'. This would involve a four-year 'trial period' between 1994 and 1998 with a choice between 'two organisational structures': the Commission's TPA model or 'a more regulated model'. The regulated model would offer 'a more limited form of liberalisation and TPA', in the sense that 'a strict separation of generation and networks would not be required as part of this option'. This retaintained some of the Commission's ideas, such as 'the abolition of exclusive rights for electricity generation', whilst shying away 'from much of the rest, such as the licensing system for building and operating new gas and power transmission and distribution lines'. The alternative model would involve the creation of a new European regulator with a wide remit to oversee harmonisation in the areas of 'the organization of markets, rules on environmental protection, principally on land use, accounts transparency and public service obligations'. Desama argued that for those who do not favour TPA, they should be free to maintain the 'three pillars of economic wisdom: the possibility of concluding long term contracts, sufficient volume of captive demand and the ability to assume public service obligations'. The idea of a two-track approach was described by critics as 'a la carte legislation'.[57]

Socialists, including Desama himself, were the powerful force in the European Parliament at this time and held the majority of seats on CERT. However, there was significant disagreement amongst the committee members. Criticisms of Desama's proposals were led by Christian Rovsing, a Danish MEP of the European Peoples Party (EPP), who called for parliament to tone down its criticisms and act as a friendly broker between the Council and the Commission. Rovsing was concerned that if parliament could not broker a compromise, the Commission would pursue liberalisation via the courts, in his view, to the detriment of Danish energy sector interests. The ECJ would unlikely take energy security criteria into account in its decisions, which had been the basis for much of the Danish government's energy consumption taxes; effectively subsidies which were introduced following the 1970s oil crises in order to favour domestic sources, especially gas.

By the time CERT met in October 1993, MEPs were faced with in the region of 600 amendments to the Commission's proposals for the liberalisation of each Member States' electricity and gas sectors, most of which were put forward by Desama and Rovsing. Unsurprisingly, given its political composition, CERT sided with Desama at this meeting, while Rosving's amendments for more competition, in line with the Commission's ideas, were rejected.

In the revised version of his report, Desama backed away from the 'two systems' model and instead proposed a 'common core' where 'all Member States adhere to a minimum degree of mostly harmonisation, along with some liberalisation, over a four year trial period (1994-1998)',[58] covering three main areas: harmonisation, liberalisation and public service obligations. The CERT proposals would allow distribution companies to retain their monopoly franchises and exclusive rights, whilst allowing electricity generators to directly contract with energy-intensive users, but this would require approval from the local distributor. This then was some distance away from the European Commission's original intentions.

The European Parliament would need 260 votes for the Commission's proposals to be altered in this fundamental way, and at this stage the MEPs were divided; the threshold could not be reached on the opinion before a vote on the first reading. Although the number of amendments was now whittled down to 240, the EPP group viewed Desama's draft as extreme and counter to the original proposal, and were looking for agreement along the lines of the Commission's proposals. They abstained in the final vote held during the parliament's plenary session, making it difficult for Desama to obtain the required votes.

Given the sequencing of decision making and the Council meetings, a common position between the Council, Commission and European Parliament was not looking likely until mid-1994. The Commission, for its part, was unwilling to accept the maintenance of local distribution/supply monopolies, as CERT had insisted. However, Matutes was showing signs of an openness to compromise by backing down on compulsory TPA and signalling a willingness to accept 'negotiated' TPA (nTPA)—as opposed to regulated TPA (rTPA). He argued that the harmonisation proposals that CERT had put forward would need to be accompanied by meaningful liberalisation reforms. He addressed the members of CERT on 27 July 1993, outlining that 'he could agree to a system of voluntary TPA on a negotiated basis', with disputes to be 'subject to compulsory arbitration'.[59] At an industry conference held shortly afterwards, Matutes outlined the benefits of the nTPA approach, as avoiding top-down imposed reform and excessive regulation, and respecting subsidiarity: 'Each Member State will adopt a system that suits its own situation and traditions';[60] so, for example,

Germany could rely on its anti-trust legislation while the UK pursued its regime based on licencing and independent regulation.

Despite these overtures to the parliament, the Commission did not give up on its carrot and stick approach. Karel Van Miert, the new Competition Commissioner, was frustrated with lack of progress and it was announced in May 1993 that the commission would take a number of member states to court over import/export monopolies.[61] This followed the initial letters sent in 1991 setting out infringement proceedings. Meanwhile, Matutes was looking for the ECJ to provide a clearer definition of public service obligations and how far it could be used as a justification for exclusive rights and monopolies.[62] The need for clarity in this respect was pressing, as in 1993 the Commission was dealing with 1250 cases which involved accusations of restrictions on market access and monopoly abuse in the electricity sector alone.

However, in June of 1993 Van Miert agreed to put on hold proceedings against the six Member States, a decision which had been demanded by the French Industry Minister, Gérard Longuet. This followed an announcement by France and the Netherlands that, as a result of the Commission's move, they would be willing to review their legislation; Matutes stated that he wanted 'to give them a chance to confirm their good intentions'.[63] The Dutch promised to change their legislation and remove Article 34 of their 1989 Electricity Law which granted an import monopoly to SEP, a cooperative of the four largest producers.[64] There were signals that the Dutch may now switch sides in the TPA debate.

Although Van Miert had suspended the proceedings in June 1993, the Commission became increasingly frustrated with a lack of movement. A key motivating factor was the need to speed up the process in order to get agreement at the May 1994 Energy Council, in advance of the upcoming elections for the European Parliament, after which there would be a new European Commission appointed, which perhaps would be less inclined to push through the liberalisation reforms. The Commission was also worried about being cut out of a potential deal between the Council and the European Parliament. MEPs had been very critical of the Commission for taking the Member States to court and threatened a vote on a resolution calling on the Commission to pull back. The view was that this is was not appropriate at a time when the co-decision procedure around the TPA proposals was underway.

In this new spirit of compromise and consensus seeking, the DG Energy developed a new internal document which floated an idea about splitting the market between franchise and free market areas. This would leave public supply—with franchises and exemptions—largely untouched. The proposals involved negotiated—not compulsory—TPA to be largely limited to the 'independent or non-public sector', that is, independent producers, large customers (over 100 GWh consumption) and distribution companies, but only over an agreed threshold of their total supply. The Commission wanted distribution companies to have TPA so that small consumers could benefit, although with some provisions to limit access to the market on the basis of public service obligations (PSOs). The Commission also took on board counter-proposals that CERT had made in relation to constructing new power lines and generation capacity: that competition for new lines and plants could be either through licencing—like the UK—or by a central planner which would identify capacity requirements and put the projects out to tender. Compulsory unbundling between generation and transmission was watered down in favour of a requirement to maintain separate accounts and greater transparency. These elements were what the Commission saw as the minimum baseline for electricity liberalisation.

Although these revised proposals on nTPA and limited market access were presented by the European Commission and discussed at the Energy Council meeting of 10 December 1993, this was mostly dominated by coal/hydrocarbon issues. The scope for significant movement was also limited at the next Energy Council (May 1994 in Greece) due to uncertainty presented by the upcoming European elections (scheduled for June 1994). As it was difficult to see how a second reading could happen before the elections, it was no surprise that there was little progress made on achieving a common position at the May Energy Council. An energy working group discussed several of the most contentious issues—'public service, access to networks, the transmission system operator, unbundling, and how competition in generation was actually going to work'—but 'there was little agreement on any of these points, and the only conclusions that emerged were from the Presidency rather than the Council, meaning there was little unanimity'.[65]

In the run up to this meeting a rival to TPA model known as the 'single buyer model' had been proposed by France and was tabled by Greece at the May 1994 Energy Council. Under this access regime, eligible customers—only the very large electricity-intensive consumers in the French proposal—would be able to enter into contracts for power imports, but only via the 'single buyer' who would purchase the power on their behalf and settle the transaction. The customer would effectively sell the imported power to the single buyer and be compensated for any price difference against supply via the public grid, with the single buyer making the decision about which sources of generation would meet the demand. The background to this was the Mandil Committee, which had been set up in 1993 by Eduaord Balldur, the newly elected conservative French Prime Minister, and tasked with reviewing the scope for electricity sector competition and contributing to a new White Paper on broader French industrial policy. The *Rapport Mandil*[66] was published in January 1994 and presented to the European Commission later that year. The approach they advocated would effectively leave the monopolies of national companies, like *Électricité de France* (EDF), intact; they would be responsible for central planning of the system, issuing tenders for new capacity and coordinating the majority of cross-border flows, in a manner very similar to the UCPTE model of trade between utilities discussed previously.

France was not the only country in favour such an approach. Greece saw the model as a means of protecting their highly centralised and publicly owned electricity system, an issue which was seen to be of strategic national importance given their relative electricity isolation and longstanding national security concerns. A number of countries had already begun to open up their generation markets and allow independent power producers (IPPs) compete; the single buyer concept was appealing as it would enable them to retain a strong element of central planning and control. In Ireland the national electricity company, the Electricity Supply Board (ESB), was in the process of being split into separate business units in a way which aligned with the approach, with one of the units being a central power purchaser for the entire market. Italy were also discussing restructuring proposals along these lines, while recent Spanish and Dutch reforms both retained a centralised purchaser of imports.

However, critics argued that it would give too much power to the single buyer who, as an effective monopoly, would act to limit competition and favour its own generation sources. Comparisons were made with the UK's failed 1983 Energy Act which, as outlined in Chap. 2, attempted to introduce competition into the generation market whilst maintaining the authority of the Central Electricity Generating Board (CEGB) over the system. A concern held by the UK and Portugal was that it simply recreated import/export monopolies which were already deemed to contravene the treaties, so it was decided at this meeting to investigate the legality of the single buyer concept. Under the Greek proposal, each Member State would have the choice between nTPA and the single buyer model and it was left open whether the single buyer needed to also be the transmission system operator (TSO). If it was to be integrated within the incumbent, a key requirement was that the single buyer unit would make purchasing decisions in an independent and non-discriminatory manner, particularly in relation to the decision of whether to procure power from domestic or foreign generators to fulfil the customer's contract.

Following the European elections of June 1994, there were personnel changes at the European Commission with two new commissioners responsible for energy being appointed in quick succession. Marcelino Oreja (Spanish, centre right) took up office in May 1994, followed quickly by Christos Papoutsis (Greek, socialist) who was part of the new Commission convened in January 1995. At this time energy was not a prestigious or particularly desirable job within the Commission. It was clearly a highly complex sector with conflicting agendas and interests; much political capital would need to be expended in forcing through radical reform, but it was gaining more prestige as the environmental issue rose up the agenda.[67] With respect to competition, Both Oreja and Papoutsis were closer to Matutes than to Cardoso e Cunha; focused more on aligning themselves with the changing political dynamic following Maastricht, as opposed to getting mired in the technical and legal details of the IEM.

The European elections of 1994 also changed the dynamic within CERT.[68] Only 16 of 31 Committee members were re-elected, but there was an element of continuity, with socialists remaining the largest group. There was however a significant dispute about who would act as the chair, which delayed the commencement of the committee's work. Initially a *Forza Europa* candidate (an independent group of Italian MEPs led by Silvio Berlusconi) looked to have been elected following a deal cut between political parties which meant they did not gain control of the Media Affairs Committee. Given Berlusconi's dominance of the Italian media sector, this was a concern for many. German socialist MEP Rolf Linkohr forced a vote and Desama was elected by 13 to 12 votes. The EPP MEPs subsequently walked out in protest that the *d'Hondt* method for allocating top jobs within the European Parliament was undermined and Desama subsequently resigned. A new election for a chair followed, with socialists initially seeking to compromise and vote for an EPP candidate. The EPP grouping refused the overtures and Umberto Scapagnini of Forza was eventually elected. The socialists remained an influential force however, with Gordan Adam as vice-chair and Desama as coordinator of the socialist MEPs on the committee.

At the following Energy Council meeting held in November 1994, there was broad agreement around a number of issues: introducing competition in generation, accounting unbundling and the need for a separate TSO, but debate continued about the coexistence of the single buyer and nTPA models, along with the definition of PSOs in the context of Article 90(2). Denmark and the Netherlands were lobbying for environmental goals to be explicitly linked to PSOs, but the opposing view was that a vague definition of the environment in relation to PSOs would leave the door open for a refusal of network access; for example, Denmark could refuse access on the basis of protecting its combined heat and power (CHP) plants, while France could protect its nuclear industry using similar criteria. The main contentious issue remained the meaning and extent of competition however. Germany, in particular, was concerned that those countries going down the single buyer route would have an advantage over states who opened up their markets more fully. There was talk that TPA countries should have the ability to restrict imports from single buyer countries. The issue was becoming more sensitive in Germany at this time and Helmut Kohl, who had just won an election but with a narrow majority, was increasingly aware of the sensitivities of the issue within his government and was keen to kick it into the long grass. As a result, a conclusion was not reached; unsurprising given the scheduled arrival of a new European Commission in January 1995.

Following the November 1994 meeting, the DG Energy undertook an investigation into whether the two models could coexist. There were divisions within the Commission, with Van Miert calling the single buyer model 'unacceptable', whereas Oreja seemed more accommodating. Van Miert subsequently gave a speech at Chatham House in London which was very critical of the single buyer concept, saying it would violate 'two fundamental principles for opening up the electricity market; first, that distributors should be independent of producers, and second that there should be no import/export monopoly'.[69] Shortly after, the Commission published its report. This included a further elaboration of the two models: nTPA was split into a licencing and tendering approach, with the latter enabling a Member State to influence more directly what new power plants and lines were to be constructed. Under the alternative model, the single buyer would tender for new capacity, with foreign capacity entitled to bid. As they purchased on behalf of consumers, the single buyer could decide on the type of generation (baseload, middle and peak) and fuel required, and in the tender document they could indicate whether domestic or imports were desired. If imports won the bid, the single buyer could not specify the fuel type, while the final decision would be made by an independent body who would issue and evaluate any tenders. The Commission also called for full unbundling of management between the single buyer and the integrated utility, along with independent oversight of its activities. The report suggested some balance between the two models as customers would likely have more choice under nTPA, but the single buyer model compared more favourably against the licencing/nTPA approach as, through its tendering process, generators inside and outside the market may have more access to contracts for new plant.

Overall, however, the Commission's working paper was highly critical of the single buyer approach and viewed the two models as incompatible. The view was that the singly buyer was contrary to treaty articles covering import restrictions and the Commission proposed significant changes to it if it was to be a viable option. They called for independent power producers to be able to enter the market on the basis of licensing, with tendering running alongside this. With this approach the singly buyer would still be a central planner, as the IPPs would need to deliver power via the central purchaser, but the IPPs would be able to contract directly with consumers, therefore a more competitive approach than the original French proposal. Also, worried that small consumers would lose out, the Commission were also calling for distributors to be able to shop around; France did not include this in their original proposal, most likely because they wished to retain the country's long history of uniform pricing for domestic customers.

The French government were of course critical of what they saw as a watering down of their proposed model, arguing it would undermine its ability for long-term planning and the fundamental principles of the French system since its nationalisation in 1946. The presidency of the Council of Ministers was now held by France and the next Energy Council meeting was scheduled for June 1995. This took place in the context of an ongoing French presidential election in which the liberalisation of public services was a hot political issue. During the campaign, Jacques Chirac had promised to protect the 'French style' of public services. At this next meeting ministers agreed on a number of broad points, agreeing that the two models could co-exist, but they were vague about the extent to which the single buyer model would have to be adjusted to make it equivalent to TPA.

The general view was that although there are many issues to be resolved, the outcome, which recognised the validity of the two models, was a victory for France. Others, such as the UK, were simply happy that the process hadn't collapsed. The upcoming December meeting was seen to be a fork in the road; if no progress was made the whole electricity liberalisation programme was likely to require a fundamental rethink. Papoutsis was signalling that if the issue was not resolved ten years after the inception of the original single market agenda, the Commission would recommend a reference back to the heads of government to decide if they wanted an IEM at all.

By this point Spain held the presidency and was looking to pin down a legal text on the two models. The Spanish, and the subsequent Italian presidency, ended up playing a key mediating role between the various Member States at the next two Energy Council meetings where agreement on liberalisation was finally reached. The December 1995 meeting took place amidst political turmoil, leading both France and Germany to request that the issue of electricity liberalisation be dropped from the meeting agenda entirely. In France mass public sector strikes were underway, while in Germany the political uncertainty following the recent Federal election saw the composition of the new government in flux, with Gunter Rexrodt, German economics minister and part of Free Democratic Party in Kohl's coalition, unsure of his job. Papoutsis was pushing for a one-off meeting dedicated to the IEM agenda to be held in the following months.

In the run up to the December Council meeting, debate was particularly focused on the question of distributor access to the market. The Spanish were floating a 'two-model' proposal with respect to distributor access, with one option to include them as eligible customers, but limited to 20% of their supply, and the second with no access for distributors but to compensate by lifting the threshold—provisionally agreed at 100 GWh/year electricity consumption—for industrial and commercial customers. This was unlikely to be accepted as the second option was very unpopular amongst single buyer model advocates, which now included an alliance of France, Greece, Luxembourg and Ireland. The alternative French proposal was a 'positive reciprocity' model; countries that didn't allow distributors access could not sell to distributors in other countries.

The next Energy Council meeting was in May of 1996 with an Italian presidency. Distributor access was still a key issue, with the Spanish compromise still in play. Meanwhile, new compromise solutions around the distribution issue were being floated by Italy and France. Italy was proposing that each country open up their markets according to an agreed and fixed percentage—somewhere in the range of 22–40% initially, to increase according to a 'progressivity clause'—with the composition of the eligible customers and whether distributors would be included being left to each Member State to decide.

The Italians also proposed an additional 'safeguard clause', which would offer some protection against cherry-picking to the Member State that decided to liberalise at a quicker rate. France was wary of this safeguard clause because they already had contracts in place with the British Regional Electricity Companies. Most countries supported this Italian proposal, but the UK and Germany were somewhat concerned and were calling for a high minimum market opening threshold to make the liberalisation process meaningful. They wanted a significant opening at the higher end of the range, of at least 40%, and at minimum a commitment to distributor access in the near future. France and Greece were opposed, with the French concerned that it would lead to a slippery slope where the percentage of market opening required would be continually ratcheted up. France proposed instead that the baseline should be decided on the basis of the size of the industrial customers. They were willing to agree that consumers over 100 GWh/year could shop around, constituting 22% of French market, but to have no market access for distributors. France signalled that they may be willing to compromise somewhat on this consumption threshold and to go down to 40 GWh/year—which would only increase market opening to 25% of the market—but distribution access was a red line. So, the Italian compromise proposal was based on a fixed percentage of the market while the French proposal was based on a consumption threshold.

One month prior to the May 1996 Energy Council meeting, a dialogue took place between the representative ministers from Italy, France and Germany (Alberto Clò, Franck Borotra and Gunter Rexrodt, respectively). They accepted the Italian proposed compromise as the basis for finalising an agreement, with specific details such as eligibility and the progressivity clause to be finalised. The basis of this compromise took the lower French figure for a consumption threshold of 40 GWh/year (equivalent to a 25% market share) and combined it with the earlier Italian proposal of a fixed percentage of the market. Distributors would only be guaranteed access to the market to supply those customers consuming above the 40 GWh/year threshold. Each country could then decide the composition of customers who would be eligible.

The ratcheting clause in the Italian proposal was subsequently revised, where market opening would then be expanded as the 40 GWh/year threshold was reduced by 10 GWh/year every three years, such that in nine years roughly 30% of the market would be opened. All parties agreed on the need for some kind of safeguard clause, but there were doubts about whether this was compatible with the treaties. The UK, who had wanted a transition to full competition within five years, were moving to the point where they were willing to accept minimal initial market opening as a way of getting the process started and concentrated on securing a more ambitious progressivity clause. Both the UK and Germany considered the threshold as far too high as this part of the market was already quite competitive, thus reducing the incentive to switch and delaying the ratcheting up of competition.

A decision was made to hold an extraordinary Energy Council meeting on 29 June in Luxembourg, but before this a bilateral meeting between France and Germany was held on 5 June in Dijon at which an outline compromise was agreed. This was based on the 40 GWh/year threshold—recalculated as 22% of market share across the Member States—but with a more accelerated market opening: the initial threshold would half to 20 GWh/year after three years and to 9 GWh/year after a further three. The market opening process would not commence until two years after the adoption of the new directive; Belgium and Ireland were to get an additional year and Greece an extra two years due to the specifics of their electricity systems. For countries opting for the single buyer model, this entity would need to operate separately from the vertically integrated supplier.

The view at the time was that Germany compromised more than France, which may have been partly due to the pressure exerted by French trade unions during this period, with French public sector workers staging a one-day strike, with approximately half of GDF's and EDF's employees involved. This then formed the basis of a common position which was unanimous and was to be presented to the European Parliament for second reading in September. Despite attempts by Desema and his colleagues on CERT to amend the proposal,[70] it was passed by parliament on 11 December 1996.[71]

An Evolving Market

This was not the end of the politics of Europe's electricity market; political shaping and intervention turned out to be an endemic feature of the market itself, rather than just part of this early negotiation phase. Following on from the implementation of the first electricity directive, the European Commission sought to provide further impetus to the electricity liberalisation project and decided in 2001 to table new proposals to accelerate the timeline towards full competition, with a view to allowing market access to all electricity consumers. What followed in 2003 was a second directive which required that from 1 July 2007 all consumers have access to the electricity market across the EU states.[72] This also included stricter 'unbundling' rules. Arising from the entrenched positions of some Member States, a necessary ambiguity in the first directive was the nature of the relationship between the generation and transmission activities; this merely required integrated companies to have separate functional divisions within their companies and to publish separate accounts. (In the end, no country implemented the single buyer due to the practical and administrative difficulties of doing so whilst complying with the directive).

The second directive placed a focus on legal separation of these entities, so while generation and transmission could be part of a wider corporate structure, they had to be distinct legal entities. Full 'ownership unbundling' was not made a requirement until 2009 following a third directive; and even at this stage countries were given the option to choose an alternative model—the creation of a separate, fully independent system operator (ISO). The second directive also saw steps towards a more robust regulatory regime for TPA. Countries had initially been given the choice between a regulated or negotiated TPA regime, but the Commission proposed to beef this up and mandate the regulated model. Therefore, all Member States were required to have an independent regulator and a European body for coordination across these National Regulatory Authorities was subsequently created in 2009—the Agency for the Cooperation of Energy Regulators [ACER].

The general problem driving these successive directives was that most countries were unenthusiastic about the model of competition initially envisaged by the European Commission. As Thomas explains: 'Only for the UK, Portugal, Sweden, Finland and perhaps the Netherlands could it be argued that the governments enthusiastically pushed for the implementation of the EU Electricity Directive. The other governments simply followed the letter of the Directive and had no real commitment to creating a competitive electricity market'.[73]

Change in the market was driven as much by corporate dynamics as government initiative as the energy companies with the largest balance sheets took advantage of the new opportunities presented to them. Rather than leading to greater diversity in these markets and direct competition between the incumbent energy (electricity and gas) companies, the main outcome of the reforms was a wave of M&A activity across the continent. As Cameron summarises, there were 'about 135 merger and acquisition transactions in the EU electricity and gas sector'[74] between 1998 and 2003. A notable effect of this was increasing concentration in many key markets and a reduction in the number of smaller utilities as they were taken over by larger conglomerates. As we saw in Chap. 4, this market dynamic began in Britain, initially as US companies entered the market by buying a number of the Regional Electricity Companies, but by the mid-2000s the market there was increasingly dominated by European players such as EDF, RWE and E.ON.

The late 1990s/early 2000s, just following the implementation of the first electricity directive, saw a radical shakeup of the German power market in particular, resulting from the business strategies pursued by the already dominant utilities in this new institutional environment. As discussed in the previous chapter, liberalisation was a double-edged sword for the large integrated utilities there; they would lose their protected markets, but it unleashed them to expand beyond their geographical confines and dominate the regional/local companies, and later to expand abroad. The process began when *PreussenElektra* and *Bayernwerk*, part of the VEBA and VIAG industrial groups respectively, were merged in 2000 to form E.ON., the same year that RWE and VEW[75] had proposed a merger. The mergers of VEBA/VIAG and RWE/VEW were highly controversial and scrutinised closely by the European Commission, as the two groups would hold over 80% of the supply market. A condition of approving these mergers was that the large former West German electricity utilities sell their stakes in VEAG (*Vereinigte Energiewerke AG*) in the former East, as otherwise the two groups dominating the German market would be commercially linked.[76] VEAG was subsequently purchased by HEW, by then a subsidiary of Vattenfall, the Swedish state utility. Vattenfall had in the early 2000s entered the German power market after it purchased the electricity utilities of Hamburg (HEW) and Berlin (BEWAG), along with a number of lignite power plants and mines in East Germany (the former LAUBAG company). These separate Vattenfall holdings were later brought together to form *Vattenfall Europe AG*. The subsequent creation of *Energie Baden-Württemberg AG* (EnBW) following the merger of *Energie-Versorgung Schwaben* (EVS) and *Badenwerk* (see below) saw the emergence of a 'big four' German electricity utilities (E.ON, Vattenfall, RWE and EnBW), who over the 2000s increased their market shares. Part of the reason for this was their integration into the local supply market and purchase of many local Stadwerke.

The trend towards concentration was not only confined to electricity as mergers between gas and electricity companies began to transform the wider German energy market. Most notable was the 2003 merger of E.ON with the gas importer and supplier *Ruhrgas*. While the German competition authority opposed this move, on the basis that it would diminish competition and potentially discriminate against other electricity generators reliant on *Ruhrgas*, the German government overruled and pushed it through. Brunekreeft and Twelemann speculate that the trend towards concentration in the energy market may have been a strategy pursued by the government; it would enable the creation of energy companies capable of competing in newly internationalising markets and strengthen the bargaining position of gas importers in the face of Russian market power.[77] Clearly, the German government struck a different balance between the benefits of diversity in the market versus integration and scale than the UK.

What characterised the German approach to liberalisation was this trend towards concentration combined with a very swift transition to competition and a weak regulatory regime. The Energy Act of 1998 went further than the minimum requirements to comply with the electricity liberalisation directive and opened up the market fully from the end of 1999. However, the TPA regime was weak—on the basis of negotiated rather than regulated access—with little or no regulatory oversight of network access until 2004. The 'Association Agreement' (*Verbändevereinbar*) for negotiated access (nTPA) clearly favoured the incumbents and was 'riddled with discrimination'.[78] Also, there was no organised wholesale power market in Germany until 2000. The introduction of competition, whilst failing to create robust market institutions, was taken advantage of by the dominant utilities who were willing to accept low margins in the short term, expanding their market share rather than raising prices. Unlike National Power and PowerGen in Britain, who were faced with greater regulatory scrutiny, they adopted the classic monopolistic strategy of vertical integration and low margins to see off a competitive threat. As the Economist noted:

> In no time, wholesale prices have been cut in half, and industrial users have won discounts of up to 60%, often from existing suppliers that wanted to stem defections to upstart rivals ... the real fear is that today's furious price-cutting is not so much real liberalisation as the start of a stitch-up ... With no regulator to keep them in check, they could easily establish a tight oligopoly, then quietly start to fleece consumers once again.[79]

Along with divesting of their holdings in the former East, the European Commission had made a condition of approval of the mergers additional measures to enable trading between the two extensive transmission areas which would be controlled by RWE and E.ON. This pressure, combined with the 2003 and 2009 directives, which placed tighter restrictions on generation/transmission integration, meant that, slowly but surely, and very reluctantly, these companies separated out their transmission operations. RWE sold a 74.9% stake in its transmission grid (then operated under *RWE Transportnetz Strom GmbH*) to a group of institutional investors (*M31 Beteiligungsgesellschaft mbH & Co. Energie KG)* in 2003 to form *Amprion Gmbh.* The former East German transmission grid was later sold by Vattenfall and *50Hertz* was formed—initially a joint venture between the Belgian utility Elia and IFM Global Infrastructure, who later sold their stake to the public development Bank, KfW. Later, in 2010, E.ON, following a long legal dispute with the European Commission, sold its extensive transmission grid (*Transpower Stromübertragungs GmbH)* which stretched from northern to southern Germany, to *TENNET*, the TSO owned by the Dutch state. This bargaining between the German utilities and the European Commission, which saw the ownership unbundling of the transmission networks, to some extent bypassed the national level as the German government at this time was actively opposing such strict separation.[80]

The early 2000s also saw a greater integration of the French and German markets. In 2000, EDF purchased a major shareholding (34%) in the newly formed integrated utility operating in the south-west of Germany, *Energie Baden-Württemberg AG* (EnBW). EnBW itself had emerged as a large player in 1997 following a merger of two regional utilities in Baden-Württemberg (*Badenwerk* based around Karlsruhe and

Energie-Versorgung Schwaben [EVS] from Stuttgart). EDF bought the landers' (state governments) share in the new company in 2000 and was then joint owner of the utility along with OEW (*Zweckverband Oberschwäbische Elektrizitätswerke),* a grouping of municipal investors.[81]

The EnBW system is located just on the border with France, so EDF's move was generally viewed as having competition implications for both markets, as the French utility was snuffing out a potential competitor in its domestic market. While the transaction was eventually approved by the European Commission, they required EDF to divest some of its generation assets (6000 MW of capacity) within France in order to offset the adverse implications for competition there. Rather than actually sell the capacity, the French government, EDF's major shareholder, devised a scheme whereby the plant would be leased; EDF's competitors were given the right to bid for the use of these assets through competitive tenders, known as virtual power plant auctions.

The nuclear structure of the French system continued to be a barrier to competition as no new entrant could compete against this low marginal cost source and offer competitive prices to customers. Under pressure from the European Commission, in 2010 the French government passed the NOME law (*Nouvelle Organisation du Marché de l'Electricité*) which extended this quasi-leasing scheme for competitors to access the output of EDF's nuclear fleet, with each retailer seeking to supply domestic customers being entitled to a share of up to one quarter of this output at a regulated price.[82]

This is but a selection of the many takeovers and mergers which took place in the immediate years following the first electricity directive.[83] EU anti-trust legislation and the activist role of the European Commission in placing conditions on such mergers, requiring divestments of assets, acted as a countervailing force and played a role similar to that of the British energy regulator during the mid-1990s (see Chap. 4). This tension between the reluctant liberalisers amongst the EU Member States and the European Commission culminated in a sector-wide inquiry, published in 2007, followed shortly by a new directive in 2009. The 2007 inquiry found that there was

> too much market concentration in most national markets; a lack of liquidity, preventing successful new entry; too little integration between Member States' markets; an absence of transparently available market information, leading to distrust in the pricing mechanisms; an inadequate current level of unbundling between network and supply interests which has negative reper-

cussions on market functioning and investment incentives; customers being tied to suppliers through long-term downstream contracts; current balancing markets and small balancing zones which favour incumbents.[84]

Competition was certainly not a 'natural' outcome of the process, rather, to the extent that it came about, it was the result of continual regulatory oversight and intervention by the European Commission and some national governments. The decision for European nations was whether they would follow the British lead and actively dismantle the legacy incumbents, in theory benefiting the consumer, or use the opportunity to provide a favourable regulatory environment for the emergence of 'national champions', with sufficient financial resources and scale to compete in international markets. Creating the market through this corporate-regulatory dynamic has been, as Hancher and Hauteclocque describe, 'an ongoing process of "trial-and-error"'.[85]

Since the directive of 2003, a second front was created by the European Commission in its efforts to open up national electricity regimes; to develop a more sophisticated and harmonised cross-border trading platform, enabling exchanges between its Member States. It is perhaps surprising that this issue did not feature more prominently in the early directive, and as a result cross-border trading relied largely on the legacy UCPTE system for connecting buyers and sellers and allocating capacity on the interconnectors. Rather than introduce new directives for this purpose, requiring each Member State to implement the new legislation, the Commission has gone down the road of introducing 'Regulations' which have general applicability. This has necessarily restricted their focus somewhat, to the cross-border aspects of trading, in particular placing requirements on the transmission system operators to ensure that market transactions requiring the use of the interconnector capacity can be facilitated.

A 2003 regulation, introduced alongside the second electricity directive—together termed a 'package'—saw the creation of an 'inter-TSO compensation mechanism' to better account for transit flows. Following this, in 2006, the European Commission published guidelines to create a common approach to 'capacity allocation and congestion management' (CACM). An updated regulation in 2009[86] formalised requirements on TSOs, which set in train a process lasting at least five years of writing the detailed network codes to enable such a system to operate.

While it is not possible within the scope of this book to account for the details of this complex market arrangement—from the mid-2000s to the late 2010s—we can set out to explore the origins of cross-border trade in Europe. To do this we must once again return to the early history of electricity markets, this time in Norway and the wider Nordic region. Here, during the 1990s, the world's first power exchange (*Nord Pool*) was created. In the following two chapters we will discuss the political origins of this exchange-based market model, and how, through its flexible design, it came to form the basis of the cross-border market functioning across the continent of Europe today.

PART III

The Nordic Region

Part III contains two chapters on the development of the Nordic electricity market model, examining the origins of electricity liberalisation in Norway which was implemented in the early 1990s, and how neighbouring systems were integrated with this 'power exchange'. Nordic electricity supply industries, particularly in Norway and Sweden, had multi-tiered configurations and a history of municipal control over distribution and supply functions, but in these cases there was also a strong role for publicly owned power producers and transmission monopolies. Amongst the most electro-intensive societies in the world, electricity supply became strongly embedded in the narrative of national economic development since the early twentieth century. The first chapter explores the history and distinctive features of the Norwegian electricity system which created the conditions for its pioneering market reform of 1990. Following this, the extension of the Norwegian model across the wider Nordic region during the 1990s is explored, a process which led to the creation of *Nord Pool*, the world's first multinational electricity market.

The Nordic Region

CHAPTER 8

Power Exchange: Norwegian Origins

The market reform which took place in Norway in the early 1990s was particularly notable, not only because the country was one of the first to go down the road of introducing competition to its electricity sector, but also because the Norwegian market was later extended across the Nordic region, creating the world's first multinational electricity market, later known as *Nord Pool.* A key characteristic of the early Norwegian market, and a critical factor in its successful expansion across the wider region, was that it was designed around an exchange-based model, with a quasi-separation of transmission system operation from market trading, enabling power trade to be conducted in a manner similar to a conventional commodities market. This was quite different from the highly complex and bespoke Electricity Pool in England and Wales (discussed in Chap. 4). This separation enabled critical system functions to be 'managed on a national basis while commercial trading between the market participants is multinational',[1] an appealing feature of the market for countries in the Nordic region which had a long history of public ownership and state control of their electricity systems.

In the post-war decades in Norway and Sweden, state-controlled electricity generation and transmission companies had been created to pursue economic growth. They became deeply embedded in the state-apparatus, becoming a means of industrial development and job creation in remote geographic regions. State-led electricity expansion was a key factor behind the high proportion of hydroelectric capacity across the Nordic region,

R. Bolton, *Making Energy Markets*,
https://doi.org/10.1007/978-3-030-90075-5_8

particularly in Norway and Sweden. In 1990, for example, hydropower produced around 60% of output across the entire Nordic region (208 TWh), with 24% coming from the nuclear plants located in Sweden and Finland, and fossil fuels (mainly coal and oil) providing only 15%.

However, this strong emphasis on national hydro resources and energy security in the different countries, with each being largely self-sufficient in terms of electricity supply, created surpluses and deficits which the transmission system operators (TSOs) had difficulties in managing. In certain years, when rainfall was high, this created significant imbalances and electricity would spill across the borders. Conversely, the Norwegian system was particularly vulnerable if there was a dry year or the water in its reservoirs was frozen for a protracted period. A key natural advantage and motivation behind deeper electricity integration across the Nordic region was therefore the ability to take advantage of the complementarities between the different sources of electricity production and to deal with seasonal fluctuations due to unusually wet, dry or cold years.

The next chapter will outline in more detail how the Norwegian exchange-based model was evolved and expanded over the course of the 1990s in order to exploit these synergies across the Nordic national systems. This chapter focuses on the Norwegian origins of the highly flexible and transferrable power exchange model.

Since the large-scale exploitation of its hydro resources for electricity generation, particularly during the 1950s and 1960s, Norway became a highly electricity-intensive society. Its total electricity consumption was over 100 TWh/year, with 23,400 kWh per capita consumption, amongst the highest in the world.[2] Electricity-intensive industries, which played a key role in the development of the nation's economy during the twentieth century, had benefited from low priced power on the basis of long-term contracts which were politically sanctioned by the state. Statkraft (*Statskraftverkene*), the state-controlled electricity producer, dominated this market for supplying large industry. But the sector as a whole was quite diverse, particularly at the regional and local levels. Similar in ways to the configuration of the German electricity regime, there were a number of medium-sized integrated regional companies and many small local distributors, holding 70% of the supply market between them.

Unlike the British case, the Norwegian government did not set out to fundamentally shift the balance of power between different industry actors and dramatically change the relationship between the state and the market. The nature of the reform meant that it appeared that competition could be achieved without the disruptive structural changes which took place in Britain. The pre-existing diversity of its electricity supply industry, along with the fact that Statkraft was not privatised during the reform process, meant that there was less need for transition arrangements to protect a single incumbent or domestic energy industries—coal or nuclear—reliant on the electricity generation market, which, as we have seen in the British case, cast a long shadow over its electricity market. In Norway, ownership was kept in public hands and the reforms had a 'negotiated character'.[3]

In a wider sense, while the British model was to a large extent based on the fundamental principles of Austrian economics, with its scepticism of market equilibrium and state intervention, the Norwegian market was based more on the classical economic idea of perfect competition.[4] The latter requires a designed market structure which realises the preconditions for this market equilibrium: low concentration in the market, ease of entry and exit, and perfect information. It will be outlined how a team of industrial economists based at the Norwegian School of Economics at Bergen (NHH) was particularly influential in articulating this concept of an exchange-based power market in the late 1980s. This built on a pre-existing trading arrangement—in place since 1971—for managing hydro resources between Norwegian electricity generators, known as *Samkjøringen av Kraftverkene I Norge* (the market for occasional power). In the next chapter we will see how the *Nord Pool* market, as it is today, was evolved through a process of gradual reform and decision making to exploit opportunities and respond to immediate practical problems. This loose framework enabled the quite different structural systems and cultures of the Nordic systems to be accommodated, hence the reason why the exchange-based model became widely applied across Europe's IEM during the 2010s.

We begin our discussion of the Norwegian market reforms of the early 1990s by providing a short introduction to Norway's distinctive electricity regime.

Norway's Electricity Regime

Like many countries in the late nineteenth and early twentieth centuries, the early development of electricity supply in Norway was driven by private investment in small-scale localised systems. Lars Thue, a historian of the Norwegian electricity system, characterised this early period, prior to the 1920s, as a 'dual regime',[5] consisting both of large energy-intensive industries with their own generation and supply systems operating alongside many small-scale utilities for general supply, the first of which had been established in 1885 in Skien by a *Laugstol Brug*, a private company. Favourable geographic conditions—'excellent reservoirs in the mountains combined with very high waterfalls, often close to the seashore'[6]—made hydropower exploitation at this small-scale technically and economically feasible. This was in contrast to Norway's neighbours—Sweden and Finland—where the nature of the hydro resource required the construction of long high-voltage transmission links to remote locations, a technology which was not available at this early stage of the industry.

Due to the proliferation of the smaller scale systems in Norway, state-controlled electricity came late to the country in comparative western European terms. But it rose in prominence after WWII as the construction of larger dams and high-voltage transmission lines became more feasible. Continuing tensions between these different and often competing sub-regimes (industry, local supply and state sponsored projects) characterised the politics of the industry right through to the market liberalisation period.

Going back to the origins of the Norwegian electricity supply industry, the institutional framework governing the exploiting of hydro resources was developed shortly after the dissolution of the union with Sweden in 1905. A series of laws were passed which set out the role of the new state in defining property rights for water courses, a key natural resource of the fledging nation. Since the 1880s waterfalls had been treated as private property and, following the 'Concession Laws' of 1909 and 1917, a process was instituted requiring any private development exploiting water power (over 1000 horse power) to hold a licence—a time-limited concession—and to conform to strict regulations regarding the nature of the development and the allocation of any economic rents from it. Many of the early licences awarded were for 60 or 70 years, so the secure and long-term nature of the property rights regime enabled companies to exploit waterfalls for commercial purposes, providing an impetus to the early development of hydroelectric schemes to service private industry. Lars Thue outlines how distinctive ideas about the management of national resources came to influence the Norwegian approach in the early twentieth century:

> Strong nationalism went hand in hand with a policy inspired by American politician, journalist, and political economist Henry George. His main

> message was that natural resources belonged to society. Economic rent of land and natural resources should not be expropriated by private property owners. George's economics inspired a "water movement" in Europe, and in many European countries the use of hydropower became strictly regulated and subject to duties. ... As a reaction to the invasion of foreign capital, the [Norwegian] parliament passed several bills to secure national and public ownership of hydropower resources. The majority of legislators wanted to limit the influence of big business and encouraged a widespread electrification of households, agriculture, crafts, and small industry. It was a battle between a "small-scale" and a more "large-scale" modernization strategy ...[7]

Soon after, similar forms of state intervention were expanded across the natural resource economy, in particular forestry and mineral resources. This led to increasing state oversight over the exploitation of the country's resources, which expanded rapidly, in particular between 1916 and 1920 as the economy prospered. The prime minister for much of the 1910s, Gunnar Knudsen,[8] became associated with this activist state with respect to the exploitation of natural resources and the macroeconomy of the newly independent nation. The period also saw increasing state intervention in the electricity supply industry: an Electricity Supply Commission was established in 1918 'to work out a national plan for the entire electricity sector ... with the mandate to provide an in principle framework for the future electricity system, a general plan for the developments in each region, and a financial plan'.[9] Then, in 1921, the Norwegian Water Resource and Energy Administration (NVE)[10] was formed to administer the state's functions in relation to water resources and to develop hydroelectric power projects on behalf of the state—NVE being a body within the economics ministry but with a good deal of operational independence.

By 1924, '90-95% of investments in large scale industrial electricity generation were private, whereas 83% of investments in general supply were municipal, 7% were state investments and 10% were private'.[11] There was tension between the different sides of the emerging national electricity regime, characterised by Olsen as rival 'state-hierarchical' and 'local-cooperative' coalitions of actors. The former involved the government along with the NVE, as guardian of the 'Concession Law' system, while the latter compromised a network of 'local banks, municipal electricity companies and local enterprises', these 'small units were integrated in local politico-economic systems where financial resources, electrical power and political decisions supported each other'.[12] Olsen summarises the political character of the dual regime and these actor coalitions as follows:

> The sector has been thorn [sic] between a programmatic cooperative collective largely associated with a small scale vision of modernization which came to dominate the general supply industry at the early stage, and a state hierarchical collective for national, political and professional control and large scale modernization which mainly emerged in the wake of the two world wars, and with the growth of state capacities and resources.[13]

Back in 1922, following the development of a national plan by the Electricity Supply Commission, a political turf war began between the two coalitions, with the advocates of localism seeming to win out and become established as a powerful collective actor. The commission had recommended further centralisation and state coordination of the fledgling electricity industry, in some cases to force smaller local undertakings—both private and municipally owned—to merge and form larger units at the county level in order to exploit economies of scale. This was controversial and seen to be undermining local autonomy; in the end, the proposals were dropped.

This setback for state-coordinated and centralised electricity governance led to a continuance of a decentralised industry structure for much longer than many western European contemporaries, many of whom had begun to centralise their systems in the inter-war period. This was a key factor in Norway's relatively slow development of a national transmission system (discussed further below) and centralised generation: by 1939 the total electricity output across the country was in the region of 12 TWh, with only 10% of this being from NVE-developed sources, which were generally confined to the more densely populated and wealthier south-eastern areas of the country.

A notable later development was the construction of the state-owned Nore power plant, which became a key node in an increasingly interconnected system.[14] However, many such large-scale investments by the state had proved to be uneconomic as they were made with a view to accessing rural customers in adjacent areas served by the local cooperatives who successfully defended their systems against state encroachment. The state's role became increasingly important however as the accessible hydro resources were exploited by private and municipal actors, leaving more expensive projects which required significant capital injection and long transmission lines for market access.

An example of the coordinating role played by the state was the development of a regionally integrated system centred around Buskerund county, just south of Oslo.[15] In the early 1920s government proposed a new 100 km transmission line from a large plant at Rjukan to Buskerund so they could benefit from this excess, and later municipalities around Oslo and Drammen were integrated after a 60-km line was built from the plant to Oslo. This embryonic system connected with the Nore plant further to the north-east, which had been financed by the state in 1928. This integration became an early example of a regional system with a power pool, enabling exchanges between the different power stations—60 were connected by the mid-1930s—and local suppliers.

Partly due to Norway's geography and dispersed load centres, the development of a fragmented electricity regime was a likely outcome, but its persistence well into the post-WWII period resulted in significant duplication of assets and a failure to exploit economies of scale in electricity system development. The failure to centralise the electricity industry in the inter-war years—along British or French lines—created the conditions for later tension between the various coalitions and ultimately the liberalisation reforms discussed below.

The state's role in the electricity sector had until WWII been focused largely on domestic customers, but in the post-war decades the electricity system began to be utilised as a key instrument of state power with respect to industrial development, employment and macroeconomic stabilisation. The development of Norway's heavy industry sector had become institutionalised as a means of accelerating economic recovery and a way of earning foreign currency, accounting for 40% of exports by the late 1970s. There was a strong regional element to this co-location of hydropower and industry due to high transmission costs, especially in the west. The development of dams and hydro schemes therefore opened up economic opportunities locally, enabled by a degree of cooperation between the competing electricity sub-regimes. As Olsen notes, projects like 'Tokke in Telemark and Sira- Kvina in Vest-Agder and Rogaland, typically involved cooperation between the state and a large number of local and regional electricity companies as well as negotiated agreements on where to locate new industries'.[16] This new alignment between the state, industry and municipal actors around a regional economic development logic to some extent side-lined the private developers who had established a foothold in the market for supplying large industrial customers.

Given the advances which were being made in electrical systems engineering and the low interest rates of the 1950s and 1960s, focus shifted to the development of large-scale hydro projects. Hydropower expanded as both the central state and local/regional power companies pursued separate investment strategies, with around 80/90 individual plants in Norway being constructed by the 1970s. Another contributor to Norway's 'hydropower complex'[17] was the political control of Statkraft's electricity prices which, as we discuss in a later section, was a key driver behind the economics of electricity supply and demand across the entire Norwegian power market. The political pressure to have competitive electricity supplied to the country's large industries meant that power prices were not in line with the long-run marginal cost (LRMC) of hydropower capacity. While pricing based on the LRMC was eventually adopted as an investment rule in the late 1970s, the continual subsidisation of industrial prices kept average prices well below this. This should, in theory, have stalled investment, but government adjusted its investment appraisal methodology, with a low discount rate applied to enable new investment, whilst keeping prices low.

In order to deal with the resulting overcapacity on the system, once the storage capacity in the reservoirs was reached (circa 82 TWh),[18] much of the excess power was sold cheaply on the short-term spot market, where prices were extremely low, and in some cases water in reservoirs which could have been used to generate power was simply spilt.[19] Due to the lack of a centrally controlled transmission system, it was difficult to manage the surpluses within Norway and as a result municipal companies started exporting to Sweden at prices well below costs, a practice which the government later banned after it granted exclusive rights to Statkraft to export and import power. Low price exports to Sweden resulted in price discrimination as Norwegian customers had paid for the assets, as Bredesen et al. summarise:

> Investments and potential profits for the companies literally disappeared 'straight into the ocean'. Excess power was exported to Sweden at a lower price than that paid by Norwegian industry and households. Norway was in a surplus situation, with a production capacity that far exceeded power consumption. The end-users paid the tariff price that had been agreed with the local power company and did not profit from the surplus situation by being offered lower prices.[20]

Alongside the imbalances at the production level, there were significant regional variations in tariffs within Norway due to the fragmentation of the electricity industry. The key reason for this was the structural diversity the local supply companies: some were integrated into generation and could cover all of their needs in-house, whereas others in less favourable geographical locations were heavily reliant on supply from larger regional utilities. These inequalities created political pressure for reform, which added to the argument which had been forwarded by NVE about the benefits of sharing resources and exploiting economies of scale.

The creation of a unified national grid in 1970 was the culmination of a long process of amalgamating a number of fragmented systems which had been built up in a rather haphazard and uncoordinated fashion. This process began after WWII when a number of regional cooperatives created four cross-regional power pools—known as *Samkjøringen* organisations. Alongside *Samkjøringen for kraftverkene på Østlandet*, which, as already discussed, had been operating since the early 1930s in the south-eastern region, there was *Nordenfjeldske Kraftsamband*, established in 1947, *Vestlandske Kraftsamband* (1955), *Samkjøringen Nord-Norge* (1960) and *Vest-Norges Samkjøringsselskap* (1961).[21] NVE was a member of all of these organisations, representing the growing influence of the state in aligning with the cooperative network of local and regional actors. These regional power pools later formed the basis of the national grid, and for the first time the large number of hydropower plants could be connected under a single control system.

The grid was operated by an organisation called *Samkjøringen av Kraftwerkene I Norge,* established on 1 January 1971, of which the vast majority of the public and private generating companies across the country, including Statkraft, were members. Statkraft, which had been formed as a division within the NVE—only becoming independent in 1986[22]—was clearly the dominant actor; it initially owned 55% of the transmission grid, expanding to 85% by the early 1990s, as the grid itself had expanded significantly. It effectively controlled the entire system as it had agreements in place to operate the other 15%, which was owned by smaller regional suppliers and some large industries. As we will discuss in more detail, a mechanism for trading production surpluses and deficits between members of this organisation was also introduced—the market for occasional power—which later became the embryo for the newly liberalised market in the early 1990s.

By end of 1990 total installed capacity in Norway was 26,913 MW, with only 278 MW of this thermal. Over half of this capacity was owned by town- or county-level local authorities (55.5%), the state, via Statkraft, had 29.1% and the remainder, just over 15%, was private undertakings and industry auto-generation. Statkraft's output in 1990 was 33.6 TWh, with 14.9 TWh sold to power-intensive customers, accounting for just under half the consumption of this sector of 30.3 TWh.

While Statkraft had less than half of the overall capacity, it could exert a strong influence over the industry because of its role in delivering government objectives around industrial development and macroeconomic stabilisation. Along with owning the majority of the transmission grid, it had a monopoly on any exports to neighbours, and its long-term contracts with large industrial users were regulated by the government. Also, its contracts with local distributors, although not a significant proportion of overall supply, typically set a benchmark price for the rest of the market.

Despite the increasing centralisation of the system, the Norwegian electricity industry in terms of ownership of power plants remained diverse. The industry was organised around three levels: below Statkraft, at the national level, were around 30 publicly owned regional utilities which had emerged following the amalgamation of local utilities in earlier decades; 20 of these were vertically integrated utilities which also supplied smaller distributors. At the local level were 230 or so small distribution and supply companies.[23] This diverse set of publicly owned distribution companies were obliged by law to cover demand in their areas and were organised around three types of networks:[24] city-based vertically integrated companies, such as *Oslo Energi AS* and *Drammen Kraft AS*, who traded in-house, covered about 45% of demand; then there were distributors who owned a share in production assets but could not cover all of their demand from this, about 25% of demand; and finally there were distributors who had no ownership of generation (about 15% of demand), and typically collaborated with other small suppliers to form collective purchasing companies who then entered into long-term contracts with generators on their behalf. The largest 34 of the generators contributed up to 96% of the country's power output.[25]

Similar to the ownership of the power plants, Norway's electricity market structure was quite fragmented and diverse. The main segment of the market was power contracts between generators and distributors to cover general supply, accounting for about 60% of generation output. The contracts were usually long term and for firm power—as distributors had an obligation to supply—which 'were negotiated individually and were predominantly bilateral, nonstandardised contracts between buyers and sellers'.[26] As Bye and Hope have highlighted, while the market for such contracts was diverse in terms of the number of buyers and sellers participating, the participation of Statkraft had a strong centralising effect.[27] The administered 'Statkraft price', determined by government, essentially set a benchmark for the rest of the industry. Prior to 1979, government set this price in line with Statkraft's average costs, but then switched to the LRMC principle, as outlined earlier.

A second segment of the market, covering circa. 10% of output, was the *Samkjøringen* market—the market for occasional power. This was an arrangement for hydropower producers to trade short-term surpluses and deficits, with access limited to those members of the organisation with an output of at least 100 GWh/year. Danish and Swedish producers could also access the market, although this trade had to be via Statkraft. As discussed earlier, this market had its origins in the highly dispersed nature of the local energy collectives, as small-scale producers sought to deal with variations in hydropower output whilst avoiding amalgamation and centralised control of their operations. The ability to trade was particularly useful in the event that a producer could not meet its obligation to supply under a firm power contract with a local distributor. At weekly intervals producers would submit information about reservoir levels which would then be used to calculate prices based on marginal cost pricing principles—essentially, the 'the calculated marginal value of stored water'—which 'signalled to each reservoir owner whether to sell or buy, as well as indicating whether to use electricity or oil for heating the large industrial boilers that were usually linked to electricity companies on special flexible contracts'.[28] Unlike the long-term contract markets in Norway, this decentralised trading arrangement was based on liberal and free-trade principles and was enabled by a limited form of common carriage on the transmission system. There were in the region of 120 producers trading on this market by the early 1990s.[29]

The origins of this spot market dated back to the 1960s when Vidkunn Hveding, then Director of NVE, and previously Professor of Hydroelectric Engineering at NTH and international consultant at the World Bank, was asked by the government to write a report on the organisation of the industry and to recommend proposals for improving its efficiency. Hveding, along with colleagues, wrote an influential report in 1969 which first introduced economic concepts to the problem of electricity industry organisation to Norway.[30] He was influenced by the work of *Électricité de France* (EDF) economists on marginal cost pricing as a means of welfare maximisation and its application to the specifics of the electricity industry. As part of his early work, a model of the Norwegian electricity system—the EFI model—was developed, jointly by the NVE and the Norwegian Electric Power Research Institute (EFI), whose 'Multi-area Power-market Simulator' underpinned the calculations. Based on meteorological and hydrological data, the model was attuned to the highly weather sensitive and disaggregated Norwegian system.[31] Simulations showed that the hydro-based system could be run more efficiently if there was a means of short-term trading introduced.

Hveding recognised that a model of pricing based on the centralised French approach would not work; his decentralised exchange proposal was therefore rooted in the highly fragmented and diverse Norwegian context. As discussed in more detail later, the crux of the Norwegian electricity reform was that this pre-existing market was liberalised; so, rather than being an exclusive member-only organisation, access was opened up and consumers of power were able to participate, mainly large industries and distributors. With the trading period shortened to day-ahead, the price in this short-term market then became the reference price for long-term contracts, replacing the administered 'Statkraft price'.

Alongside the bilateral contracts market and the short-term market for occasional power, the third key market segment was the supply of power to large industrial customers. This accounted for around 30% of generation output and was dominated by Statkraft. Similar to the case of West Germany discussed in Chap. 6, as competitive electricity pricing was a critical component of the national economy, there was a set of contracts in place with large industrial users with prices set at highly preferential rates. By 1990 around half of Statkraft's output was for industrial customers, serving in the region of 50% of the industrial load, the other half being from their own private systems. The scale of these industrial operations and the regulated nature of the Statkraft sales operation meant they were vulnerable to companies switching to own-supply, providing an additional rationale for below cost prices in their contracts. This vulnerability to competition from auto-generation was growing as Statkraft's prices became increasingly determined by marginal cost pricing principles, limiting their ability to sell at below cost.

Despite the move towards economic pricing, there was a strong degree of lock-in as these contracts with industry, which in some cases were 'one-tenth of the price to the "ordinary" consumption market',[32] had been agreed in different rounds in 1950, 1960, 1976 and 1983, with a significant amount of Statkraft's output being tied up in contracts running out to 1995, and some even into the 2000s. This contractual structure came under pressure as prices in the spot market (occasional power) declined in the 1980s due to new capacity investments and a number of wet years. In 1988 there was record levels of output, up 7.2% on 1987, resulting in depressed prices. Although under pressure from industry to revise down contract prices, government refused to cut industry prices agreed under the '1983 contracts'. A key issue was the tranche of contracts which had been agreed in 1976, when oil prices were high. These were 'among the most highly-priced of Statkraft's firm power contracts with industry'.[33] Along with switching to auto-production, some industrial consumers began to look to the market for occasional power as their main source of supply. Electricity purchased on this spot market was tax exempt, so the ability to purchase via this route was proving increasingly attractive to some large industries, one prominent example being Hydro Aluminium who turned down Statkraft's offer for supply of firm power on a long-term contract. There was also increasing competition between Statkraft and Norsk Hydro, another state-owned company who were becoming more aggressive in the market.

By the end of the 1980s, the tension between economic pricing of Statkraft's output and the need to ensure industrial competitiveness was a key feature of the politics of electricity reform in Norway. For example, one study published in 1987 showed that if Statkraft's prices had been calculated according to the LRMC principle, as opposed to at subsided rates, as many economists had been demanding, many electricity-intensive industries would be in the red, apart from the aluminium industry 'at the top of a business cycle'.[34] On the other side of the argument was the price discrimination effect of subsidised contracts to industry; in 1983, for example, the per unit power price paid by the average household was over three times that paid by power-intensive industries on average.[35] While small- and medium-sized industrial consumers were generally in support of market liberalisation, as many of them did not qualify for the subsidised rates and were tied to local monopolies,[36] the question facing large industry was whether, under any model of reform, they would be willing to substitute the security of regulated tariffs for the short-term benefits of lower prices, with the associated risks of market volatility.

New Economic Ideas

Under the control of the Norwegian Ministry of Industry, electricity pricing, as we have discussed, was traditionally viewed as a tool to achieve wider industrial strategy and macroeconomic goals for the nation, with the efficiency of the sector itself taking somewhat a backseat. This changed in 1978 when the Ministry of Petroleum and Energy was formed and took responsibility for electricity policy. Led by developments in the oil industry, which was moving towards a more market-based approach during the 1980s, this ministry and its key officials tended to have a strong microeconomic focus, which was part of a wider Norwegian shift towards neoliberalism in the 1980s. As a result, the traditional link between electricity pricing and industrial policy was weakened and the electricity industry was increasingly judged on its own merits, creating an opening for economists to propose market reforms.

A key source of intellectual ideas for the political reform of the industry which followed was a study led by Prof Einar Hope (published in March 1989) of the Center for Applied Research (SAF), an affiliate centre of the Norwegian School of Economics (NHH) in Bergen. Throughout the 1980s, as Norway began to liberalise its banking and credit markets, Hope's group 'grew into a position as perhaps the most influential economic research center in Norway at the time, with a strong academic profile and tight relationships to the state central administration'.[37] Hope was an empirical, rather than a theoretical, economist, with a focus on industrial economics and firm performance in relation to market structures, as viewed through the lens of the structure–conduct–performance (SCP) paradigm. He had created the group as a way of directly informing government and company strategy about industry reform, and under his directorship the group became quite flexible and could draw on expertise from across NHH, enabling them to integrate research on financial and industrial economics.[38]

As recounted in an interview with the author, Hope had a specific interest in the electricity sector. Born in 1937 on a farm, his father had an engineering mindset and built a small electricity generation unit at the nearby river, 25 years before the rest of the area was electrified. From this he learned about the basics of electricity supply, for example, the need for backup if there was a risk that the river source was dry in winter. Later, a large hydro plant was developed near his village and he worked there as a student. He therefore understood the technical limitations of any market design given the physical constraints and uncertainties of hydro-based electricity systems, and was aware of drought risks and the fact that it can be wet in the west and dry in the east, thus giving rise to complex organisational challenges for the industry. He was initially trained as an economist at Bergen but spent a year at the University of Minnesota whilst doing a PhD on economies of scale in banking (1967)—an econometric empirical study influenced by work in the field of industrial organisation which had been pioneered by Fred Scherer. Following this, he spent a year of sabbatical leave at the University of Cambridge in 1971/72, which was also influential in developing his analytical framework for industry restructuring and regulatory reform.

Later in his career, Hope was influenced by Vidkunn Hveding and began to study the operation of the *Samkjøringen* market for occasional power, publishing an article in 1983 called 'Markets for power exchange in Norway: An in principal discussion'.[39] In this, he discussed how to improve the market by addressing key issues, such as 'the need to study how market actors reacted to changes in administratively set prices, how market equilibrium was actually achieved under such conditions and what happened when markets did not clear'.[40] This pre-existing exchange looked to him like a 'perfect market', with a demand and supply curve intersecting to determine the equilibrium price, describing it as if it was taken directly out of a textbook on microeconomics.[41]

Hope did have a fundamental difference of viewpoint to Hveding however, in relation to the need for a policy on electricity pricing. In Hveding's view, the *Samkjøringen* market should only play a minor role and he was in favour of a planned system approach where prices approximated a calculated LRMC. In contrast, for Hope the short-term market should be central to the economics of the new system; LRMC, in this view, should be an investment signal based on actual demand, rather than a centralised pricing policy.[42] In any case, while the LRMC pricing principle had been acknowledged by the Norwegian government, in Hope's view electricity prices were politically negotiated and were rarely, if ever, subject to rational calculation.[43] The 'Statkraft price' was essentially set to cover the company's costs, rather than send a signal to the industry to operate and invest efficiently.[44] Hope and his team analysed the important relationship between the bilateral market for firm power contracts and the occasional power market. In theory, and over time, the two should converge at a market equilibrium, equating to the LRMC, but they were not doing so, in their view due to excessive state intervention which resulted in overcapacity. This overcapacity was partly a result of the political nature of the contracts with industry, but also obligations which had been placed on utilities to contract for a sufficient amount of generation output—to be 95% self-sufficient in a dry year—to ensure they met universal service obligations.

The Bergen economists came to the view that 'there should be the option for market participants either to use the market or to have contracts'.[45] They recognised the risk of giving this choice, although they were concerned about whether key market participants would choose to stick with bilateral contracts rather than transact via the exchange, meaning 'there would not be enough liquidity in the market [for it] to function'.[46] As part of his research, Hope had travelled to New Zealand to study the experience of its electricity industry, as an element of market reform had been introduced there in 1987 (they kept intact the major producer which had 90% of the market, a close analogue to the Norwegian case). Hope's conceptual scheme for a competitive electricity market in Norway was to take the existing market for occasional power and to bring in the demand side explicitly into the exchange. The group of economists also proposed a long-term futures market to align with investment timescales in the electricity sector, but for pragmatic purposes the day-ahead physical market was the main focus early on.

In 1987/88 the discussion about the industry and its reorganisation was intensified at the governmental level. Tormod Hermansen, an economist with close links to Hope, was appointed as Secretary General of the Ministry of Finance.[47] Hermansen had written a large report on the efficiency of the Norwegian economy, with the electricity sector featuring prominently in this. He then initiated a study to be undertaken as background research for an eventual deregulation of the electricity industry, appointing an economist within the Ministry to conduct dedicated research on the issue and awarding a research grant to the SAF group to write their report. As Hope recalls, his group was given significant freedom; he was essentially asked to outline the project proposal himself.[48]

One key issue the Ministry was particularly concerned with was excess capacity and cheap exports to Sweden. In their view, this was blatant price discrimination as they 'gave it more or less away'. Overall, the three main concerns were the efficiency of the system, price discrimination—keeping up the price in Norway—and the technical issues around intermittency and technical vulnerability of the predominantly hydro-based system. Excess capacity had developed due to a lack of national coordination; thus, uncoordinated investment in a decentralised system was viewed as the main problem by people like Hermansen. Hope had done estimates of the efficiency losses, the extent of the problem varied depending on hydro resources, and even with the significant level of overcapacity, the system remained vulnerable to seasonal conditions.

The report, 'Market based power exchange in Norway',[49] was based on a nine-month study, with one main report and nine sub-reports. Although Hope was not aware of it initially, this would form the basis of the subsequent legislation which liberalised the Norwegian electricity market. The report proposed the creation of a new public organisation to coordinate the exchange—provisionally christened *Kraftsentralen AS*—which would involve trading in both physical and financial power products. This would 'both function as a clearing house and as the operator of the electric pool system in coordination with a national transmission company'.[50] They recommended the creation of a new transmission company, separating Statkraft's generation and networks divisions, and to rationalise and reorganise the distribution sector. They also outlined a number of high-level principles for the regulation of the new market, emphasising the priorities of mitigating producer power and removing what they saw as distorting government interventions in price-setting processes. The report essentially outlined the basic principles of a commodities market, whilst taking into account the special characteristics of electricity systems: that electrical energy cannot be stored in bulk, the need for instantaneous balancing, very low short-run elasticity of demand and supply, capital-intensive investments, and so on.

Their concept of regulation involved a strict split between technical and market oversight, in part as a means of side-lining the powerful NVE. This would involve competition policy on the market side and then technical regulation on the water/resources side, which NVE would be in charge of.[51] NVE at the time was the dominant regulator, organised on a regional basis and staffed with engineers with little training in economics. Hope wanted the competition authority to be more central to the industry's governance; he was essentially concerned with how to assign responsibilities between the market and hydro/technical regulator.[52] Hope also played an important role in 'selling' the ideas to the industry, giving in the region of 50 presentations around the country to industry bodies and other stakeholders, at which he talked about the 'characteristics of the electricity as a commodity'.[53]

The Norwegian Energy Law

The first attempt at restructuring the Norwegian electricity industry, somewhat along market lines, was a 1985 reform proposal by the Energy Law Commission which recommended an amalgamation of the multiple suppliers and distributors of various sizes into '20 regional vertically integrated companies with exclusive service areas'.[54] This was highly contested and eventually dropped, partly because the proposal largely originated from within the NVE, hence a feeling of it being imposed on the industry.[55] Later, a government energy white paper was published in April 1987 which emphasised the prospects of gas-fired plant to deal with demand growth over the next few decades, to be located near the industrial heartland of the country. This was spearheaded by the Norwegian Labour Party, but the Norwegian Conservatives mounted a successful opposition campaign. The major energy reform proposal of the Brundtland Labour government, tabled in April 1989, just before the election of that year, was centred on industry rationalisation, involving mergers between local distributors and forcing greater uniformity of pricing across the country. It also sought to tackle the issue of poor investment appraisal and was to be accompanied by a high degree of centralised political control over the industry. These proposals had the effect of building support amongst many of the local and smaller regional utilities for a more decentralised 'free market' approach through which they could retain their independence.

After the 1989 election, a minority coalition government, led by Jan Syse of the Conservative Party of Norway, and with support from the right-wing Progress Party, withdrew the draft bill, with a view to table a more liberal market-based reform. The new government took over on 16 October 1989 and remained in power only until 4 November 1990, so it exploited a very short window of opportunity; the revised Norwegian Energy Act was approved on 29 June 1990 and came into force on 1 January 1991,[56] under a subsequent Norwegian Labour Government. Magnus and Midttun argue that the shifts between the Norwegian Labour and Conservative-led reforms were less dramatic and ideological than may seem apparent from the headline political arguments made. While the framings were ideological on the surface, 'the same arguments that supported the centralistic planned economy approach in 1985 were adduced to motivate the competitive market reform three or four years later'.[57] So, very similar proposals were branded as planned or market based within the space of a few years.

A key challenge for the economists in favour of market-based reform was to convince MPs in parliament of the need for the economic approach, as Einar Hope and his team had articulated. They had to, in Hope's words, 'fight with the engineers', who were the dominant voice influencing politicians at the time and who saw economists as ignorant of the physical characteristics of electricity.[58] While many of the political actors didn't foresee the ramifications of the proposals and were happy to 'leave it to the experts', the argument that Norway was 'giving power away to Sweden' cut through politically. A key alliance of pro-market actors formed across the Ministry of Finance, the Norwegian School of Economics and Business Administration, and the Ministry of Petroleum and Energy; the key individuals being Einar Hope, Tormod Hermansen (senior civil servant in the finance ministry) and Eivind Reiten, for a short but crucial period (late 1989–late 1990) the Minister of Petroleum and Energy, having previously been in the private sector as a divisional director at Norsk Hydro, Statkraft's main competitor.

Reiten had been critical of what he saw as excessive and uncoordinated hydropower development and the lack of any price mechanism inputting into investment decisions. An economics graduate, he didn't like the Brundtland proposals 'so he rewrote the Act and based it on a different framework … [with] … a clearer description of future ownership and responsibility relations in the industry'.[59] An important decision was to leave the question of how many power companies there should be up to the market, with the aim of the reform being to 'ensure social economical rational utilization of energy resources, facilitating secure electricity supply and reduced prices to the consumers'.[60]

Largely based on the work of the SAF group, a key concern underpinning the 1990 Energy Act was price discrimination between the different consumer categories; the aim was to develop a mechanism whereby those consumers who placed the highest value on electricity when it was scarce paid the highest price. Arising from the act, the occasional power spot market was opened up to non-members and to demand-side participation; generation was separated from transmission operation and a common carrier principle was introduced, with uniform tariffs for the use of the transmission system. The Energy Act also introduced a regulatory regime—with NVE as the regulator—to determine the rates-of-return on investments in the networks[61] and to ensure non-discriminatory access for competing suppliers. However, the regulatory division within NVE was small, with only around 100 employees, with regulation 'based on principles, not detailed rules'[62]—the licence document for market participants was just five pages long.

The licensed distribution companies were to be 'responsible for metering and for reporting information on network flows to the system operator according to rules laid down by the regulator'.[63] As the retail market was fully opened on day one of the market, on the basis that price reductions in the spot market should be passed on to consumers (discussed further at the end of this chapter), the electricity consumer's bill would then show separately charges for distribution and supply.

The market-based reform, however, involved a weak split of distribution and supply functions, along accounting lines. Fundamental reform of the distribution sector had featured strongly in the earlier SAF report—with a strict split of distribution, generation and supply activities—and in previous reform proposals under the Norwegian Labour Government which sought to centralise activities and achieve economies of scale, but this aspect of the reform proved too politically difficult and was dropped in the interests of achieving the main priority of reducing producer power and addressing price discrimination.

The 1990 Energy Act set out the broad contours of the new industry, but left the specific future of Statkraft somewhat ambiguous.[64] It set out the need for a national transmission tariff to be regulated, but said little about the functioning of the grid otherwise. This was part of Reiten's general strategy of incremental reform and not confronting highly contentious structural questions in the interests of achieving the main objective of market-based pricing. After the reform was passed and the Norwegian Labour Government had taken over the reins of power, just shortly before the Energy Act was due to come into effect on 1 January 1991, the most politically divisive aspect of the reforms emerged as the splitting of Statkraft into separate divisions for generation and transmission. This process eventually led to the dismantling of *Statskraftverkene* and the formation of *Statnett SF*, a transmission system operator (TSO) with no generation assets.

Statkraft, as already outlined, had been for many decades the key instrument of state power with regard to directing the electricity industry to achieve key industrial policy and macroeconomic goals. It had been created following a reorganisation of NVE in 1960, essentially a separate department within that broader organisation. It was subsequently separated out in 1986, such that there would be a clearer distinction between asset ownership and the technical coordination and regulation of the system within NVE. Statkraft was then denoted as a 'semi autonomous state company', directly under the control and direction of the Ministry of Petroleum and Energy, and tasked with pursuing commercial objectives, the first major shift towards a more economic framing of the industry.

The origin of the Statkraft split was essentially political; in the view of the pro-market constituency, the organisation could not become the neutral market facilitator if it also had such a dominant position in the electricity generation market. The priority was to split the company into two, separating out the natural monopoly; Hope's team initially christened this Transkraft.[65] From a purely economic viewpoint, this was a prerequisite for a functioning 'free market'; in the view of advocates, if you mixed the natural monopoly with the market function you there would be a significant market distortion. Hope's general preference was for a clear split with the market settlement function and then dealing with any transmission constraints that arose. Otherwise, the view was that in the absence of this split between market and system operation, the transmission side, in the interests of system security and seamless functioning of the high-voltage grid, may be intervening in the market settlement procedure. This structural decision was in contrast to the Electricity Pool in England/Wales which integrated the market and the operation of the transmission system; the market price became input into a wider system optimisation (see Chap. 4).

The Norwegian Conservatives' proposals for restructuring therefore involved a splitting of Statkraft according to the economic logic of open access competition: 'splitting the company [Statkraft] into divisions based on its various functions',[66] some of which could possibly be privatised in the future. The privatisation of Statkraft had been considered early on in the process, but Statkraft was so politically powerful that Hope's team was strongly advised against using privatisation as a word in the report; there was a concern that even raising the possibility 'could have stopped it' [the entire reform process].[67] The task was to reform the industry whilst retaining public ownership. This is not to say that reform of Statkraft, even though it was to remain in public hands, was uncontroversial; if Statkraft was no longer in charge of the transmission system and was not the vehicle through which government effectively regulated the electricity price, it would lose its status as the strategic linchpin of the electricity system.

The question of the future industry structure and role of Statkraft was also highly politicised due to the concerns of smaller-scale electricity companies who were worried that Statkraft would retain control of the transmission grid and exclude competition. The mayors of a number of municipal areas with significant electricity interests expressed concern directly to the minister,[68] arguing that in order to avoid market dominance by one player who would be able to undercut smaller competitors, the new Statkraft should be restricted to sales to industrial customers, leaving the general market open to local and regional suppliers.

Following the passing of the Energy Act in June 1990, working groups were established: one considered the details of market operation and the second covered the transmission grid. Later, a project group was established to consider unbundling of generation and transmission; known as 'the band of four',[69] they held their meetings in an old transformer station. The issue was also discussed through the *Hoeisveen Committee*, composed of representatives of the finance ministry, oil and energy, Statkraft management and employees. What emerged from these discussions was a three-way split: the new Statkraft as a 100% state-owned joint-stock company which would take over the generating plant[70] and operate it commercially, the planning and construction division to be a subsidiary of this new company, and the national grid as a separate state-owned company under the direction of the relevant ministry.

The proposal for structural reform, due to go before Storting (Norwegian Parliament) by 14 June 1991, was delayed however, as the 'Energy minister Finn Kristensen was understood to be still in doubt about the wisdom of splitting the company'. There had been a work stoppage at Statkraft on 12 June in protest against the proposals and 'disagreement about Statkraft's future role and structure within both the Norwegian Labour Party and its traditional ally, the national trade union federation (LO). Many influential people in both organisations support[ed] the utility's plea that it be allowed to retain control of the grid, and its monopoly of electricity exports and imports'.[71] Statkraft's Board meanwhile were making the argument that a 'weakening' of the company was the wrong strategy, given the opening up of European energy markets for trade and investment.

> The board believes (such a weakening) would be unfortunate, and points out that other countries are pushing a completely opposite policy, by building up large national energy utilities. In a future European market it will be important for Norway, too, to have a strong national energy utility able to safeguard Norwegian interests (as) international competition increases ...[72]

Another contentious issue was the future legal status of Statkraft. The previous conservative-led coalition had put forward a joint-stock option, with Reiten holding the view that the model—like Statoil—would enable the state-owned company to operate in a commercial way. However, the subsequent Norwegian Labour Government became concerned that this could lead to privatisation down the road. They favoured something between a purely state-owned organisation and the joint-stock model. This would involve reorganising the utility under the provisions of a 1965 law regarding state-owned companies—the *foretaks* law—enabling the government of the day to intervene and direct the state enterprise if strategic and macroeconomic issues were at stake. This, for example, would allow government to dictate prices charged by the company for power supplied to energy-intensive industry. The idea was that Statkraft SF (SF for *statsforetak)* would generate and trade power, along with owning the country's waterfall rights and having the first right to buy any hydro plants once a concession had expired. Statkraft SF and Statnett SF were subsequently formed, with the change coming into effect on 1 January 1992. Statkraft was valued at NKr 32 bn and Statnett at 9.5 bn.

There was also a decision to be made about the future governance and operation of the *Samkjøringen* market (*Samkjøringen av Kraftverkene I Norge*). From January 1992, the market timeframe was to be shortened from a week-ahead delivery to day-ahead, and distribution companies and large industries could also participate, forming a demand side to the previously producer-only market. Unlike the Electricity Pool in Britain, there was no requirement to trade physical power through this market, so it needed to operate alongside an over-the-counter market for contracts 'with different suppliers/customers, with different lengths and varying degrees of interruptibility'.[73]

In the immediate aftermath of the legislative reform, there was a discussion over who would own and control the spot market institution. Energy minister Finn Kristensen favoured Statnett taking it over from the member-owned *Samkjøringen* organisation, while utilities favoured a retention of the existing governance approach and greater independence. The coalition government and its key economic advisors in Hope's group believed that 'the market institution should be owned and operated by the market actors rather than the state. This could be obtained through a restructuring of Samkjøringen into a joint stock company'. However, the new Norwegian Labour Government 'took Statkraft's position that operation and balancing of the network system should be coordinated closely with the network owner – the new Statnett S.F. company'.[74] The politics of the issue of whether the market should be essentially separated from the grid in the Norwegian Parliament was particularly intense, as outlined by Olsen:

> The parliamentary debate and voting on this issue turned out to be the only incident of parliamentary drama during the entire market reform process. In the end, the market liberal party FrP fell down on the government's side – apparently because its leader Carl I. Hagen had been provoked by the intensity of the massive lobbying campaign put forward by Samkjøringen and its members – and chose rather to support a state takeover of the market institution from Samkjøringen.[75]

Statnett Marked, or *Kraftsentralen AS*, was subsequently created, becoming operational in 1993 as a subsidiary of Statnett S.F. *Samkjoeringen av Kraftverkene I Norge* was essentially dissolved and its staff and functions were moved into Statnett.[76]

The decision to have *Statnett Marked* as a functional unit within the wider TSO umbrella helped to facilitate a crucial information exchange which enabled the market to function in its early years, particularly important being the level of transmission network capacity which could be allocated in line with price signals in the power market, an issue we discuss further in the next chapter. Overall, this relationship between market operation and the TSO, although close, was not at the same level of integration as was the case in the English/Welsh Electricity Pool where the price formation procedure and final settlement was a function of the National Grid Company. The decision to have a rather looser TSO/market relationship, but with an operational link—an outcome which arose from the intense political debate in Norway—along with the voluntary nature of the exchange, set a trend for the development of power exchanges in many European countries during the 2000s.[77] The *Nord Pool* market, whose evolution we discuss in the next chapter, rather than the 'British Model', became the template for how to liberalise power markets, whilst retaining a strong degree of state control over the physical power systems.

* * *

While the main focus of these two chapters is on the creation of the wider Nordic regional market, it is worth briefly noting that the introduction of full retail competition occurred on day one of the new Norwegian market, following the implementation of the 1990 Energy Act. This was of course in stark contrast to the English/Welsh and EEC-level reform cases discussed in Parts I and II. It seems that in the Norwegian case retail competition was not politicised to the same extent as these other cases, rather the political bandwidth was taken up by the horizontal splitting of Statkraft and the governance of the wholesale power market, as discussed above.

The rapid transition to full competition was enabled as the metering and settlement procedure in the Norwegian market was highly simplified: for the majority of customers, those without an hourly meter, consumption was calculated based on estimated profiles and, given the scope for former monopoly suppliers to interfere with the switching process, the role of the distribution network operators in relation to the retail market was strictly regulated.[78] This enabled a relatively seamless move to a form of retail competition without a transition period, as was required in Britain and most other countries.

However, there were significant transaction costs—in the form of switching fees—imposed on customers in the new retail market, which were not removed until 1997.[79] So, although all customers could, in theory, switch, the transaction costs and inertia in the market ensured that incumbent suppliers could continue to hold the majority of their customers, at least for the first number of years. From the late 1990s onwards switching rates increased; this was unsurprising given the significant regional differentials in electricity prices and the removal of the punitive transaction costs. The majority of contracts in the market conformed to a 'Standard Agreement', with a standardised fixed price, a variable and a spot price linked contract; and from the late 1990s, the tariff rate of each supplier under this agreement was published on the national competition authority's website. An interesting feature of the market in more recent years has been the willingness of customers to take risks by entering into supply contracts with tariffs linked to spot market fluctuations. This commitment to the market was tested in the early 2000s—and in particular the winter of 2002/03—when spot prices rise sharply due to a dry weather.[80]

CHAPTER 9

Constructing a Multinational Market

During the mid and late 1990s, the Norwegian market model was evolved and expanded across the Nordic region, eventually encompassing Sweden (in 1996), Finland (in 1999), Western Denmark (in 1999) and Eastern Denmark (in 2000). A key basis for the development of this regional-level trade was the technical synergies which existed between the different national systems: the Norwegian pumped hydropower could displace more expensive thermal stations in the region and provide a cheaper means of meeting peak loads, whilst the more diversified mix of plant across the region could help Norway as its system was prone to swing drastically between under and over-production of power, depending on seasonal weather conditions. Building nuclear or thermal power in Norway in order to optimise its system would have been extremely expensive as it would have had a low capacity factor, only used for occasional periods during dry years. Overall, cross-border exchanges reduced the need for each country to hold spare reserves and improved the security of the individual systems.

While they shared a common interest in cross-border trade, each of the Nordic countries had experienced different energy histories and the technical configurations of their systems had evolved in line with particular national priorities and circumstances. Influenced by a range of factors, there were different approaches to state involvement in the electricity industry in each case. As we have seen for the case of Norway, state involvement arose in large part from a desire to improve the coordination and

R. Bolton, *Making Energy Markets*,
https://doi.org/10.1007/978-3-030-90075-5_9

efficiency of a highly disaggregated industry, while in Sweden and Finland, the role of the state was stronger and intervention occurred earlier, linked to the development of large hydroelectric schemes. Unlike the Norwegian case, where the resource was more distributed, in Sweden and Finland larger rivers and lower river heads imposed restraints on smaller-scale developments and, as a result, generation projects were largely beyond the financial means of municipal or private sector actors. Capital-intensive development at scale required either direct state investment or the creation of large-scale regional joint-stock companies. The remote and capital-intensive nature of hydro resources in Sweden and Finland also meant that their systems became more technologically diversified, with more of a role for thermal sources, and later nuclear (Figs. 9.1 and 9.2).

Norway, Finland and Sweden had in common a strong emphasis on electro-intensive industries and a high level of concentration in their industries, with a small number of key sectors accounting for 80–90% of industrial demand. This included pulp and paper, metals and machinery fabrication (e.g. shipping, machine tools), chemicals, non-ferrous metal basic industries (e.g. aluminium), and iron and steel.[1] Enabled by the increasing availability of abundant and low marginal cost power supply from hydroelectric schemes, by the 1950s industry consumed about 70% of Swedish electricity production and circa. 60% in Norway and Finland. Although overall industrial demand continued to increase, by 1990 it was down to a 50% relative share in Finland and Norway, and 40% in Sweden.

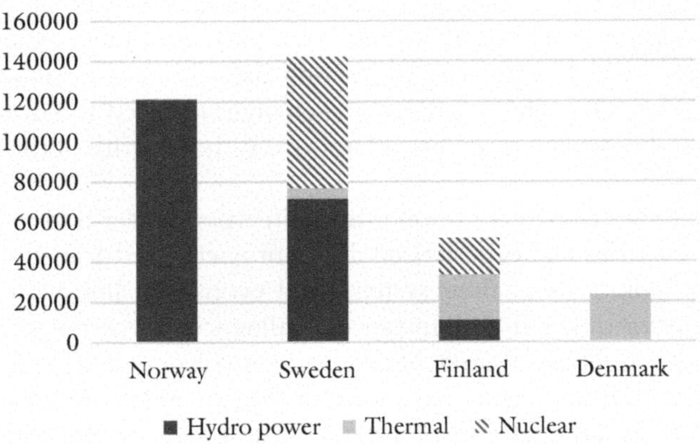

Fig. 9.1 Electricity production in Nordic countries in 1990 (GWh). (Data from: Nordel Annual Report, 1990)

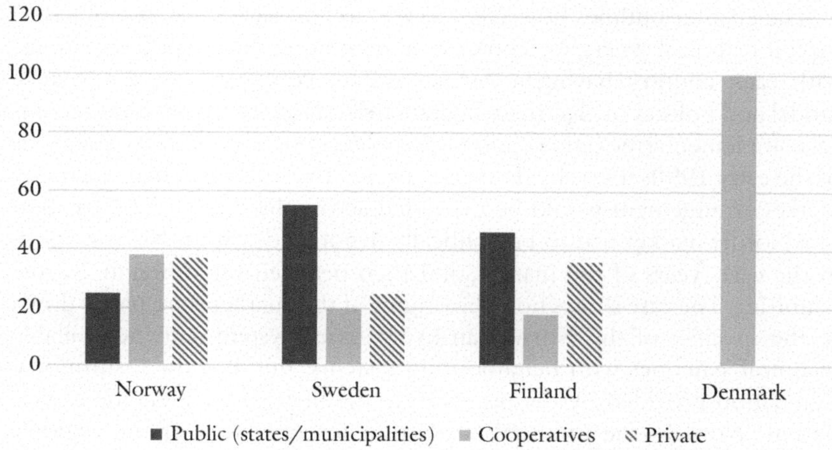

Fig. 9.2 Ownership of generation as a percentage share of the market in the Nordic countries (1990). (Figures from Table 4.1 of Hjalmarsson, L. (1996) *From Club-Regulation to Market Competition in the Scandinavian Electricity Supply Industry*. In Gilbert, R.J., Kahn, P. (Eds.) International Comparisons of Electricity Regulation. Cambridge University Press, Cambridge, 1996, p. 133). (In the Danish case municipal ownership was via larger cooperatives)

This pattern of industry-led electricity development did not take place in Denmark whose economy remained largely agriculture based. Electricity schemes were developed by rural electricity cooperatives (known as *andelslag*) and by municipalities in the larger towns and cities, which over time began to cooperate as part of two large power pools (Eastern and Western Denmark). Even more so than the Norwegian case, the electricity industry remained disaggregated, with limited direct state control.

Political institutions influenced how these national electricity regimes developed in different ways: municipal-led growth in Norway was partly a result of an earlier extension of democratic rights which, unlike Sweden or Finland, came to be viewed as a means of economic advancement in the early twentieth century.[2] The countries did have in common a liberal approach which sought to protect the rights of non-state actors and enabled a good degree of industry self-regulation. This common culture of energy regulation proved to be important as the Nordic market developed during the 1990s.

The chapter outlines how *Nord Pool's* 'architecture'[3] was assembled to exploit technical synergies, a process of integrating diverse power systems, with each country having a distinct system configuration, governance model and politics of electricity liberalisation. Despite the obvious technical complementarities and economic benefits, even after Norway's reforms of the early 1990s it was by no means a given that this particular electricity market arrangement would be expanded across the region. The creation of a Nordic market had to be politically negotiated, within Norway itself, in the early years of the market, and then between the different Nordic countries. The case shows how the origins of this market were partly down to the specifics of the Norwegian hydro-based system and the available technical synergies with neighbouring systems, but also the institutional foundation provided by the pre-existing multilateral technocratic organisation, Nordel—the industry association for operators of the region's high-voltage transmission systems. Nordel created the setting and the venues for practical technocratic discussions to take place, enabling the incumbent state-backed integrated generation-transmission companies to shape this new market. The sections which follow will chart in detail how the *Nord Pool* market was also politically shaped through this process of system integration as the different nations across the region sought to retain a strong degree of autonomy with regard to the control of their systems, whilst reaping the benefits of participating in a wider market, which, as all markets do, became more attractive to producers and consumers as it expanded and became more 'liquid'.

The chapter begins by discussing the Norwegian electricity system in a wider Nordic context, outlining the pre-existing integration of the Nordic systems and how pressures within Norway to alter its approach to managing cross-border trade emerged following the 1990 market reform. The following sections then examine the particular circumstances of the region which led to the power exchange model being adopted, along with some of the technical features of the market which enabled it to become a transferrable model.

Following a discussion of the particular liberalisation trajectories of Sweden, Finland and Denmark, it is shown how the outcome was a form of 'Nordic' integration which enabled countries to engage in organised electricity trading, but in a way which allowed them to retain significant autonomy over their national transmission systems and regulatory regimes. This delicate balance between integration through markets and national system autonomy was facilitated by the exchange-based market model which had been developed by the Norwegians and later emerged as a key feature of *Nord Pool*. This, in later years, had a wider applicability across Europe and became the basis of the European Union's internal energy market (IEM) from the 2010s onwards. A short section at the end of this chapter provides a summary of these wider European developments and their links to the story of the world's first multinational power market.

Norwegian Electricity in a Nordic Context

The Norwegian hydropower-based system had an average annual output of 111 TWh,[4] but as illustrated in the first figure below for the years 1975–90, excess production and the level of exports varied significantly depending on weather conditions (Fig. 9.3). Across the entire Nordic region, in a wet year, there could be a surplus of 100 TWh, or 60 TWh for an average year in terms of rainfall,[5] creating a strong impetus behind the economic logic of trade between Norway and its neighbours.

Alongside this production-side logic of exporting low marginal cost power from Norway, there was a significant demand-side driver as electricity consumption across the wider Nordic region was rising, at a rate of around 1% per year during the 1980s. This growth was particularly strong

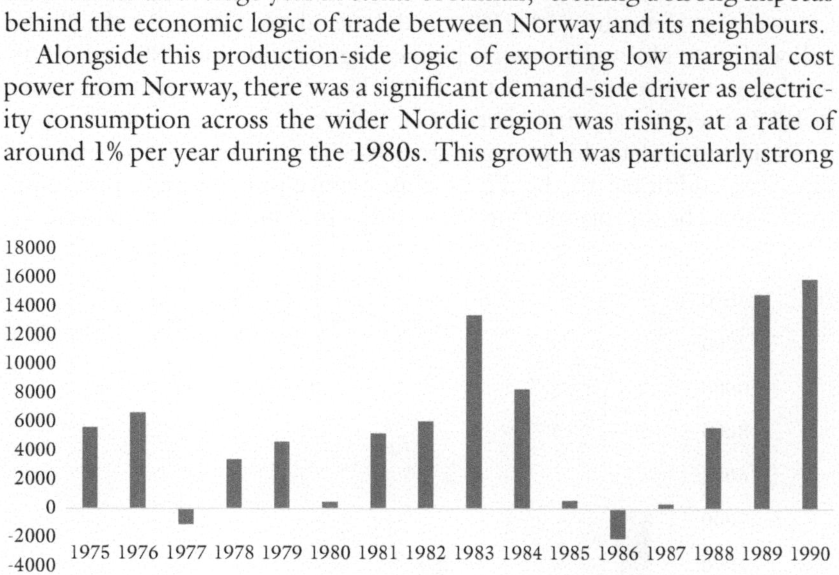

Fig. 9.3 Electricity exports (GWh) from Norway 1975 to 1990. (Figure developed from data presented in Olsen P.I., (2000) *Transforming Economies: The Case of the Norwegian Electricity Market Reform*. Dissertation for the Degree of Dr. Oecon. Norwegian School of Management BI: 120/121/256. Original sources cited by Olsen are Central Statistical Bureau (SSB) and Historical Statistics, 1992).

in Finland which saw a 4.1% increase in 1989–90. Partly as a result of this growing demand, there were concerns about capacity shortages across the region by the late 1980s; a particular concern for Finland was its increasing reliance on the Soviet Union for imports. Finland also imported significant amounts of power from Sweden, which itself vied with Norway to be the largest exporter in the region. Denmark, with its two separate transmission systems—east and west—was a significant importer from both Norway and Sweden, reaching 3.6 TWh in 1987. The rationale for increasing exchanges between Norway and its capacity constrained neighbours was therefore growing throughout the 1980s; by 1987 10 TWh was traded across these borders, of a total consumed of just over 327 TWh.

Later, in 1990, there was a further increase in trade between the systems due to high output from hydro plants in Sweden and Norway, exporting over 15 and 16 TWh respectively, reaching almost 10% of production across the region. The main importers were Sweden (13 TWh), followed by Denmark (12 TWh) and Finland (6 TWh). As the figure below shows, Norway's exports jumped significantly in 1989 and 1990, beating the previous record set in 1983 (Fig. 9.4). This increased further in 1991 when its exports reached 16.4 TWh.[6]

To accommodate this growing cross-border trade, new interconnector capacity—additional to the 22 existing connections between the countries[7]—was being planned in line with the uneven distribution of

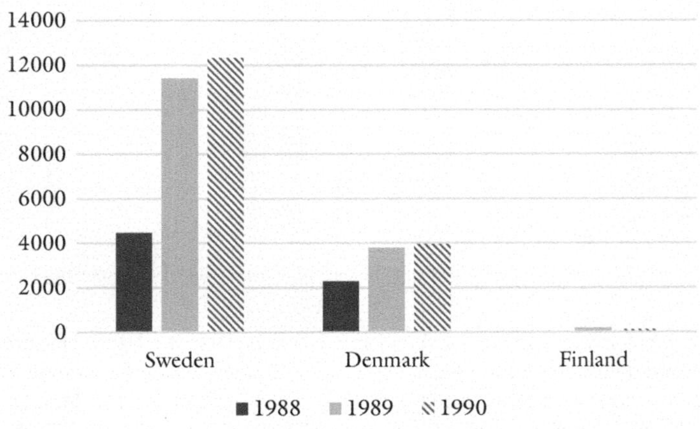

Fig. 9.4 Exports (GWh) from Norway across the Nordic region: 1988, 1989 and 1990. (NORDEL Annual Reports 1988, 89 and 90).

production and demand-side growth across the Nordic region.[8] For example, the 230 km Ivalo-Varangerbotn link between Norway and Finland was in planning by this time, along with a second subsea cable linking Sweden and Finland. A new link between Sweden and Denmark had recently become operational—the 285 kV Konti-Skan 2 line—replacing an older link owned by Vattenfall, the Swedish state-owned monopoly producer. Statkraft also had plans for a new link to Denmark. The deal with Denmark was to be based on a contract for firm power to run from 1993 to 1998 and was also to include transit rights such that the Norwegian exporter could access the large German market via Jutland. In 1990 Denmark imported 3.78 TWh from Norway through spot trades, but proposals for long-term firm power contracts—for non-interruptible power—required political approval from the Norwegian Parliament (*Storting*), an issue which was politically contentious (discussed further below).

The majority of these cross-border exchanges were coordinated via Nordel,[9] the association for electricity cooperation between the Nordic countries. It was created in 1963 to formalise cooperation between Sweden, Norway, Finland, Denmark and Iceland. Nordel set down governing principles in 1971 covering exchanges between the systems. These included 'prices based on variable production costs', 'comparable methods to determine the worth of various power sources among member countries', 'calculated worth of power as the base for exchange of electricity' and 'those exchanging power bilaterally share the profits'.[10] This inter-utility trading was organised through Nordel's 'Nordic despatch cooperation', with short-term exchanges between members taking place 'on a spot buying basis, with prices set according to variable production costs'; the buyer and seller agreed payment based on the 'median price between production costs of the prospective buyer and the lower production costs of the seller'.[11] Each utility had to maintain an agreed level of reserves to participate in the system and there was a price-cap imposed in order to reduce risks and mitigate against market power and price manipulation. However, as Norwegian electricity production costs were largely composed of fixed costs, and so were cheap at the margin, this provided an arbitrage opportunity as cheap Norwegian power could be sold on to Germany at higher prices by Danish and Swedish companies.

Despite these loopholes, the underlying principle was one of cooperation, in line with the 1971 principles; buyers and sellers would share the costs and profits of the exchanges. Like UCPTE (Union for the Co-ordination of Production and Transmission of Electricity), as discussed in Chap. 5, the amount of exchanges was high, but the net flow was comparatively low, and in many cases the same amount of power was sold back from buyer to seller within a 24-h period. Nordel's spot trading wasn't linked to the market segment for long-term delivery between producers and end-users and, as we discuss next, the Norwegian government was reluctant to provide consent for 'firm power' contracts, placing a political limitation on the extent of trade.

The Political Control of Exports

The political control of Norwegian electricity exports had a long history, going as far back as the early concession laws of 1909 which 'explicitly forbade export of electricity without government permission'.[12] Self-sufficiency and energy security became a mantra in Norway, associated with its welfare state and political culture of managing and socialising risks.[13] Contracts for firm power were particularly contentious, with only one contract being approved for exports to Sweden in 1955—330 GWh annually to Stockholm—with an associated joint-investment deal to 'finance the exploitation of the Nea watercourse in the county of Sør-Trøndelag'. As Thue outlines, 'no further Norwegian power export deal was implemented. Instead, national self-sufficiency and the cross-border exchange of "occasional power", in combination with the provision of mutual reserves, became the golden rule for Nordic electricity cooperation'.[14]

Later, the management of surplus electricity in years of excess was a key driver of industry reform during the 1980s. Pro-market reformists had been arguing that the surplus had a perverse effect on the domestic market by, for example, depressing prices on the occasional market and creating an incentive for large industrial consumers to refuse Statkraft's firm power contract offers. The resulting downward pressure on prices made it difficult for Statkraft and other large producers to cover the high capital costs associated with generating hydropower. Even after the 1990 Energy Act, the Storting retained control over Statkraft's contract prices for supplying large industrial users on the basis that potentially high and volatile prices would impact employment and regional economic stability. Government could intervene if, for example, a factory was at risk of closure in a particular region. A key concern for the Norwegian politicians was that Statkraft could become financially unstable if it could no longer hold on to industrial customers via its long-term contracts, accounting for up to 17 GWh/

year of its production by 1991. There was therefore a conflict between government's desire for Statkraft to commit to renew these long-term contracts after they expired later in the 1990s and early 2000s, and the desire for Statkraft to transition to a commercial operator and to compete in the market.

Due to this politicisation, within Norway there were different constituencies organised around the issue of exporting power. There were those who argued in favour of pricing at the margin and that electricity price inflation resulting from increasing exports would reflect the market fundamentals, while, on the other hand, there were those who argued for price controls in line with the long-run marginal cost (LRMC) to maintain the mutually supportive link between electricity production and energy-intensive industries. Those seeking to continue setting power prices in line with a national industrial strategy were calling for Statkraft to publish guideline prices for those contracts which were due to expire in 1995—accounting for 7.7 TWh/year—to be set once the market came into operation in January 1991. The Norwegian Labour Government, under 'Proposition 104', then before the *Storting*, were in favour of placing Statkraft on a more stable footing and calling for these contracts to be renewed 'with a gradual real increase in price per kWh from about NKr 0.13/0.14 (1991 money) in 1996 to NKr 0.18/kWh (1991 money) by 2010'.[15] Backed by some of the key power-intensive industries,[16] opposition conservatives voted against this proposal and argued that if the prices in the contracts were to be regulated, the rate should fluctuate in line with commodity prices, the economic basis for industries like aluminium, magnesium, paper and pulp, steel, and so on.

Alongside the continuing debate about the role of government in regulating industry's electricity prices in the new market context, exports from Norway remained politically controlled, and Statkraft had a monopoly on any foreign trade. The logic for this was that in the past, in excess years, power had been exported to Sweden at a lower price than that paid by Norwegian industry and households. So, while there was ample interconnector capacity available to enable an expansion of trade, with Sweden in particular, the political control of exports from Norway meant that a market framework to value this output adequately was not in place, and following the 1990 Energy Act the strict control of the export market remained unchanged. However, the Norwegian market price became increasingly important in the wider Nordic region, as from 1991 Nordel's trading arrangement 'was replaced by a new mechanism, where both

Danish and Swedish producers were allowed to trade at prices related to the Norwegian spot market'.[17] While exports from Norway continued to be tightly controlled, imports were free to flow, and on many occasions the excess variable production from Denmark and Sweden spilled into the Norwegian system, further depressing prices on the exchange market and undermining Statkraft's position. Following the electricity liberalisation reform within Norway, there was therefore a vigorous debate about long-term contracts for firm power exports. Until this point Statkraft were only allowed to export 'occasional' power via Nordel, the key question now being whether such long-term contracts would be sanctioned and, more generally, whether foreign trade would be liberalised at all.

Prior to the reform, as it was faced with a significant surplus in 1989, Statkraft had requested the Norwegian government that it be allowed to enter into contracts for firm power exports. Part of the rationale for agreeing such contracts was to improve the capacity factor of a number of new gas plants located around the Haltenbanken area in central Norway which were designated to supply Finland via a new link. In 1991 Statkraft eventually received approval from the minority Norwegian Labour Government to export via firm power contracts, one each with Denmark and Sweden, with the deals signed in 1995. Trade with Western Denmark—the Elsam system covering Jutland and Funen—was directly with Statkraft, while Vattenfall, the Swedish state-owned utility which also had a monopoly on international trade, transacted 'via Statnett Utland, another subsidiary of Statnett'.[18]

The contract with the Danish utility Elsam was the most significant in terms of volume of power, involving exports of 1 TWh/year for three years from 1993 to 1996 and transit rights for exports on to Germany. This created the economic foundation for a new cable link (440 MW, 127 km), the third between the two countries—the existing links were built in 1976 and 1977 and had a combined capacity of 500 MW. The new link was to connect Bulbjerg on the Danish coast to east Kristiansand, at a total project cost of NKr 1.3 bn, and was planned to be operational by October 1993.

Proposed deals with Swedish utilities proved to be more controversial as a number of Norwegian producers sought to bypass the Statnett export monopoly. One proposed deal was between two municipalities; Hedmark Energi A/S (HEAS) in Norway, 'a county-owned utility, and Sweden's Uddelholm' for '440 GWh/yr for 25 years'. The second involved Oppland who 'applied for permission to sell 270 GWh/yr, for 25 years, to Swedish utility AB Skandinaviska Elverk'.[19] Although recommended by government, the Norwegian Labour Party was in a minority and the *Storting* refused to endorse the two deals. There were divisions within the Labour Party and some of its MPs sitting on the *Storting* energy and industry committee came out against the Swedish export proposals, based on a view that the contracts would result in more pressure to construct additional new hydro projects dedicated to the new export market, an outcome they were keen to avoid.

There was conflicting evidence presented around the profitability of exporting firm power from Norway to Sweden. Power-intensive industries had lobbied strongly against these new deals because, as discussed earlier, they benefited from the low prices if there were restrictions on exporting the Norwegian surplus. But there was a significant industry lobby in favour of such electricity exports: the Norwegian Federation of Business and Industry (NHO) had issued a policy paper on the benefits to their members of more exports, in particular for the electrical equipment industry if there was an expansion of new hydro build and a programme to upgrade existing plant, providing over 35,000 new jobs. Advocates like the *Kværner Group*, a large power industry equipment manufacturer, were lobbying for expansion of hydro capacity to exploit European market opportunities and support job creation, a powerful argument given the high unemployment levels of the period. A counter-argument made was that the cost of additional generating and transmission capacity to deliver firm power would outweigh the benefits, while the lack of full European electricity market liberalisation meant that the envisioned market opportunities simply did not exist at the time (see Chap. 7). Norway, it was argued, should instead focus on providing flexibility via the existing short-term spot market.[20]

Similar to the French case (see Chap. 6), the technical risks of entering into firm power contracts were highlighted by sceptics. There had been a recent period when Norway, due to falling water levels in its reservoirs, had to import significant volumes (1 TWh) from Sweden during May/June 1991[21]—although Swedish power happened to be cheap at this time due to the steady output of its nuclear plants. Firm power contracts with Sweden and Denmark would be lucrative for Norwegian producers however, with per unit prices up to five times greater than the average spot price; the extent to which this was enough to cover the additional capital costs required to cover the obligations in the firm power contracts was debated.

This bottom-up pressure for the liberalisation of cross-border trade created an incentive on the state-owned electricity producers in Norway and Sweden—Statnett and Vattenfall respectively—to cooperate via an organised trading platform. Rather than allow a free-for-all type of trading which undermined their monopolies, an organised exchange would maintain a level of centralised control to handle the variability of their systems, whilst aligning with the political limitations on their export activities. During their ongoing discussions within the Nordel organisation, they began to see the newly liberalised Norwegian market exchange as a convenient vehicle for this.

The potential for the embryonic Norwegian exchange market to fulfil this function became apparent shortly after it came into operation in January 1991. Liquidity on the spot market was high from the beginning, largely because Statkraft decided to sell into the market—over 30% of its capacity initially—a decision which encouraged the other producers to participate also. Prior to this there had been a concern that the close historic association between generation and transmission divisions within Statkraft would limit competition, but once Statnett was formed and the split was made, it was observed rigorously. Statkraft's decision to commit to the market may have been partly about displaying this to the politicians.[22] A few years into the operation of the new market, the independence of the market was further enhanced as *Statnett Marked* became an increasingly autonomous unit, having its own organisational structure and CEO, whilst remaining within the wider Statnett organisation. Another factor increasing trade in the market was the co-ownership model of generation assets and distribution businesses in Norway. Many of the new participants in the market where smaller Norwegian distribution companies who also owned generation assets; they could now use the market as a means of managing variability of their hydro plants, deciding when to self-generate and sell into the market, or purchase from the exchange.[23]

Intermediaries also began to enter the market, one example being *Skankraft*, which from 1992 was brokering the sale of power supply contracts and trading in the new market. Another company, *Norsk Kraftmarked* (*Skankraft* owned 50% of its shares), started offering services in the 'trading and clearing of financial contracts'. They were the 'first to offer the power industry a derivatives market based on an underlying reference price from the physical power market'.[24] This was the start of a financialisation of the exchange. The ability of independent brokers to settle contracts via the exchange's clearing service also increased participation; one prominent early example was *Bergen Energie* which helped large industries operate in the market. Liquidity on the exchange steadily increased throughout the early 1990s: the volume traded more than doubled between 1993 and 1995, rising to over 40 TWh, but the majority of power was still traded over-the-counter (OTC).[25]

The unsurprising outcome of healthy participation in the power exchange was a reduction in prices in the early years of the market, a fall from 40–50 ore/Kwh to 10 in the first four years.[26] This price drop reinforced political support for the market and had been part of the economists' argument against political interference.[27] A reason for the early price declines, cited by Midttun and Thomas, was the relatively wet years of 1992 and 1993.[28] Price dynamics were also driven by the early emergence of the trading companies as 'there were considerable arbitrage profits to be made by buying from the spot market and selling to industrial end-users and distribution companies. New trading companies flourished during this period, and triggered market competition'.[29] However, following this early period, prices began to rise in the mid-1990s, partly because of lower water inflow, but also because the arbitrage opportunities between the exchange and bilateral markets faced diminishing returns. The liberalisation of the Swedish market (discussed later) also had a further effect on price inflation in the Norwegian market as the Swedish utilities, under increasing competitive pressure, were less keen on spilling cheap electricity into Norway.

Organised trade via the embryonic Norwegian exchange provided an alternative to long-term firm power contracts for accessing export markets, an option which was viewed as risky and disruptive by many politicians and the monopoly producers in Norway and Sweden. Statnett in particular were faced with politically imposed limitations on firm power exports and the inherent instability of their hydro-based system, vulnerable to seasonal weather fluctuations, required a more flexible solution.

Accommodating Diversity

The following sections explain how the Norwegian market was evolved and adapted in order to accommodate and integrate the markets of Sweden, Finland and then Denmark during the 1990s. It discusses the specific liberalisation trajectories of these countries and how the market which became known as *Nord Pool* was shaped during the process.

Sweden[30]

There were many similarities between Sweden and Norway with respect to the characteristics of their national electricity regimes and the internal tensions which characterised them. Since 1902 monopoly rights to supply designated areas in Sweden had been granted to local distributors who were given an obligation to supply. By the early 1990s, 'the Swedish electricity market comprised roughly 100 generators and 300 distributors of power',[31] being organised around three layers: 'national (220-400 kV), regional (20-130 kV), and local (0.4-20 kV)'.[32] The majority of the generators were connected to regional networks, but in many cases large industrial loads were connected to both local and regional networks and so could avail of the cheapest power depending on market conditions. The Swedish system was slightly larger than Norway's, in the region of 140 TWh annual production, and was more diverse, with a significant amount of nuclear and decentralised co-generation thermal plant. Nuclear was politically contentious; in 1980 there had been a decision made to phase it out by 2010, but uncertainty persisted over the future of the industry, which by 1985 comprised 12 reactors (BWRs [boiling water reactors] of a Swedish design and three PWRs [pressurised water reactors] based on US technology).

Even more so than in Norway, the electricity regime was dominated by a state-owned electricity generating and transmission company - Vattenfall; founded in 1909 to exploit the *Trollhättan* falls resource. Similar to Statkraft, the Swedish state company had operated as an arm of state power during much of the twentieth century. The Swedish high-voltage grid, operated by Vattenfall, was established by the Social Democratic Government in 1947, and over the following decades, this network linked the hydro plants in the north and the thermal/nuclear generators in the south, where the main population centres were located. Vattenfall, along with a number of other large Swedish producers, defined the rules for accessing the National Grid, excluding many small players and reinforcing the hierarchical structure of the country's electricity regime.[33] The uneasy tension between the dominant Vattenfall at the national level, the regional utilities and smaller supply companies had been a key feature of energy politics in Sweden since its inception.

There were strong similarities in the technical character of the Swedish and Norwegian systems, with the northern part of Sweden being hydro dominated, and much of the investment coming from regional-level integrated companies and local suppliers. However, the Swedish market was more concentrated than Norway's, with the twelve largest companies—five of which operated under the KGS banner—producing around 90% of all electric power. These large producers had a history of close cooperation, forming a 'power club' in the early decades of the industry, and in 1964 a voluntary power pool was created which operated under a split-savings rule.

By the early 1990s, when debates about liberalisation reforms were beginning to heat up in Sweden, Vattenfall had around 50% of the power production in the market.[34] The other half consisted of '20% municipal, 20%, private and 10% institutional (i.e. insurance companies, pension funds)'.[35] Vattenfall, plus the other nine large producers, continued to generate the vast majority of electricity, still in the region of 90% of the total. At this time there were in the region of 270 small distribution companies; of these 56% were 'wholly municipally owned', 16% private, 18% 'associations or co-operatives', 9% 'state owned' and 1% 'jointly state-municipally owned'.[36] The majority of the municipally owned companies also ran combined heat and power (CHP) production facilities to supply heat locally.

Vattenfall, along with the other large producers, were by this time tending towards vertical integration, while distributors were seeking more freedom to choose their suppliers, opposing trends which were leading to tensions within the industry and pressures for reform. From the early 1990s, a particular source of tension was Vattenfall's aggressive entry into the distribution market through the purchase of municipal supply companies. Overall, around '20 mergers and acquisitions were reported to be under negotiation in June 1991'.[37] Municipalities adopted different strategies during this period, with some seeking to integrate with larger payers, such as Vattenfall, while others sought to remain independent and switch between suppliers in the market, raising the difficult issue of how access to the Vattenfall network would be negotiated.[38] A highly controversial move by Vattenfall was their attempt to purchase the local supply company in Gothenburg, but this proved to be politically contentious and was later cancelled. Gothenburg then signed a long-term supply contract which tied some of the large consumers in the city to Vattenfall for five years.

Other large producer companies were also undergoing such restructuring and repositioning within the market, most notably Sydkraft, a key player with 25% of production capacity and Vattenfall's main competitor. With a mixed public/private ownership model, in the German vein, Sydkraft had entered into a cooperation agreement with the large German utility *PreussenElektra*, who took a 10% equity stake after the Helsingborg municipality sold its share of Sydkraft. In 1991 Sydkraft also purchased *Malmö Energi*, the municipal supply company of Malmo, for 1.7 bn SEK.

Swedish energy historians Högselius and Kaijser have argued that the consolidation trend of the early 1990s was a strategic move by the large players, a means of strengthening their position in anticipation of liberalisation reforms.[39] Amongst this emerging competitive dynamic, there were also disputes about access to Vattenfall's network, as municipalities, which had previously been long-standing Vattenfall customers, sought to enter into contracts with alternative producers. A notable case was *Järfälla Energi's* attempt purchase from *Stockholm Energi*. Both parties had signed a contract in November 1991, but Vattenfall, the existing supplier who also owned the regional grid through which the power would need to be wheeled, refused to facilitate the transaction. Meanwhile, Vattenfall signed a contract to supply Ericsson, one of the largest commercial consumers in Stockholm; but the city energy company refused access to its local distribution grid. In the end, Vattenfall agreed to allow *Stockholm Energi* access to its regional grid for 1992–94 at an agreed tariff, and the Ericsson deal was put on hold.[40]

A similar issue arose in 1993 when four Swedish municipalities located north of Gothenburg, near the Norwegian border,[41] clubbed together and struck a supply deal—for 1 TWh/year—with a consortium of 22 Norwegian producers (*Eurokraft Norge AS*). The price in the contract was one-fifth less than Vattenfall's contract offer, who then refused transit access via its transmission network.[42] Following a dispute, the Swedish competition authority sided with Vattenfall as transit rights had not been written into law at this point in Sweden.[43]

This wave of M&A activity and the trend towards vertical integration between large producers and distributors prompted the Swedish competition authority to recommend to government to accelerate market reforms in order to protect customers, as the market was becoming increasingly concentrated. This was then followed by the election of a liberal/right coalition government after the September 1991 elections, thus opening up a political window of opportunity for electricity liberalisation.

Reform-orientated politicians in the early 1990s saw competition as a means of mitigating Vattenfall's growing market power in the context of a trend towards increasing concentration in the market. This was also part of a wider process of economic reform following the country's property market bust and credit crunch of the early 1990s. Similar to the cases of Britain and Norway, a key question which the politicians had to grapple with initially was the future structure and legal status of the incumbent producer, with some calling for Vattenfall to be transformed from a state-controlled public organisation and be recognised in law as a commercial entity. Vattenfall itself 'had for decades lobbied for a "corporatization" – i.e. a transformation of the commercial agency into a joint-stock company – arguing that the government agency form reduced its flexibility',[44] along with its ability to exploit opportunities as European markets opened up.

The issue proved to be highly politically contentious. Some of the municipal suppliers had been demanding a horizontal splitting of Vattenfall into a number of smaller units, as in the CEGB case (see Chap. 2), while voices on the right of the political spectrum were calling for Vattenfall to be privatised and possibly split up into regional divisions. Meanwhile, the Swedish Social Democratic Party, like the Norwegian Labour Party, sought to retain political control over the energy system. Since its foundation, Vattenfall had been designated as a '"commercial government agency" ("*affärsverk*"), which among other things meant that all major investment decisions had to be formally approved by the Parliament'.[45] Ultimately, it was decided that Vattenfall remain intact at the generation level and for it to be made into a joint-stock company, with the state as the sole shareholder. A separate state-owned grid operator, later called *Svenska Kraftnät*, was then formed. Svenska Kraftnät was not as powerful or integrated as Norway's Statnett, as many of its functions were contracted out to various service providers. This decision to restructure Vatenfall, enacted in January 1992, was the prelude to a wider market liberalisation which was eventually agreed in 1995. The eventual reform package drew heavily from an earlier NUTEK report—'The electricity markets under change' (1991) - and a subsequent White Paper (June 1992)—'An electricity market with competition'.[46]

From 1992, with the Norwegian market already in operation, there had been growing calls for a liberalisation of the existing member-only exchange in Sweden, but with key producer interests, led by Vattenfall, arguing against. In their submission to the debate, Vattenfall put forward the argument that 'the established "production optimization" led to an optimal use of the country's electricity resources and that an electricity exchange would lead to lower efficiency'.[47] As environmental issues were rising up the political agenda at the time, they argued that with 'a deregulated market the power companies would be more restrictive in their use of hydropower resources, and the result would be an increased use of fossil fuels, with negative effects in terms of sulphur and CO2 emissions'.[48] There was also an argument made against a liberalised Swedish market on the basis that if cheap imports were allowed to come into the market uncontrolled, particularly in a wet year, this would threaten the economic viability of nuclear and thermal generators in the south of the country.

The reality was that, given the failure to break-up the dominant Vattenfall and the continuation of a highly concentrated electricity generation market following the liberalisation reforms,[49] the creation of a competitive Swedish-only exchange would not have been viable. Although a Swedish exchange was not created and Vattenfall retained its dominant position after the reform, the producer interests lost the debate about a liberalisation of the wholesale power market as it was decided to integrate with the existing Norwegian exchange. This came on the back of a commitment which had been made in June 1995 at a meeting of Nordic energy minister's in Denmark to establish a common cross-border market from 1996. Prior to this, in 1994, Statnett and *Svenka Kraftnät* had entered into an agreement for a joint exchange—based on an earlier work done by Noderl's 'Nordic Exchange Study Group'—which ultimately led to the creation of Nord Pool in 1996 as a regulated market place under Norwegian law and 'subject to inspection by NVE'.[50] There were also discussions with the Finnish and Danish members of Nordel underway from 1995.

The integration between Sweden and Norway officially took place on 1 January 1996, following approval from the Norwegian *Storting*, which saw the creation of the world's first competitive cross-border wholesale electricity market. This change had been due to come into effect on 1 January 1995, as the Swedish Parliament had voted through a reform package in early 1994. However, following the election later in September 1994, the Social Democrats won back power and put a halt to the reform. They then requested that the 'Electricity Legislation Commission' consider further the impacts of competition reforms, particularly in light of developments at the European level. Ultimately, the Swedish market was opened a year later, in January 1996, broadly according to the plans which had been agreed in 1994.

The financial arrangements underpinning this market integration involved each transmission system operator (TSO) taking an equity stake in Nord Pool as they joined, and an agreement not to charge fees on cross-border flows, thus creating the common market area. Essentially, *Svenka Kraftnät* bought a 50% equity stake in the new Nord Pool organisation, an ownership model which continued as the market expanded across the borders to Finland and Denmark (see below). The agreement between Norway and Sweden involved the development of a 'prototype exchange for electronic trading of Nordic electricity contracts' which was developed by 'the OM Group, the Swedish securities and derivatives exchanges operator in association with Norway's Statnett and Sweden's Svenka Kraftnät'.[51]

In the Swedish case, the government's decision to retain Vattenfall as the dominant producer was key as it meant that a Swedish domestic market would unlikely have been viable. In part, a reason why the Nordic solution was attractive to the Swedes was because of their own difficulties with market reform and the reluctance of politicians to address the issue of its highly concentrated electricity industry.

Finland

Similar to Norway and Sweden, the Finnish system was dominated by a state-owned company, *Imatran Voima Oy* (IVO). IVO, later Fortum, owned in the region of 30% of the country's production capacity, approx. 5000 MW, with a similar amount owned by smaller utilities—mainly ten regional systems—and the rest split between industry own-production and local distribution companies. There were around one hundred of these in operation, mainly municipally owned monopolies. The generation mix was more balanced than in Norway and Sweden, split between nuclear, thermal—with a lot of CHP—and a limited amount of hydropower (see figure presented in the introduction to this chapter). Electricity trade was taking place between these actors, mainly via bilateral contracts, but there was a number of power pools operating in Finland, and unlike Norway and Sweden, there was historically little state oversight of the electricity system. This changed somewhat in the 1970s: in 1973 cooperation agreements were signed between private and state producers, and in 1979 the state became more active and instigated a process of amalgamation. This saw the creation of 20 regional systems, each with a grouping of stakeholders responsible for grid planning and operations, with investment plans having to be approved by the national Ministry of Trade and Industry.

A distinctive feature of the Finnish system was the presence of two large transmission systems: the IVS (*Imatran Voimansiirto Oy*) and TVS (*Teollisuuden Voimansiirto*) grids. IVS mainly served the IVO generators, but this also had features of a public grid, with an open access regime and published tariffs, although these were not applied to IVO-owned generators, the main users of the grid. The IVS grid was initially build in 1929 to deliver power from the large Imatra plant near the Russian border to towns in the west of the country.[52] The TVS grid, on the other hand, was operated by large industry players, along with 'a consortium of generators who wanted to avoid using IVO's network. Hence, no real open access to third party was available in this network'.[53] In all, there were about 60 private companies using this grid, under the terms of a private contract which specified rules and tariffs; the dominant shareholder was PVO (*Pohjolan Voima*). Even though the IVS grid had somewhat of an open access regime, the scope for market trading was limited; firm power contracts took precedent and spot trades 'were subordinate to long-term contracts, so they took place only if there was no conflict with them'; this of course 'limited spot transactions and was not providing an efficient signal to the producer of electricity because there was no short-term indication regarding the losses and constraints'.[54]

In line with the history of electricity system development in Finland, there was generally a liberal, hands-off approach to the construction of new transmission links; this was open to anyone, but there was an obligation on IVO to connect and integrate any new power lines. Government did seek to control this somewhat by regulating the prices charged for accessing the IVS grid. These were regulated according to a 'cost plus' formula—covering the costs plus a limited rate of return on investment for IVO—in part due to government concerns that high fees would create an incentive for the creation of private transmission grids and further fragmentation of the industry.

Finnish international electricity trade had been quite limited, in part because the two transmission grid operators had exclusive rights over foreign trade. In 1996 Finland 'imported 2% of its total consumption of electricity from Sweden and no imports were made either from Norway or Denmark. Total imports were 8.5% of which 6% was imported by IVO from Russia'.[55] In light of developments, firstly in Norway and then in

Sweden, there had been a growing commercial driver for integration: Vattenfall was increasingly involved in asset purchases in the Finnish market and had already signed 'long-term power supply agreements' with 'two Finnish industrial groups, Enso-Gutzeit and Outokumpu',[56] while IVO was buying generation capacity in Sweden.

A key driver for this increasing integration between the Swedish and Finnish systems was risk management as there was growing uncertainty over the future of nuclear power in both countries—the Finnish IVO had purchased Swedish reactor technology, providing crucial support for its indigenous BWR technology. Also, the Norwegian exchange spot price was emerging as the key benchmark price for contracts across the region, so any barriers—such as transmission charges for cross-border trade—were disadvantageous for Finnish suppliers, particularly as electricity demand was growing relative to domestic production. This commercial logic, which incentivised Finnish companies to own Swedish assets, grew as the Norwegian market became increasingly liquid, and in 1995 the Finnish legislature passed the Electricity Market Act. This introduced accounting unbundling of IVO and created a regulatory agency for awarding licences and monopoly price regulation, to be conducted within the Ministry of Trade and Industry. From 1997 there was full retail competition and an open access regime for the transmission grid was introduced, along with the creation of Fingrid following a merger of IVO and PVO: Ownership of Fingrid was 'at an equal level of 25% by IVO and PVO, the state (12%) and by institutional investors (38%)'.[57]

Since October of 1996, before its official entry into Nord Pool in 1999, when Fingrid took an equity stake in Nord Pool, Finnish energy companies had been participating in the joint Norway-Sweden exchange, but with transmission tariffs charged at the Finnish/Swedish border. A key reason for Finland's delayed integration into the Nordic market was the question of how the pre-existing Finnish exchange, which had only been created in 1996, could operate alongside Nord Pool. A number of financial institutions in Finland, led by the Finnish Stock Exchange (Bourse) and the SOM clearing house, and in partnership with Svenska Kraftnät and Fingrid, had established their own exchange, *EL-EX*. This was similar to Nord Pool, in that hourly and weekly products were offered, but it was not based on a uniform pricing principle as in the Nord Pool day-ahead spot market, rather on the basis of continuous hourly trading (intraday) where buyers and sellers were 'matched' in real time. This resulted in differential pricing based on the submission and matching of bids and offers for contracts.

In February 1998 Fingrid purchased El-EX, primarily as a means of easing the merger with Nord Pool. El-EX, as a newly established market platform, was unsurprisingly reluctant to be taken over by Nord Pool, seeking to preserve its independence and protect its share of the market. When Finland joined Nord Pool in 1999, EL-EX initially operated alongside the Nord Pool market segments, with each acting 'as agents for each other's products, which complement one another'.[58] El-EX agreed to operate its market under the Nord Pool banner; the intraday (Elbas) market was then introduced in 1999, enabling continuous trade in '1 MWh electricity during a specific hour'[59] in a particular market region up to 1 h before physical delivery. It was initially extended only to Swedish participants, replacing an earlier '"adjustment" market operated by Svenska Kraftnät'.[60] It was later extended across the Nordic region following a merger of 'Nord Pool spot market and EL-EX to form a new company – Nord Pool Nordic Elspot – to be owned 20% each by Nord Pool, Statnett, Svenska Kraftnät and Fingrid and 10% each by Eltra and Elkraft System, the Danish system operators'.[61]

The Danish Systems

The Danish electricity industry, unlike thone of the other Nordic countries, was less dominated by a single state-owned production company, rather the industry was organised in a bottom-up fashion, with rural and municipal utilities cooperating as part of larger units. This was, in part, due to the mainly rural economy and consequent lack of large industrial loads on a Norwegian or Swedish scale. Another contributory factor was the fragmentation of the networks, with two separate high-voltage transmission systems emerging during the twentieth century: *Elsam*—covering Jutland and Funen and synchronised with UCPTE—and *Elkraft*—covering Zealand and synchronised with Nordel. Centralisation had occurred much earlier in the eastern system—in the 1920s—while on the western side this did not occur until the 1950s. These centralisation processes led to the creation of the two systems which operated as cooperatives, with a bottom-up governance structure. On the western side, the 30 or so municipal producers and many rural cooperatives pooled their production into six regional generators, who in turn relied on Elsam to carry out system operation and other collective functions (financing, purchasing fuels for plants and operating the 150 Kv transmission system, including the *Konti-Skan* cable which had linked the west to Lindome in Sweden since

1965). There was 'no real competition between the power companies in Jutland and on Funen in the period prior to deregulation of the power industry',[62] so Elsam was essentially a cooperative, being characterised organisationally as 'decentralised co-operation'.[63] Elkraft was formed in 1978 out of a cooperation between the City of Copenhagen utility and a large generator (*Sjællandske Kraftværker*), which in turn was owned by a number of municipalities and rural cooperatives across the region.

Whilst being entirely physically separated—until 1999—the two systems had developed their own distinctive organisational cultures and systems of operation and control: Elsam, in the west, had been particularly innovative in developing control systems for its own purposes; it was an early developer of an 'optimal power flow' model in 1977 which was used for its economic dispatch.[64] Elkraft had a closer cooperation with Sydkraft—the Swedish utility—than with the neighbouring Danish system. The first subsea electricity connection between Nordic countries was between the north-east Zealand coast and southern Sweden under the *Øresund* strait in 1915, constructed in order to take advantage of surplus power produced by a number of Swedish municipalities at the time. The link was operated by a company called NESA; and the NESA system later became the backbone for the western Danish regional integration.[65] Elkraft's strategy with the Swedish cooperation was to keep power prices lower than they were in Jutland and Funen, so they were more in competition than cooperating with their Danish neighbour.

Denmark was also slower to liberalise than the other Nordic countries, partly because of policy support for domestic fuel sources, the rationale for which was often linked to environmental protection. Combined heat and power plants burning domestic gas and biomass fuel, and later wind power, were granted priority in the economic dispatch. The large amount of medium- and small-scale CHP plants on the systems also created complications for the centralised system operators as the requirement to meet peak heat demands often did not coincide with peak electricity demand. These constraints placed an incentive on plant operators to conserve fuel and invest in highly efficient plant, whilst the complexity of the decentralised system and the need to consider the interaction of the power and heating markets reinforced the production-side emphasis of the system operators. Given the distinctiveness of the Danish electricity industry, there was little appetite to go down the road of liberalised market pricing, as noted by Bredesen and colleagues; 'Danish electricity suppliers realized early on how deregulation and a free power market in Norway shifted influence from the producers to the consumers – a development which at the time was uninteresting for the Danish producers. Danish optimizing of local production capacity and supply agreements clearly conflicted with the Norwegian view of rationalization and efficiency'.[66]

However, as Denmark had been a member of the EEC since 1973, it was required to adopt the new electricity liberalisation directive (see Chap. 7). In 1999 the Electricity Supply Act was passed which, again in line with the directive, reduced the threshold of consumption from 100 to 10 GWh, subsequently allowing all consumers access to the market by January 2003, although obligations on suppliers to buy a certain share of renewables/CHP output—the 'CHP guarantee'—remained in place. It also placed obligations on transmission owners to ensure efficient supply and facilitate competition. Both systems were then split operationally, in line with the competitive industry model: Elsam (Jutland and Funen) was split into a system operator, a transmission owner and a generation company (Elkraft System, Elkraft Transmission and EK Energi, respectively), while 'on 1 January 1998 the production and transmission company Elsam was divided into the production company ELSAM and the transmission company Eltra' (the transmission companies Eltra and Elkraft were later merged to form *Energinet.DK* in 2005).[67]

Denmark joined Nord Pool in phases, with the western region joining first in 1999, and the eastern system following in October 2000. The integration of the western Danish system into Nord Pool was partly motivated by the opportunities that some senior managers in Elsam saw arising from deeper Nordic integration—it was also physically linked to the Norwegian system—combined with European-level liberalisation. As already outlined in this chapter, Elsam and Nord Pool had already entered into a long-term contract for firm power supply, which also granted Statkraft transit rights to access the German market. Elsam later established a 'trading agreement' with Nord Pool and started participating in June 1999.

A key consequence of the Danish (and Finnish) integration in terms of the structure of the power exchange was the splitting of Nord Pool into physical (Elspot) and financial market (Eltermin) segments. The split came as a way of enabling the Danish companies (and Fingrid) to buy shares in Nord Pool; otherwise, it would have been too expensive, given the high value of the company and the need for a large equity stake to secure the clearing house for financial contracts.[68] This was facilitated by a reorganisation of Nord Pool, separating the clearing house function, which was finalised in 2003, and creating a company jointly owned by the TSOs:

Nord Pool Spot AS. The clearing house company, *Nord Pool ASA*, was fully owned by Statnett.[69]

A Case Study of Market Design Within Institutional Constraints

By the late 1990s, through this process of integrating across the Nordic region, Nord Pool was evolved in order to accommodate the different national system characteristics and constraints of Sweden, Finland and Denmark. The addition of an intraday trading component in order to accommodate the inclusion of the pre-existing Finnish exchange, along with the separation of the financial/clearing house functions from the physical power market, shows how the overall *Nord Pool* 'architecture' emerged as a result of a process of integrating these national electricity regimes and accommodating different approaches to, and trajectories of, market liberalisation.

The ways in which the operation of the Nord Pool market has been designed to interact with the physical power system of each country illustrates how each nation-state's desire to retain a degree of autonomy over electricity system control is balanced against the benefits of participating in a wider regional market. This trade-off has been designed into Nord Pool by incorporating within the market operation a procedure known as 'market splitting'—separating the market into a number of distinct 'price zones'—and became more sophisticated over the following years. Rather than being centralised and top down, this is a rather flexible and decentralised market arrangement: a price zone can be an entire country (e.g. Finland), or there can be a number of price zones per country, depending on the likelihood of congestion occurring within a national system.

The market-splitting approach had been in use since the early years of Norwegian market in the 1990s. Its roots are in the pre-liberalised system where, owing to the decentralised structure of the Norwegian electricity industry previously discussed, separate 'sub-pools' were formed in the event of grid bottlenecks, for which the *Samkjøringen* computer programme would deliver individual clearing prices. This had been used as a means of system balancing in situations where hydropower output created severe imbalances on the Norwegian system. The extension of such a method became logical in the new Nordic market context, particularly after the creation of Nord Pool in 1996 when the Swedish and Norwegian systems were integrated. Very early on it became apparent that there would be problems encountered at the border between the two countries due to the annual variations in hydro output. There were problems experienced in the first years of the new market—in 1996 and 1997—due to low rainfall and a deficit in Norway, resulting in more significant inflow from Sweden. The opposite occurred in 2000 due to heavy rainfall, having knock-on effects within the Swedish system as there was a supply shortfall in the southern part of the country due to the temporary shutdown of a nuclear plant. These seasonal variations and the effects at the Norwegian/Swedish border created the impetus for a managed solution.

The market-splitting procedure essentially sets the boundaries of the market and the physical systems of the Nordic countries. Normal—'unconstrained'—market operation would see a single clearing price for the entire Nordic market region, but in the event that a transmission constraint becomes significant, the market operator has the ability to 'split' the market into separate trading zones either side of the constraint (see Fig. 9.5 for a recent bidding zone configuration). Scarce capacity on the constrained interconnectors can then be allocated. In such a scenario, Nord Pool receives information from the various TSOs about the situation on the transmission lines and informs market participants a week in advance about the configuration of bidding zones. With separate bids being submitted, in the zone with a surplus seeking to export, the price will be lower, and vice versa, for the zone with a deficit seeking to import. This price differential between the different zones is then used to calculate a fee for use of the scarce transmission capacity. This is done such that the electricity 'flowing over the bottleneck is in effect taxed, with revenue from the process of allocating transmission capacity (energy flow multiplied by the price difference between the two regions) accruing to the grid company'[70] and used to invest in new grid capacity to alleviate the bottlenecks. In the Nordic market, the cost of interconnector capacity is therefore 'implicit' in the market price for electricity on the power exchange. That is, Nord Pool offers a 'one-stop shop' where 'all buying and selling of power and auctioning of capacity on an interconnector is performed in one and the same operation'.[71]

After information about the likely zonal configuration is known by market participants, cross-border trades in the intraday (Elbas) market can then take place until the transfer capacity of the interconnector has been reached, thus, in theory, making the most efficient use of the available capacity and approximating as closely as is physically possible the optimal uncongested market where there is a single system price dictated by supply and demand for electricity—in theory maximising economic welfare. Market participants, wary of the risks involved with this market-splitting

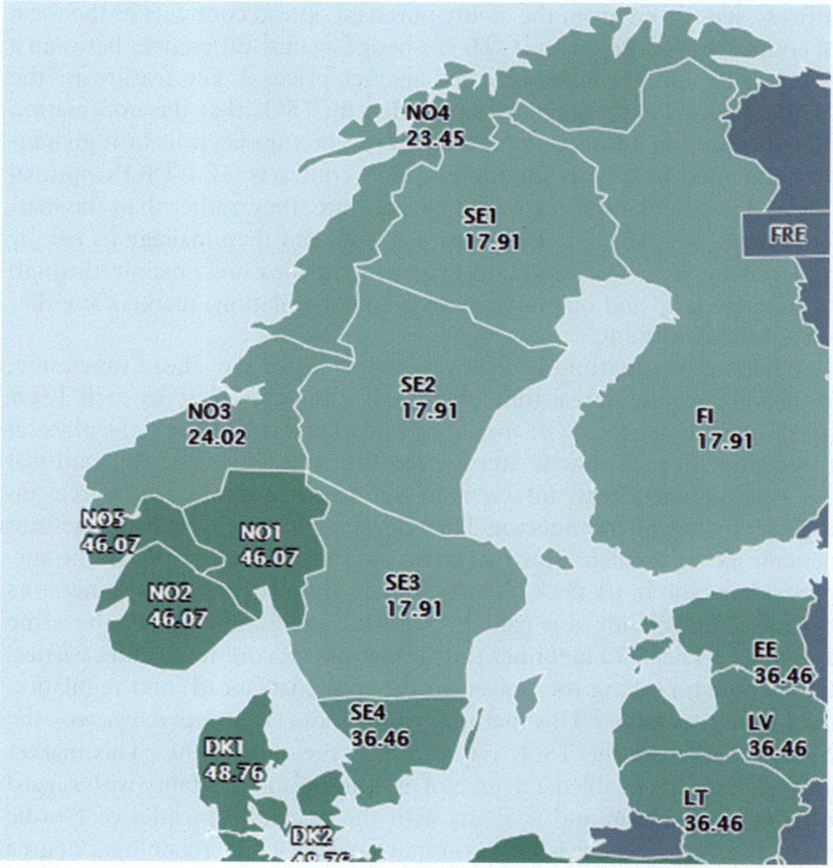

Fig. 9.5 An example of a price zone configuration in the Elspot market. (Courtesy of Nord Pool). (From Nord Pool: https://www.nordpoolgroup.com/Market-data 1/#/nordic/map (Accessed 5.5.21. Reproduced here courtesy of Nord Pool). This market configuration is included for illustrative purposes only. Price zones are occasionally redefined. Sweden, for example, originally started as a single price zone but is now separated into due to transmission constraints arising from imbalances between the north [excess production] and south [a capacity shortage] of the country. The figures also shows that the Baltic states have been integrated into Nord Pool in more recent years)

process, have been given the ability purchase option contracts in the form of contracts for differences (CfDs) to hedge against differences between a zonal price and the unconstrained market price. A key feature of the Nordic process is the guarantee provided by TSOs that the information they provided in advance to Nord Pool can be translated to firm guarantees and used as a basis for these option contracts. If a TSO's optimal power flow calculations prove to be inaccurate, they, rather than the market traders, bear the risk. Each national TSO can then manage its risk by undertaking its own congestion management measures, mainly through 'countertrading' and operating short-term (Regulation) markets at either side of the constraint.

While market splitting is deployed mainly in the day-ahead timeframe, as markets operate in real-time, the use of 'countertrading' by each TSOs has developed as a means of aligning the market outcome with the physical constraints on each system. In essence, if there is a bottleneck, a national TSO can independently intervene in the market in a way which frees up capacity on the interconnector. The relevant TSO does this by requesting generators 'to regulate down a certain amount of generation on the surplus side of the bottleneck, for which they are paid. Similarly, generators on the shortfall side are paid to regulate generation up by the same amount'.[72] The TSO identifies the 'lowest-priced counter-trading parties' by buying and selling the power on the spot (day-ahead) and regulation (real-time) markets.[73] This method was introduced extensively across the Nordic market by the TSOs via Nordel in the early 2000s. This market arrangement has enabled a degree of autonomy and flexibility with regard to system operation and it aligns with the general principles of Nordic integration—to benefit from a common market whilst retaining a degree of strategic national autonomy.

However, it has its critics. Countertrading was initially introduced with a view to resolving temporary bottlenecks (such as a line outage), while market splitting would be used to address congestion management issues arising from more structural supply/demand imbalances. A potential source of inefficiency in the system, and the basis of many critiques, is that combining market splitting with counter-trading leads to price distortions. The overuse of counter-trading within each market can skew these locational signals and dampen the signals to investors that new capacity is required.[74] As Nordel explain, the market actors 'receive no signal as to where in the grid the congestion is actually located when counter-trading is used, it is up to the TSO concerned to do something about the congestion that occurs, regardless of whether it is of a temporary or structural nature'.[75] There have been calls for a clearer delineation of structural constraints, those for which market splitting should be used, and temporary constraints, for which counter-trading should be deployed.

While the market arrangement is highly flexible and able to accommodate different national approaches to congestion management and system operation, a key quasi-political constraint on its operation has been the determination of, and process for, revising the price zone borders. There was a strong element of path dependency in how these zones were initially delineated as they corresponded to national systems for the cases of Finland and Sweden, with Denmark and Norway typically being split into two zones.[76] In an ideal world, one with no limitations on transporting power from producers to end-users, there would be a single price zone covering the market, thus enabling maximum liquidity and hence efficiency. In order to approximate this ideal as closely as possible, given the physical constraints, it is 'therefore important to locate the boundary between price areas at the place where there is a physical constraint, so that we can ensure full utilisation of transmission capacity over the bottleneck with the aid of price mechanisms'.[77]

As a general principle, the larger the price zone, the less bottlenecks within a zone will be reflected in the market prices. Proposals to redefine these price zone borders in a way which corresponded to physical constraints, rather than national borders, were put forward in 2001, with the number of bidding areas 'being increased to ten',[78] but there was little support amongst stakeholders for price zones which took no account of national borders. However, very frequent changes to price zone configurations can be problematic as it introduces uncertainty for market participants, as Nordel explained: 'During 1998 and 1999, there were for a period frequent changes in the division into bid areas in Norway. Trading in some areas could also vary greatly over the course of 24 hours, so that bottlenecks arose for parts of the day in one place, only to disappear at other times of the day. Information about price area division over the course of a week became very complicated'.[79] Following this, what was intended to be a 'flexible zonal pricing system' was changed to 'a system with a few a priori determined zones'.[80]

The issue of price zone delineation and revision has proved to be highly politicised and a problematic aspect of the Nord Pool market model. The trade-off made between national autonomy via control of transmission systems and the idealised operation of the market exchange is a legacy of the processes of Nordic market integration and the continuing influence of national electricity regimes.

Europeanisation of the Nordic Model

The story of how the Nordic power exchange model expanded further and became a template for today's European IEM would require an extensive and dedicated study.[81] What can be said here is that the replicability of the original Norwegian power exchange was not confined to the Nordic region and by the late 1990s Nord Pool had expanded significantly. This was achieved through the purchase of ownership shares in smaller European power exchanges, by selling its expertise and IT services, and licencing its trading platform across the wider region. It was also involved in international knowledge transfer process through Nord Pool Consulting which was established in 1996. This provided technical support to new exchanges around the world; for example, the South African Power Pool (SAPP) was initially designed based on the Nord Pool market, a project partly funded by Norwegian and Swedish development agencies, along with the Indian Power Exchange and California's ill-fated power exchange (Cal PX). The Nord Pool exchange also played a key role in the start-up phase of a number of European power exchanges; most notably, it's trading platform and IT systems were licensed to Powernext, the French power exchange initiated in 2001 by a number of TSOs, including RTE (the French TSO owned by EDF), Euronext (a stock exchange) and a number of financial institutions. For the first number of years of its existence, much of the operation of the French exchange was performed from Nord Pool's head office in Oslo.

As the European electricity markets were progressively opened up from the late 1990s and countries began thinking about how to link eligible customers and sellers of power products (both physical and financial), the power exchange model was implemented in a number of European countries. In some cases this involved publicly owned, quasi-national monopoly power exchanges; Spain was first off the mark in 1998 with the creation of *Compania Operadora del Mercado Espanol de Electricidad* (OMEL) and Italy followed a few years later with the creation of *Gestore del Mercato Elettrico* (GME). Both of these countries had their reasons for adopting a public sector approach; in the Spanish case the viability of a private exchange would have been questionable given the severe limitations on cross-border transmission capacity to its neighbouring markets, particularly France, while in Italy, its highly complex market configuration with multiple pricing zones perhaps required a bespoke solution.

Power exchanges also began to be developed as private initiatives. In Germany, Nord Pool played a key role in the creation of the Leipzig Power Exchange (LPX) which was launched in 2000 with the backing of the Nordic exchange and a number of regional business interests. LPX was set up as a competitor to the Frankfurt-based European Energy Exchange (EEX), an initiative of the German stock exchange. Another notable development was the establishment of the Amsterdam Power Exchange (APX) in 1999, arising from a collaboration of a number of Dutch energy companies, traders and large end-users. Like Nord Pool, it adopted an expansionary strategy, most notably through its 'tri-lateral market coupling' initiative in 2005/06. This saw the development of a technique known as 'market coupling', designed to solve a particular issue of access to the Belgian market which was problematic due to significant and unpredictable 'loop flows' arising from the transit of power between France and Germany. This saw the development of a shared algorithm which could be used simultaneously by a number of power exchanges—later called EUPHEMIA—in order to coordinate their market operations. Unlike the Nordic approach of 'market splitting', requiring a single power exchange to calculate the market equilibrium, the APX model enabled a regional market to operate whilst each national market could be serviced by a different power exchange. This clearly aligned with Europe's long history of fragmented electricity system development and the desire for national autonomy. The basic concept and algorithm developed by APX, in collaboration with Powernext and a number of TSOs, has later become the cornerstone of Europe's IEM. In the intervening years much collective effort has gone into developing the rules, codes and procurers for Europe-wide 'market coupling'.

All of this technical work has been based on a wider EU 'vision' known as the 'target model'. At its core has been the 'market coupling' approach, through which the allocation of interconnector capacity is integrated with the functioning of the power market. The main objective is to allocate capacity on the interconnectors in a way which maximises societal welfare. In basic terms, this implies that, as much as is physically possible, the flow of electricity to where it is scarce and where prices are highest should not be impeded, whilst taking into account physical transmission constraints. Similar to the Nordic case discussed above, a key deficiency of the approach arises from the limitations on the European Commission's legal powers to regulate the TSOs directly. As a result, national markets are to a significant extent 'blackboxed' during this market allocation procedure, resulting in, as many have argued, market inefficiencies.

While APX and Nord Pool entered into the British market, exchange-based trading has been less influential in this context, partly because of a more established ecosystem of brokers and independent clearing houses which could facilitate over-the-counter (OTC) trading, but also because of the structure of the New Electricity Trading Arrangements (NETA) which replaced the Electricity Pool in 1999. This placed emphasis on long-term bilateral trading—often years in advance, introduced as a reaction to the perceived failures of the highly centralised Electricity Pool—resulting in a highly decentralised process of price formation and low liquidity on centralised exchanges. A single reference price for power has less value in such a market.

The benefits of market liquidity and the increasing returns to scale of operating an IT-based market platform have made the power exchange business model highly scalable, and as a result, the continental European market quickly became more concentrated. In 2002, Nord Pool sold their interests in the LPX, which was taken over by the EEX to form a powerful continental exchange. A key development in this respect was the creation of EPEX Spot in 2009, Europe's largest market for physical trading: initially, a partnership between EEX, France's Powernext and a number of national TSOs. The EEX Group, which took a majority shareholding in Powernext, is now the dominant player in the European market, with control of EPEX Spot, a central clearing house function and a number of power exchange businesses across Europe and internationally.

While expanding and evolving significantly, the Norwegian idea of electricity as a traded commodity organised though an 'exchange' became the template for Europe's IEM. Behind all of the technical rules and operating procedures governing this complex market arrangement, the balance originally struck in the Nordic region between the autonomy of national electricity regimes and cross-border integration remains at the heart of this market.

CHAPTER 10

Conclusion: Remaking Markets

This concluding chapter returns the wider discussion about electricity systems and their transformations. Following a reflection on the period of liberalised markets covered in this book, this chapter draws out lessons for our understanding of the governance of low carbon energy transitions, emphasising the need to pay attention to the politics of electricity pricing and the distributional effects of market reforms. A historical understanding can inform us of the nature of the dynamic between states and corporate actors which emerged from the liberalisation process and the role of actors embedded across different scales of the energy system—from international to local—in reshaping energy markets and systems.

* * *

At the outset, this book sought to account for the processes through which competitive markets replaced the 'national electricity regimes' which had become embedded across western Europe in the post-war era. The inception of electricity markets was a story of interacting factors and forces of change which coincided in a western European context from the late 1980s onwards: the effects of long-running macroeconomic trends—a slowdown in demand growth, the changing relative prices of fuels on international commodity markets and innovations in energy technologies—coincided and began to undermine existing political commitments to national energy policy goals and industrial strategies. Whether, and to what extent, the nation-state was seen to be providing some kind of buffer against the fundamental uncertainties of changing global conditions, a

R. Bolton, *Making Energy Markets*,
https://doi.org/10.1007/978-3-030-90075-5_10

role that became reinforced following the 1970s oil crises, came to be an open question in a number of countries.

States had underpinned the national electricity regimes, but the vulnerability of long-established state-industry configurations to changing economic and technological circumstances was exposed, creating an opening for new ideas and arguments about alternative market arrangements. It was shown how, in different ways and in different contexts, markets came to be framed as the solution to the structural crises of state-controlled and monopoly based electricity systems. The allure of electricity markets in the late 1980s and early 1990s was that they opened up the opportunity to take advantage of what seemed to be increasingly advantageous international conditions. The ability to exploit low international energy prices and technological innovations, it was thought, would drive down electricity prices and help to make stagnant national economies more competitive in an increasingly globalising economy. Competitive forces would also drive efficiencies in what were seen by many as oversized and stagnant electricity supply industries dominated by national monopolies.

As discussions about introducing markets got underway in the late 1980s, there seemed to be a 'natural equilibrium' to be found: state control in its various guises could be replaced by the choices of distributed market agents, the implications of these choices could be internalised in prices and their consequences allocated through markets. However, as this study has shown, markets never operated as the autonomous entities driving system change that many had envisioned; this was the folly of thinking that market design could be a purely technical exercise which achieves intended outcomes. At the outset markets may have appeared to be a 'technical fix' to the structural problems of national electricity regimes, one which would depoliticise these systems, but very quickly participants involved in this process became embroiled in the 'micro-politics' of reform. This involved navigating trade-offs and politically weighted decisions about the allocation of costs and risks associated with reform, along with the implications for industries and supply chains reliant on cross-subsidies from electricity sales, and decisions about which types of consumers were to be designated as participants in the new markets and on what terms.

Various cross-subsidy arrangements which had been funded through electricity bills were typically removed, leading to significant cost reductions; the question was how the gains from liberalisation and trade arising from this decoupling would be allocated. The structural reconfiguration of national electricity regimes was to a significant extent a political process through which cost savings were distributed amongst the owners of energy companies, different classes of consumers and taxpayers. Electricity markets, in this sense, can be viewed as political constructs which reflect the uneven societal distribution of capabilities to influence the allocation of costs and risks associated with electricity supply.

Since their inception in energy policy discourse, markets quickly became enmeshed in wider political, legal and regulatory processes, along with the material orders of the systems they were designed to govern. Similar to the early electrical lighting and power systems that Thomas Hughes studied in his *Networks of Power*, electricity markets developed at different speeds and with different material configurations, reflecting the diverse geographic, political, economic and social contexts in which they evolved. It is due to these historical legacies and continuities that European electricity markets became somewhat regionally embedded around core Europe, the Nordic countries and Britain.

Despite initial intentions, the electricity liberalisation process resulted in a tendency towards vertical integration and increasing concentration in many markets as large and diversified energy corporations began to dominate European energy markets. Freed from the constraints of national regimes and monopolistic structures, their ability to deal with the risks endemic in markets became a key competitive advantage, and many of the smaller regional and local utilities became subsumed into these larger organisations. Their substantial balance sheets and sophisticated corporate structures meant that they could more effectively manage risks associated with fuel price fluctuations by integrating downstream and expanding geographically. As we saw in the German case, for example, contrary to predictions that liberalised markets would see greater diversity, the changing risk profile of the electricity industry due to the introduction of markets favoured the traditional attributes of the incumbent electricity (and gas) utilities—the economies of scale and scope they could achieve. In the British case, where regulatory intervention was more of a feature, the dynamic was towards de-concentration at the generation level, while supply and distribution became increasingly concentrated. This was, to a large extent, the result of a trade-off made by politicians and the regulator as they forced the generators to divest of assets if they wanted to integrate downwards.

Another dimension of the reconfiguration of national electricity regimes and the electricity liberalisation agenda has been the establishment of a

European-scale electricity market, the IEM. Power exchanges, those organisations that operate wholesale power markets, took up a strategically important position in this new cross-border market as countries sought to develop practical ways to link buyers and sellers of power and utilise interconnector capacity in line with market principles. As transnational actors with relatively low capital costs, they have emerged as key 'system builders' in this new configuration, developing partnerships with transmission system operators, financial institutions and stock exchanges, and influencing how the EU-level operational procedures and rules which govern trading across international boundaries have been formulated. The success of this new market collective has been as a facilitator of more efficient cross-border trade, whilst enabling countries to retain a level of national control over their systems.

While this more recent cross-border market dynamic has only been briefly touch upon, readers of this book will at least have gained some insight into the reasons why European markets were 'coupled' at a regional level and never fully 'integrated'. As we have seen, national electricity regimes, both their technical character and political foundations in historic state-industry alignments, could not be dismantled and replaced by a single legally enforceable 'European model'. The regional markets which evolved were built upon existing relationships and infrastructure, and as a result these markets developed incrementally; reform was a slow and political process which maintained continuities with the previous era of national electricity regimes.

* * *

Systems are being transformed today of course; this time their fundamental material constitution is changing as the use of fossil fuels for electricity generation is in rapid decline across parts of western Europe. What has of course happened in the intervening decades has been a reversal of the original economic logic of electricity markets: the impact of fossil-fuel-based electricity use on the climate has meant that the internalisation of economic decisions and their consequences within the market is no longer possible. Electricity systems once again need direction; not for the purposes of economic modernisation, as was the case in post-war western Europe, rather to decarbonise energy supply and societies. The reasons behind this ongoing shift—which has accelerated since the signing of the Paris Agreement in 2015—are of course many and would require a substantial study to account for fully. In a European context, the most important contributory factors have been the operation of an increasingly effective emissions trading scheme covering large power plants and industrial installations across much of the continent, along with the introduction by many countries of subsidy schemes to support investments in renewables and other low carbon sources in various ways, contributing to an acceleration of cost reductions in these technologies.

The transition to low carbon energy will not be a clean break however. The book emphasises the importance of studying the legacy organisational frameworks build up around fossil-based energy supply systems which govern financial flows and the allocation of economic costs and risks of energy systems amongst producers, consumers and taxpayers. In a western European context at least, historical studies such as the one presented here can provide a resource for uncovering the origins and basic contours of such frameworks. As has been shown, they were not neutral, or the outcome of a new equilibrium between technologies and markets, rather they were born out of political processes and trade-offs made during the process of reform. The links between political reforms, risk reallocation and technological change need to be made transparent as we conceptualise and investigate future energy transitions. This points to a critical research agenda—perhaps a new politics of electricity markets—which draws back from a discussion of fuel choices, individual behaviours and favoured technological solutions, to widen the analytical lens, emphasising the economic logics and organising frameworks of the systems themselves.

While the markets studied in this book belong to the fossil fuel age, there are some important historical resonances with the early period of liberalisation which should be borne in mind as we discuss transitions between the present and future of electricity supply. The first is the political dynamics of energy markets during an era of energy price deflation. As we have discussed, in some countries a key early driver in the move towards markets was the desire of large consumers of power to break free from regulated tariffs which had been in place to subsidise national industries and to access cheaper sources of energy that were increasingly available on globalising energy markets. This deflationary era had its roots in the earlier oil crises of the 1970s which prompted substantial investments in oil and gas exploration and coal export infrastructure. This, alongside depressed demand due to energy efficiency and slow economic growth, lead to a supply glut from the mid-1980s.

Today, we are witnessing a similar disjuncture between energy costs and the prices consumers pay for their electricity as renewables—in particular wind and solar power with their low marginal costs—push down average wholesale energy prices. With renewables there is a deflationary negative feedback loop at work: the more low or zero marginal-cost renewables that come onto the system at one time, the more prices fall. Then, as renewables push other sources out of the market and begin to set prices more often, average prices are pushed down even further. This 'price cannibalisation effect' can be exacerbated by policy mechanisms which provide guaranteed grid access at all times and provide hedges against low prices, incentivising renewables operators to continue producing even when prices are low, or even negative. In the medium and long-term, prices for electricity may no longer be kept in check by demand for scarce fossil fuels.

This is a long-run deflationary dynamic, most likely characterised by periods of extreme price volatility while fossil fuels continue to play an important role in balancing supply and demand at the margin. The long-run trend has two key implications for the politics of electricity markets. Firstly, it severs the link between markets and investment, creating a strong impetus behind increasing state intervention to direct long-term system change. The theory behind competitive markets was that high prices would enable fixed costs to be recouped and loans to be repaid, and if they were persistent, they indicated scarcity, with the availability of economic rents then triggering new investments. This link between the short and long-run was of course theoretical, but whether it was in reality as strong as some have suggested is a moot point, as state-controlled systems had built in significant capacity margins, so low prices rarely threatened security of supply. There is no doubt that this situation has now changed and the link between the short and long-run is severed. These dynamics may 'cannibalise' the market institutions themselves, as low average prices threaten the recovery of fixed costs made by private investors; governments are then forced to step in to ensure security of supply and meet climate change targets.

The nature of state involvement in the context of liberalised energy markets may take two forms. Step-by-step we are already seeing a return to regulated prices as policy supports are introduced to fix these 'flaws' in the market. In various ways, interventions are made in order to reallocate risks between investors, consumers and taxpayers, thus ensuring that new investments in capacity are made. These costs then need to be reallocated across society. This creeping re-regulation of energy prices is unsurprising given that, historically, the economic logic for regulated tariffs was to compensate investors in situations when average costs are greater than marginal costs. An alternative approach available to governments is to reconceptualise the basic design and purpose of these markets. The foundation of a more fundamental market-based solution would involve the incorporation of the demand side into these markets, in such a way that price levels are reinflated through increasing the temporal flexibility of energy use; that is, using energy more when it is cheap, in line with the fluctuations of variable sources of production. As industrial processes, transport and heating are increasingly electrified, the scope for such 'flexibility' will undoubtedly be enhanced. Also, as we saw from the Norwegian case, supply side flexibility and resilience against seasonal fluctuations can also be achieved through the integration of different national markets. It is as yet unclear whether electricity markets need to be refined or fundamentally reformed to address this pricing problem. Valuing flexibility is one thing, incorporating it into a new conceptual frame for a reliable and equitable low carbon energy market is another.

A second implication of this long-run deflation of average power prices is a growing discrepancy between prices in wholesale and retail markets; the question being how this plays out in terms of the politics of market reform. As we have seen in the British nuclear case, the use of levies on electricity bills became a key means of maintaining a technology policy in a liberalised market setting, and the use of such levies has been extended across many countries as a means of supporting investment in renewables. The need to cover the fixed costs of infrastructure expansion and the increases in balancing costs associated with more complex systems are non-energy costs which also add to final bills. So, while wholesale prices may be on a downward trend, the same cannot be said for the prices that final end-users pay for their electricity.

How will this discrepancy play out? Who will reap the benefits of renewables and associated low electricity prices? As we have seen from history, powerful actors will make moves to bypass levies and fixed charges, using arguments such as the need to maintain industrial competitiveness. The effects of such moves will be to undermine the collective nature of such systems as charges are imposed on a smaller customer base, an outcome which is likely to exacerbate inequalities. If markets are to be relied upon to allocate such system costs, as well as the benefits of low energy prices, this cannot be a free-for-all; there is a need for discussion of the basic principles and social objectives guiding any technical reforms to markets and, as far as possible, to reduce the influence of sector lobbyists.

* * *

A second lesson from the early history of electricity markets is that we should not think only of governments when we consider which actors have agency to transform markets, rather they are shaped through complex multi-actor processes characterised by an evolving relationship between public and private actors.

Underpinning the early reform processes was legislation which set out the new ground rules for the industry; regulatory agencies and competition authorities would have powers to enforce market rules and anti-trust laws. A paradox of the free market for electricity was that competition was certainly not a natural outcome of the liberalisation process, rather it required ongoing regulatory oversight and political intervention. In determining the appropriate role and scope of regulation, the essential trade-off to be made was a political one; whether the benefits of economies of scale and scope, enabled through a loose form of industry self-regulation, would be sacrificed in order to reduce the market power of incumbents and bring about diversity in the market, enabling consumers to benefit from the greater competition.

As we have seen, there was no uniform approach adopted as countries made different political judgements about the benefits, or otherwise, of competitive and contestable electricity markets. The British energy regulator and the European Commission were particularly active in placing conditions on high-profile mergers and acquisitions, leading in some cases to asset divestment and voluntary unbundling of networks. Arising from this process, we can no longer view electricity supply as a single industry, or regime, rather it is now a set of interconnected markets shaped by these corporate-regulatory dynamics. Political interventions or business strategies do not determine market outcomes; these factors can be seen to interact, or 'co-evolve', continually reshaping these markets which have become increasingly layered and hybridised through this process.

More recently, this dynamic has taken new forms, particularly as some nation-states and the EU have become increasingly proactive in their efforts to mitigate greenhouse gas emissions arising from electricity generation. Recent developments in the German power market provide some illustration of the nature of this new dynamic. Here, as has been widely commented upon, the German government has introduced policies to subsidise renewables deployment and phase-out nuclear generation, and as result we have seen an increasing specialisation of German electricity companies in either networks/services businesses, renewables or upstream fossil fuel assets. This process was initiated in 2015 when *Rheinisch-Westfälisches Elektrizitätswerk* (RWE) split its renewables, networks and retail businesses into a separate company called Innogy SE. Its majority share in Innogy was then used as part of a swap deal with E.ON, with RWE taking over a large part of E.ON's renewables business along with a shareholding in E.ON itself. Prior to this deal with RWE, E.ON had separated its fossil fuel plant into a separate company called Uniper, which is now majority owned by the Finish utility Fortum. So today, in 2021, E.ON is largely focused on the downstream distribution and services market while RWE specialises in the generation business. Meanwhile, southern European companies, in particular Enel (Italy) and Iberdrola (Spain), seem to have adopted a strategy of diversification and international expansion, whilst retaining an integrated structure in their home markets. Both have invested heavily in renewables, successfully developing large wind and solar projects in both Europe and South America as governments have begun to offer long-term contracts via auction mechanisms. The market valuation of these companies is now as high as the faltering oil majors.

Large energy generation and supply corporations may now be facing a choice: to remain diversified across fuels and sectors, or to specialise in either low carbon or fossil-fuel-based energy. The future market size and risk profile of these two energy regimes are fundamentally different of course, and it remains highly uncertain what form energy markets will take in the future and the nature of the corporations which dominate them. An intriguing question is how these dynamics will play out in the long run: Will increasing specialisation lead to a bifurcation of the energy market into discrete segments dominated by specialised companies? Or will large diversified players, perhaps similar in scale to the oil majors, come to dominate markets for low carbon technologies and services? The nature of competition and the coordination needs of such models would be radically different; these questions are worthy of consideration as governments look to reform regulatory frameworks.

* * *

A final lesson from history is the need to pay attention to 'scales' as we consider the role of markets in a low carbon future.

In the introduction we highlighted the variation of European electricity industries; these national regimes were multi-tiered configurations, held together by relationships across scales. To a significant extent it was how pre-existing tensions across the local, regional, national and international scales played out that shaped the transition to markets and their varied structural characteristics. In the British case, for example, its hierarchical regime was dismantled as the Regional Electricity Companies came to the fore in the new market during the 1990s. In the German case, the multi-tiered national regime fragmented as the large integrated utilities came to see the opportunities of liberalisation and used it as an opportunity to reinforce their dominance by taking over many of the local utilities. The Nordic case shows how the desire to reap the benefits of cross-border trading, whilst retaining a strong element of national system control, was incorporated into the technical features of the market itself. Markets, in many ways, were borne out of the tensions across these scales, but they can, in turn, be useful devices to achieve alignments and accommodations between them.

The question of scales is particularly important today because of the increasing electrification of transport and heating demands, and the uptake of distributed energy resources (DERs). There are of course many technical issues brought up by the demands of integrating these technologies (electric vehicles, heat pumps, rooftop solar PV, etc.) into low-voltage distribution systems which were certainly not designed for this purpose. But this technological trend also brings to the fore important organisational and governance challenges for the energy system as a whole. While it may be the case that DERs can be integrated into hierarchical systems, with transmission-level system operators extending their control downwards to the local level and managing the integration process, there is a potential for DERs to be disruptive innovations which radically and rapidly transform energy markets. This could lead to a new dynamic between incumbent firms and new entrant challengers in these markets, with the latter focusing on consumer-centred business models and innovations which create novel value propositions.

If systems are to be fundamentally transformed in this way, with the emphasis of markets moving downwards, to the local and consumer level, the risks associated with a further hollowing out of the national level should not be discounted. Building on our earlier point about the need for a principles-based approach to market reform, if this is not done carefully, DERs may undermine established mechanisms of cost socialisation which were designed for centralised systems, with early DER adaptors in effect free-riding on non-adaptors. A further disassociation of energy markets from the redistributive mechanisms inherent in welfare states raises difficult questions about fairness and equality, which may come into tension with techno-optimist visions of a more 'distributed' and 'democratic' energy system. A progressive reform approach should seek to incentivise this type of innovation, but balance this with an equitable allocation of shared system costs. It is unlikely that this can be achieved without recourse to the mechanisms of cost socialisation embedded in the nation-state.

While mapping the contours of a new market framework which can achieve this is well beyond the scope of this book, perhaps lessons can be learned from the early phase of market design in the late 1980s and early 1990s when quite new and radical ideas about competition, markets and the organisation of electricity systems interacted with the political process. Developing and institutionalising new ideas about the organisation of energy markets will be an important part of any system reinvention around low carbon energy; but a lesson from the early period of competitive markets is that the drivers of such reforms are multiple and it is difficult to identify a single causal factor. Rather than a reaction to an immediate set of drivers, liberalised electricity markets were in many ways an outcome of deeply rooted and historically embedded structural tensions within national regimes, a working out of poor technology choices and investment decisions which had been made decades earlier in the 1960s and 1970s.

* * *

In the midst of great uncertainty about the future of electricity systems and markets, what can at least be said is that markets, and the decisions of distributed agents which constitute them, are no longer seen as the driving force of low carbon systems as long-term system change is increasingly driven by government decisions. Competitive electricity markets were created by governments, part of a trend towards non-deterministic energy policy, with powerful actors keen to open up national electricity regimes, to exploit opportunities and navigate uncertainties. However, in the context of low carbon transitions, the role of electricity markets is transforming; they are becoming the means through which governments are seeking to redirect systems, part of a wider state project to 'manage' energy system transitions and a means of achieving pre-defined, long-term system goals.[1] With governments once again seeking to direct long-term system change for wider economic, societal and environmental purposes, the main role of markets now is to allocate the costs and risks of investing in and operating power systems. Energy markets no longer drive investment decisions.

Perhaps electricity market liberalisation will come to be viewed as a phase—an interregnum—bookended by eras of state planning of these large technical systems. In this new era of system change, electricity supply will increasingly be met by variable renewable sources, in particular wind and solar power, whose cost base is fundamentally different to fuel-based sources of generation, being more akin to infrastructure investments with high upfront capital costs and low running costs. Traditional markets designed around marginal costs and valuing energy output are no longer fit for purpose. How are state and market actors dealing with this new risk profile of low carbon electricity systems? In what ways are established market frameworks being reconfigured around the reallocation of costs and risks associated with low carbon energy transitions? The age-old question: who will be the winners and losers following these reform processes? These, amongst others, are the critical questions for studying electricity markets in an era of transition.

Notes

Chapter 1

1. Lagendijk, V. and Van Der Vleuten, V. (2013) *Inventing Electrical Europe: Interdependencies, Borders, Vulnerabilities.* In: The making of Europe's Critical Infrastructure: Common Connections and Shared Vulnerabilities. Eds Hogselius, P., Hommels, A., Kaijser, A. and Van Der Vleuten, V. Palgrave Macmillan, London.
2. Chandler, A.D. (1990) *Scale and Scope: The Dynamics of Industrial Capitalism.* Harvard University Press, Cambridge MA.
3. An argument most eloquently expressed by Langdon Winner. Winner (1977) *Autonomous Technology: Technics-out-of-Control as a Theme in Political Thought.* MIT Press, Cambridge MA.
4. Hirsh characterises this alignment of political and industrial elites around an expansionary logic as the 'Utility Consensus'. Hirsh, R. (1999). *Power Loss: The Origins of Deregulation and Restructuring in the American Utility System.* MIT Press, Cambridge MA.
5. Fligstein, N. (1996) Markets as Politics: A Political-Cultural Approach to Market Institutions. *American Sociological Review*, 61(4), pp. 656–673.
6. This national-level framing is chosen to articulate the realities of how electricity systems were actually governed during this period. Geels' defines 'socio-technical regimes' much more broadly as 'the locus of established practices and associated rules that stabilize existing systems'. The Geels (2011) The Multi-level Perspective on Sustainability

R. Bolton, *Making Energy Markets*,
https://doi.org/10.1007/978-3-030-90075-5

Transitions: Responses to Seven Criticisms. *Environmental Innovations and Societal Transitions*, 1(1), p. 26.

7. Granovetter, M., and McGuire, P., (1998) The Making of an Industry: Electricity in the United States. *The Sociological Review*, 46(1), pp. 147–173.
8. Hirsh's *Power Loss* is a notable exception (Hirsh, R. (1999) *Op. cit.*). Published in 1999, this provides a rich account of the introduction of market reforms in the USA from the 1970s to the mid-1990s. The Utility Regulatory Policies Act (PURPA) of 1978 was a landmark in the move towards competition in US electricity supply industry as it enabled unregulated companies to compete against the incumbent utilities, beginning a process of dismantling the 'utility elites'. An early study of the effects of the British reforms on technological change is: Winskel, M. (1998) *Privatisation and Technological Change: The case of the British electricity supply industry*. PhD Thesis, University of Edinburgh. https://era.ed.ac.uk/handle/1842/7511. This work situates the British privatisation and liberalisation reform as a broader socio-technical system dynamic, demonstrating the co-evolution of these institutional reforms and technology choices. Winskel emphases the usefulness of the Hughesian LTS framework for this purpose and highlights the need for future work on the particular dynamics of mature/late stage systems.
9. Although the use of gas turbines for generating electricity had been proposed as early as the 1940s, the technology was immature, a particular problem being the inability of turbine blades to withstand the very high inlet temperatures required to achieve the high efficiency potential of the technology. However, as the technology could be deployed for a range of uses, for example as part of pumping systems in oil and gas industry, and benefited from knowledge spill-overs from the jet engine industry, blade performance and the reliability of the turbines were gradually improved. These industrial scale CCGT units (100–150 MW, as opposed to the 8–900 MW coal-fired units being proposed by some utilities during th e 1980s) could be deployed in a modular way and operated flexibly. Their competitive advantage lay in the improved efficiency of the thermal conversion process—through recycling the exhaust gases via a heat exchanger and used to power a steam generator—being in the region of 50% higher than conventional steam generators of the day. For an overview of this technology in the context of changes to the wider electricity industry, see Watson (2004) Selection Environments, Flexibility, and the success of the Gas Turbine. *Research Policy* 33(8): 1065–1080.
10. See, for example, Künneke, R. W. (1999) Electricity Networks: How 'Natural' Is the Monopoly? *Utilities Policy*, 8(2), pp. 99–108.

11. See, for example, Voß, J. P. (2007) *Designs on Governance: Development of Policy Instruments and Dynamics in Governance*. PhD Thesis, University of Twente. Science and Technology Studies scholars refer to such processes as 'performativity', whereby economists do not merely describe and analyse, but actually shape reality through the design of policies and markets, in line with the assumptions of their theories. See Callon, Michel (1998) *The Laws of the Markets*. Blackwell, Oxford.
12. See, for example, Meek, J. (2012) How We Happened to Sell Off Our Electricity. *London Review of Books*, 34 (17).
13. Rip, A., Kemp, R. (1998) *Technological Change*. In: Rayner, S., Malone, E.L. (Eds), Human Choice and Climate Change, Vol. 2. Battelle Press, Columbus, OH, p. 365. Hughes, T. (1986) The Seamless Web: Technology, Science, Etcetera, Etcetera. *Social Studies of Science*, 16(2): 281–292. The systems approach has been drawn upon more recently by a group of historians of European infrastructure who have developed the concept of 'Hidden Integration': The word 'hidden' here alludes to the fact that technical integration processes often took place behind the scenes, somewhat removed from 'high politics' of the day. This approach offers an alternative to mainstream political science and international relations accounts of European integration, one which places science and technology alongside political, economic, cultural and societal factors in the creation of modern Europe. See, for example, Misa T.J. and Schot, J. (2005) Introduction. *History and Technology*, 21(1): 1–19. Lagendijk, V. (2008) *Electrifying Europe: The Power of Europe in the Construction of Electricity Networks*. Amsterdam University Press, Amsterdam. Høgselius, P., Kaijser, A., van der Vleuten, E. (2015) *Europe's Infrastructure Transition Economy, War, Nature*. Palgrave Macmillan, London. A very useful overview of the vast literature on 'Large Technical Systems' is provided in Van der Vleuten, E. (2004) Infrastructures and Societal Change. A View from the Large Technical Systems Field. *Technology Analysis & Strategic Management*, 16(3), pp. 395–414.
14. Çalişkan, K. and Callon, M. (2009) Economization, Part 1: Shifting Attention from the Economy Towards Processes of Economization. *Economy and Society*, 38(30), pp. 369–398. Çalişkan, K. and Callon, M. (2009) Economization, Part 2: A Research Programme for the Study of Markets. *Economy and Society*, 39(1), pp. 1–32.
15. Çalişkan, K. and Callon, M. (2009) Economization, Part 2: A Research Programme for the Study of Markets. *Economy and Society*, 39(1), p. 2.
16. 'Market devices' is a term used by sociologists of markets to describe the various pieces of equipment and tools—both in the physical sense and in

the use of intellectual tools like mathematical formulae—deployed by actors for conducting calculations and making decisions in a market context. When interconnected, these myriad of devices form the infrastructure of the market. See Muniesa, F., Millo, Y. and Callon M. (2007) An Introduction to Market Devices. In: Callon, M., Millo, Y. and Muniesa, F. (eds.) Market Devices. Oxford: Blackwell, pp. 1–12.

17. A difference between these two perspectives should be noted here. As outlined by Hughes (Hughes, T. (1986) Op. cit), in his 'systems view', there is an interaction between a 'system' and its 'environment'. As systems develop, key actors—system builders—incorporate aspects of this broader environment into their systems and seek to understand it as they develop strategies to manage 'uncertainty'. There is no such external 'environment' in the actor-network view, in which there are no presumptions about the presence of such pre-existing 'macro' influences, rather it focuses on the empirical study of networks, as formed solely through connections made between materials and people. Making Energy Markets broadly aligns with the Hughesian 'systems view', in the sense that an analytical boundary is placed around 'national electricity regimes', and interactions with broader factors, for example, processes of Europeanisation and the dynamics of international commodity markets, are analysed. Also, in line with a Hughesian view, this book analyses electricity system change over a long timespan, with the creation and establishment of liberalised markets viewed as a distinct 'phase', but one which was characterised by continuities with the previous era of state-directed systems. Worthy of note here is Russell's critique of actor-network theory as a frame for the study of long run changes in energy systems. Here, the convincing and evidence-based argument is made that outcomes, in terms of which technologies are adopted, as opposed to others, can only be explained with reference to context and 'broader structures'. Russell, S. (1993) Writing Energy History: Explaining the Neglect of CHP/DH in Britain. British Journal for the History of Science, 26(1), pp. 33–54.

18. Austrian economists emphasise the role of competition as the most effective route to problem solving and innovation. Entrepreneurs exploit incalculable uncertainties as part of a continual discovery process, so unlike traditional classical economics, there is a scepticism of static market equilibria, and quantitative approaches more generally. Public choice theory questions the motivations of politicians and public officials with respect to economic enterprises. The theory predicts that in pursuit of their rational self-interest, they will tend to develop projects for political gain and create unnecessarily large bureaucracies. Property rights theory, or agency theory, places emphasis on the owner-manager relationship and the behaviour of managers under incentives. The theory predicts that in

the presence of incomplete contracts, information asymmetries and a lack of accountability, as is often the case in publicly owned enterprises, economic performance will diminish. New regulatory economics emerged from analyses of public service regulation as practised in the USA during the 1960s and 1970s. This began to emphasise the risks of over-investment associated with traditional rate-of-return regulation—the 'Averch-Johnson effect'—while Harold Demzetz, in his famous article 'Why Regulate Utilities?', questioned the theory of natural monopoly as a foundation of utility regulation, proposing that competition for the market could replace ex-post regulation in many instances. These theoretical summaries draw from Chap. 2 of Parker D. (2009) The Official History of Privatisation Vol. I: The formative years 1970–1987. Government Official History Series. Routledge, Abingdon. In a correspondence with the author, Professor Stephen Littlechild, a prominent British economist during the reform process (see Chaps. 2, 3 and 4), pointed to a number of influential studies which looked to apply these theoretical insights and develop practical proposals for market reform: Lovejoy, W. F. (1971) The Impact of Competition Among Public Utilities: Gas Versus Electricity. In H. Trebing (Ed.) Essays on Public Utility Pricing and Regulation. East Lansing, MI: Institute of Public Utilities, Michigan State University, 1971. Phillips, A. (Ed.) Promoting Competition in Regulated Markets. Brookings Institution, Washington DC, 1975. Two chapters in particular: 'Antitrust in the Electric Power Industry' by Leonard Weiss, and 'A Re-examination of the Monopoly Market Structure for Electric Utilities' by W.J. Primeaux. An influential study of the prospects of liberalisation reforms in the USA was Joskow, P. & Schmalensee, R. (1983) Markets for Power: An Analysis of Electric Utility Deregulation. MIT Press, Cambridge MA.

19. Pearson, P., Watson, J. (2012) UK Energy Policy 1980–2010: A history and lessons to be learnt. Parliamentary Group for Energy Studies, London, p. 8.
20. The EEC as a whole was importing aver 70% of its oil.
21. The British coal mining industry, for example, saw dramatic productivity improvements, particularly following the 1984/85 miners' strike. For example, 'underground productivity in UK mines in 1989 was 90% above the 1987 level'. Surrey, J. (1990) Beyond 1992—the single market and EC energy issues. Energy Policy, 18(1), pp. 42–54.
22. Lignite coal was also extracted in large volumes (circa. 1200 mt) but not internationally traded owing to its lower quality.
23. The Large Combustion Plant Directive (LCPD) was agreed by EEC members in 1988, requiring a progressive reduction in SO2 and NOx

emissions by 2003. These targets varied per country. See Directive 88/609/EEC.

4 Winskel M. (2002a) Autonomy's End: Nuclear Power and the Privatization of the British Electricity Supply Industry. Social Studies of Science, 32(3), pp. 439–467.

25. While the volume of internationally traded hard coal was quite small—for steam coal about 133 million tonnes (mt), or 4% of total production, and a roughly equal volume for coking coal—it was a significant increase on a decade earlier, with roughly only 1% traded in the early 1970s. Partly because the USA was imposing import restrictions to protect its domestic coal industry, almost half of this coal was sipped into European ports and by 1986 prices had fallen to $30/tonne, significantly lower than levels reached just a few years earlier in the early 1980s when prices were in the region of $80. Key reasons for these depressed prices were the oil price collapse, the high value of the pound and the deutschmark relative to the US dollar, and the increasing volumes from low cost mines in China and Colombia. Parker, M., and Surrey, J. (1995) Contrasting British policies for coal and nuclear power, 1979–1992. *Energy Policy*, 23(9), pp. 821–850.

26. Surrey, J. (1990), *Op. cit.*

27. Ibid., p. 43.

Chapter 2

1. As already noted in the Introduction, the Scottish electricity industry was organised differently to England/Wales. Both of them came under the jurisdiction of the UK government, with the Scottish industry being run through the Scottish Office and the English/Welsh through the Department of Energy. For simplicity, the 'British' electricity industry will refer to the system in England/Wales, unless otherwise indicated in the text.

2. For a history of the wider privatisation programme, see Parker's two-volume history of British privatisation. Parker D. (2009) *The Official History of Privatisation Vol. I: The formative years 1970–1987.* Government Official History Series. Routledge, Abingdon. Parker D. (2012) *The Official History of Privatisation, Vol. II: Popular Capitalism, 1987–97.* Government Official History Series. Routledge, Abingdon.

3. Director of Atomic Energy Research Establishment (Harwell Laboratory) (1966–75); Chief Scientist at the Department of Energy (1974–77); Deputy Chairman, then Chairman, of UKAEA (1975–82); Chairman of

CEGB (1982–89); Chairman of World Nuclear Operator's Association (1989–93).

4. Walter Marshall evidence to Energy Committee. Energy Committee (1988) *Third Report: The Structure, Regulation and Economic Consequences of Electricity Supply in the Private Sector.* HMSO. 6 July 1988.
5. 'By the 1980s the CEGB had a capital programme of some £750 million per annum'. Parker (2012) *Op. cit.*, p. 252.
6. The background to this was a failed agreement between Iran and the UK regarding nuclear cooperation. For a detailed history of Marshall's role in negotiating this, see Ansari, A. M. (2017). The Curious Case of the Nuclear Company of Britain and Iran. *Iran: Journal of the British Institute of Persian Studies.* 55 (1), pp. 73–86.
7. Just before it was privatised in 1990 the CEGB had '34 coal, 6 oil 5 dual-fired, 9 open-cycle gas turbine, 6 hydro, 1 wind, 2 pumped storage, 7 (nuclear) magnox, and 5 (nuclear) advanced gas-cooled reactor stations (AGR) stations' (p30). Newbery, D. and Green, R. (1996*) Regulation, Public Ownership and Privatisation of the England Electricity Industry.* In Gilbert, J. and Kahn, E. (Eds.) International Comparisons of Electricity Regulation. Cambridge University Press.
8. Financial Times Publishing Ltd. (1987) *Power in Europe* (issue 6). 'Power in Europe' was published on a bi-monthly basis during this period by the *Financial Times* and it cited extensively in the chapters.
9. Power in Europe (94), 1991.
10. Henney, A. (1994) *A Study of the Privatisation of the Electricity Supply Industry in England and Wales.* EEE Ltd., London.
11. CEGB Memorandum, Energy Committee (1988) *Op. cit.*
12. In current cost accounting terms.
13. The short-run marginal cost (SRMC) is the incremental cost of producing an additional unit to meet a change in demand with the existing installed capacity. For the long-run marginal cost (LRMC) all inputs are variable, so the cost of modifying capacity is incorporated. This is done by calculating the difference in present value between the costs of future systems with and without the change in demand. On average, in an economically optimal system, the SRMC should equal the LRMC, as high marginal prices, above the LRMC, indicate a shortage of capacity and thus send a signal for future investment, bringing the SRMC back in line with the LRMC. This condition relies on free price formation and perfect information, conditions which are difficult to achieve in an electricity market. There is a long-running debate within the electricity economics field about whether to set prices according to the SRMC or the LRMC. For an overview of different approaches as applied in France,

Britain and the USA, see Joskow, P. (1976) Contributions to the Theory of Marginal Cost Pricing. *The Bell Journal of Economics, 7(1)*, pp. 197–206.

14. MMC (1981) *Central Electricity Generating Board: A Report on the Operation by the Board of its System for the Generation and Supply of Electricity in Bulk.* Monopolies and Mergers Commission, May 1981. HMSO, London, p. 285.
15. Parkinson, C. (1992) *Right at the Centre.* Weidenfeld & Nicolson, London, p262.
16. Littlechild, S. (1986) *The Fallacy of the Mixed Economy: An Austrian Critique of Conventional Mainstream Economics and of British Economic Policy.* Institute of Economic Affairs, p. 57. (First published in 1978).
17. John Baker, interview (British Library). From the British Library's project 'An Oral History of the Electricity Supply Industry in the UK'. This archive includes interviews form a wide range of participants in the electricity privatisation project. Project page (accessed 6.4.21): https://www.bl.uk/projects/national-life-stories-an-oral-history-of-the-electricity-supply-industry-in-the-uk#
18. MMC (1981) *Op. cit.* The MMC had been set up a year previously following the 1980 Competition Act.
19. Ibid., pp. 292–293.
20. Jones, P. (1987) Energy Policy: Government vs Industry? *Long Range Planning*, 20(1), pp. 15–16.
21. The industry achieved only 2.44% in 1988–89, below the compromise target of 3.75% target. (All of these figures are on current cost accounting terms).
22. Power in Europe (12), 1987.
23. Power in Europe (12), 1987.
24. Energy Committee, 1988 *Op. cit.*
25. Reported in Power in Europe (12), 1987.
26. Power in Europe (94), 1991.
27. This section draws extensively from Parker (2012) *Op. cit.*
28. Plowden Committee (1976) *The Structure of the Electricity Supply Industry in England and Wales*, Cmnd 6.188, January 1976.
29. Power in Europe (10), 1987.
30. MMC (1987) *Central Electricity Generating Board: A Report on the Efficiency and Costs of the CEGB in Discharging its Functions for the Transmission of Electricity in Bulk.* Monopolies and Mergers Commission, June 1987. HMSO, London, p. 132
31. From Marshall a paper to the CEGB Board in 1983. Quoted in Power in Europe (10), 1987. By the early 1980s the CEGB operated 90 power plants.
32. Power in Europe (10) 1987.

33. Parker (2012) *Op. cit.*, p. 255.
34. Lawson, N., *The Market for Energy*. Speech to the British Institute of Energy Economics, Cambridge, June 1982.
35. This 'ended British Gas's statutory monopoly in gas supply and distribution, forced the British Gas Corporation (BGC) to dispose of its oil interests (Enterprise Oil), and provided for common-carrier provision and hence competitive entry' (p. 53). It was followed in 1986 by the Gas Act which set out the terms of privatisation of BGC as a single entity. Helm, D. Kay, J., and Thompson, D. (1988) Energy Policy and the Role of the State in the Market for Energy. *Fiscal Studies*, 9(1), pp. 41–61.
36. The Act 'abolished the monopoly dating back to the 1909 Electric Lighting Act, which had prohibited persons other than Electricity Boards from commencing to supply or distribute electricity, and to the 1911 Electricity (Supply) Act, which had restricted the establishment and extension of generating plants'. Private generation was legal prior to the 1983 Act but could not be the 'main business' of the company. Hammond, E., Helm, D, and Thompson, D. (1986) Competition in Electricity Supply: Has the Energy Act Failed? *Fiscal Studies* 7 (1): p. 12
37. Ibid., p. 11.
38. Ibid., p. 31.
39. Walter Marshall's evidence to Energy Committee. Energy Committee (1988) *Op. cit.*
40. 'Report on the review of the bulk supply tariff'. The report was delivered to the department in May 1983. The report authors were Roger Chorley and Prof Christopher Foster.
41. Power in Europe (10) 1987.
42. 'Denationalisation' was a term used by critics of the mixed economy and public ownership of industries prior to the common use of the term 'privatisation' which became associated with the Thatcher government. For a first-hand account of how his thinking evolved during this period, see Littlechild, S. (2019) *Life Before Economic Regulation*. Centre for Competition Policy Research Bulletin. Issue 38, Winter 2019. In this piece he references his influential 1978 monograph *The Fallacy of the Mixed Economy*, which outlines his views about the need to bring insights from Austrian economics, public choice and property rights theory to bear on policy towards natural monopoly industries. This signalled his move away from the prevailing economic approach to electricity pricing which had been pioneered by economists such as Marcel Boiteaux, James Meade and Ralph Turvey from the 1940s onwards.
43. Littlechild (1983) *Regulation of British Telecommunications' Profitability*. A Report to the Secretary of State, London: Department of Industry. The RPI-X regulatory formula was first proposed in this report and has come

to be viewed as a landmark in regulatory economics. In 2003 a seminar was held at the University of Bath to mark the 20th anniversary of the report and its impact on regulatory practice in the UK and internationally: *The UK Model of Utility Regulation – A 20th Anniversary Collection to Mark the 'Littlechild Report' – Retrospect and Prospect.*

44. Byatt had published a book on the history of the electricity industry which was based on PhD at Oxford: Byatt, I. C. R. (1979) *The British Electrical Industry, 1875–1914: The Economic Returns to a New Technology.* Oxford University Press.
45. Robinson and Sykes (1987) *Current Choices: Good and Bad Ways to Privatise Electricity.* Centre for Policy Studies, London.
46. Henney, A. (1987) *Privatise Power.* Centre for Policy Studies, London. Available at https://www.cps.org.uk/research/privatise-power/ (Accessed 5.4.21).
47. Power in Europe (8) 1987.
48. Electricity Council Memorandum to Energy Committee. Energy Committee (1988) *Op. cit.*
49. Parkinson, C. (1992) *Op. cit.*, p. 260.
50. Philip Jones' evidence to Energy Committee. Energy Committee (1988) *Op. cit.*
51. Power in Europe (7), 1987.
52. Ibid.
53. CEGB memorandum to Energy Committee. Energy Committee (1988) *Op. cit.*
54. Ibid.
55. Power in Europe (7), 1987.
56. Power in Europe (8), 1987 .
57. Interview, Stephen Littlechild (British Library).
58. Power in Europe (7), 1987.
59. *The Next Moves Forward: The Conservative Manifesto 1987.*
60. See Parkinson's autobiography. Parkinson, C. (1992) *Op. cit.*
61. Interview, Cecil Parkinson (British Library).
62. TV interview given by Parkinson on 2 August 1987. Face the Press, Tyne Tees Television. Reported in the Guardian newspaper, 3 August 1987, p. 28.
63. With demand of over 25,000 therms/year.
64. Waddams Price (1997). Competition and Regulation in the UK Gas Industry. *Oxford Review of Economic Policy*, 13(1), pp. 47–63.
65. Walker, P. (1991) *Staying Power.* Bloomsbury, London, p. 133.
66. Department of Energy (1992) *History of Electricity Privatisation (England and Wales).* Section 3.09 (no page numbers in the copy). The 'History' was written by department officials in order to reflect on the

process and has not been widely published. I am grateful to Stephen Littlechild for providing me with a copy.
67. Power in Europe (10), 1987.
68. Hannah, L. (1987) *Electricity privatisation and the Area Boards: the case for 12: a report*. London Economics.
69. Power in Europe (15), 1987.
70. Interview, Cecil Parkinson (British Library).
71. Ibid.
72. Interview, John Harris (British Library). Harris was Chairman of East Midlands Area Board.
73. Interview, Cecil Parkinson (British Library).
74. Interview, William Rickett (British Library).
75. Figures for numbers of staff allocated to the Electricity Division: 71.5 by end of 1987, 106.5 by end of 1988, peaking at 130 in Mar 1989 and falling to 55 in April 1991. As the privatisation process evolved the Division reorganised itself on a number of occasions. In June 1988 the Division was split into two groups, A and B. With B Division focusing exclusively on privatisation matters. In September 1988 the B Division was split into 4 (ELB1, 2, 3 and 4). During the process Rickett was promoted, taking over responsibility for transition to vesting, contracts and regulation. In 1992, the year after the final privatisations, the Department of Energy was dissolved and merged into the Department of Trade and Industry. Department of Energy (1992) *History of Electricity privatisation*.
76. Interview, William Rickett (British Library).
77. Walter Marshall quoted in Department of Energy (1992) *Op. cit.*
78. Interviews, Cecil Parkinson and William Rickett (British Library).
79. Parkinson (1992) *Op. cit.*, p. 263.
80. Department of Energy (1992) *Op. cit.*
81. Interview, Stephen Littlechild (British Library).
82. Department of Energy (1992) *Op. cit.*
83. Interview, Stephen Littlechild (British Library).
84. Parker, D. (2012) *Op. cit.*
85. Along with one Permanent Secretary, the department had two Deputy Secretaries.
86. *Privatisation of the Scottish Electricity Industry,* Cm 327 (London: HMSO, 1988).
87. Power in Europe (19), 1988.
88. *Privatising Electricity,* Cm 322 (London: HMSO, 1988).
89. Ibid., p. 2.
90. Interview, Cecil Parkinson (British Library).
91. HC Deb 07 March 1988.

92. Power in Europe (19), 1988.
93. Power in Europe (21), 1988.
94. Interview, Stephen Littlechild (British Library).
95. *Privatising Electricity*, p. 11.
96. Interview, Bryan Townsend (British Library). Townsend was Chairman of Midlands Electricity.

Chapter 3

1. The Area Boards were renamed Regional Electricity Companies (RECs) following the vesting of the industry on 31 March 1990. For the purposes of clarity, I will use the RECs term from now on.
2. British Coal Memorandum, Energy Committee (1988) *Third Report: The Structure, Regulation and Economic Consequences of Electricity Supply in the Private Sector*. HMSO. 6 July 1988.
3. Power in Europe (5), 1987.
4. Walter Marshall evidence, Energy Committee (1988) *Op. cit.*
5. There were only two collieries operating: Longannet and Bilston Glen.
6. Jeffry summarises that 'Essentially the process involves calculating a cash value at some pre-determined date for all payments (expenditures and receipts) over the whole span from the start of construction until the end of the station's useful life, and in the case of nuclear stations, for a further 25 years or so until decommissioning costs have to be met' (p8). Jeffery (1982). The Real Cost of Nuclear Electricity in the UK. *Energy Policy*, 10 (4), pp. 76–100.
7. Ibid.
8. Interview, William Rickett (British Library).
9. Power in Europe (36), 1988.
10. Six per cent in the first year of the contract, 5.5 in the second and 5 in the third.
11. Department of Energy (1992) *History of Electricity Privatisation (England and Wales)*.
12. British Coal Memorandum, Energy Committee (1988) *Op. cit.*
13. Littlechild, S. (2010) *The Creation of a Market for Retail Electricity Supply*. Working paper (CWPE 1035 & EPRG 1017): 8 https://core.ac.uk/download/pdf/77057111.pdf (Accessed 5.4.21).
14. Ibid.
15. Department of Energy (1992) *History of Electricity Privatisation (England and Wales)*.

16. Walter Marshall, quoted in Winskel, M. (2002a) Winskel M. (2002a) Autonomy's End: Nuclear Power and the Privatization of the British Electricity Supply Industry. *Social Studies of Science*, 32(3), p. 445.
17. Power in Europe (94), 1991.
18. For an overview of nuclear technology choices made in the UK post-war decades, see Williams (1980). *The Nuclear Power Decisions: British Policies 1953–1978.* Croom Helm, London.
19. Energy Committee (1990). *Fourth Report: The Cost of Nuclear Power.* House of Commons. 7 June 1990, p. xiii.
20. For a history of the UK's fast breeder programme and the test facility at Dounreay in Scotland, see MacKenzie, N. G., Knox, S. & Hannon, M. (2020): Fast breeder reactor technology and the entrepreneurial state in the UK, *Business History* (early online publication). https://doi.org/10.1080/00076791.2020.1809653
21. Power in Europe (51), 1989.
22. Mackerron, G. (1996) *Nuclear Power under Review.* In Surrey, J. (Ed.) The British Electricity Experiment. Privatisation: The Record, the Issues, The Lessons. Earthscan, London, 1996.
23. Written into Clause 12 of the 1989 Electricity Act.
24. For a study of this inquiry, see O'Riordan, T., Kemp, R., & Purdue, M. (1988) *Sizewell B: An Anatomy of Inquiry.* Macmillan Press, Basingstoke and London.
25. Power in Europe (63), 1989.
26. Mackerron, G. (1996) *Op. cit.*, pp. 141–142.
27. For example, Mackerron, G. (1982) *Nuclear Power and the Economic Interests of Consumers.* Electricity Consumers Council. Jeffery (1982) *Op. cit.*
28. Mackerron, G. (1996) *Op. cit.*, p. 143.
29. Energy Committee (1990) *Op. cit.*, p. xxxviii.
30. The public sector price was slightly higher than the economic resource cost (at 2.24–3.09 p/kWh, depending on whether a 5% or 8% discount rate was used) as in order to directly compare project costs Marshall adjusted for inflation and added overheads and other construction-related costs.
31. Energy Committee (1990) *Op. cit.*, p. xiv.
32. Energy Committee (1990) *Op. cit.*, p. xv.
33. Cecil Parkinson later claimed in his memoir that the idea for this levy came about following a conversation with a Californian businessman who explained the mechanism through which the state had been subsiding the nascent wind industry there.
34. Department of Energy (1992) *History of Electricity Privatisation (England and Wales).*

35. Ibid.
36. Power in Europe (64), 1989.
37. Energy Committee (1990) *Op. cit.*, p. xiii.
38. Department of Energy (1992) *Op. cit.*
39. Ibid.
40. John Baker, quoted in Power in Europe (44), 1989.
41. Lawson, N. (1993) *The View from No. 11: Memoirs of at Tory Radical.* Corgi Books, London, p. 169.
42. Department of Energy (1992) *History of Electricity Privatisation (England and Wales).*
43. Parkinson's speech to the House announcing the decision was made on 24th July 1989.
44. Summarised from Energy Committee (1990) *Op. cit.*, p. xxii/xxiii.
45. Energy Committee (1990) *Op. cit.*, p. xxiv
46. Ibid.
47. Department of Energy (1992) *History of Electricity Privatisation (England and Wales).*
48. Energy Committee (1990) *Op. cit.*, p. xvi.
49. Interview, John Baker (British Library).
50. John Wakeham, in Power in Europe (62), 1989.
51. Although the Secretary of State lobbied for him to take over as head of the World Association of Nuclear Operators.
52. Henney, A. (1994) *A Study of the Privatisation of the Electricity Supply Industry in England and Wales.* EEE Ltd., London.
53. Power in Europe (64), 1989.
54. Noted in Parker (2012) *Op. cit.*, p. 304.
55. Littlechild, S. (2010) The Creation of a Market for Retail Electricity Supply. *Working Paper (EPRG, 1017; CWPE, 1035),* p. 19.
56. Power in Europe (58), 1989.
57. Interviews, John Baker, David Jefferies, Joh Wakeham (British Library). Jefferies was former Deputy Chairman of the Electricity Council until 1990 and then became the first Chairman of the National Grid Company.
58. Green (2005) *Market power mitigation in the UK power market.* https://spiral.imperial.ac.uk/bitstream/10044/1/10432/2/Market%20Power%20Mitigation%2005.pdf (accessed 5.4.21).
59. Power in Europe (60), 1989.
60. Department of Energy (1992) *Op. cit.*
61. Littlechild, S. (2010) *Op. cit.*, p. 21.
62. Offer (1998a) *Review of Energy Sources for Power Stations.* Office of Electricity Regulation, Birmingham.

63. For a thorough analysis of the different contracts and evolution throughout the 1990s, see Lowery (1999) *Electricity Pricing and Regulation*. PhD thesis, Brunel University, pp. 32–55.
64. National Consumer Council figures presented in Energy Committee (1992) *Second Report: Consequences of Electricity Privatisation*. HMSO, para 16.
65. Three hundred of the largest industrial consumers of power had since 1982 been included in the 'Qualified Industrial Consumers Scheme (QUICS)', benefiting from cheap supplies linked to world coal prices.
66. See Henney, A (1994) *Op. cit.*
67. Energy Committee (1990) *Op. cit.*, p. xxxv.
68. Interview, John Wakeham (British Library).
69. Department of Energy (1992) *Op. cit.*
70. See National Audit Office reports for overviews of the sales: NAO (1992a) *The Sale of National Power and PowerGen*. Report by the Comptroller and Auditor General. HMSO: NAO (1992b) *The Sale of the Twelve Regional Electricity Companies*. Report by the Comptroller and Auditor General. HMSO.
71. Meek, J. (2012) *How We Happened to Sell Off Our Electricity*. London Review of Books, 34(17).
72. The company, with 6200 employees, included the CEGB's transmission system, the Dinorwig and Ffestiniog pumped storage stations, along with a corporate planning division and a research unit.
73. NAO (1992b) *Op. cit.*, p. 11.
74. Kleinwort Benson (1990) *The Regional Electricity Companies Share Offers*.
75. The idea behind the split being to have companies of similar value through allocating plant based on size, age, efficiency, fuel source and likely position in the dispatch merit order. There were of course many factors considered in determining the allocation of plant between the two companies. The overarching one was fuel costs as this accounted for approx. 70% of total generation costs, so an equitable split would need to see plants with a similar fuel cost base split between the companies. For example, plants located along the Thames Estuary could access cheaper coal imports, so these needed to be split according to the 70:30 share. Similarly, inland plants, such as those supplied by the Yorkshire coal fields, were split. An account of this process if provided by John Wooley, former CEGB and PowerGen executive: Interview, John Wooley (British Library).

Chapter 4

1. For a full analysis of distributional aspects of the market throughout the 1990s, see Mackerron, G. (2003) *Electricity in England and Wales: Efficiency and Equity.* In Glachant, J.M & Finon, D. (Eds.) Competition in European Electricity Markets. Edward Elgar, Cheltenham, 2003. Mackerron outlines that the combined operating profits of National Power and PowerGen in 1990/91 stood at £351 m, £753 in 1994/95 and £1000 m in 1996/97; while for the RECs' distribution businesses, profits rose from £636 m in 1990/91, to £1291 m in 1994/95, falling back to £1093 in 1996/97 due to the more stringent price control taking effect.
2. Joskow and Schmalensee note that such power pools could be 'tight'—rules-based systems placing formal requirements on members; for example, centralised dispatch, coordination of spare capacity and coordinated system planning, or 'loose'—typically voluntary arrangements with no central despatch or penalties. Joskow, P. & Schmalensee, R. (1983) *Markets for Power: An Analysis of Electric Utility Deregulation.* MIT Press, Cambridge MA, p. 66.
3. Interviews, Nick Winser & Fiona Woolf (British Library).
4. Power in Europe (42), 1989.
5. Power in Europe (56), 1989.
6. Henney, A. (1994) *A Study of the Privatisation of the Electricity Supply Industry in England and Wales.* EEE Ltd., London.
7. Department of Energy (1992) *History of Electricity Privatisation (England and Wales).*
8. Interview, Brian Pomeroy (British Library).
9. Bunn, D. (1994) Evaluating the Effects of Privatizing Electricity. *Journal of the Operational Research Society*, 45 (4), pp. 367–375.
10. Interview, Brian Pomeroy (British Library).
11. Early calculations of LOLP which were with reference to a baseline of the prior seven days 'resulted in a very steep curve' which meant that 'small changes in demand or availability would result in large changes in the value of LOLP in the capacity element of the Pool price'—potentially giving generators an incentive to 'gain from manipulation of availability'. RECs proposed that the LOLP should be made more predictable and the curve smoother such that at 'higher plant margins, the probability of loss of load would be less'. Department of Energy (1992) *Op. cit.*
12. Newbery, D. (1997) *Pool Reform and Competition in Electricity.* Paper presented to the IEA\LBS Lectures on Regulation Series VII 1997 on 11 November 1997, p. 15.

13. This included the RECs who held public electricity supply licences to supply the franchise customers in their areas, and the 'second-tier' suppliers who were in market to supply eligible customers.
14. Generator bids contained a number of different components to its price offer; its start-up, no-load prices and additional prices for incremental increases in output. They also included information about key technical parameters such as their minimum level of output and their ramp rates (how quickly they could increase or decrease their output).
15. See Hunt, S., Shuttleworth, G. (1993) *Op. cit*, pp. 2–8.
16. Power in Europe (62), 1989.
17. Ibid.
18. Interview, William Rickett (British Library).
19. For project details see Winskel, M. (2002b) When Systems are Overthrown: The 'Dash for Gas' in the British Electricity Supply Industry. *Social Studies of Science,* 32 (4), pp. 563–598.
20. Bunn, D. (1994) *Op. cit.*
21. Green, R. (2005) *Market Power Mitigation in the UK Power Market.* Available at: https://spiral.imperial.ac.uk/bitstream/10044/1/10432/2/Market%20Power%20Mitigation%2005.pdf (Accessed 12.4.21).
22. The Electricity Forwards Agreement (EFA) was a trading place through which brokers matched buyers and sellers of standardised forwards contracts. These were two-way CfDs around the Pool price which were settled weekly. Unlike an exchange, there was no central clearing house so the identities of the parties was revealed before the transaction. The main brokers involved were Gerrard & National Intercommodities (GNI) Ltd., who were later in 1995 joined by Tradition Financial Services and Euro Brokers. Overall trading volumes were low and the marketplace did not have a significant effect on the competitive industry.
23. NAO (1992b) *The Sale of the Twelve Regional Electricity Companies.* Report by the Comptroller and Auditor General. HMSO, London.
24. Green, R. (2006) Electricity Liberalisation in Europe – How Competitive Will It Be? *Energy Policy*, 34 (16), pp. 2532–2541.
25. Offer (1998a) *Review of Energy Sources for Power Stations.* Office of Electricity Regulation, Birmingham, p. 10.
26. Ibid.
27. Henney, A. (1994) *Op. cit.*
28. It was not until the introduction of a different market arrangement which replaced the Pool in the late 1990s (the New Electricity Trading Arrangements) that a business model for gas peaking plant became viable.
29. For sulphur, Directive 88/609/EEC required 'a three-stage cut of a total 60%, on 1980 levels of emission, by 2003. The basic target is for a 20% reduction by 1993, 40% by 1998 and 60% by 2003'. For NOx, a reduc-

tion 'on 1980 emission levels, of 15% by 1993, and a further 15% by 1998' (Power in Europe (27), 1988). It was initially thought that meeting this would require FGD retrofits on 12 GW capacity, but the UK successfully negotiated for derogations due to the relatively higher sulphur content of British coal.

30. The threatened pits were later closed in 1994 when the coal industry was privatised. RJB mining bought most of the pits.
31. A detailed overview of the policy debate around subsidisation of the British coal industry during this period is provided by Helm. Dieter Helm, D. (2003). *Energy, the State, and the Market: British Energy Policy since 1979*. Oxford University Press, Oxford.
32. 'The coal labour force had fallen from nearly 200 000 at the time of the 1984–5 coal miners' strike to about 70 000 by 1990, but pit closures reduced numbers to 20 000 by 1993 and less than 10 000 by 1998'. Newbery, D. (1999) *The UK Experience: Privatization with Market Power*. In CEPR (1999) A European Market for Electricity? Monitoring European Deregulation 2. Centre for Economic Policy Research, London, p. 97. Job losses were also seen in the electricity industry itself: Nuclear Electric and the RECs had planned to reduce their workforce by 30% while National Power quickly shed 60% of its allocation of CEGB staff.
33. Energy Committee (1992) *Second Report: Consequences of Electricity Privatisation*. HMSO, para 147.
34. Bunn, D. (1994) *Op. cit.*
35. British Coal Memorandum, Energy Committee (1992) *Op. cit.*
36. Ibid.
37. Energy Committee (1992) *Op. cit.*, para 148.
38. British Coal Memorandum, Energy Committee (1992) *Op. cit.*
39. Energy Committee (1992) *Op. cit.*, para 51.
40. National Power Memorandum, Energy Committee (1992) *Op. cit.*
41. John Baker evidence to Energy Committee (1992) *Op. cit.*
42. Ibid.
43. As set out in 'Horton IV', the department's central scenario developed by Geoff Horton. See Helm (2003) Op. cit., p. 164.
44. Green estimates that 'around 90% of the electricity traded through the Pool was covered by CfDs'. Green, R. (2003) Failing electricity markets: should we shoot the Pools? *Utilities Policy,* 11 (3), pp. 155–167.
45. Offer (1998b) *Op. cit*
46. Green (2005) *Op. cit.*
47. Offer (1998b) *Op. cit.*
48. Energy Committee (1992) *Op. cit.*, para 13.
49. The three were: *Report on Constrained-on Plant* (1992); *Review of Pool Prices* (1992); *Review of Economic Purchasing: Further Statement* (1993).

50. Offer, quoted in Henney, A. (1994) *Op. cit.*, p. 244.
51. Offer, quoted in Energy Committee (1992) *Op. cit.*, para 104.
52. Ed Wallis, evidence to Energy Committee (1992) *Op. cit.*, paras 384, 398 and 401.
53. Green, R. (2005) *Op. cit.*, p. 5.
54. National Power Memorandum, Energy Committee (1992) *Op. cit.*
55. The percentage of National Power and PowerGen's total capacity tied up in CfDs was, respectively, 84.3 and 89.1 in 1991, and 72.7 and 70.6 in 1992 and 1993. Helm, D. & Powell, A. (1992) Pool Prices, Contracts and Regulation in the British Electricity Supply Industry. Fiscal *Studies*, 13 (1), pp. 89–105.
56. Newbery, D. (1999) *Op. cit.*, p. 98.
57. The regulator subsequently estimated that for 1997 the avoidable cost to coal stations of running was in the region of 1.6–1.7 p/kWh, whereas average pool prices were '2.45 p/kWh time-weighted and 2.6 p/kWh demand-weighted in 1997'. Offer (1998a) *Op. cit.*, p. 21.
58. For a detailed economic analysis, see Green and Newbery (1992) Competition in the British Electricity Spot Market. *Journal of Political Economy*, 100, (5): 929–953. Here Green and Newbery argue that this would not have been the case if the CEGB was split into five rather than two competing generators. Somewhat of a counter argument was later put forward by the regulator who argued that the REC/IPP contracts for new gas plant may have been a sensible strategy given the uncertainties at the time, but acknowledged the constraints on competition imposed by the earlier political decision to have only two competitors. 'It has been argued that the RECs' IPP contracts have turned out to be more expensive over the past few years than other possible contracts which subsequently became available, and that the DGES should revisit the economic purchasing review. However, the only reasonable basis for assessing compliance with the economic purchasing condition in REC licences is against other possibilities open at the time. Alternative contracts were not on offer at the time the IPP contracts were signed. The fact that National Power and PowerGen themselves invested heavily in early CCGT stations suggests that the judgements and decisions of RECs and IPPs were not without foundation at the time'. Offer (1998a) *Op. cit.*, p. 15.
59. Energy Committee (1992) *Op. cit.*, paras 53 & 54.
60. In this case the regulator 'agreed that National Power had based its bids on estimates of each station's costs, and had sometimes reduced its bids in order to avoid over-recovery against its targets. He viewed this as a responsible strategy'. Green (2005) *Op. cit.*, p. 6.
61. Ibid.
62. Henney, A. (1994) *Op. cit.*

63. Offer (1992) *Report on constrained-on plant.* Office of Electricity Regulation, Birmingham.
64. Energy Committee (1992) *Op. cit.*, para 168.
65. A commitment 'to bid into the Pool during financial years 1994/95 and 1995/96 in such a way that, under reasonable assumptions of other generators' bids and taking seasonal fluctuations into account, average annual Pool Purchase Price would in normal circumstances reasonably be expected not to exceed 24 £/MWh time weighted and 25.5 £/MWh demand weighted (both in October 1993 prices)'. Offer (1998b) *Op. cit.*, p. 46.
66. Interview, Brian Townsend (British Library). Chairman of Midlands Electricity.
67. 1995: Hansen bought Eastern; Scottish Power bought Manweb; North Western merged with the regional water utility to form United Utilities; SWEB bought by Southern Company (US). 1996: London bought by Entergy (US); South Eastern purchased by Central and South West (US); Northern bought by CalEnergy (US) creating CE Electric; SWALEC bought by Welsh Water to create Hyder; Midlands purchased by Avon Energy (US) to form GPU Power UK; East Midlands purchased by Dominion Resources (US). 1997: Yorkshire bought by AEP (US). 1998: London bought by EDF; Scottish-Hydro merged with Southern to form SSE; Eastern bought by TXU (US), creating TXI Energi; National Power bought Midlands, creating nPower; PowerGen bought East Midlands. 1999: SWEB bought by Western Power Distribution (US).
68. It later bought 'the RyeHouse gas-fired power station from PowerGen'. Green (2006) *Op. cit.*, p. 2538.
69. Newbery, D. (1999) *Op. cit.*, p. 92.
70. Ibid. EDF, after buying London Electricity, bought a total of 4800 MW of thermal generation plant, including the '2 GW Cottam power station from PowerGen in 2000. EDF had also acquired the SWEB supply business, in the SouthWest of England'. Later, EDF bought the REC in the South East (Seeboard) in 2002 and a year later created EDF Energy, the consolidated arm of its UK operations. It bought a majority share in the AGR fleet in 2008, then part of the privatised British Energy which had been created in 1996, with the Magnox stations staying in the public sector. Green (2006) *Op. cit.*, p. 2538.
71. For a critical appraisal see: Helm, D. (2003) *Op. cit.*
72. Green (2006) *Op. cit.*, p. 2537.
73. Newbery, D. (1999) *Op.cit.*, (p. 91)'.
74. National Power then split its international (International Power) and UK (Innogy) operations. Innogy was later taken over by RWE. In 2001 Innogy had 'bought Yorkshire Electricity, and then swapped its distribu-

tion business for Northern Electric's supply business'. Green (2006) *Op. cit.*, p. 2538.

75. 2000: TXU bought North Western's supply business; WPD bought Hyder's distribution business; SSE bought Hyder's retail business; nPower separated into Innogy and International Power; Central & South West merged with AEP. 2001: Innogy purchased Yorkshire; Swap deal between Innogy and CE Electric, Innogy took the Northern supply business and CE Electric took the Yorkshire distribution business. 2002: E. ON purchased PowerGen, along with Eastern's supply business; RWE purchased Innogy (nPower); EDF purchased Eastern distribution. 2003: EDF purchased the SWALEC retail business and South Eastern distribution
76. Green (2006) *Op. cit.*, p. 2538.
77. The philosophy behind NETA/BETTA was quite different to the original Electricity Pool. NETA/BETTA more closely resembled gas markets than traditional power pools. Unlike the Electricity Pool which was a 'gross' market, requiring all trades for physical power to be routed through it, BETTA is a decentralised market where buyers and sellers of power are free to enter into bilateral contracts or transact via an organised power exchange. They simply need to notify National Grid of their positions 1 hour prior to gate closure. The bids then become 'firm', and based on the costs of balancing the system close to real time, system prices are calculated which are then used as a basis to charge licensed generators and suppliers (the balancing responsible parties) for their role in creating deviations between trading positions and actual physical exchanges. So alongside its decentralised structure, BETTA is characterised as a 'net' pool, where system pricing is based on the final positions of the traders rather than the overall, or gross, economic dispatch.

Chapter 5

1. Single European Act, 1986, Article 13.
2. European Commission (1985) *Completing the Internal Market.* COM (85) 310.
3. The background to the White Paper is outlined in Cockfield's account of his time as commissioner. Cockfield, F.A. (1994) *The European Union: Creating the Single Market.* Wiley, London.
4. Cameron, P. (2002) *Competition in energy markets: law and regulation in the European Union.* Oxford University Press, Oxford, p. 48.

5. The SEA was an amendment to EEC, ECSC and EURATOM—the three foundational treaties of the EEC—not an Act in the strictest sense of the term.
6. Power in Europe (46), 1989.
7. In the late 1980s the existing power pools in Europe were UCPTE (Austria, Belgium, France, Germany, Italy, Lux, Spain, Netherlands, Switzerland, Denmark, Greece, Portugal, Yugoslavia); UFPTES (France, Iberian Union); SUDEL (Austria, Italy, Yugoslavia); NORDEL (Denmark, Norway, Sweden, Finland, Iceland).
8. UCTE (2003) *The 50 Year Success Story – Evolution of a European Interconnected Grid,* Secretariat of UCTE, Brussels, p. 10. (UCTE became the successor organisation to UCPTE following the unbundling of electricity generation and transmission across the European Union).
9. Lagendijk, V. and Van Der Vleuten, V. (2013) *Inventing Electrical Europe: Interdependencies, Borders, Vulnerabilities.* In Hogselius, P., Hommels, A., Kaijser, A. and Van Der Vleuten, V. (Eds.) The Making of Europe's Critical Infrastructure: Common Connections and Shared Vulnerabilities. Palgrave Macmillan, London, p. 74.
10. Ibid.
11. Bolton, R., Lagendijk, V., Silvast, A. (2019) Grand Visions and Pragmatic Integration: Exploring the Evolution of Europe's Electricity Regime. *Environmental Innovation and Societal Transitions.* 32, pp. 55–68.
12. UCTE (2003) *Op. cit,* p. 15.
13. Ibid, p. 16.
14. Hunt, S., Shuttleworth, G. (2001) *Competition and Choice in Electricity.* Wiley, Chichester, p. 40.
15. Ibid: See p. 41 for and overview of issues of free-riding in pools and other problematic economic issues with pooling arrangements, particularly around incentives for excess capacity.
16. See Lagendijk, V. and Van Der Vleuten, V. (2013) *Op. cit.*
17. Ibid, p. 80.
18. Ibid.
19. Finon, D. (1990) Opening access to European grids: In search of solid ground. *Energy Policy,* 18 (5), pp. 428–442.
20. See Finon, (1990) *Op. cit.*
21. Ibid., p. 432.
22. Ibid., p. 433.
23. European Commission (1988) *The Internal Energy Market.* COM (88) 238, p. 6.
24. Key outputs of the WG were the 'Protocol of Agreement on Energy Matters' (1964) and the community's policy for oil and natural gas (1967).

25. European Commission (1988) *First Guidelines for a Community Energy Policy*. COM (68) 1040.
26. Ibid., p. 5.
27. Cameron, P. (2002) *Op. cit.*, p. 46.
28. Ibid.
29. Ibid.
30. European legislation has been amended significantly following the Maastricht (1992), Amsterdam (1997) and Lisbon Treaties (2007). I will use the original EEC Treaty Article numbers throughout these chapters.
31. Most notably 'Directive 73/278 was adopted, implementing the rules of the International Energy Agency'. Cameron, P. (2002) *Op. cit.*, p. 47.
32. Power in Europe (35), 1988.
33. European Commission (1981) *The Development of an Energy Strategy for the Community. Communication from the Commission to the Council.* COM (81) 540.
34. Cameron, P. (2002) *Op. cit.*, p. 47.
35. This was later written into key Articles of the Treaty on the Functioning of the European Union (TFEU—signed in December 2007 and coming into effect on 1 December 2009) in relation to energy policy: Article 194 TFEU outlines that European cooperation in relation to energy markets, security of supply and cross-border networks 'shall not affect a Member State's right to determine the conditions for exploiting its energy resources, its choice between different energy sources and the general structure of its energy supply …'
36. Power in Europe (11), 1987.
37. European Council (1986) *Council Resolution of 16 September 1986 concerning new Community energy policy objectives for 1995 and convergence of the policies of the Member States.* 86/C 241/01.
38. Hancher, L. (1990) *Towards a free market for energy? A Legal Perspective.* Energy Policy, 18 (3), p. 233.
39. Power in Europe (11), 1987.
40. European Commission (1988) *Op. cit.*, p. 2.
41. European Commission (1988) *Op. cit.*
42. European Commission (1987), *Towards a dynamic European economy – green paper on the development of the common market for telecommunications services and equipment.* COM (87) 290.
43. European Commission (1988) *Op. cit.*, pp. 8–9.
44. European Commission (1988) *Op. cit.*, p. 72.
45. European Commission (1988) *Op. cit.*, pp. 73–74.
46. Press Release (8880/88 (Presse 160)). 1270th meeting of the Council and of the Representatives of the Governments of the Member States meeting within the Council. Brussels, 4 December 1988.

47. Ibid, p. 4
48. Power in Europe (29), 1988.
49. Power in Europe (39), 1988.
50. Ibid.
51. Ibid.
52. Finon (1990) *Op. cit.* describes him as 'an eager partisan of open access.'
53. Draft directive on price transparency (COM (89) 332); Electricity exchanges and transit (COM (89) 336); Investment coordination (COM (89) 335).
54. Cardoso e Cunha, quoted in Power in Europe (54), 1989.
55. Power in Europe (45), 1988.
56. Power in Europe (63), 1989.
57. Power in Europe (63), 1989.
58. Ibid.
59. Power in Europe (86), 1990.
60. Power in Europe (62), 1989.
61. Power in Europe (85), 1989: A contribution by Leigh Hancher.
62. This issue is related to the way that electricity flows according to the laws of physics. Cameron summarises the fundamentals of the issue: 'The flow of electricity over wires follows different physical laws to that of gas, giving rise to "loop flows". These are intrinsic to electricity transmission and affect the way that access to transmission capacity is made available to buyers and the way it is controlled by the system operator. So-called wheeling transactions along one part of the path can have an effect on the availability of transmission capacity along an interconnected path. In the EU context, "transit" has recently been defined as a physical flow of electricity hosted on the transmission system of a Member State, neither produced nor destined for consumption in this Member State, and including transit flows commonly denominated as loop-flows'. Cameron, P. (2002) *Op. cit.*, p. 22.
63. Financial Times Ltd. (1989) *EC Energy Monthly*, Issue 5.
64. Rent extracted 'by charging a price equal to the difference between the cost of the power and its value in the receiving zone'. Hunt, P. & Shuttleworth, G. (2001) *Op. cit.*, pp. 32–33.
65. McGowan, F. (1993) *The Struggle for Power in Europe: Competition and Regulation in the EC Electricity Industry*. Royal Institute of International Affairs, London.
66. Power in Europe (85), 1989: A contribution by Leigh Hancher.
67. Council Directive 90/547/EEC of 29 October 1990 on the transit of electricity through transmission grids. There was also a Directive on price transparency passed in June 1990. A gas transit directive was subsequently passed in May 1991.

68. Power in Europe (85), 1989: A contribution by Leigh Hancher.
69. Transit Directive, 1990, Article 2.
70. Transit Directive, 1990, Article 3, Para 3.
71. Hancher, L. (1990) *Op. cit.*, p. 243.
72. Commission Decision 92/167/EEC.

Chapter 6

1. Chick, M. (2009) *Electricity and energy policy in Britain, France and the United States since 1945.* Edward Elgar, Cheltenham, p. 9.
2. Ibid., p. 11.
3. Ibid., p. 9.
4. For data on the nuclear programme, see Grubler, A. (2010) The Costs of the French Nuclear Scale-up: A case of negative learning by doing. *Energy Policy,* 38(9).
5. See Ibid.: Table 1 provides details of how the French reactor design evolved.
6. The CEA had a shareholding in Framatome and became the parent company of COGEMA. Subsequently, as Grubler outlines, 'In 2001, Framatome and COGEMA (now AREVA NC) merged to form AREVA, essentially owned by the CEA, i.e., the French government. Also, AREVA entered a joint venture with Siemens of Germany in the development of the European Pressurized Water Reactor (EPR), and Framatome ANP was founded with a minority Siemens stake, renamed AREVA NP in 2006. In 2009, Siemens announced its intention to end its partnership, selling its 34% share back to AREVA': Grubler, A. (2010) *Op. cit.*, p. 5176.
7. Laffont, J.J. (1996) *The French Electricity Industry.* In Gilbert, J. and Kahn, E. (Eds.). International Comparisons of Electricity Regulation. Cambridge University Press.
8. Thomas, S. (1988) *The Realities of Nuclear Power: International Economic and Regulatory Experience.* Cambridge University Press, Cambridge, p. 206.
9. Ibid., p. 209.
10. Ibid.: Figures from Table 1.1. Original source listed as Nuclear Engineering International, Power Reactors. August 1985.
11. Power in Europe (66), 1990.
12. Thomas, S. (1988) *Op. cit.*, p. 198.
13. Ibid.
14. Ibid., p. 215.
15. Ibid., p. 215.

16. Finon, D. (1990) Opening access to European grids: In search of solid ground. *Energy Policy*, 18 (5), pp. 428–442.
17. Power in Europe (76), 1990.
18. EC Energy Monthly (5), 1989.
19. Power in Europe (62), 1990.
20. Power in Europe (46), 1989.
21. 'In 1991, Switzerland bought 14 TWh, Italy 13.1 TWh, Germany 5.4 TWh, Benelux 4.4 TWh, and Spain/Portugal 0.2 TWh'. Power in Europe (120), 1991.
22. Power in Europe (71), 1990.
23. Power in Europe (92), 1991.
24. For a full description of the event, see Lagendijk, V. and Van Der Vleuten, V. (2013) *Inventing Electrical Europe: Interdependencies, Borders, Vulnerabilities*. In Hogselius, P., Hommels, A., Kaijser, A. and Van Der Vleuten, V. (Eds.) The making of Europe's Critical Infrastructure: Common Connections and Shared Vulnerabilities. Palgrave Macmillan, London.
25. Thomas, S. (1988) *Op. cit.*, pp. 226–7.
26. Power in Europe (66), 1990.
27. Thomas, S. (1988) *Op. cit.*, p. 222.
28. Herpich, P., Brauers, H. & Oei, P. (2018) *A Historical Case Study of Previous Coal Transitions in Germany*. Coal Transitions project. IDDRI and Climate Strategies.
29. Gustafson, T. (2020) *The Bridge: Natural gas in a redivided Europe*. Harvard University Press. Cambridge MA.
30. Herpich et al., (2018) *Op. cit.*
31. Parnell, M. (1994) *The German Tradition of Organized Capitalism*. Clarendon Press, Oxford, p. 105.
32. Ibid., pp. 98–99.
33. Ibid., pp. 98–100.
34. Ibid., p. 100.
35. Ibid., p. 100.
36. Herpich et al., (2018) *Op. cit.*, pp. 14.
37. Ibid., p. 8.
38. Parnell, M. (1994) *Op. cit.*, p. 111.
39. Parnell, M. (1994) *Op. cit.*, p. 135 & 138.
40. OECD (2004) *Germany – Regulatory Reform in Electricity, Gas, and Pharmacies*. Organisation for Economic Co-operation and Development (OECD), Country Studies, p. 11.
41. Parnell, M. (1994) *Op. cit.*, pp. 201–2.
42. Parnell, M. (1994) *Op. cit.*, p. 140.
43. Parnell, M. (1994) *Op. cit.*, p. 142.

44. Power in Europe (96), 1991.
45. Power in Europe (96), 1991.
46. The 41 mt was divided into three tiers; for 23 mt the price was to be 'subsidised to match the world market price of oil'; for 11 mt 'subsidised to nearly match the price of world market coal'; and for the remaining 7 mt there was to be 'no compensation'; however, 'every tonne of domestic coal used by a utility in this category entitles it to use one tonne of imported coal'. Power in Europe (60), 1989.
47. Padgett, S. (1992) The Single European Energy Market: The Politics of Realization. *Journal of Common Market Studies*, 30(1), p. 63.
48. Ibid., p. 65.
49. 55 mt by 2005, sustaining the 1995 level (the 1990 level was 70 mt); 35 mt of this for electricity and the rest for steel.
50. Power in Europe (112), 1991.
51. Ibid.
52. Power in Europe (114), 1991.
53. EC Energy Monthly (49), 1993. Following this, 'under the March 1997 *Kohlekompromiss* (coal compromise), a political agreement among the federal government, the coal-producing *Länder*, the coal industry and the unions', it was agreed that employment would drop to 36,000 by 2005, from 84,000 at the time.
54. Lagendijk, V. and Van Der Vleuten, V. (2013) *Op. cit.*
55. OECD (2004) Op. cit., p. 10
56. Ibid.
57. *Marktöffnung und Wettbewerb* (Opening of Markets and Competition), 1991.
58. Deregulation Commission 1991, para. 316. Quote from OECD (2004) *Op. cit.*, p. 12.
59. One prominent example of this was the case of Kleve, a locality close to the Dutch border. The municipality there had wanted to import cheaper power from the Netherlands but were obstructed from doing so by RWE who claimed that they could not do so under the terms of their concession contract with them. Kleve, along with Nordhorns, a neighbouring municipality, were looking for exemption from the commission under Article 85 of the Treaty of Rome.
60. Padgett, S. (1992) *Op. cit.*, p. 65.
61. Ibid.
62. Ibid., p. 68.

CHAPTER 7

1. Part of the reason why common carriage was toxic for European electricity utilities was that the term originated in the context of radical reform of the US gas sector where opening up the networks led to intense competition. The US interstate gas system, regulated by FERC, provided a precedent which was transformational and the extreme case which the European energy industry was keen to avoid. In this case the network began to be operated as a pure market, with network capacity begin defined as a property right which could be traded; a type of 'Coasian' market with 'deregulated trade in capacity rights'. Makholm outlines the historical evolution of this market for gas pipeline capacity rights from the 1930s to its final completion in 2000. Early in the process the interstate pipeline industry was separated from local distributors so that 'those regulated local distributors could buy gas in the field for themselves and simply contract with pipelines for the needed inland transport service'. The pipeline owners were transformed 'from gas merchants to simply contract transporters for hire'. In essence, their role was diminished to became service providers to market participants, effectively passive intermediaries, a fate the European energy utilities wished to avoid. Makholm J. D. (2017) *Institutions, to Property Rights, to High-Technology Gas Markets.* NERA Economic Consulting, p. 8.
2. TPA was defined by the commission as 'a regime providing for an obligation, to the extent that there is capacity available, on companies operating transmission and distribution networks for electricity and gas to offer terms for the use of their grid, in particular to individual consumers or to distribution companies, in return for payment'. European Commission (1992) *Proposal for a Council Directive Concerning Common Rules for the Internal Market in Electricity and Gas.* COM(91) 548. 21 February 1992, p. 6.
3. European Commission (1991a) *Reports of the Consultative Committees on Third Party Access to Electricity Networks.* May 1991, p. 4.
4. UNIPEDE congress (10 June). Reported in EC Energy Monthly (30), 1990.
5. The commission had decided to set up the committees during discussions around the transit directive in 1989. The idea of the committees is mentioned in COM(89) 336 which was a communication by the commission to the Council of Ministers alongside the draft Transit Directive.
6. *Comité Consultatif Etats Membres Electricité* and *Comité Consultatif Etats Membres Gaz.*
7. Professional Consultative Committee on Electricity and Gas.
8. European Commission (1991a) *Op. cit.*

9. McGowan, F. (1993) *The Struggle for Power in Europe: Competition and Regulation in the EC Electricity Industry.* Royal Institute of International Affairs, London, p. 56.
10. European Commission (1991b) *Final Report: Professional Consultative Committee on Electricity.* April 1991, p. 6
11. Ibid., p. 14.
12. Ibid., p. 11–12.
13. Ibid., p. 12.
14. Eurelectric (1991) *Submission to TPA Consultative Committees.* Appendix II of European Commission (1991a) *Op. cit.*
15. Ibid., p. 3.
16. Ibid., p. 12.
17. Ibid., p. 15.
18. Ibid., p. 15.
19. Ibid., p. 5.
20. Ibid., p. 7.
21. Ibid., p. 7–8.
22. IFIEC, *Submission to TPA Consultative Committees.* Appendix III of European Commission (1991a) *Op. cit.*, p. 3.
23. Ibid., p. 3.
24. Power in Europe (58), 1989. (An article written by Leigh Hancher).
25. Particularly relevant to electricity in this respect was Costa v ENEL (1964). Cameron cites a number of relevant cases to electricity markets: 'Case 6/64 *Costa v Enel* [1964] ECR 1251. At a later date, this was reinforced by Case C-393/92 *Almelo Gemeente v NV Energiebedrijf Ijsselmij* [1994] ECR-1477, and cases C-157/94 *Commission v Netherlands*, C-158/94 *Commission v Italy* [1997] ECR 1-5789, C-159/94 *Commission v France* C-160/94 *Commission v Spain* [1997] ECR I-5699 *et seq*'. Cameron, P. (2002) *Competition in energy markets: law and regulation in the European Union.* Oxford University Press, Oxford, p. 40.
26. As outlined by Waller, 'The major weakness in the Article is the nature of the enforcement process. The language of Article 37 gives the European Commission only advisory powers in setting the timetable for compliance by state trading countries. Consequently, enforcement efforts have shifted to the European Court of Justice. The European Court is limited to developing the law on a case-by-case basis in accordance with the peculiar mechanics of Article 177 of the EEC Treaty. When the European Court of Justice is referred a case from a national court under Article 177 it may deliver only an abstract interpretation of Community law rather than a decision on the merits. The abstract nature of these rulings has hindered the development of a consistent and effective judicial doctrine interpreting Article 37'. Waller S. W. (1981) Article 37 of the EEC Treaty: State

Trading under Scrutiny. *Northwestern Journal of International Law and Business*, 3 (2), p. 672.

27. *Article 86* 'prohibits companies in a dominant position from abusing that position', for example 'possible refusal of access to networks', and *Article 85* 'prohibits anti-competitive agreements'. *Articles 87, 88* and *89* were also related to competition, but in the area of state-aids: 'They prohibit the provision of state aids where they threaten to distort trade, but create exceptions and are subject to EC policing'. Cameron, P. (2002) *Op. cit.*, p. 45–46.
28. Power in Europe (29), 1988.
29. Article 90(2), EC.
30. Hancher, L. (1990) *Towards a free market for energy? A Legal Perspective.* Energy Policy, 18 (3), p. 241.
31. Directive 88/301/EEC.
32. Ruling on Case C-202/88: France v Commission [1991], ECR I-1223.
33. Report in Power in Europe (96), 1991.
34. The divisional structure of DG Energy at this time: around 450 staff, more than half working in Luxembourg on Euratom and nuclear safeguards. Policy Directorate (A)—cross-cutting and international issues, Energy 2010 strategy. Directorate B—coal. C—hydrocarbons (a key area here was liberalisation of refining and oil import industries; countries like France and Italy were concerned about damage to their domestic industries. The EC, as part of the IEA, had agreed to an open door policy with Japan and the US in this area. Directorate C also covered security of supply and diversification). Directorates D&F—nuclear. Directorate E—electricity/efficiency.
35. Cameron, P. (2002) *Op. cit.*, p. 52.
36. This was later replaced by a *co-decision procedure* which came into force on 1 November 1993 after Germany's constitutional court ruled to allow ratification of the Maastricht Treaty.
37. Padgett, S. (1992) The Single European Energy Market: The Politics of Realization. *Journal of Common Market Studies*, 30 (1), p. 62.
38. Power in Europe (111), 1991.
39. EC Energy Monthly (33), 1992.
40. '... over 1mcm/yr of gas and 5 GWh/yr of power until 1995'. Ibid.
41. Power in Europe (117), 1991 (An article by Leigh Hancher).
42. Reported in Power in Europe (104), 1991.
43. EC Energy Monthly (35), 1991.
44. His speech is reproduced in Energy Committee (1992) *Second Report: Consequences of Electricity Privatisation.* HMSO, London.
45. Ibid.
46. Power in Europe (112), 1991.

47. Deputy Secretary and Director General of Energy Resources in the UK Department of Energy and Trade and Industry.
48. Abel Matutes (Spanish): end 1992–Spring 1994; Marcelino Oreja (Spanish) from May 1994; Christos Papoutsis (Greek) from Jan 1995. Karel van Miert (Belgian, socialist) took over from Leon Brittan as Competition Commissioner in 1992.
49. McGowan (1993) *Op. cit.*, p. 65.
50. The Maastricht Treaty was agreed in December 1991, signed in February 1992, and entered into force on 1 Nov 1993. A detailed overview of co-decision procedure is available here: https://publications.parliament.uk/pa/ld200809/ldselect/ldeucom/125/12504.htm#n3 (Accessed 27.4.21). Here, it is outlined that the three stages of the legislative process were as follows: *First reading*—presentation of proposal by Commission to European Council and Parliament. 'There are no formal time limits to this stage so the speed of the negotiations depends on political impetus coming, usually, from the Council Presidency'. During this phase the Parliament submits its report, compiled by the rapporteur and containing amendments, to the Council which then either accepts and passes the legislation or adopts a common position either rejecting the Parliament's report and/or suggesting its own amendments. *Second reading*—the Parliament considers the Council's common position. This 'must be completed within six months, extendible to eight'. The Parliament considers the Council's common position and 'can (i) approve the Common Position and adopt the Proposal as set out there' ... (ii) 'reject the Common Position entirely, in which case the Proposal falls; or (iii) adopt amendments to the Common Position'. *Third Reading (or conciliation)*—If the Parliament decides to suggest amendments to the common position, a third reading with the aim of producing a 'joint text' between the Council and Parliament is required. This 'must be completed within 18 weeks, extendible to 24, of the Council's second reading'. During this stage 'informal three-way meetings, or trilogues, between the Parliament, Council and Commission' are initially held, and if required a 'formal conciliation committee meeting is held'. Following the Lisbon Treaty the procedure was renamed 'the Ordinary Legislative Procedure' and extended further 'into areas including agriculture, fisheries, justice and home affairs and the budget'.
51. Cameron, P. (2002) *Op. cit.*, p. 53.
52. Quoted in EC Energy Monthly (48), 1992.
53. Desama quoted EC Energy Monthly (51), 1993.
54. EC Energy Monthly (46), 1992.
55. McGowan (1993) *Op. cit.*, p. 59.
56. Ibid.

57. EC Energy Monthly (51), 1993.
58. EC Energy Monthly (53), 1993.
59. Ibid.
60. Matutes, quoted in EC Energy Monthly (55), 1993.
61. France, Italy, Ireland, the Netherlands and Spain (electricity); France and Germany (gas).
62. Key cases in this respect being the *Corbeau case (C320/91)* and *Commune Almelo and others v NV Energiebedrijf IJsselmij (C393/92)*; both requiring the Court to provide definition to the PSO concept.
63. Quote from Van Miert in EC Energy Monthly (56), 1993.
64. The ruling of the Almelo v Ijsselmij case which challenged SEP's monopoly was due in 1994.
65. EC Energy Monthly (66), 1994.
66. DGEMP (*Ministere de l'Industrie*) *Rapport du groups de travail sur la reforme de l'organisation electrique et gaziere francaise* (1994).
67. A Green Paper on energy policy was issued in January 1995, to lead to White Paper on energy policy published in December 1995, an update of 1986 energy policy guidelines.
68. The committee was renamed Research, Technological Development and Energy Committee.
69. EC Energy Monthly (72), 1994.
70. A report in Politico summarised these final attempts to amend the common position: 'In spite of his fear that this deal could be threatened, Desama has nevertheless tabled three amendments to the text aimed at beefing-up distributors' public service obligations to consumers in remote areas, encouraging environmentally-friendly electricity production and avoiding the competitive downgrading of employment rights for power workers ... MEPs from the European People's Party on the Parliament's energy committee have already decided to oppose all these amendments when Desama's report on the directive is put to a vote on 18–19 November ... However, the Greens and the Liberals have both come forward with proposed changes to the text, and German Social Democrats have even suggested that not only large industrial concerns but distributors consuming a set amount of electricity every year should have freedom to choose in the market-place ... The amendments from Desama, as the rapporteur on the legislation, are being taken more seriously. Right at the beginning of the directive – before the rule-making even starts – Desama wants to add a commitment to undertake Community harmonisation of rules concerning environmental protection, safety and social protection of workers on the basis of the highest possible standards ... This is intended to prevent social dumping, with electricity suppliers in some member states offering much lower prices because their wage bills

are lower, the benefits they offer their staff are less generous and their environmental standards are weaker ... As part of this environmental guarantee, Desama wants generating installations using renewable energy sources or waste, or producing combined heat and power, to be allowed subsidies to keep their prices competitive ... He is also dissatisfied with the guarantee of universal service written into the proposed directive, which only allows member states to impose an obligation on distribution companies to supply customers in certain high-cost and remote areas at a regulated tariff. In his final amendment, Desama adds a commitment by distribution companies to "safeguard [customers] against excessive tariff increases"'. Reported in Politico: on 6.11.96 https://www.politico.eu/article/high-tension-in-electricity-deal/ (Accessed 28.4.21).

71. Directive 96/92/EC.
72. Directive 2003/64/EC.
73. Thomas, S. (2003) The Seven Brothers. *Energy Policy*, 31 (5), p. 398.
74. Cameron, P. (2007) *Competition in Energy Markets: Law and Regulation in the European Union*. OUP, Oxford, p. 368.
75. VEW (*Vereinigte Elektrizitätswerke Westfalen*) was a smaller company which had been created by municipalities in the north-western region.
76. As outlined in the previous chapter, the main West German utilities had earlier joined to take a majority (75%) stake in VEAG (Verinigte Energiewerke AG), which was the dominant player in East Germany following reunification. Other West Germany utilities owned the remaining 25% stake in the holding company, this included VEW, BEWAG, Badenwerk, EVS and HEW.
77. Brunekreeft, G., & Twelemann, S. (2005) Regulation, competition and investment in the German electricity market: RegTP or REGTP, *Energy Journal*, 26(1), p. 99–126.
78. Ibid.
79. The Economist, *Germany's Electrical Storm*. Nov 13th 1999.
80. Hancher, L. and De Hauteclocque, A. (2010) Manufacturing the EU Energy Markets: the Current Dynamics of Regulatory Practice. *Competition and Regulation in Network Industries*, 11(3), p. 307–334.
81. EDF subsequently sold it back to the state government in 2010.
82. For an overview of its introduction, see Reverdy, T. & Breslau, D. (2019) Making an exception: market design and the politics of re-regulation in the French electricity sector. *Economy and Society*, 48(2), p. 197–220.
83. For an overview of electricity sector mergers and acquisitions across the continent, see Codognet, M.K., Glachant, J.M., Leveque, F., Plagnet, M.A., (2002) *Mergers and Acquisitions in the European Electricity Sector: Cases and Patterns*. CERNA, Centre d'economie industrielle, Ecole Nationale Superieure des Mines de Paris, Paris. For an overview and dis-

cussion of effects on consumer prices see: Dias, M.F., Jorge, S.F. (2016) Mergers Between Natural Gas Suppliers and Electricity Generators: Should European Consumers be Concerned? *Energy Procedia,* 106, pp. 185–203.

84. EU Commission quotes in Pollitt, M. (2019) *The European Single Market in Electricity: An Economic Assessment.* Journal of Industrial Organization (55), p. 69: The EU's sector inquiry can be accessed here: https://ec.europa.eu/competition/sectors/energy/2005_inquiry/index_en.html (Accessed 10.5.21).
85. Hancher, L. and De Hauteclocque, A., (2010) Manufacturing the EU Energy Markets: the Current Dynamics of Regulatory Practice. *Competition and Regulation in Network Industries,* 11(3), pp. 307–334.
86. The full list of directives and regulations discussed in this chapter is as follows: *Transit and price transparency (1990):* Directive 90/377/EC of 29 June 1990 concerning a community procedure to improve the transparency of gas and electricity prices charged to industrial customers, O.J. 17.7.1990, L185/16; Directive 90/547/EC of 29 October 1990 on the transit of electricity through transmission grids, O.J. 13.11.1990, L 313/30. *First Directive (1996):* Directive 96/92/EC of 19 December 1996 concerning common rules for the internal market in electricity, O.J. 30.1.1997, L 27/20: *Second Package (2003):* Directive 2003/54/EC of the European Parliament and of the Council of 26 June 2003 concerning common rules for the internal market in electricity and repealing Directive 96/92/EC, O.J. 15.7.2003, L 176/37; Regulation 1228/2003 of the European Parliament and of the Council of 26 June 2003 on conditions for access to the network for cross-border exchanges in electricity. *Third Package (2009):* Directive 2009/72 of the European Parliament and of the Council of 13 July 2009 concerning common rules for the internal market in electricity and repealing Directive 2003/54/EC, O.J. 14.8.2009, L 211/55; Regulation 713/2009 of the European Parliament and of the Council of 13 July 2009 establishing an Agency for the Cooperation of Energy Regulators, O.J. 14.8.2009, L 211/1; Regulation 714/2009 of the European Parliament and of the Council of 13 July 2009 on conditions for access to the network for cross-border exchanges in electricity and repealing Regulation 1228/2003, O.J. 14.8.2009, L. 211/15. List developed from Hancher, L. and De Hauteclocque, A., (2010) *Op. cit.*

CHAPTER 8

1. Bergman, L. and von der Fehr, N.H.M (1999) *The Nordic Experience: Diluting Market Power by Integrating Markets.* In: CEPR. A European Market for Electricity? Monitoring European Deregulation. Centre for Economic Policy Research, London, 1999, p. 118.
2. Sweden was at 15,000 TWh/year, while Denmark, with more gas use for heating, was at 6000 TWh/year.
3. Magnus, E. & Midttun, A. (2000) *The Norwegian Model: Competitive Public Economy.* In: Magnus, E. & Midttun, A. (Eds.) Electricity Market Reform in Norway. Palgrave Macmillan, Basingstoke, 2000, p. 5.
4. An argument made by Midttun and Thomas. Midttun, A. & Thomas, S. (1998) *Theoretical Ambiguity and the Weight of Historical Heritage: A Comparative Study of the British and Norwegian Electricity Liberalisation.* Energy Policy, 26(3), pp. 179–197.
5. Thue, L. (1995) *Electricity Rules: The Formation and Development of the Nordic Electricity Regimes.* In Kaijser, A. & Hedin, M. (Eds.) Nordic Energy Systems: Historical Perspectives and Current Issues. Science History Publications, Canton, MA, 1995.
6. Thue, L. (2013) *Connections, Criticality, and Complexity: Norwegian Electricity in its European Context.* In Högselius, P., Hommels, A., Kaijser, A. and Van Der Vleuten, E. (Eds.) The Making of Europe's Critical Infrastructure: Common Connections and Shared Vulnerabilities. Palgrave Macmillan, Basingstoke, 2013, p. 220.
7. Ibid., p. 221.
8. 'Shipowner and industrialist Gunnar Knudsen, who later became prime-minister for Venstre (1908–1910 and 1913–1920). He was probably the most important entrepreneur behind the active state engagement in the electricity sector at the time, with substantial influences on the shaping of state electricity policies, regulatory systems and the choice of state projects. He was a true "developer" and "network constructor" across politics as well as industry, had participated in the first electricity distribution project in Norway already in 1885 and also initiated the first inter-municipal electricity organization in his home region in Telemark with the establishing of Skiensfjordens Kommunale Kraftselskap'. Olsen P.I., (2000) *Transforming Economies: The Case of the Norwegian Electricity Market Reform.* Dissertation for the Degree of Dr. Oecon. Norwegian School of Management BI, p. 88.
9. Ibid., p. 95.
10. *Norges vassdrags- og energidirektorat.*
11. Olsen P.I., (2000) *Op. cit.*, p. 89.
12. Magnus, E. & Midttun, A. (2000) *Op. cit.*, p. 3.

13. Olsen, P.I (2000) *Op. cit.*, p. 122.
14. Christened *Samkjøringen for kraftverkene på Østlandet.* It emerged initially in the early 1930s around 'the private Hafslund system in Østfold, then from the interaction of Norsk Hydro in Rjukan (Telemark) with Drammen, Oslo and other population centers in Buskerud and Akershus, and from the interaction between the private Treschow-Fritzøe company in Vestfold and «Skiensfjorden Kommunale Kraftselskap» in Telemark during the post-war period'. Olsen, P.I (2000) *Op. cit.*, p. 100.
15. Kaiser, A. (1995) *Controlling the Grid: The Development of High-Tension Power Lines in the Nordic Countries.* In Kaijser, A. & Hedin, M. (Eds.) Nordic Energy Systems: Historical Perspectives and Current Issues. Science History Publications, Canton, MA, 1995.
16. Olsen, P.I (2000) *Op. cit.*, p. 113.
17. Midttun, A. (1988) The Negotiated Political Economy of a Heavy Industrial Sector: The Norwegian Hydropower Complex in the 1970s and 1980s. *Scandinavian Political Studies*, 11(2), pp. 115–144.
18. Thue, L. (2013) *Connections, Criticality, and Complexity: Norwegian Electricity in Its European Context.* In The Making of Europe's Critical Infrastructure: Common Connections and Shared Vulnerabilities. Eds. Högselius, P., Hommels, A., Kaijser, A. and Van Der Vleuten, E.
19. One estimate put this in the region of 5% in the late 1980s. Bye, T. & Hope, E. (2005) *Deregulation of Electricity Markets: The Norwegian Experience.* Discussion Papers No. 433, September 2005 Statistics Norway, Research Department.
20. Bredesen, H. A. and Nilsen, T. (2013) *Power to the People: The First 20 Years of Nordic Power-Market Integration.* Oslo: Nord Pool Spot/Nasdaq OMX, p. 12
21. Olsen, P.I. (2000) *Op. cit.*, p. 113
22. For mere details on this see Bredesen, H. A. and Nilsen, T. (2013) *Op. cit.*, pp. 24–5
23. Magnus, E. & Midttun, A. (2000) *Op. cit.*
24. Midttun, A. & Summerton, J (1998) Loyalty or Competition? A Comparative Analysis of Norwegian and Swedish Electricity Distributors' Adaptation to Market Reform. *Energy Policy*, 26(2), pp. 143–158.
25. Hjalmarsson, L. (1996) *From Club-Regulation to Market Competition in the Scandinavian Electricity Supply Industry.* In Gilbert, R.J., Kahn, P. (Eds.) International Comparisons of Electricity Regulation. Cambridge University Press, Cambridge, 1996. Hjalmarsson originally extracted data from NUTEK, the Swedish business agency.
26. Bye, T. & Hope, E. (2005) *Op. cit.*, p. 4.
27. Ibid.
28. Magnus, E. & Midttun, A. (2000) *Op. cit.*, p. 10.

29. Thue, L. (1995) *Op. cit.*
30. 'Report regarding Norway's energy supply industry'.
31. Thue, L. (2013) *Op. cit.*
32. Power in Europe (111), 1991.
33. Power in Europe (102), 1991.
34. Midttun, A. (1988) *Op. cit.*, p. 134.
35. Bye, T. & Hope, E. (2005) *Op. cit.* (See Table 1).
36. Midttun, A (1995) *(Mis) Understanding Change: electricity liberalization policies in Norway and Sweden.* In Nordic Energy Systems: Historical Perspectives and Current Issues by Kaijser, Arne, Hedin, Marika. Science History Publications, Canton, MA, 1995.
37. Olsen, P. I. (2000) *Op. cit.*, p.188.
38. Author's interview with Einar Hope. Olsen's study also provides insights about the backgroup to the SAF report. Olsen, P. I. (2000) *Op. cit.*
39. Hope, E. (1983) *Markeder for kraftomsetning i Norge: En prinsippiell drøfting*, Statsøkonomisk Tidsskrift, hefte 1. A later research report from Hope's group was influential in setting out the ideas: Morten, B, Kåre Petter Hagen, K. P. & Hope, E. (1986) *Elektrisitetspriser og energiøkonomisering*, SAF rapport nr. 7. Cited in Olsen, P. I. (2000) *Op. cit.*, p. 192. In a correspondence with the author Professor Hope also highlighted a 1984 report initiated by *Statkraftverkene* and developed with his research assistant Tufte: 'Markets for power exchange in Norway: An analysis of the market strategic role and behaviour of Statskraftverkene in the market for occasional power', SAF Report 6-84. This report was later drawn upon during the discussion about the Statkraftverkene/Statkraft split discussed later in this chapter.
40. Olsen, P. I. (2000) *Op. cit.*, p. 188.
41. Author's interview with Einar Hope.
42. See Bye and Hope (2005) for an articulation of this argument. Bye, T. & Hope, E. (2005) *Op. cit.*
43. Evidence for this is provided by Midttun. Midttun, A. (1988) *Op. cit.*
44. Ferdinand Banks provides a succinct summary of the basic assumptions behind the abstract notion of 'efficiency' in textbook economics: 'efficiency is usually pictured as being obtainable in a world featuring atomistic consumers and very large numbers of profit maximizing producers, where utility curves (for consumers) and production functions (for producers) have the "right" mathematical properties, where there is a complete system of "contingency" and/or derivatives markets to hedge uncertainty, and where things like "spillovers" (i.e. externalities) are conspicuous by their absence'. Banks, F.E. (2004) Economic theory and the failure of electricity deregulation in Sweden. *Energy and Environment*, 15(1), pp. 31–32.

45. Author's interview with Einar Hope.
46. Ibid.
47. Ibid.
48. Ibid.
49. Bjørndalen, Jørgen, Einar Hope, Eivind Tandberg and Berit Tennbakk, 1989: *Markedsbasert kraftomsetning i Norge*, SAF rapport nr. 7. Olsen (2000) provides an extensive summary of the contents of the report from p. 233.
50. Olsen, P. I. (2000) *Op. cit.*, p. 237.
51. Later a new division for the grid was created within the NVE.
52. Hope himself became the head of Norway's competition authority in 1995, so had a hands on role in pushing through reforms in areas such as ease of entry to the market, consumer information issues and market dominance. Hope has written extensively, in Norwegian and English, on power sector reform, regulation and policy, and also on competition regulation and policy. Some of these writings are collected in *Studier i markedsbasert kraftomsetning og regulering* (Studies in market based power exchange and regulation), Fagbokforlaget, 2000, and *Studier i konkurranse- og energpolitikk. 2004–2016* (Studies in competition and energy polices), NHH-SNF, 2018.
53. Author's interview with Einar Hope.
54. Magnus, E. and Midttun, A. (2000) *Op. cit.*, p. 4.
55. Author's interview with Einar Hope.
56. Magnus and Midttun include list of the key legislative documents at the end of their bibliography. Magnus, E. & Midttun, A. (Eds.) Electricity Market Reform in Norway. Palgrave Macmillan, Basingstoke, 2000, p. 237.
57. Magnus, E. & Midttun, A. (2000) *Op. cit.*, p. 4.
58. Author's interview with Einar Hope.
59. Bredesen, H. A. and Nilsen, T. (2013) *Op. cit.*, p. 14.
60. Translated text from the 1990 Norwegian Energy Act, from Ibid.
61. The rate was initially set at the interest on government bonds plus a small risk margin of 1%. In 1997 this rate-of-return regime was replaced with an incentive-based approach which compared the many distribution networks against an efficiency frontier.
62. Bredesen, H. A. (2016) *The Nord Pool Market Model.* ASEAN Energy Market Integration (AEMI), Energy Security and Connectivity: The Nordic and European Union Approaches, Forum Paper, p. 16.
63. Bergman, L. and von der Fehr, N.H.M (1999) *Op. cit.*, p. 126.
64. At this time the state company 'controlled approximately 30% of national electricity production, 40% of generating capacity and 50% of hydro-res-

ervoir capacities and around 85% of the national grid system'. Olsen, P. I. (2000) *Op. cit.*, p. 182.

65. Author's interview with Einar Hope.
66. Power in Europe (56), 1989.
67. Author's interview with Einar Hope.
68. Nordland, Telemark, Soer-Troendelag, Sogn of Fjordane, Nord-Troendelag and Hordaland.
69. Bredesen, H. A. and Nilsen, T. (2013) *Op. cit.*
70. By this time, 29.8 TWh output and 33% of Norway's capacity.
71. Power in Europe (101), 1991.
72. Statkraft Board, reported in Ibid.
73. Power in Europe (111), 1991.
74. Olsen, P. I. (2000) *Op. cit.*, p. 277.
75. Ibid.
76. Bredesen, H. A. and Nilsen, T. (2013) *Op. cit.*, p. 21.
77. The structural differences between the Norwegian and British models are explained in more detail by Hunt and Shuttleworth: in the Norwegian, and later the Nord Pool, market, 'the participants have the choice as to whether to use the spot market, or whether to schedule physical contracts. They may choose to do both or they may choose to buy at spot and hedge the price risk with financial contracts. This mixed system requires the transmission settlement system to settle the contract amounts as well as the spot purchases, which is what the Norway pool does. The UK Pool was an alternative to this "mixed system"; the approach in the more centralised model "is to treat all sales as spot sales, to schedule only by bid, and to force all contracts to be financial hedges"'. Hunt, S., Shuttleworth, G. (1993) *Op. cit.*, p. 84.
78. The 380 or so distribution companies were given the right to compete for customers, whilst retaining an obligation to supply a certain area. Enabling switching within these constraints required a central role for the distribution companies in the market: each distributor calculated and reported weekly to the market operator an estimated net load which was then 'divided between retailers according to the profiles of their respective consumers'. The profiled customers were metered once a year and any differences 'between actual consumption and estimated consumption based on profiles [we]re adjusted for in the financial settlement between the local distribution utility and the respective external retailer' and then valued at the associated price in the day-ahead market. von der Fehr, N. H. M. & Hansen, P.V. (2010). Electricity Retailing in Norway. *The Energy Journal*, 31(1), pp. 129–130.

79. These 'were first capped in 1992, at a level of Norwegian kroner (NOK) 5000, and were gradually brought down to NOK 246 in 1995; in 1997, switching fees were abolished altogether ...'. Ibid., p. 28.
80. Studies examine the dynamics of the retail market: von der Fehr, N. H. & Hansen, P. V. (2010) *Op. cit.* Littlechild, S. (2006) Competition and Contracts in the Nordic Residential Electricity Markets. *Utilities Policy*, 14(3), pp. 135–147.

Chapter 9

1. Myllyntaus, T. (1995) *Kilowatts at Work: Electricity and industrial transformation in the Nordic Countries.* In Kaijser, A. & Hedin, M. (Eds.) Nordic Energy Systems: Historical Perspectives and Current Issues. Science History Publications, Canton, MA, 1995.
2. For an overview of political institutions and their influence on electricity development across the Nordic region, see Thue, L. (1995) *Electricity Rules: The Formation and Development of the Nordic Electricity Regimes.* In Kaijser, A. & Hedin, M. (Eds.) Nordic Energy Systems: Historical Perspectives and Current Issues. Science History Publications, Canton, MA, 1995.
3. Wilson, R (2002) Architecture of Power Markets. *Econometrica*, Vol. 70, No. 4, pp. 1299–1340.
4. Based on figures for 1931–90. Midttun, A. & Summerton, J (1998) Loyalty or Competition? A Comparative Analysis of Norwegian and Swedish Electricity Distributors' Adaptation to Market Reform. *Energy Policy*, 26(2), pp. 143–158.
5. Thue, L. (2013) *Connections, Criticality, and Complexity: Norwegian Electricity in its European Context.* In Hogselius, P., Hommels, A., Kaijser, A. and Van Der Vleuten, E. (Eds.) The Making of Europe's Critical Infrastructure: Common Connections and Shared Vulnerabilities. Palgrave Macmillan, Basingstoke, 2013.
6. Power in Europe (92), 1991.
7. Approx. 5000 MW capacity in total.
8. This resulted in a more than doubling of interconnector capacity across the region by 2001 to 10,000 MW. Thue, L. (2013) *Op. cit.*
9. A notable exception was a long-term supply contract between Denmark and Norway which was outside of the Nordel agreement.
10. Power in Europe (52), 1989.
11. Power in Europe (120), 1991.
12. Thue, L. (2013) *Op. cit.*, p. 221.

13. Ibid.
14. Ibid., p. 226.
15. Power in Europe (108), 1991.
16. Some of the key producers were Norsk Hydro (aluminium and magnesium producer), Norske Skog (paper and pulp) and Elkem (aluminium and ferro alloys).
17. Magnus, E. & Midttun, A. (2000) *The Norwegian Model: Competitive Public Economy.* In: Magnus, E. & Midttun, A. (Eds.) Electricity Market Reform in Norway. Palgrave Macmillan, Basingstoke, 2000, p. 19.
18. Bergman, L. and von der Fehr, N.H.M (1999) *The Nordic Experience: Diluting Market Power by Integrating Markets.* In: CEPR. A European Market for Electricity? Monitoring European Deregulation. Centre for Economic Policy Research, London, 1999, p. 126.
19. Power in Europe (99), 1991.
20. In 1991 spot prices were up, at NKr 0.102/kWh, while at 0.061 and 0.052 in 1990 and 1989, respectively. And by 1991, 'although exports were sharply down in January/June 1990 levels – 4.5 TWh, compared with 7.7 TWh – they earned a total of NKr 464 m, against 1990's NKr 460 m'. Power in Europe (104), 1991.
21. Power in Europe (105), 1991.
22. Author's interview with Einar Hope.
23. Newbery, D. (1997) *Pool Reform and Competition in Electricity.* Paper presented to the IEA\LBS Lectures on Regulation Series VII 1997 on 11 November 1997.
24. Bredesen, H. A. and Nilsen, T. (2013) *Power to the People: The First 20 Years of Nordic Power-Market Integration.* Oslo: Nord Pool Spot/ Nasdaq OMX, p. 44.
25. Liquidity on Nord Pool increased further, reaching 20% in 1998, 60% in 2005 and 80% by 2010. Ibid., p. 210.
26. Ibid., p.100.
27. Author's interview with Einar Hope.
28. Midttun, A. & Thomas, S. (1998) *Theoretical Ambiguity and the Weight of Historical Heritage: A Comparative Study of the British and Norwegian Electricity Liberalisation.* Energy Policy, 26(3), pp. 179–197.
29. Magnus, E. & Midttun, A. (2000) *Op. cit.*, p. 18.
30. This section draws extensively from Högselius, P. & Kaiser, A. (2010). The Politics of Electricity Deregulation in Sweden: The Art of Acting on Multiple Arenas. *Energy Policy*, 38(5), pp. 2245–2254.
31. Olerup, B. (1995) *Cooperate or Compete: The Swedish Electricity Market in Transition.* Energy, 20(12), p. 1238.
32. Ibid., p. 1239.

33. Kaiser, A. (1995) *Controlling the Grid: The Development of High-Tension Power Lines in the Nordic Countries.* In Kaijser, A. & Hedin, M. (Eds.) Nordic Energy Systems: Historical Perspectives and Current Issues. Science History Publications, Canton, MA, 1995.
34. Market shares in 1991 were 'Vattenfall 53%, Sydkraft 17%, Stockholm Energi 5%, Stora Kraft 5%, B&ab Energi 3%, Gullsptigs Kraft 3%, Uddeholm Kraft 3%, Graningeverken 2%, Skelleftei Kraft 2%, and Skandinaviska Elverk 1%'. Olerup, B. (1995) *Op. cit.*, p. 1238.
35. Midttun, A. & Summerton, J (1998) Loyalty or Competition? A Comparative Analysis of Norwegian and Swedish Electricity Distributors' Adaptation to Market Reform. *Energy Policy*, 26(2), p. 147.
36. Ibid.
37. Högselius and Kaijser (2010) *Op. cit.* Olerup provides further detail on the industry's M&A activity of the time: 'Vattenfall bought Solna/ Sundbyberg in 1992, Soderkiiping in 1993, 99% of the shares in Huddinge Elverk and 93% of the shares in Drefvikens Energi in 1994, and Wnersborg in 1995. Sydkraft acquired MalmS Energi in 1991. Graningeverken bought Roslags Energi in 1991, and both Malarkraft and Upplands-Bro in 1993. Gullsplng bought the distribution section of Stora Kraft in 1992. Smhlands Kraft bought Eksjij Energiverk in 1993'. Olerup, B. (1995) *Op. cit.*, p. 1240.
38. Summerton, J. (1995) *Coalitions and Conflicts: Swedish Municipal Energy Companies on the Eve of Deregulation.* In Kaijser, A. & Hedin, M. (Eds.) Nordic Energy Systems: Historical Perspectives and Current Issues. Science History Publications, Canton, MA, 1995.
39. Högselius and Kaijser (2010) *Op. cit.*
40. Summerton, J. (1995) *Op. cit.*
41. The Fyrstad Kraft AB purchasing company: led by Uddevalla and involving Trollhättan, Vänersborg and Lysekil, along with a number of large industrial consumers.
42. Sweden did not join the European Union until 1995 so Vattenfall was not subject to the Transit Directive (see Chap. 5).
43. Summerton, J. (1995) *Op. cit.*
44. Högselius, P. and Kaijser, A. (2010) *Op. cit.*, p. 2247.
45. Ibid.
46. Midttun, A. (1995) *(Mis)Understanding Change: electricity liberalization policies in Norway and Sweden.* In Kaijser, A. & Hedin, M. (Eds.) Nordic Energy Systems: Historical Perspectives and Current Issues. Science History Publications, Canton, MA, 1995, p. 145.
47. Högselius, P. and Kaijser, A. (2010) *Op. cit.*, p. 2251.
48. Ibid.

49. Similar to the British and German cases, the trend towards concentration was in fact reinforced by the market reforms. Högselius and Kaijser note that shortly after the implementation of the reform in 1996 there was a 'dramatic wave of mergers and acquisitions' which 'radically increased market concentration on the production side, with three large producers – Vattenfall, Fortum and E.ON – controlling around 90% of power generation'. Over the 1990s, 'in the period from 1991 to 2002, 100 of Sweden's 286 municipalities divested their energy production, while 51 municipalities also divested their distribution networks'. Högselius, P. and Kaijser, A. (2010) *Op. cit.*, p. 2253.
50. Bredesen, H. A. and Nilsen, T. (2013), p. 43.
51. EC Energy Monthly (79) 1995.
52. Kaiser, A. (1995) *Op. Cit.*, p. 55.
53. Pineau, P.O. & Hämäläinen, R.P. (2000a). A Perspective on the Restructuring of the Finnish Electricity Market. *Energy Policy*, 28(3), p. 184.
54. Pineau, P.O. & Hämäläinen, R.P. (1999). A Perspective on the Restructuring of the Finnish Electricity Market, p. 6. Pre-print version available at https://sal.aalto.fi/publications/pdf-files/mpina.pdf (Accessed 5.5.21).
55. European Commission (1998) Commission Decision Regarding Case No IV/M.931 – NESTE/IVO, p. 5.
56. EC Energy Monthly (79), 1995.
57. Pineau, P.O. & Hämäläinen, R.P. (1999) *Op. cit.*, p. 10.
58. Svenska Kraftnät (2001) *The Swedish Electricity Market and the Role of Svenska Kraftnät*. Svenska Kraftnät, p. 3.
59. Bergman, L. and von der Fehr, N.H.M (1999) *The Nordic Experience: Diluting Market Power by Integrating Markets*. In CEPR. A European Market for Electricity? Monitoring European Deregulation. Centre for Economic Policy Research, London, 1999, p. 119.
60. Ibid.
61. Svenska Kraftnät (2001) Op. cit. *The Swedish Electricity Market and the Role of Svenska Kraftnät. Svenska Kraftnät*: 3. By 2015 the market had expanded across to the Baltic region. Ownership of Nord Pool consisted of Statnett 28.2%; Svenska Kraftnat 28.2%; Fingrid and Energinet.dk 18.8; 2% each for Estonia, Lituania and Latvia (Breseden, 2016). In 2019 Euronext, the stock exchange company, took a majority equity stake in Nord Pool, with the TSOs above retaining a minority share.
62. Bredesen, H. A. and Nilsen, T. (2013) *Op. cit.*, p. 139.
63. Van Der Vleuten, E. (1999) Op. cit., p. 22.
64. For more on the Danish culture of electricity system control, see Lehtonen, M. & Nye, S. (2009) *Op. cit.*

65. Kaiser, A. (1995) *Op. cit.*
66. Bredesen, H. A. and Nilsen, T. (2013) *Op. cit.*, p. 138.
67. Ibid., p. 144.
68. This financial settlement facility could be accessed directly by market participants engaging in one of Nord Pool's organised markets (automatic settlement) and by brokers organising OTC contracts as a separate service which they pay for. A new organisation was established in 1999 for clearing financial transactions—Nordic Electricity Clearing (NEC), bringing together the functions of a number of previous organisations (NOS and OMX), but this never got off the ground. Nord Pool Clearing was established a few years later. Trading of financial contracts was initiated in Norway by *Norsk Kraftmarked*, a company 50% owned by Skankraft. *Norsk Kraftmarked* was purchased by Statnedd Marked in 1994 and trading in its financial derivatives market (called *Eltermin*) commenced in 1995. As part of this, a clearing service for contracts was offered to manage counterparty risk, which was open to both over-the-counter and traded financial contracts. There were two types of contract traded on *Eltermin* (forwards and futures), both of which specified, but did not require, a physical delivery of power, that is, not settlement through a physical exchange of power, rather a cash exchange. Electricity forwards contracts, which although standardised, are more akin to bilateral contracts as they are settled once the term of the contract has been reached, while with futures there is daily mark-to-market and settlement. Futures 'can be traded as "single weeks" up to between 4–7 weeks in advance, as "blocks of four weeks" from between 5–8 weeks and up to 52 weeks in advance, and as "seasons of several blocks" 1–3 years in advance', while less standardised *forward* contracts 'can be traded as seasons ("winter 1", "winter 2" and "summer") or a full year'. Standardised futures contracts are financially settled daily and are more liquid, whereas forward contracts 'do not have cash settlement before the delivery period starts'. A number of firms, apart from Nord Pool, were offering such contracts; these were independent brokers, for example, 'Skandinavisk Kraftmegling and Markedskraft'. When it opened, two types of futures contracts were traded on Eltermin, 'one for base-load power and one for peak-load power. Trade in the latter type of contract was, however, very limited and was eventually closed'. The baseload contracts 'cover 24 hours of each day for a full week' and can also be traded in blocks to cover an entire season or year. Option contracts were traded via the exchange also. These types of financial contracts essentially enable market participants to manage their risk without the responsibilities and obligations which come with trading physical power. The markets tend to be dominated by traders rather than conventional power companies. Across liberalised electric-

ity markets, the latter have tended to manage the risks of buying or selling power through more traditional means, that is, vertical integration. Bergman, L. and von der Fehr, N.H.M (1999) *The Nordic Experience: Diluting Market Power by Integrating Markets.* In: CEPR. A European Market for Electricity? Monitoring European Deregulation. Centre for Economic Policy Research, London, 1999: 122. The financialisation of Nord Pool, and electricity markets more generally, is not discussed in detail in this book. For a useful overview, see Banks, F.E. (2004) Economic theory and the failure of electricity deregulation in Sweden. *Energy and Environment*, 15(1), pp. 25–35.

69. Nord Pool ASA, along with Nord Pool's consulting arm, was subsequently sold by Statnett to OMX in 2007, which in turn was taken over by NASDAQ in 2010.
70. Bergman, L. and von der Fehr, N.H.M (1999) *The Nordic Experience: Diluting Market Power by Integrating Markets.* In CEPR. A European Market for Electricity? Monitoring European Deregulation. Centre for Economic Policy Research, London, 1999, p. 127.
71. Nordel Annual Report, 2000.
72. Ibid.
73. The regulation market (*Regulerkraftmarkedet*) 'was previously operated by Nord Pool on behalf of the system operator, but is now run by the system operator himself. Before each trading day, bids are accepted for the regulation market. These represent the prices at which participants are prepared to increase/reduce their output (or increase/reduce their demand) on the central grid. Participants are required to respond to notification of the need to adjust their production/demand within 15 minutes. Regulation prices are used to price discrepancies between participants' contracted quantities (including the spot contracts) and their actual generation or consumption' (Bergman, L. and von der Fehr, N.H.M (1999) *The Nordic Experience: Diluting Market Power by Integrating Markets.* In: CEPR. A European Market for Electricity? Monitoring European Deregulation. Centre for Economic Policy Research, London, 1999, p. 127). There have been different pricing approaches used in each country: 'Norway uses a "one-price model" according to which the same price applies to both the purchase and sale of balancing power. The other countries use a "two-price model" according to which the price of the purchase or sale of the individual balance responsible player depends on whether the purchase or the sale has been to the advantage or disadvantage of the total regulation of the power system for the hour concerned' (Nordel Annual Report, 2002, p. 25). The prices for upward or downward regulation are then used by TSOs as reference prices for imbalance pricing in the local balancing markets.

There is an inter-TSO settlement system to account for cross-border exchanges at this timeframe. After 2002 there has been increasing harmonisation of this regulating market. Turvey makes a relevant point about the relationship between system and market integration in this context: it is possible for neighbouring TSOs to operate a common interconnector, even if the market structures are quite different on both sides, but there does need to be an element of harmonisation, such as 'the same gate closure time in the two systems and agreement about the net transfer capacity of the interconnector'. Turvey, R. (2006) Interconnector Economics. *Energy Policy*, 34(13), p. 1462.

74. For an overviews of this issue, see Newbery, D. & Strbac, G. (2011) *Physical and Financial Capacity Rights for Cross-border Trade.* Booz and Co., London.
75. Nordel Annual Report, 2000.
76. Note that in the following years there have been changes to this and the delineation of price zones in Norway was always more flexible.
77. Nordel Annual Report, 2000.
78. Nordel Annual Report, 2001.
79. Nordel Annual Report, 2000.
80. Bjørndal, M. and Jørnsten, K. (2001) Zonal Pricing in a Deregulated Market. *The Energy Journal*, 22(1), p. 72.
81. For an overview see Boisseleau, F. (2004) *The Role of Power Exchanges for the Creation of a Single European Electricity Market. Market Design and Market Regulation.* Delft University Press.

Chapter 10

1. These comments relate mainly to high-income countries with extensive and mature electricity systems. The role of the state with regard to electricity system development will be quite different in contexts where electricity supply is less extensive and/or reliable.

Index

R. Bolton, *Making Energy Markets*,
https://doi.org/10.1007/978-3-030-90075-5

C

H

I

L

M

N

Q

R

The manufacturer's authorised representative in the EU is Springer Nature Customer Service Centre GmbH, Europaplatz 3, 69115 Heidelberg, Germany. If you have any concerns regarding our products, please contact ProductSafety@springernature.com

Printed and bound by CPI Group (UK) Ltd, Croydon, CR0 4YY
30/09/2026
02225492-0009